The Scots in early Stuart Ireland

Manchester University Press

Series editors

DAVID EDWARDS & MICHEÁL Ó SIOCHRÚ

The study of Early Modern Irish History has experienced something of a renaissance in the last decade. However, studies tend to group around traditional topics in political or military history and significant gaps remain. The idea behind this series is to identify key themes and set the agenda for future research.

Each volume in this series comes from leading scholars from Ireland, Britain, North America and elsewhere, addressing a particular subject. We aim to bring the best of Irish historical research to a wider audience, by engaging with international themes of empire, colonisation, religious change and social transformation.

Already published

The plantation of Ulster: Ideology and practice	Micheál Ó Siochrú and Éamonn Ó Ciardha (eds)
Ireland, 1641: Contexts and reactions	Micheál Ó Siochrú and Jane Ohlmeyer (eds)

The Scots in early Stuart Ireland

Union and separation in two kingdoms

Edited by
DAVID EDWARDS
with
SIMON EGAN

Manchester University Press

Published by Manchester University Press
Altrincham Street, Manchester M1 7JA
www.manchesteruniversitypress.co.uk

British Library Cataloguing-in-Publication Data
A catalogue record for this book is available from the British Library

Library of Congress Cataloging-in-Publication Data applied for

ISBN 978 0 7190 9721 8 hardback

First published 2016

ISBN 978 1 5261 3933 7 paperback

First published 2019

Typeset
by Frances Hackeson Freelance Publishing Services,
Brinscall, Lancs

Contents

List of tables

Contributors

Robert Armstrong is a Fellow of Trinity College Dublin, where he is Associate Professor of History. He is the author of *Protestant War: The British of Ireland and the Wars of the Three Kingdoms* (2005) and editor of a number of volumes including, most recently (with Tadhg Ó hAnnracháin) *Christianities in the Early Modern Celtic World* (2014). His current research focuses mostly on the Presbyterian experience in seventeenth-century Ireland.

Aoife Duignan currently manages the Bachelor of Arts Degree Programme at University College Dublin. Her doctoral thesis is a study of politics and war in Connacht during the 1640s. Her article 'Shifting allegiances: the protestant community in Connacht, 1643–5' appeared in Robert Armstrong and Tadhg Ó hAnnracháin (eds), *Community in Early Modern Ireland* (2006), and she has contributed to the *Dictionary of Irish Biography* (2009–).

David Edwards is Senior Lecturer in History at University College Cork, and a Director of the Irish Manuscripts Commission. His books include *The Ormond Lordship in County Kilkenny, 1515–1642: The Rise and Fall of Butler Feudal Power* (2003), *Age of Atrocity: Violence and Political Conflict in Early Modern Ireland* (2007), *The Tipperary Hero: Dermot O'Meara's Ormonius (1615)* (2012). His latest book is *Campaign Journals of the Elizabethan Irish Wars* (2014).

Simon Egan is Irish Research Council Government of Ireland Postgraduate Scholar in the School of History, University College Cork. His PhD thesis investigates the resurgence of the wider Gaeltacht in the British Isles during the later medieval period.

Alan Ford is Professor of Theology in the Theology and Religious Studies Department, University of Nottingham. He has published widely on the religious history of Ireland since the Reformation. Besides numerous articles in peer-review journals he has published *James Ussher: Theology, History, and Politics in Early Modern Ireland and England* (2007), *The Origins of Sectarianism in Early Modern Ireland* (2005), and *The Protestant Reformation in Ireland, 1590–1641* (1997).

Jason Harris is a lecturer in the School of History, University College Cork, and Director of the Centre for Neo-Latin Studies, Cork. His research interests are Renaissance humanism and Latin writing *c.*1450–1750, with a particular focus on authors of Irish origin. His principal publications include *Making Ireland Roman: Irish Neo-Latin Writers and the Republic of Letters* (2009), co-edited with Keith Sidwell, and *Transmission and Transformation in the Middle Ages* (2007), co-edited with Kathleen Cawsey. He is currently working with Nóirín Ní Bheaglaoi on an edition of the *Historia Missionis Hibernicae Capucinorum* of Robert O'Connell (forthcoming), and with Joad Raymond on *Milton's Latin Defences* (forthcoming).

Brian Mac Cuarta SJ is director, Archivum Romanum Societatis Iesu, Rome. His publications focus on the Catholic community, and on recent immigrants, in early seventeenth-century Ireland. Author of *Catholic Revival in the North of Ireland 1603–41* (2007), he has edited *Reshaping Ireland 1550–1700: Essays Presented to Nicholas Canny* (2011).

Jane Ohlmeyer MRIA is Erasmus Smith's Professor of Modern History at Trinity College Dublin and for 2014–15 is Parnell Fellow at Magdalene College Cambridge and a Visiting Professor of History at Jawaharlal Nehru University in Delhi. She has published on a number of themes in early modern Irish and British history. Her books include *Civil War and Restoration in the Three Stuart Kingdoms* (1993) and *Making Ireland English: The Irish Aristocracy in the Seventeenth Century* (2012). She has also edited *Ireland from Independence to Occupation, 1641–1660* (1995); *Political Thought in Seventeenth-Century Ireland* (2000); and co-edited *Ireland 1641: Contexts and Reactions* (2013). She is one of the editors of *The 1641 Depositions* (12 vols, forthcoming 2014–17), www.1641.tcd.ie. She is currently working on a study of Colonial Ireland, Colonial India and editing volume 2 (1550–1730) of the *Cambridge History of Ireland*.

William Roulston is Research Director of the Ulster Historical Foundation and is active in a number of other organisations in the heritage field. His most recent book is *Abercorn: The Hamiltons of Barons Court* (2014). He is also the author of *Restoration Strabane: Economy and Society in Provincial Ireland* (2007), and co-edited with Eileen Murphy *Fermanagh: History and Society* (2004).

Scott Spurlock is lecturer in Religious Studies at the University of Glasgow and convener of the Scottish Religious Cultures Network. He is author of *Cromwell and Scotland: Conquest and Religion, 1650–1660* (2007) as well as articles and book chapters on the role of religion in early modern Irish and Scottish history.

Series editors' preface

The study of Early Modern Irish history has experienced something of a renaissance since the 1990s, with the publication of a number of major monographs examining developments in Ireland during the sixteenth and seventeenth centuries from a variety of different perspectives. Nonetheless, these works still tend to group around traditional topics in political, military or religious history and significant gaps remain. The idea behind this new series is to identify key themes for exploration and thereby set the agenda for future research. Manchester University Press, a leading academic press with a strong record of publishing Irish related material, is the ideal home for this venture.

This third volume in the series builds on its predecessors by exploring the relationship between the Scots and Ireland in the first half of the seventeenth century, a subject that has had little attention for many years. Despite the recent surge of interest in early modern 'British History', studies of Ireland's place in the Three Kingdoms of the Stuarts after 1603 have tended to obscure the ongoing and developing links between Scottish and Irish people of the period by concentrating mostly on English engagement with the country. These nine chapters, by a select panel of established and upcoming scholars, pay only passing attention to the English in order to reveal the broad range of issues affecting Hiberno-Scottish relations at a time of enormous political, social, economic and religious change on both sides of the North Channel. By turning the spotlight in other directions the volume succeeds in revealing the dynamic nature of Scottish involvement in Ireland, and Irish involvement in Scotland. In doing so it exposes some of the very real limitations that deflected and stymied the growth of English power across the northern and western 'British Isles' before and after the Anglo-Scottish Bishops' Wars, the Irish rebellion of 1641, and the Civil Wars of the 1640s and 1650s.

Acknowledgements

The seeds for this book were planted in 2000, when John Young asked me to present a paper at his conference 'Scotland and Ulster: Connections and Interactions, c.1585–1750', held at the University of Strathclyde as part of the Irish-Scottish Academic Initiative. In writing my paper I quickly became aware of just how under-developed the study of Irish-Scottish relations for the early seventeenth century remained, despite the brilliant pioneering forays of a previous generation, particularly Michael Perceval-Maxwell and David Stevenson, and also Robert Hunter and Raymond Gillespie. Typical of Irish historiography not so very long ago, major contributions such as theirs had not stirred others to follow their lead very far, to seriously develop the field. Even with the advent of the much-vaunted 'New British History' questions abounded, unasked and unanswered. Eventually, I set about trying to rectify this situation by hosting a conference, 'The Scots and Stuart Ireland', held at University College Cork in 2007. This volume is partly derived from that conference, and I would like to thank all the participants for making it such a worthwhile (and enjoyable) event. I must also, of course, thank John Young for first encouraging me to enter the fray.

The conference was supported by grants from the College of Arts, Celtic Studies and Social Sciences, and the Department of History at UCC, for which I am very grateful. Margaret Curtis assisted me in organising the event, handling the logistics with her usual efficiency and positivity; the departmental secretaries Deirdre O'Sullivan and Charlotte Holland provided excellent administrative support. When searching for a suitable publisher Professor Dermot Keogh helped to steer me towards Manchester University Press; indeed, without his input, the Studies in Early Modern British History series to which this volume belongs might not exist. At Manchester I wish to thank Emma Brennan for bringing the book along, and also the two anonymous readers whose comments were so empathetic and constructive. Finally, an especial thank you is due to Simon Egan, who did so much to carry the book through its final stages when I was not always able to give it my full attention due to other pressing commitments.

David Edwards

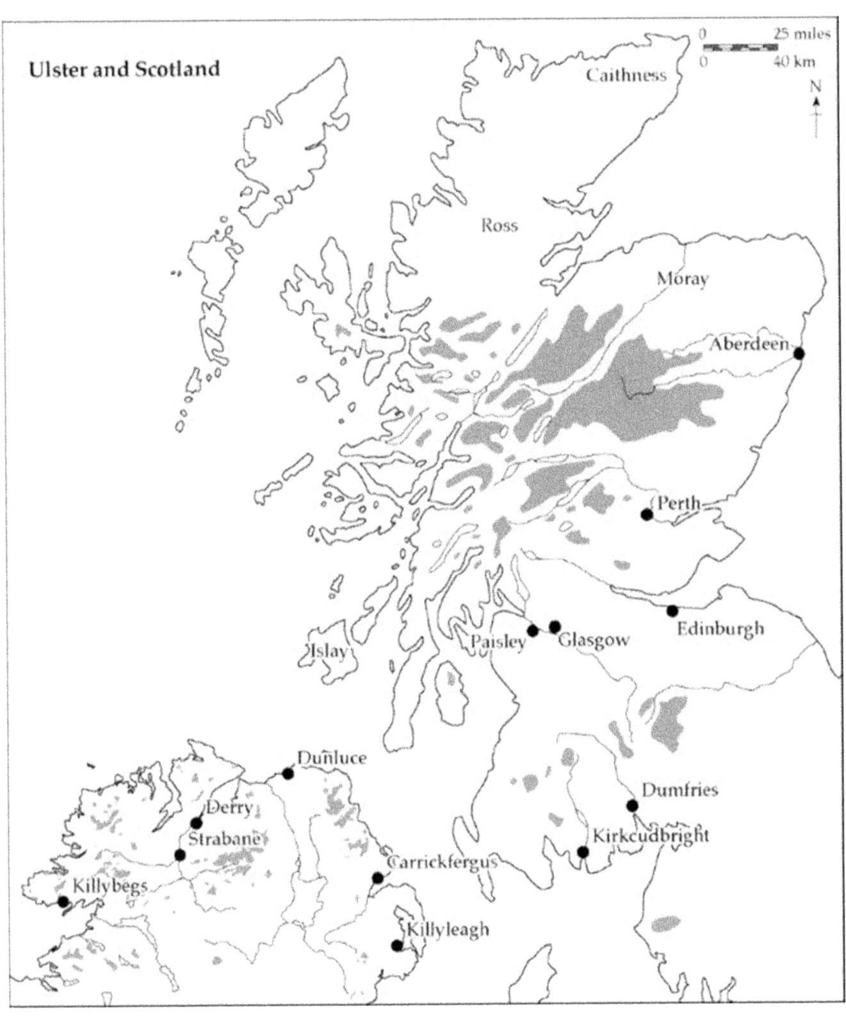
Ulster and Scotland
0
25 miles
0
40 km
N
Caithness
Ross
Moray
Aberdeen
Perth
Edinburgh
Glasgow
Paisley
Islay
Dunluce
Derry
Strabane
Killybegs
Carrickfergus
Killyleagh
Dumfries
Kirkcudbright

Introduction
Union and separation

DAVID EDWARDS

On 16 February 1642 Henry Boyne, an English cleric from Yorkshire,[1] approached the forbidding walls of Dublin Castle, the administrative centre of the Stuart kingdom in Ireland. Allowed entry by the armed guards stationed at the gatehouse, he was pointed towards a chamber where two government officials were waiting to hear the testimony that he had travelled all the way from northern England, after fleeing Ulster, to make. A written account of what he said survives.[2]

It is one of thousands of testimonies among the collection known as the '1641 Depositions' held in the library of Trinity College Dublin and that are now available as an online digitised resource. In several respects Boyne's is one of the most revealing of all the depositions regarding the troubled state of the country. Whereas most speak of atrocities perpetrated by the rebel Catholic Irish on Protestant English (and some Scottish) settlers in the autumn and winter of 1641–42, his story tells a different tale. It goes something like this: on 25 October 1641, barely forty-eight hours after the outbreak of the Ulster rising, Boyne left the house of a Scotsman in Co. Tyrone, responding to a summons issued to all settlers in the area to assemble for their common defence at the hill of Tullahogue. Before setting out he had ascertained that it would be safe to travel out of doors. He was understandably worried. The previous evening a neighbour, another Scot, had come to his house to tell him that the rebels intended to leave the Scots alone and confine their attacks to the English.

On reaching Tullahogue Boyne found a very considerable armed gathering, mostly Scottish, 'about 300 Scots assembled together'.[3] He presumed, he said, that they were preparing to join the English, as fellow colonists and fellow Protestants. They were not. On the contrary he learned that they meant to stay out of the fighting, to honour a parley that in the meantime they had made with Sir Phelim O'Neill, the Irish rebel leader; the English could look to themselves.

It got worse. Some of the Scots at Tullahogue were not content with mere neutrality; sympathising with O'Neill and the Irish, they wished to help the rebellion. With his own eyes Henry Boyne witnessed a number of Scots 'rescuing' cattle from the possession of another Englishman, who was badly treated; at almost the same time he learned that a party of O'Quinns were out looking for him too, and that some local Scots were abetting the search. Boyne ran for it. The better to avoid suspicion he headed for Scotland, not England. At his wife's insistence he left her and their children behind (a decision he later had cause to regret). When, months afterwards, he arrived in Dublin, he went hoping for news of his family, but by the time he made his deposition he had yet to find them or learn of their fate. Besides the fear and trauma he had experienced the main point to be gleaned from his story was this: by 25 October 1641 the Irish rebellion in Co. Tyrone included a Scottish component.

The second element of Boyne's deposition is equally curious. Switching his emphasis from occurrences he had witnessed himself to things he had heard about before his escape, he recounted a rumour. It concerned Robert Stewart, a prominent Scottish gentleman in Tyrone, who allegedly had gone to Mountjoy Castle to join the Irish there, and had been seen drinking with them to celebrate its capture from the English. From other sources we know that the storming of Mountjoy had been one of the very first episodes of the Ulster rebellion, occurring on Saturday 23 October.[4] According to Boyne's testimony Stewart was at the castle by the Sunday (24 October) at the latest. Given the strength of anti-English sentiment among the Scots assembled at Tullahogue, a question immediately presents itself: had some Scottish planters been complicit in the Irish rebellion from the start?

Henry Boyne's words must have unsettled the English officials who listened to him, not least because they had already heard something very like it, just two days previously. On 14 February 1642 another English colonist named Roger Markham had arrived at Dublin Castle from Ulster, claiming that in October the great majority of the Scots in Tyrone had deliberately stood aside while the Irish ran amok, burning and looting English houses, killing English men, women and children.[5] Boyne's subsequent testimony confirmed Markham's story of Scottish collusion with the Irish rebels. It was not just a wild tale: now an English clergyman said so, and from first-hand experience in Tyrone provided important details to corroborate it.

Though modern Unionist mythology continues to commemorate 1641 simply as an 'Irish papist' outrage perpetrated against innocent 'British Protestants', Henry Boyne's tale should not surprise students of seventeenth-century Irish, Scottish, or 'British' history. Since the path-breaking work of Michael

Perceval-Maxwell and David Stevenson in the 1970s the *fact* of Scottish settler neutrality and/or participation in the early stages of the 1641 Irish rising has been revealed in scholarly literature.[6] Revealed, but, alas, not entirely accepted. Even with the 1990s vogue for 'British' perspectives placing a much greater emphasis on the role of English, Scottish, Irish and Welsh inter-relations to better explain the often complex historical evolution of the islands of Great Britain and Ireland, several major surveys of the early modern period have overlooked this curious aspect of the Irish rebellion. (Has this, perhaps, contributed to the strength and endurance of the Unionist myth?)[7]

Apart from Perceval-Maxwell himself, who provided further information about it in a major study of the rising published in 1994,[8] and a penetrating discussion of some of the evidence by Nicholas Canny in 2001,[9] few historians have acknowledged the initial relations of the Ulster Scots with the Ulster Irish in October 1641.[10] Rather, a much older narrative, traceable to the Victorian period – and earlier – has persisted, stressing an automatic merger of Scottish and English settler interests when the Irish rose up. According to this tradition, Scottish neutrality/participation in the rising is not worth mentioning; instead, what matters was the rapid growth of Anglo-Scottish cooperation against the Irish in the final weeks of 1641, following reports of the rebel massacre of Scots gathered at Augher in mid-November, and then the continuation of this cooperation until the arrival in Ulster of a Scottish Covenanter army under Robert Monroe in April 1642.[11]

A major attraction of this older narrative is that it provides a clear line through the squall of events during the winter and spring of 1641–42. However it is surprising that it has prevailed so long, beset as it is by a number of conspicuous shortcomings. For instance, in terms of basic historical methodology it manages to telescope developments, so that the combined Anglo-Scottish military initiatives after December 1641 appear to flow directly from the events of October, omitting from view those very different happenings described by Henry Boyne and other witnesses. Just as problematical, it conforms to a version of events carefully constructed by the English parliamentary leadership and the London publishing industry it controlled in 1642. We now know that printed 'reports' of occurrences in Ireland had little to do with actual developments in the country. Rather (besides making money for the publishers) the 'reports' helped bolster parliament's position in an escalating constitutional crisis in England in which it, not the king, Charles I, could pose as the architect of a new political and military understanding with the Covenanter regime in Scotland. Its propaganda had no place for news of Anglo-Scottish hostilities in Ireland as Anglo-Scottish relations on the British mainland inched closer to resolution.[12]

A third, and final, shortcoming of the old narrative is the sheer scale of Scottish collusion in the rebellion. In plain terms it is fast becoming clear that

Scottish support for the Irish rebels and/or indifference to the plight of the English was actually more widespread than has previously been suggested. Perceval-Maxwell highlighted Co. Fermanagh as an area where the Scots appear to have been particularly supportive of the rebels, while Canny paid especially close attention to occurrences in Co. Tyrone, the rebellion's epicentre. More recently, however, William Roulston has shown that there was also a considerable degree of pro-rebel/anti-English sentiment among Scots living in Co. Cavan,[13] and evidence for Co. Down suggests that the apparent defection of the local notable Sir James Montgomery caused alarm among the English there as fears grew that a wider Scottish action was in train.[14] Then there was the situation in Co. Antrim. In a major re-examination of the career of Randal MacDonnell, first earl of Antrim, Jane Ohlmeyer has shown that the earl only succeeded for a few months in preventing his Gaelic Scottish Catholic followers from joining in the rebellion. Eventually, in the first days of 1642, as his influence waned, the MacDonnells rose in arms in Antrim to join forces with the Irish in Co. Derry/Londonderry[15] (where, incidentally, one of the leading rebel captains under the O'Cahans was another Scot, John Mortimer. Also associated with members of the O'Reilly lineage, Mortimer appears to have joined the Irish soon after 23 October, with about 30 followers).[16]

By continuing to overlook this sort of evidence in favour of an established, less complicated narrative some historians risk failing to do justice to the intricacy and diversity of Scottish involvement in early Stuart Ireland. The everyday stresses and strains, the attraction and repulsion that the Scots experienced in their relations with the New English, the Gaelic Irish, and the Old English have been too often left unexplored. Given that Ireland was the most multi-ethnic of the Stuart's three kingdoms, and where the monarchy tried hardest to create a new 'British' political order based on closer Anglo-Scottish union, the fact that significant numbers of Scottish colonists chose to join with the Gaelic Irish – whose former lands they were occupying – rather than their New English colonial partners can hardly be disregarded, or dismissed as an inconvenient aberration. The pro-Irish and/or anti-English actions of the Ulster Scots in October 1641 were the antithesis of what Stuart policy for Ireland – and for England and Scotland – was intended to achieve. It requires wider notice, and a place in any general account of the period. Besides what it reveals of the fragmented state of the north of Ireland by the time of the rebellion, with colonists helping the colonized attack fellow colonists, it shows the extent to which the Stuart experiment in political union and archipelagic regime-building through colonization had collapsed.

When the crown encouraged large-scale Scottish migration into Ireland in the years immediately following James Stuart's succession to the English and Irish thrones in 1603, closer Scottish involvement with the Gaelic Irish, let alone collusion with rebels, was hardly the intended outcome; neither was neutrality. From early in the reign of James VI and I it had been assumed that, especially in Ulster, increased Scottish settlement would serve to extend government control over the most restive of his three kingdoms. Ireland had only recently been brought under the heel of the English military after more than six decades of bloodshed.[17] Throughout much of that conflict Irish resistance to English dominance had been partly sustained by a steady supply of fighting men and weapons from western Scotland and the Isles, at least as much as – and probably more than – the prospect of foreign aid from France, Spain, or Italy.[18] Indeed, since the late 1540s Ireland had surpassed Scandinavia as the main export market for Scottish mercenary soldiers.[19] In 1595–96, anxious to reassure the English that he would never support Irish rebels, King James had taken steps in Edinburgh to interrupt the supply line.[20] After 1603, successfully ensconced at Whitehall, he and his advisers had calculated that an influx of Scottish settlers into Ulster would help bring an end to Scottish military involvement with Irish lords and chieftains once and for all. Where formerly it had threatened it, henceforth Scottish migration would serve to consolidate English power in Ireland.

But, of course, such mundane security considerations had been spiced up with a generous measure of crown posturing and grandiosity. As every student of the period knows, the Scots who migrated to Ireland after James Stuart's succession had been nominal partners of the English. According to various officially sanctioned proposals and projects, together the two nations had been set the lofty task of 'civilizing' Gaelic and gaelicized Ireland. The Gaelic regions of Scotland were also to be 'civilized'. It had been hoped that by cooperating closely the English and Scots might finally succeed in subduing the entire *Gaedhealtacht* – 'those rude partes' – that stretched nearly 700 miles from Lewis in the Outer Hebrides to the Skellig Islands off the south Munster coast.[21] Moreover, it had been envisaged that therein they would advance the cause of Anglo-Scottish/'British' union, strengthen the new monarchy, and make all three kingdoms safe for the spread of Protestantism.

In the event, as the occurrences of October 1641 indicate, far from shoring up a new political order in Ireland based on Anglo-Scottish power sharing, many Scots not only rejected it, but even provided military support to an attempted Gaelic resurgence. What caused this development? Why, for these Scots, had Anglo-Scottish union ended in separation? Or, to put it another way, why had a different union entirely, with the Irish, trumped it, even if only halfheartedly? And why, for that matter, had the understanding they had apparently reached with the Irish broken down so quickly, after just a few weeks?

To fully comprehend the Scottish predicament in Ulster or elsewhere in Ireland in the period before 1641, it is of course vital to consider the position of those many other Scots who had drawn close to their English fellow settlers, as the government had desired, and who had retained that connection throughout the Bishops' Wars of 1639–41 on the British mainland and the Irish rebellion that followed. Since 1603, not just in Ulster but in many parts of the country, significant numbers of Scots had formed effectual, even warm, relations with English neighbours, business associates, and officials.[22] In Co. Kilkenny, for instance, individual Scotsmen such as Patrick Wemyss had been able to settle into the local regime that emerged in the south-east around the twelfth earl (future duke) of Ormond in the 1630s, working closely with New English and Old English servitors in the area.[23] Others, such as Sir James Craig, had cooperated closely with English officers and adventurers in more than a dozen Irish counties after arriving in Ireland from Edinburgh, amassing a considerable if scattered estate, and when the Irish rebellion began he was one of two Scottish landowners in Co. Cavan to offer protection to English families fleeing the onslaught.[24] Nor should it be overlooked that some Scottish arrivals had entered very fully into the spirit of the crown's 'briticizing' programme: George Montgomery, the bishop of Derry, worked tirelessly to have the local Gaelic Irish driven off his episcopal land so as to create a model Protestant colony peopled by English and Scottish newcomers, while of Andrew Knox, bishop of Raphoe, it was said he was responsible for importing more English and Scottish tenants into Co. Donegal than any other figure.[25]

However, it is no longer certain that *most* of the Scottish settlers in early Stuart Ireland drew close to the English with whom they lived. Though precise figures are unattainable, recent research tends towards a different impression. The scale of pro-Irish activity among the Ulster Scots in 1641 suggests that, by that time at least, a deep division had emerged among the Scots living in Ireland. For all the rhetoric of union after 1603 the Scottish colonists had themselves become hugely disunited – that is, if they weren't disunited already, on their arrival in the country.

When mentioning the Scots, general accounts of the period in Ireland rarely notice the wide variety of their backgrounds beyond the standard observation that the settlers included both Lowland Scots and Highland Scots. However, as the pioneering work of Perceval-Maxwell indicated in the early 1970s, it is possible to apply a much higher degree of differentiation to the Scottish arrivals. Whether major planters or ordinary tenants, surviving records show that the migrants came from Kincardine in the east of Scotland; from Jedburgh in the south, near the frontier with England; from Dumbarton and the Isles in the west; and from numerous places in between.[26] Strictly speaking, relatively few came from the central or northern Highlands, suggesting that Irish historians would be better advised to specify the *western* Highlands and Isles as one of the principal areas of Scottish settler recruitment. Moreover, in recent years local and regional studies conducted by Scottish historians have revealed the degree of political and religious fragmentation affecting different parts of Scotland during the late sixteenth and early seventeenth centuries – developments that had a bearing on migration patterns, whether in the Lowlands or Highlands, the east or the west.[27] Such tensions helped ensure that many different types of Scot went to Ireland in the early 1600s, fleeing different pressures, seeking different opportunities. That they followed different trajectories on their arrival, and reacted differently to English and Gaelic groups (or to other Scots) was only to be expected.

Ideally, greater awareness of the regional and other differences that helped propel individual Scotsmen and women to sail to Ireland after 1603 should be factored into any consideration of their experiences upon settling in the country. Similarly, it should inform analysis of the Irish who went to Scotland in the same period. The Scottish experience of early seventeenth-century Ireland was not a one-way relationship; nor did it only revolve around the mainly Gaelic inhabitants of Ulster and Connacht.[28] Since medieval times Old English merchants from Leinster ports such as Drogheda, Dublin and Wexford had traded into Ayr and Glasgow, and this despite much English government opposition at the time.[29] This traffic very likely increased after 1603, with extant evidence suggesting growing commercial links with merchants from the main Munster ports of Waterford, Cork and Youghal, and also from lesser ones like Kenmare and Bantry.[30]

Encounters with different types of Irish people would have helped shape the attitudes of individual Scots to Ireland beyond the Stuart government's agenda-driven representations, fostering a largely self-directed calculation of how and where to engage with Irish opportunities, and with whom. While some saw political or religious fulfilment in working with the English to advance the cause of Britishness and Protestantism in Ireland, many – possibly the majority – gave this little consideration. For most, obtaining land and wealth was what mattered. Moreover, for those Scots with deep religious convictions Ireland seemed to offer something Scotland did not: freedom to practise either a version of Protestantism that was out of step with the government-controlled Church of Scotland, or to practise Catholicism more safely in a country where Catholics greatly outnumbered Protestants and where Continentally trained Counter-Reformation clergy were in growing supply.

Awareness of the diverging influences that lay behind Scottish migration is important to understanding their subsequent experience in Ireland and in identifying more accurately the impact they had on the sort of society emerging in Ireland before 1641 and how this deviated from what the royal authorities had intended. It also helps to locate aspects of something else that is at last beginning to feature, tentatively, in seventeenth-century studies: the effect that the Scottish experience of Ireland and the Irish had on Scotland, both in terms of its internal developments, within the regions,[31] and also externally, concerning its relations with Protestant and Catholic Europe.[32]

Thanks to a recent resurgence of interest in the Scottish role in Ireland, and that of the Irish in Scotland, it has become possible to explore their interrelationship in greater depth. Spurred by the creation of a major research partnership linking the University of Aberdeen, Queen's University, Belfast, and Trinity College, Dublin and also by the formal establishment of the Institute of Ulster Scots Studies at the University of Ulster, the Centre for Irish-Scottish Studies at Trinity College Dublin, the Micheál Ó Cleirigh Institute at University College Dublin, and the Centre for Neo-Latin Studies at University College Cork,[33] there has been a flurry of publications discussing aspects of late medieval and early modern Hiberno-Scottish affairs from a variety of perspectives. These can be divided into five broad categories: studies (i) that emphasize the close historic links between Scotland and Ireland in the Middle Ages;[34] (ii) that investigate the extent of the subsequent cultural and political contact between the Irish Gaelic world and its Scottish counterpart in the Highlands and Western Isles;[35] (iii) that explore the inter-connections between the Protestant and Catholic Reformations in Ireland and Scotland from the later sixteenth century onwards;[36] (iv) that examine the Scottish contribution to 'British' colonisation and elite formation in Ireland after 1603;[37] and (v) that detail the role of the Ireland-based Scottish forces and Scotland-based Irish forces in the Wars of the Three Kingdoms of the 1640s.[38]

As yet there has been no attempt to encapsulate the new levels of understanding achieved by all this research within the covers of a single collection. Instead papers have appeared here and there across a wide array of publications – chiefly journal articles and conference proceedings – so that what scholars now think about growing Irish-Scottish links in the wake of the Stuart succession is not fully appreciated by a more general audience. This volume is intended to rectify the problem by providing a concentrated focus on Irish-Scottish affairs between 1603 and 1660 – the years when the government's hopes of using Scottish migrants to forge a more manageable political order in Ireland, and to make Ireland a flagship of wider British union, led to determined action, the consequences of which were destined to have a widespread impact on all three of the Stuart kingdoms. The book is organised thematically in order to draw forth the underlying web of connections between Ireland and Scotland that so often are under-represented or even omitted in choronological narrative-driven studies. It has three distinct sections, dealing in turn with secular power and land acquisition, religious movements and identities, and the political and military turmoil of the 1640s and 1650s.

The opening chapter grapples with a key aspect of the intended political partnership between the Scottish newcomers and the English in Ireland after 1603 – the extent to which the Scots were able to enjoy a role in the secular government of the country. Strangely, the matter of Scottish office-holding has never been closely investigated by historians of early Stuart Ireland.

In recent years it has drawn some comment as part of the trajectory of the 'British history' debate, and heavy emphasis has been placed on the numbers of prominent Scottish figures granted positions by King James on the Irish Privy Council and further down the administration in Dublin Castle. On close examination this emerges as mostly a mirage. While King James did indeed appoint numerous Scots as Irish privy councillors, few of them appear to have actually taken up their postings. Attendance records of Council meetings, scattered all through the state papers, record a minimal Scottish presence. For much of the period after 1606, when the first Scottish councillor was appointed, there was usually just one Scotsman involved in Council deliberations – if any. For the final years of King James's reign, from 1618 until 1625, there was effectively no Scottish presence at all in the Irish Council chamber. Things remained much the same under Charles I.

On one level, this need not detract very much from the notion of Anglo-Scottish political union deployed in most histories of the period. After all, their presence in Dublin notwithstanding, the Scots attained something very close to parity with the English in the divvying-up of forfeited Irish land, most famously in the Plantation of Ulster (1609–10), but also in the grants of land made by the crown in Antrim and Down, strategically important coastal counties east of the main plantation area. There is no doubt that the business of acquiring land, peopling it, and exploiting it consumed most of the energies of the Scots who settled in early seventeenth-century Ireland. It is as colonists and tenants, developers and house-builders that they chiefly appear in records of the time. Likewise the growth of Scottish settled communities across Ulster encouraged Scottish merchants and vendors to supply their needs, and those of others too – much to the chagrin of English merchants, who seem to have struggled to compete. According to a report of the English Surveyor-General made in 1637, by that date the Ulster coastline from Carrickfergus west to Rathmullan in Donegal was infested with Scottish pedlars and 'renegadoes', involved in a widespread smuggling trade to the detriment of law-abiding (and allegedly tax-compliant) English traders and shopkeepers.[39]

However the success of the Scots in terms of economic power should not be permitted to obscure their lack of political or executive power; in fact, as Chapter 1 indicates, by the early 1620s, just as it was becoming apparent that in many parts of Ulster the Scottish settlements were out-performing the English ones, the leaders of the various Scottish enclaves began to press for greater official agency in Dublin. Long overlooked as a petty squabble, a dispute in 1624 over the office of Clerk of the Irish Council grew into bitter inter-ethnic bickering between the Scots and the New English (and Protestant Old English) that rumbled on for more than six years. After demanding a separate clerk to deal with Scottish petitions, but failing to secure one, the Scottish pressure for representation eventually died down, but not before other tensions had added to their sense of alienation.

The attainment of military office had likewise proved a disappointment, with numerous Scottish candidates bypassed for captaincies in the crown forces, and at local level, in some of the counties where Scottish settlers outnumbered English ones, the Scots found themselves under the rule of English governors. Far, then, from forming a 'British' governmental elite with the English, the Scots found themselves effectively excluded from the formal apparatus of state power, nationally and regionally. At best, they were junior partners in the new colonial order. The advent of the Wentworth administration in 1633 saw their position further constrained.

Chapter 2, by Jane Ohlmeyer, explores the progress of Anglo-Scottish political union in Ireland from another essential angle – the acquisition of Irish noble titles by leading Scots and the role this played in the formation of the new colonial elite.[40] The better to demonstrate how the interests of dynasticism operated slowly, over succeeding generations, Ohlmeyer's study stretches well beyond 1649, into the Restoration period; in the process it helps reveal the foundations laid by the peers for the next major phase of Scottish migration to Ireland, in the 1690s.

Chapter 1 begins with the chronology of the Irish peerage creations, before proceeding systematically through the evidence for the peers' Scottish origins, their links to the monarchy and the Stuart court, their marriages and levels of procreation, their economic activities, their military service records, and their role as local lords and patrons. It soon emerges that the Scottish peerage families in Ireland behaved very differently after 1660 to how they had before 1649. Their 'British' leanings were fairly pronounced in the later period, and their Scottish origins 'bleeched out', as it was chiefly then that they sought marital alliances with English settler dynasties in order to retain their high status and consolidate their (precarious) place in Restoration Ireland. Significantly, such tendencies had been almost entirely absent in the earlier timeframe. Between 1617, when the first Irish peerage was granted, and the outbreak of the Bishops' Wars in 1639,the founding generation of 'Scottish peers' in Ireland paid little regard to their English counterparts when seeking marriage partners for themselves or their children. Almost without exception they sought their spouses across the North Channel, at home in Scotland.

Accordingly, in the period before the 1640s the Scottish peers in Ireland tended to construct a society that the crown did not want.Rather than make their Irish presence serve a new Anglo-Scottish/'British' state they sought mostly to attach it to Scotland. The Montgomerys, viscounts Ards, the Hamiltons, viscounts Clandeboy, and the MacDonnells, earls of Antrim, created what amounted to a Little Scotland or Scottish Pale in Counties Antrim and Down. Enjoying as they did uninterrupted access to south-western Scotland and the Western Isles – the very regions of Scotland most at odds with the direction of the Scottish church and state – they headed up a society in east Ulster that in some respects embodied an alternative version of Scotland, and that attracted a steady stream of immigrants. For much of the period before the advent of Viceroy Wentworth the English barely featured in their world. In the case of at least one of the peers, Lord Balfour of Glenawley, this was entirely intentional. He is known to have advised other Scottish settlers never to trust English people.

William Roulston's Chapter 3 rounds out this first section of the book on Scottish secular power in early Stuart Ireland. Drilling down into local Ulster conditions, he succeeds in retrieving a sense of the variety of ground-level problems experienced by Scottish settlers of modest size as well as those of noble status. Echoing Ohlmeyer's earlier comments on how before the 1640s the Scottish peers had hoped mostly to populate their estates with Scottish tenants, Roulston notes that this outlook characterized the lesser Scottish landowners also.

On most Scottish estates Scottish tenants and artisans proved their worth because of the similarity of climate and land quality between Ulster and Scotland, and – equally – because of their sheer availability. The capacity to bring tenants over to Ulster gave the Scottish landlords, large and small, a competitive edge over their English counterparts in the province, who often struggled to find suitable tenants in England (especially southern and western England, where Munster was a far more familiar and more attractive location for emigration). Even so, Roulston reveals, Scottish tenant recruitment was itself slow and uneven. Uncertainty over legal title to a number of Scottish estates, combined with a proliferation of time-consuming and costly legal disputes, discouraged settlement in some areas. Landowner absenteeism was another deterrent. But ultimately such obstacles were of only limited effect. Entering the 1630s the numbers of Scots living in Ulster was steadily rising, aided partly by the emergence of several 'great estates', such as the Hamilton/Acheson dominance of the Fews or the growing Annandale interest in west Donegal, but also by the stream of ordinary migrants leaving Scotland to take up tenancies all over Ulster. English influence, such as it was, stalled and contracted. Roulston's work supports Perceval-Maxwell's once-controversial contention that by 1622 approximately 40 per cent of Scots residing in Ulster lived either on English-owned land or on land that had been acquired from English grantees by Scottish investors; the evidence for this seems very strong. Moreover it emerges that in several districts Scottish tenancy pre-dated Scottish ownership of the land – or, to put it another way, when some of the English planters accepted Scottish tenants they were not attempting to develop their holdings as a 'British' entity, but rather were moving towards selling up to the Scots and getting out of Ulster altogether.

Chapter 3 also gives brief consideration to the evidence for Scottish interaction with the Ulster Irish population. Suggestively Roulston notes that while the barriers separating Scottish colonists from Irish natives remained firmly in place, there was also a significant amount of constructive interplay between the two groups. From early in the Ulster Plantation Scottish freeholders with large estates had been willing to recruit Irish under-tenants to ensure their lands were farmed; though some English freeholders adopted the same attitude it seems that the Scots were generally quicker to do so. Remarkably, on one Scottish plantation holding – the Hamilton portion of Strabane, Co. Tyrone – it was decided to hand over the management of the entire estate to a local Gaelic Irish middleman. The fact that the estate survived and subsequently expanded may, then, be due to strong Irish participation in its development. Similarly, other evidence unearthed by Roulston, of Scottish and Irish cooperation in the provision of bail for a Scottish prisoner in Tyrone in 1628, points the way towards a deeper, more localized understanding of Hiberno-Scottish relations in early Stuart Ireland. Additionally, it has obvious implications for exploring the lead-up to the events of October 1641.

The second section of the book deals with religious matters. The years 1603–49 witnessed a number of attempts by both central government and opposition religious groups to alter the balance of confessional allegiances in Ireland and Scotland. Significantly these efforts often revolved around increasing the contact between the people of both countries, through migration and missionising. In the main the outcomes often proved disappointing for the organisers, yet they were of profound importance otherwise. It is widely accepted that they helped to set the underlying social tensions behind later political crises such as the Bishops' Wars of 1639–41 and the 1641 Irish rebellion. Less particularly, but of equal significance, they revealed one of the crucial shortcomings of the early Stuart monarchy, which in failing to construct a properly inter-connected 'British' state apparatus with which to govern its three kingdoms, nonetheless managed to leave each kingdom more prone than ever before to troubles originating in the others, by encouraging increased movement of peoples between the three jurisdictions but failing comprehensively to control the flow. Alan Ford's Chapter 4 is a valuable addition to a growing body of work that highlights how the inflow of Scottish Calvinist ministers and settlers into Ulster in the reign of James VI and I succeeded in giving the crown the larger Protestant community it desired for reforming the province, but failed to produce a religious community amenable to government control. An important supplement to Ford's previous statement on the subject,[41] it is all the more striking for linking Scottish Calvinist non-conformity with pre-existing English non-conformity within the fledgling Church of Ireland inside and outside Ulster. Chapters 5 and 6 by Brian Mac Cuarta and Scott Spurlock respectively achieve a similar advance in comprehending the Catholic world of the North Channel, and the experiences of clergy and people travelling in both directions between Scotland and Ulster. Echoing earlier chapters by Ohlmeyer and Roulston, Chapters 4, 5 and 6 all emphasize the pivotal role of Scottish noble families in facilitating trans-insular religious movements – in Ireland the Hamiltons, the Montgomerys and the Hiberno-Scottish MacDonalds, and in Scotland the likes of the Ogilvies and McKenzies. Probably more than any other factor it was thanks to these families that Scottish expansion into Ireland and Irish movements in the western Highlands witnessed the emergence of a volatile new 'British' world in which religious defiance of the established church was a defining feature.

Ford's emphasis on the English contribution to the pre-history of Calvinism and Presbyterianism in early modern Ireland illustrates best how dynamic (and dangerous) the arrival of large number of Scottish Presbyterians was to be during the 1610s and 1620s. As he shows, since the 1590s significant numbers of English Protestant dissenters had arrived in Ireland, and were usually able to integrate reasonably comfortably into the Church of Ireland, partly because of the unity felt among all English Protestants in the country confronted by the size of the Irish Catholic population, and also because of the Puritan leanings of the church hierarchy. The Scottish settlers, however, often showed little inclination to 'merge' or integrate with their English fellow Protestants. When they arrived they stayed separate and aloof, clinging to their traditions of an independent Kirk; indeed (and as others have also shown) it was largely because of their desire to retain religious independence that they had left Scotland, where King James – who had once been kidnapped by radicals – was determined to stamp out what he saw as the excesses of non-conformity and impose stronger royal and episcopal power over the Church of Scotland.[42] To a large extent it was his introduction of the Articles of Perth (1617) imposing a new liturgy on the Scottish church that accelerated Scottish migration into Ireland, which (as Chapter 3 shows) had been progressing rather slowly to that point. When they arrived many of these new settlers – and the ministers who accompanied them – scorned the idea of communion within the Church of Ireland, even though English Puritans dominated it: which is to say, they arrived divided from other Protestants, and mostly stayed that way.

Of course, after a time the repression they had escaped in Scotland caught up with them in Ireland, when in 1634 Charles I's viceroy, Thomas Wentworth, imposed a set of canons subjecting them to the bishops and the liturgy of the established church. In doing so he helped to precipitate a crisis that led directly to the collapse of royal authority in all three kingdoms.[43] Echoing the recent work of Scottish historians, Ford shows that by driving Presbyterian and non-conformist Scots back to Scotland Wentworth supplied fresh impetus to Scottish popular resistance to the state religion and its institutions. Though it is likely that the Covenanter Revolution of 1637–38 would have occurred anyway without the input of the Ulster exiles, it would not have taken the form that it did. Among other things, the sheer diversity of non-conformity that had been possible in Ulster, mixing existing Scottish practices with English and Irish ones, gave rise to profound new ideas that, once re-exported, quickly took root. Between 1634 and 1640 the Scottish 'radical south-west' became more radical because of the strength of its links to the Irish radical north-east.

If the north of Ireland was a place for Scottish Protestants to be different, the same appears true of Scottish Catholics. Interestingly, this contrasts with English Catholic experience. Recent research has shown how, in a steady flow stretching back into the Elizabethan period, sizeable numbers of English Catholics appeared in many areas of Ireland, fleeing repression at home. By the early seventeenth century these had spread into many areas of the country, constituting a large minority of New English settlers in Leinster and Munster, but only a trickle had settled down in Ulster – presumably because of the difficulty of hiding their Catholicism from English Protestant neighbours.[44] As a result Scotland was by far the main source of Catholic immigration into Ulster. Chapter 5 by Brian Mac Cuarta breaks significant new ground, providing the most concentrated examination of the Irish documentary evidence for Scottish Catholic immigration yet attempted. Besides the usual array of sources such as the State Papers and the Depositions, it draws uniquely on the surviving Jesuit Archives to link the surge of Scottish Catholic arrivals after 1603 with growing Catholic recusancy in Scotland and the series of attempts by the Scottish government to suppress it.[45] Fearing prosecution, Scottish Catholics poured into Ulster in much higher numbers than previously realized. While the enclaves in Strabane, under Hamilton protection, and Antrim, under the MacDonnells, have long featured in studies of early Stuart Ulster, the extent to which they developed into Catholic regional hubs, controlling large hinterlands in the heart of the Ulster Plantation and along its exposed coastal border is a revelation. By the later 1620s the royal government in Dublin had become so alarmed by the rising numbers of Scottish Catholic settlers that the possibility of a Scottish Catholic revolt in Co. Tyrone was discussed in correspondence, along with concerns of a general Scottish *and* Irish Catholic dominance of central and north-east Ulster – something of obvious interest to the genesis of the 1641 rising and the curious occurrences discussed above.

Scott Spurlock's Chapter 6 delves still deeper into this Scottish Catholic world. Exploring the intricate dynastic web that existed between the western Highlands, the Isles and Ireland, his work complements that of Fiona MacDonald on Protestant and Catholic missionizing in the region to reveal how the noble patronage of Catholic migrants and clergy provided by the MacDonnells in particular was part of a wider struggle for political supremacy across the entire *Gaedhealtacht* with the Campbells and their adherents the MacKenzies. Having lost ground to the Campbells in Scotland in the later sixteenth century, and spurred on by further losses of Islay in 1607, the MacDonnells re-grouped under the leadership of Clan Donald South, in Antrim. Identifying their Campbell enemies with the spread of Protestantism, the MacDonnells utilized their secure base in Ulster to support Catholic missionary activity in the Western Isles and Highlands. It has long been thought that the Irish Franciscan missions that were undertaken from Ulster after 1619 were the result of directives from external Catholic authorities, particularly in Rome, and that the missions faltered once the hierarchy lost interest. Spurlock suggests, however, that the missions most likely originated with the MacDonnell clan leaders and that because of this they lasted much longer – and were probably more effective – than is usually thought. Instead of withering in the late 1620s, the efforts of Irish friars such as Cornelius Ward and Patrick Brady continued on for another decade or so, through MacDonnell protection. As they had intended, this greatly boosted the clan's standing among the Scottish Catholic population. Within a generation or so the friary at Bonamargy, Co. Antrim, had partly replaced Iona as the centre of Gaelic Scottish Catholicism. Up to 700 pilgrims a year visited the friary from western Scotland and the Isles, and although their achievements were disputed by their detractors, the Irish friars helped to check the advance of Calvinism in the Scottish *Gaedhealtacht,* converting, or reconverting, thousands. Though their efforts were belated, they were far from insignificant.

And yet the numbers of Irish involved in retrieving Catholic Scotland remained small throughout the period. One of the more striking aspects of the MacDonnell-sponsored mission was that it failed to establish a basis for more integrated cooperation between Irish and Scottish Catholics. The final chapter in this section, Chapter 7 by Jason Harris, helps explain at least in part why this was so. Burrowing into Continental Catholic politics and church structures Harris lays bare some of the obstacles that confronted those interested in forging closer Catholic union between the Irish and Scottish regions of the *Gaedhealtacht*. Ireland and Scotland did not figure high in Papal or Spanish priorities – no surprise there – and the institution responsible for overseeing Catholic missionary activities around the world, Propaganda Fide, sometimes redirected funds intended for the *Gaedhealtacht* to missions in Asia Minor, the Far East, Africa and North America. However, probably the most damaging obstacle to the Gaelic missions was the squabbles that characterized Irish-Scottish relations in Rome itself. In the tiny, precious academic world of Neo-Latin scholarship Irish and Scottish Catholic clerical writers traded blows over the disputed ethnic origins of the ancient Scotia. A deadly battle for papal patronage and funding lurked behind the displays of pedantry and point-scoring. Bitterly contested, neither side emerged unscathed; funds were disappointing, patrons discouraged. At home, it is likely that the Scotic dispute spilled over into relations between the Irish and Scottish Catholic hierarchies; cooperation between clergy was noticeable mainly by its absence. This is why noble patrons such as the MacDonnells were so important. But it is also why the missions failed to stir a wider enthusiasm for cooperation and integration across the pan-Gaelic world, as the missions to the western Highlands and Isles were subsumed within the factional world of secular clan politics. Just as Scottish Calvinists often kept their distance from English Calvinists, so the relations of Scottish and Irish Catholics remained semi-detached. Separation was easier than union.

The final section of the book contains two important studies of the Scottish experience of the wars in Ireland from 1641 to 1650. Though the troubles of the 1640s are at last receiving the sort of detailed scrutiny needed to make proper sense of what was by any measure a very complex period there remains much to be discovered about the various roles played by Scots in Irish events, and vice versa.

Along with Kevin Forkan, the author of a fine unpublished thesis on the subject,[46] the work of Aoife Duignan and Robert Armstrong has probably done most to lift the lid on the vicissitudes of the Scottish communities settled in Ireland and their leaders in the north and west of the country in the reign of Charles I, building on the pioneering work of Perceval-Maxwell on the earlier reign of King James.[47] By focusing on the notorious career of Sir Frederick Hamilton, in Chapter 8 Duignan succeeds in shedding fresh light on the small but sizeable Scottish population that inhabited the Connacht/Ulster borderlands, in Counties Leitrim and Fermanagh. One of seven Scottish undertakers in the plantation of Leitrim, Hamilton was a younger son and something of a maverick. Though of a noble family – his eldest brother was the earl of Abercorn – he separated from them on religious grounds, espousing a strong attachment to Protestantism while the rest of his kin (as Brian Mac Cuarta reveals in Chapter 5) remained fervently Catholic. Accordingly, his response to the 1641 Catholic rebellion in Ireland is especially interesting. Hamilton had maintained ostensibly friendly links with his Scottish Catholic relatives during the 1630s, and seems to have been beholden to them for financial assistance. As such he might have been expected to react cautiously to developments in north Connacht and west Ulster, and to have avoided bloodshed as much as possible. He did no such thing. While other English and Scottish settlers in the region adopted a siege mentality, barricading themselves into their castles, he went on the attack. Moreover he did not confine himself to punitive attacks on Irish Catholics. It seems he went out of his way to castigate Scottish Catholics, and also Scottish Protestants who had 'turned papist'. Of particular note, he seems to have strongly disapproved of Scots who had married the native Irish in the region.

The main focus of Duignan's Chapter 8 is the extent and character of Sir Frederick Hamilton's recourse to military violence. His conduct earned him a dark reputation even in the 1640s.[48] While this appears to have been at least partly exaggerated by supporters of his English enemy Sir William Cole there is no doubt that Hamilton was more than ready to go to extremes. In part his recourse to unlimited warfare, and the killing by his forces of unarmed civilians, women and children, may have been informed by his experience in northern Europe as an officer in the Swedish service, but Duignan shows that it was also in line with counter-insurgency practice in Scotland and Ireland. Indeed one factor that makes Hamilton's behaviour so striking was its unique blend of Scottish and Irish military methods; another is the response it elicited. The worst atrocities perpetrated by rebel forces in Connacht in early 1642 were in direct response to his actions during the preceding months.

The fact that Hamilton's endeavours failed to secure him promotion in government service in Ireland as a self-styled 'scourge' of rebel elements suggests that he antagonised more people than the Catholics he targeted. Of course, had he cooperated more closely with his English comrades he may have been more successful, but his tendency to quarrel with them left him dangerously isolated; by the time he returned to Scotland to seek advancement under the Covenanter regime his north Connacht estates were effectively lost.

The value of biographical studies such as this is that it facilitates richer, more nuanced understanding of key personalities and their circumstances than might otherwise only be grasped in caricature. Hamilton hardly cuts a sympathetic figure, and seems mostly to have been the author of his own (and others') misfortunes. However it is also the case that he may have chosen the hardliners' path because there was little else open to him. Echoing Chapter 1, Duignan reveals that Hamilton struggled in the 1620s and 1630s to forge a meaningful Irish career. No position was open to him beyond military office, and for a man of noble descent, he probably saw his plantation estate in Leitrim as inadequate. When the Irish rebellion began in October 1641 he seems to have calculated that exemplary harshness towards the insurgents was the surest way to earn wider recognition and obtain a better position. Initially this worked, gaining him the approval of the Lords Justices in Dublin, but his star soon waned. Despite his support for the Covenanters in Scotland, he was unable to make headway even after Robert Monroe's invasion of Ulster in 1642, and subsequently felt compelled to depart for Scotland.

It is perhaps surprising that Hamilton did not prosper more in his native homeland. Following the counter-invasion of western Scotland by an Irish and Hiberno-Scottish Catholic army recruited by the earl of Antrim in June 1644, and the boost this gave to Montrose and other Scottish enemies of the Covenanter regime in Edinburgh, he might have expected to attain a leading Scottish position because of his previous track record killing Irish rebels in Connacht and Ulster. He did not. Instead, no sooner had the enemy forces been defeated than the ground began to shift beneath Hamilton's feet because of the ties he had developed with the English parliamentary junta at Westminster. Though they had bitterly opposed Charles I over his government of the Church of Scotland, the great majority of Scottish Protestants remained strongly attached to the monarchy and the House of Stuart. The king's defeat in the English Civil War and his subsequent treatment by parliament combined with a deepening rift with Westminster over the future direction of church reform to cause a *volte face* in Edinburgh. The result was the Engagement of December 1647, which committed the Covenanters to another military intervention in England and Ireland, this time on the king's behalf.[49] Sir Frederick Hamilton was hardly the only actor caught out by this development,[50] but it ensured his career ended in obscurity all the same.

Finally, Robert Armstrong's Chapter 9 addresses the long-term consequences of the Engagement and the ultimate defeat of the Covenanter/royalist cause in Ulster. Tracing the course of events since the arrival of Monroe's army in 1642, Armstrong shows how by the time covenant and king were vanquished by parliament and Cromwell in 1649 the Scottish Protestant population of Ulster was politically and socially much more cohesive than before. In the intervening years the Scottish soldiers had overrun most of the province, and under the troops' protection Presbyterianism had spread. Ministers had busied themselves missionizing among the population – including the Gaelic Irish – and at a time of general flux and confusion the presbytery had provided crucial social order in the localities.

In the 1650s, for the victorious English parliamentarian regime, the Scottish grip on Ulster was something that had immediately to be diminished. Even after the Cromwellian conquest of Scotland and the defeat of Charles II at Worcester in 1651, fears remained that Scottish Ulster forces would emerge from the northern mist to provoke yet another war. Ongoing royalist plots in Scotland such as the Glencairn rising added to concerns of an Ulster link-up (all the more so as the earl of Glencairn's powerbase lay in western Scotland and several members of his clan, the Cunninghams, were Ulster planters and seem to have played a prominent role in the elements of the Laggan army that had turned against parliament in Ireland in 1647–49). Yet, as Armstrong shows, Cromwellian policy towards the Ulster Scots oscillated widely between severity and compromise and back again. Leading royalist lords such as Viscount Ards were targeted for punishment, and suffered confiscation, but plans to deal with the broader Ulster Scots population were intermittent and confused. Cromwellian officials determined to break the link between Ulster and Scotland by replacing the Scottish settlers with English ones; however, plans for the forced transplanting of the Ulster Scots to southern Ireland seemed to gain the ascendant in 1653 only for the scheme to stumble and lose momentum. Other voices urged negotiation, with some expecting to bring the Ulster Scots into a new partnership and even a new Protestant religious settlement, yet this too foundered.

The one consistent policy appears to have been the reduction of Presbyterian influence. Ministers were hunted and forced into exile, so that by the time of the Restoration there were barely half a dozen left according to some accounts. Otherwise indecision proved final. In 1660 the majority of Scottish Protestants in Ulster remained as they had in 1650 – royalist, numerous, Presbyterian and separate. Their very appearance could provoke unease among English visitors to the region, conscious that for every hat-wearing 'gentleman' there were dozens of bonnet-clad Scotsmen who kept to themselves and showed little or no enthusiasm for English ways or government. One consolation was that while the Scots remained the dominant 'interest' in the north, they had not drawn closer to the Catholic Irish, but remained 'sufficiently averse'. That said, just as fears of residual Scottish power in Ulster continued to haunt government policy-makers for the remainder of the seventeenth century, as often as not this was linked to suspicions that sooner or later the Scots and the Irish would form a pact. With retrospect it seems obvious that such fears and suspicions were exaggerated. Yet they were hardly groundless.

It should not be assumed from the foregoing that the nine chapters presented here are linked by a common pronounced emphasis on Irish-Scottish relations. They are not. Though all allude to it to a degree, some afford it more attention than others. It is just that in reading and re-reading the volume while preparing this Introduction it struck me that a significant point has been reached in the historiography. Hitherto most treatments of the Scottish experience of early seventeenth-century Ireland have examined the subject mostly in terms of the Scots' relationship with the English with whom they shared land and power on the island. Obviously some of the chapters are similarly oriented (especially my own, and Alan Ford's), because they have important new things to say within that context. However, most of the rest are at the least conscious of the presence of the Irish in Scottish settler life, and in Scottish affairs generally, and more than has previously been the norm.

This is exciting. We are on the cusp of something new, which, if pursued more intensively in future research, should help improve understanding of the Stuart experiment in 'British' state-building across the three kingdoms of England, Scotland and Ireland after 1603. For very good reasons treatments of this topic have focused almost entirely on *Anglo*-Scottish relations as they developed, and faltered, across space and time in the seventeenth century, in Ireland as well as on the British mainland. And for equally good reasons efforts to weave Ireland and the Irish into the story have remained predominantly focused on the *Anglo*-Irish relationship. For example, probably the best single synthesis of 'British' early modern history, Derek Hirst's recent

Dominion, presents what is essentially an Anglo-centric view, as its subtitle indicates *England and its Island Neighbours, 1500–1707*.

By extending the inquiry to consider the role of the Scots and the Irish in the fledgling 'British' state system it is possible to glimpse another 'Britishness' entirely, one hugely affected by the English, to be sure, but which nonetheless had its own independent dynamics. The Irish-Scottish world did not require English direction to exist – it had existed for millennia – but the growth and projection of English power in Ireland after 1603 greatly altered the nature of its interaction and the prospects for its development. What is now at last stealing into view is the extent to which Irish-Scottish relations deflected and challenged English-oriented 'Britishness'. The Irish and the Scots appear often to have gone their own way. They were able to draw closer together or pull further apart according to political and economic contingencies, or religious and cultural imperatives, which sometimes barely acknowledged the English presence, or consciously defied it. That such a situation could obtain between Gaelic-speaking Irish and Scots the English (and some English-speaking Lowland Scots) found unsettling; that it also obtained between the Irish and some Lowland Scots, through a shared Catholicism or some other unifying factor, was more worrying still. As several of the chapters in this book testify, successive English administrations in Ireland, from Chichester's soldier government under James VI and I to the Ormond and Essex viceroyalties following the Restoration, were sensitive to Irish-Scottish fraternization, fearing that it might spark war and rebellion across the country before spreading into Scotland, or vice versa, to England's undoing.

Hopefully, seventeenth-century Irish-Scottish relations will soon attract the study it deserves. With careful research it should be possible to gain a clearer impression of the level of Irish-Scots inter-marriage. The punitive measures taken by Sir Frederick Hamilton against Scots who had married Irish partners in north Connacht suggests the practice may have been growing there in the 1630s, and was not confined to the higher landowning classes. Irish-Scottish economic relations may be elucidated by close examination of estate papers, deeds, rentals, court and legal documents, and trading records, which, though widely dispersed, survive in greater quantities than is often appreciated. Moreover, given the availability of the 1641 Depositions online, and the posthumous completion and publication of Bob Hunter's edition of the 1630 Ulster muster rolls,[51] it may prove possible to flesh out the background to particular instances of Irish-Scottish contact, and to improve our general understanding of it through a number of well-crafted case studies. Similarly, the discovery of a large cache of Jesuit letters and reports in Rome suggests that, together with the English-Irish Catholic world, study of its Irish-Scottish counterpart may soon become a significant field in its own right, building on the work of Mac Cuarta, Spurlock and Harris that is published here.

To return to the beginning, however, and end where we started: with the plight of the English clergyman Henry Boyne in autumn 1641. Forced to flee Co. Tyrone, and leave his wife and children at the mercy of Irish rebels and their Scottish abettors, Boyne did not get to witness one of the key developments of the rebellion that occurred just a few weeks later – the Irish onslaught on the Scots. The full significance of the massacre at Augher in November 1641 and the sacking of Strabane early in December have yet to be appreciated. Rather than treat them as aberrant episodes, as awkward sideshows that interrupt the main story of the merging of Scottish and English interests against the rebels, there may be a case to reconsider them as signalling a watershed in Irish-Scottish relations. Previously, something significant had been taking place in pockets of Ulster and north Connacht for years between groups of Irish and Scottish people. The bloodshed at Augher and Strabane changed this. It destroyed the basis for any negotiation between the rebel leadership and the Covenanter regime in Scotland, and ensured Scottish military intervention in Ulster and all that that entailed for Irish hopes of victory. But did it also have a longer-term impact? To what extent was the inability of Irish and Scottish royalists to form an effective alliance after 1649 attributable, if only in part, to Scottish memories of Irish treachery in 1641? Counter-factual (or 'what if?') history has become popular in recent years, and while it has obvious limitations, it can help highlight the danger of historical writing that observes only what happened and ignores what did not happen, but was possible. The attacks on Augher and Strabane might benefit from such an approach. What if the Irish rebel leaders had left the Scots alone, and held their troops back? In Scotland, would Monroe's invasion force have materialized? If it hadn't, would the Irish have been able to attack the Pale and drive the English out of Dublin? And in England, without Monroe's army to squabble over, how would the parliamentary junta around Pym have fared in its struggle with Charles I? Could the English Civil War have been averted? Irish-Scottish relations were important. There is much still to be discovered.

NOTES

1 For Boyne's clerical status and wealth in 1641 see B. Mac Cuarta, 'Religious violence against settlers in South Ulster, 1641–2', in D. Edwards, P. Lenihan and C. Tait (eds), *Age of Atrocity: Violence and Political Conflict in Early Modern Ireland* (Dublin, 2007), pp. 159–60.

2 Deposition of Henry Boyne, 16 February 1642, Trinity College Dublin (hereafter TCD) MS 839, fols 10r–11v. All depositions are taken from the online edition http://1641.tcd.ie.

3 Another deponent reckoned there were 500 Scots at the assembly, and dates the gathering to 26 October: Deposition of Roger Markham, 14 February 1642, *ibid.*, fols 17–20.

4 The broad outline of the course of the rising is well known, yet there remains a pressing need for a comprehensive chronological regional narrative of its progress. The best account currently available is M. Perceval-Maxwell, *The Outbreak of the Irish Rebellion of 1641* (Montreal, 1994), chapter 10.

5 Deposition of Roger Markham, 14 February 1642 (TCD, MS 839, fols 17–20).

6 M. Perceval-Maxwell, 'The Ulster rising of 1641 and the Depositions', *Irish Historical Studies*, 21 (1978–79), 144–67. It is also noted in D. Stevenson, *Scottish Covenanters and Irish Confederates* (Belfast, 1981), pp. 86–90, but Stevenson sees the Scots' participation in the events as essentially defensive.

7 T.C. Barnard, 'The uses of 23 October 1641 and Irish Protestant celebrations', *English Historical Review*, 106 (1991), 889–920; J. Kelly, '"The glorious and immortal memory": commemoration and Protestant identity in Ireland, 1660–1800', *Proceedings of the Royal Irish Academy*, 94 C (1994), 25–52; I. McBride, 'Memory and national identity in Modern Ireland', in I. McBride (ed.), *History and Memory in Modern Ireland* (Cambridge, 2001), p. 21; but see now J. Gibney, *The Shadow of a Year: The 1641 Rebellion in Irish History and Memory* (Wisconsin, 2012), the fullest analysis by far.

8 Perceval-Maxwell, *The Outbreak*, pp. 216–19.

9 N. Canny, *Making Ireland British* (Oxford, 2001), pp. 477–84.

10 R. Gillespie, 'Destabilizing Ulster, 1641–2', in B. Mac Cuarta (ed.), *Ulster 1641: Aspects of the Rising* (Belfast, 1993), pp. 111–12, mentions it, but only as evidence of English paranoia about the Scots.

11 For example, R. Gillespie, *Seventeenth Century Ireland* (Dublin, 2006), pp. 142–4; P. Lenihan, *Consolidating Conquest: Ireland 1603–1727* (Harlow, 2008), pp. 94–5. See also Patrick J. Corish, 'The Rising of 1641 and the Catholic Confederacy, 1641–5', in T.W. Moody, F.X. Martin and F.J. Byrne (eds), *A New History of Ireland: Early Modern Ireland, 1534–1691* (9 vols; Oxford, 1976), iii, pp. 292–3. K. McKenny's fine book, *The Laggan Army in Ireland, 1640–1685: The Landed Interests, Political Ideologies and Military Campaigns of the North-West Ulster Settlers* (Dublin, 2005), pp. 40–1, briefly notes Scottish relations with the rebels, but focused as it is on the formation of a combined Anglo-Scottish settler army affords it little consideration; likewise S. Connolly, *Divided Kingdom: Ireland 1630–1800* (Oxford, 2008), p. 50, only notes it, more interested in Irish rebel fears of Scottish invasion.

12 Stevenson, *Scottish Covenanters*, pp. 44–65, best describes the efforts to secure financial and political control of Monro's invasion force; D. O'Hara, *English Newsbooks and Irish Rebellion, 1641–1649* (Dublin, 2006), chapter 1; I. Donovan, 'Bloody news from Ireland: the pamphlet literature of the Irish massacres of the 1640s', M.Litt thesis, Trinity College Dublin, 1995. Had the parliamentary leadership been aware of the 'Laggan Army' of English and Scots in western Ulster, hurriedly assembled during the final weeks of 1641, this failure to publicise reports of earlier Scottish indifference and/or animosity towards the English in the centre of the province might have been justified; however, as recent research has revealed, even in spring 1642 parliament was unaware of the Laggan Army's existence (McKenny, *The Laggan Army*, p. 50).

13 W. Roulston, 'The Scots in Plantation Cavan, 1610–42', and B. Scott, 'Reporting the 1641 rising in Cavan and Leitrim', both in B. Scott (ed.), *Culture and Society in Early Modern Breifne/Cavan* (Dublin, 2009), pp. 141–5 and 204–8.

14 Deposition of Valentine Pyne, 9 August 1642 (TCD, MS 837, fols 19r–20v).

15 J. Ohlmeyer, *Civil War and Restoration in the Three Stuart Kingdoms: The Career of Randal MacDonnell, Marquis of Antrim* (Dublin, 2001), pp. 101–8. See also D. Stevenson, *Highland Warrior: Alasdair MacColla and the Civil Wars* (Edinburgh, 2003), pp. 74–81.

16 Stevenson is the only historian to notice Mortimer. For more on his role see Deposition of John Turner, 7 March 1653 (TCD, MS 838, fols 65v–66r); Deposition of John Blair, 8 March 1653 (*ibid.*, fols 68v–69v).

17 D. Edwards, 'Ireland: security and conquest', in Susan Doran and Norman Jones (eds), *The Elizabethan World* (London and New York, 2011), pp. 182–200; B. Lenman, *England's Colonial Wars, 1550–1688: Conflicts, Empire and National Identity* (Harlow, 2001), chapters 2–5.

18 G.A. Hayes-McCoy, *Scots Mercenary Forces in Ireland, 1565–1603* (Dublin, 1937); K. Nicholls, 'Scottish mercenary kindreds in Ireland, 1250–1600', and W. McLeod, 'Images of Scottish warriors in later Irish bardic poetry', both in S. Duffy (ed.), *The World of the Galloglass: Kings, Warlords and Warriors in Ireland and Scotland, 1200–1600* (Dublin, 2007), pp. 86–105, 169–87.

19 J.E.A. Dawson, *Scotland Re-Formed, 1488–1587* (Edinburgh, 2007), pp. 180–2, 344–5; A. Aberg, 'Scottish soldiers in the Swedish armies in the 16th and 17th centuries', in G.G. Simpson (ed.), *Scotland & Scandinavia, 800–1800* (Edinburgh, 1990), pp. 90–1; S. Murdoch, *Britain, Denmark-Norway and the House of Stuart, 1603–1660: A Diplomatic and Military Analysis* (East Linton, 2003), pp. 187–8; D. Parrot, *The Business of War: Military Enterprise and Military Revolution in Early Modern Europe* (Cambridge, 2012), pp. 18, 110–11.

20 D. Edwards, 'Securing the Jacobean succession: the secret career of James Fullerton of Trinity College, Dublin', in Duffy (ed.), *The World of the Galloglass*, pp. 188–209.

21 J. Ohlmeyer, '"Civilizinge of those rude partes": the colonization of Ireland and Scotland, 1580s to 1640s', in N. Canny (ed.), *The Oxford History of the British Empire, i: Origins of Empire* (Oxford, 1998), pp. 124–47; J. Wormald, 'The "British" crown, the earls and the plantation of Ulster', in É. Ó Ciardha and M. Ó Siochrú (eds), *The Plantation of Ulster: Ideology and practice* (Manchester, 2012), pp. 18–32.

22 By 1641 there was a Scottish presence recorded in Counties Longford, Dublin, Kilkenny and Wexford in Leinster; Cork, Limerick and Tipperary in Munster; and Roscommon, Mayo, Sligo and Leitrim in Connacht.

23 D. Edwards, *The Ormond Lordship in County Kilkenny, 1515–1642: The Rise and Fall of Butler Feudal Power* (Dublin, 2003), pp. 291, n.303, 310.

24 Roulston, 'The Scots', pp. 124–7, 143–4; R.J. Hunter, *The Ulster Plantation in the Counties of Armagh and Cavan, 1608–1641* (Belfast, 2012), pp. 52, 66–7, 135, 139, 150–1.

25 H.A. Jefferies, 'Winners and losers: Bishop George Montgomery and Sir Cathair O'Doherty', in D. Finnegan, É. Ó Ciardha and M. Peters (eds), *The Flight of the*

Earls (Derry, 2010), pp. 20–9; A. Ford, 'Andrew Knox (1559–1633), bishop of Raphoe', in J. McGuire and J. Quinn (eds), *Dictionary of Irish Biography* (Dublin, 2009–), v, p. 246.

26 M. Perceval-Maxwell, *The Scottish Migration to Ulster in the Reign of James I* (London, 1973), pp. 317–22, map 2 p. 368.

27 S. Adams, 'James VI and the politics of south-west Scotland, 1603–1625', in J. Goodare and M. Lynch (eds), *The Reign of James VI* (East Linton, 2000), pp. 228–40; S. Adams., 'The making of the radical south-west: Charles I and his Scottish kingdom, 1625–49', in J. Young (ed.), *Celtic Dimensions of the British Civil Wars* (Edinburgh, 1997), pp. 53–74; M. Meikle, *A British Frontier? Lairds and Gentlemen in the Eastern Borders, 1540–1603* (East Linton, 2004); R.A. Dodghson, *From Chiefs to Landlords: Social and Economic Change in the Western Highlands and Islands, c.1493–1830* (Edinburgh, 1998); R. Oram, *Galloway: Land and Lordship* (Edinburgh, 1991); W.H.D. Sellar (ed.), *Moray: Province and People* (Edinburgh, 1993).

28 For similar observations focused on Scottish land-holding patterns outside Ulster, see Patrick Fitzgerald, 'Scottish migration to Ireland in the seventeenth century', in A. Grosjean and S. Murdoch (eds), *Scottish Communities Abroad in the Early Modern Period* (Brill, 2005).

29 For the later medieval period see T. O'Neill, *Merchants and Mariners in Medieval Ireland* (Dublin, 1987), pp. 23–4, 61–2. Regarding the sixteenth century, the Cocket Book of Ayr (Ayr Burgh Archives, ref. B6/29) contains numerous references to Irish merchants from Wexford, Dublin and Drogheda for the period 1577–1632, while the Dumbarton Shipping Register (Dumbarton District Library, ref. 1/3/105) contains Irish references for 1598–1607. There are also many Irish entries in the Minute Book of the Town Council of Glasgow (Strathclyde Regional Archives, MS C1/1/2). For a further description of the contents of all three sources see B. Donovan and D. Edwards, *British Sources for Irish History, 1485–1641: A Guide to Manuscripts in Local, Regional and Specialised Repositories in England, Scotland and Wales* (Dublin, 1997), pp. 308–10, 312–14.

30 See, for example, J.C. Appleby (ed.), *Calendar of Material Relating to Ireland from the High Court of Admiralty Examinations, 1536–1641* (Dublin, 1992), pp. 85, 107, 108, 120, 148, 153, 191, 257.

31 J.R. Young, '"Escaping massacre": refugees in Scotland in the aftermath of the 1641 Ulster Rebellion', in Edwards, Lenihan and Tait (eds), *Age of Atrocity*, pp. 219–41; J.R. Young, 'Scotland and Ulster in the seventeenth century: the movement of peoples over the North Channel', in W.P. Kelly and J.R. Young (eds), *Ulster and Scotland, 1600–2000: History, Language and Identity* (Dublin, 2004), pp. 11–32.

32 D. Caulfield, 'The Scotic debate: Philip O'Sullivan Beare and his *Tenebriomastix*', in J. Harris and K. Sidwell (eds), *Making Ireland Roman: Irish Neo-Latin Writers and the Republic of Letters* (Cork, 2009), pp. 109–25; D. Caulfield, 'Don Philip strikes back', in G. Petersmann and V. Oberparleiter (eds), *The Role of Latin in Early Modern Europe: Texts and Contexts II* (Salzburg 2006), pp. 65–81; Murdoch, *Britain, Denmark-Norway, and the House of Stuart.*

33 While the role of the first two is self-evident, the work of researchers attached to the Ó Cleirigh Institute at UCD and the Neo-Latin Centre at UCC has encompassed several areas of Irish-Scottish interest.

34 K. Nicholls, 'Celtic contrasts: Ireland and Scotland', *History Ireland*, 7:3 (1999), 22–6; A. Cathcart, 'Scots and Ulster: the late medieval context', in W.P. Kelly and Young (eds), *Scotland and the Ulster Plantations* (Dublin, 2009), pp. 62–83; A. Cathcart, 'James V, King of Scotland – and Ireland?', in Duffy (ed.), *The World of the Galloglass*, pp. 124–43; J.E.A. Dawson, 'Two kingdoms or three? Ireland in Anglo-Scottish relations in the sixteenth century', in R.A. Mason (ed.), *Scotland and England, 1286–1815* (Edinburgh 1987), pp. 113–38; S. Kingston, *Ulster and the Isles in the Fifteenth Century: The Lordship of the Clann Domhnaill of Antrim* (Dublin, 2004); S. Duffy, 'The Bruce brothers and the Irish sea world, 1306–29', *Cambridge Medieval Celtic Studies*, 21 (1991), 155–86; J. Wormald, *Lords and Men in Scotland: Bonds of Manrent, 1442–1603* (Edinburgh, 1985); J.M. Hill, *Fire & Sword: Sorley Boy MacDonnell and the Rise of Clan Ian Mor, 1538–90* (London, 1993); J. Goodare and M. Lynch, 'The Scottish state and its borderlands, 1567–1625', and M. Lynch, 'James VI and the "Highland Problem"', in J. Goodare and M. Lynch (eds), *The Reign of James VI* (East Linton, 2000), pp. 186–240. Going still further back, see D. Broun, *The Irish Identity of the Kingdom of the Scots* (Woodbridge, 1999); R.A. McDonald, *The Kingdom of the Isles: Scotland's Western Seaboard, c.1100–c.1336* (East Linton, 1997); M. Herbert, 'Sea-divided Gaels? Constructing relationships between the Irish and Scots, *c.*800–1169', in B. Smith (ed.), *Britain and Ireland 900–1300* (Cambridge 1999), pp. 87–97; W.D.H. Sellar, 'Hebridean Sea-kings: the successors of Somerled, 1164–1316', in E.J. Cowan and R.A. MacDonald (eds), *Alba: Celtic Scotland in the Medieval Era* (East Linton, 2000), pp. 187–218; and S. Duffy, 'The lords of Galloway, earls of Carrick, and the Bissets of the Glens: Scottish settlement in thirteenth-century Ulster', in D. Edwards (ed.), *Regions and Rulers in Ireland, 1100–1650: Essays for Kenneth Nicholls* (Dublin, 2004), pp. 37–50.

35 W. McLeod, *Divided Gaels: Gaelic Cultural Identities in Scotland and Ireland, c.1200–c.1650* (Oxford, 2004); W. McLeod, '*RíInnsiGall, RíFionnghall, Ceannas nan Gáidheal*: sovereignty and rhetoric in the Late Medieval Hebrides', *Cambrian Medieval Celtic Studies*, 43 (2002), 25–48; M. Ó Mainnín, '"The same in origin and blood": Bardic windows on the relationship between Irish and Scottish Gaels, *c.*1200–1650', *Cambrian Medieval Celtic Studies*, 38 (1999), 1–52; J. Bannerman, *The Beatons: A Medical Kindred in the Classical Gaelic Tradition* (Edinburgh, 1986); M. MacGregor, '"Lán-mara 's mile seól": Gaelic Scotland and Gaelic Ireland in the Later Middle Ages', in *Congress 99: Cultural Contacts within the Celtic Community* (Glasgow, 2000), pp. 77–97; A. Grant, 'Scotland's "Celtic Fringe" in the late Middle Ages: the MacDonald lords of the Isles and the kingdom of Scotland', in R.R. Davies (ed.), *The British Isles, 1100–1500: Comparisons, Conrasts and Connections* (Edinburgh, 1988), pp. 118–41; S.G. Ellis, 'The collapse of the Gaelic world, 1450–1650', *Irish Historical Studies*, 31 (1999), 449–69; J.E.A. Dawson, 'The fifth earl of Argyle, Gaelic lordship, and political power in sixteenth-century Scotland', *Scottish Historical Review*, 67 (1988), 1–27; N. MacLean-Bristol, *Warriors and Priests: The History of the Clan MacLean, 1300–1570* (East Linton, 1995); P. Smith,

'Hebridean settlement and activity in Ireland, *c.*1470–1565', MA dissertation, Queen's University Belfast, 1993; S. Kingston, 'Delusions of Dal Riada', in P. Duffy, D. Edwards and E. FitzPatrick (eds), *Gaelic Ireland, c.1250–1650: Land, Lordship and Settlement* (Dublin, 2001), pp. 98–114; W. Gillies, 'The invention of tradition – Highland style', in A.A. MacDonald, M. Lynch and I.B. Cowan (eds), *The Renaissance in Scotland: Studies in Literature, History & Culture* (London, 1994), pp. 144–56; A.I. MacInnes, 'Crown, clans and *Fine*: the "civilizing" of Scottish gaeldom, 1587–1603', *Northern Scotland*, 13 (1993), 31–55; A.I. MacInnes, *Clanship, Commerce and the House of Stuart, 1603–1788* (East Linton, 1996).

36 J. McCafferty, 'When Reformations collide', in A.I. Macinnes and J. Ohlmeyer (eds), *The Stuart Kingdoms in the Seventeenth Century: Awkward Neighbours* (Dublin, 2002), pp. 186–203; E. Boran and C. Gribben (eds), *Enforcing Reformation in Ireland and Scotland, 1550–1700* (Aldershot, 2006); T.M. McCoog, *The Society of Jesus in Ireland, Scotland and England, 1589–1597* (Farnham and Rome, 2012); F. MacDonald, *Missions to the Gaels: Reformation and Counter-Reformation in Ulster and the Highlands and Islands of Scotland, 1560–1760* (Edinburgh, 2006); R. Gillespie, 'Scotland and Ulster: A Presbyterian perspective, 1603–1700', in Kelly and Young (eds), *Scotland and the Ulster Plantations*, pp. 84–107; A. Ford, 'The Origins of Irish Dissent', in K. Herlihy (ed.), *The Religion of Irish Dissent, 1650–1800* (Dublin, 1996), pp. 9–30; A. Ford, 'Criticizing the Godly prince: Malcolm Hamilton's *Passages and consultations*', in V. Carey and U. Lotz-Heumann (eds), *Taking Sides: Colonial and Confessional Mentalités in Early Modern Ireland* (Dublin, 2003), pp. 116–37; J.E.A. Dawson, *The Politics of Religion in the Age of Mary, Queen of Scots: The Earl of Argyll and the Struggle for Britain and Ireland* (Cambridge, 2002); J.E.A. Dawson, 'Anglo-Scottish Protestant culture and integration in sixteenth-century Britain', in S.G. Ellis and S. Barber (eds), *Conquest & Union: Fashioning a British State, 1485–1725* (Harlow, 1995), pp. 87–114; J.E.A. Dawson, 'Calvinism and the Gaidhealtachd in Scotland', in A. Pettegree, A. Duke and G. Lewis (eds), *Calvinism in Europe, 1540–1620* (Cambridge, 1994), pp. 231–53; R. Grant, 'The Brig o' Dee affair, the sixth Earl of Huntly, and the Politics of the Counter-reformation', in Goodare and Lynch (eds), *The Reign of James VI*, pp. 93–109; P. Kilroy, 'Protestantism in Ulster, 1610–1641', in B. Mac Cuarta (ed.), *Ulster 1641: Aspects of the Rising* (Belfast, 1993), pp. 25–36; P. Kilroy, 'Radical religion in Ireland, 1641–1660', in J. Ohlmeyer (ed.), *Ireland from Independence to Occupation, 1641–1660* (Cambridge, 1995), pp. 201–17.

37 Besides the work of Canny, Ohlmeyer and Wormald cited earlier, see the comments in J. Wormald, 'James VI, James I and the identity of Britain', in B. Bradshaw and J. Morrill (eds), *The British Problem, c.1534–1707: State Formation in the Atlantic Archipelago* (Basingstoke, 1996), pp. 148–71; see also J. Johnson, 'The Scotch settlement of county Fermanagh, 1610–30', *Clogher Record*, 10:3 (1978), 367–73.

38 J. Peacey, 'The outbreak of the civil wars in the Three Kingdoms', in B. Coward (ed.), *A Companion to Stuart Britain* (Oxford, 2003). For the Scottish in Ireland see the following: K. Forkan, 'Scottish-Protestant Ulster and the crisis of the three kingdoms', PhD thesis, NUI Galway, 2003, pp. 31–3; K. Forkan, '"The fatal ingredient of the Covenant": the place of the Ulster Scottish community during

the 1640s', in B. Mac Cuarta (ed.), *Reshaping Ireland, 1550–1700: Colonization and its Consequences* (Dublin, 2011), pp. 264–6; K. Forkan, 'The Ulster Scots and the Engagement, 1647–8', *Irish Historical Studies*, 35:140 (November, 2007), 455–76; R. Armstrong, *Protestant War: The 'British' of Ireland and the Wars of the Three Kingdoms* (Manchester, 2005); R. Armstrong, 'Viscount Ards and the presbytery: politics and religion among the Scots of Ulster in the 1640s', in Kelly and Young (eds), *Scotland and the Ulster Plantations*, pp. 18–40; M. Perceval-Maxwell, 'Ireland and Scotland, 1638–1648', in John Morrill (ed.), *The Scottish National Covenant in its British Context, 1638–51* (Edinburgh, 1990), pp. 193–211; R. Gillespie, 'An army sent from God: Scots at war in Ireland, 1642–9', in N. MacDougall (ed.), *Scotland and War* (Edinburgh, 1991), pp. 113–32; P. Lenihan, 'Confederate Catholics and Covenanters, 1644–6', in Kelly and Young (eds), *Scotland and the Ulster Plantations*, pp. 108–21; E.M. Furgol, 'The military and ministers as agents of Presbyterian imperialism in England and Ireland, 1640–1648', in J. Dwyer, R.A. Mason and A. Murdoch (eds), *New Perspectives on the Politics and Culture of Modern Scotland* (Edinburgh, 1982), pp. 95–115. For the Irish military in Scotland after 1644 see Stevenson, *Highland Warrior*, chapters 4–9; Stevenson, *Scottish Covenanters and Irish Confederates*, chapter 4; E.J. Cowan, *Montrose: For Covenant and King* (London, 1977); P. Lenihan, 'Confederate military strategy, 1643–7', in M. Ó Siochrú (ed.), *Kingdoms in Crisis: Ireland in the 1640s* (Dublin, 2001), pp. 161–3.

39 Report of Charles Monck, 1637 (British Library, Harleian MS 2138).

40 This chapter is an important addendum to her recent magnum opus, *Making Ireland English: The Irish Aristocracy in the Seventeenth Century* (Yale, 2012).

41 Ford, 'The Origins of Irish Dissent'.

42 See, for example, Adams, 'James VI and the politics of south-west Scotland'; G.I.R. McMahon, 'The Scottish courts of High Commission 1610–38', *Records of the Scottish Church History Society*, 15 (1966), 193–210; D. Stevenson, 'Conventicles in the Kirk, 1619–37: the emergence of aradical party', *Records of the Scottish Church History Society*, 18 (1972–74), 99–114; E.J. Cowan, 'The making of the National Covenant', in John Morrill (ed.), *The Scottish National Covenant in its British Context, 1638–51* (Edinburgh, 1990), pp. 68–89.

43 M. Perceval-Maxwell, 'Strafford, the Ulster Scots, and the Covenanters', *Irish Historical Studies*, 18 (1973), 524–51.

44 D. Edwards, 'A haven of popery: English Catholic migration to Ireland in the age of plantations', in A. Ford and J. McCafferty (eds), *The Origins of Sectarianism in Early Modern Ireland* (Cambridge, 2005), pp. 95–126: 114–19.

45 M. Sanderson, 'Catholic Recusancy in Scotland in the sixteenth century', *Innes Review*, 21:2 (1970), 87–107; Alasdair Roberts, 'Roman Catholicism in the Highlands', in J. Kirk (ed.), *The Church in the Highlands* (Edinburgh, 1998), pp. 65–72.

46 Forkan, 'Scottish-Protestant Ulster'.

47 A. Duignan, 'All in confused opposition to each other: politics and war in Connacht, 1641–9', PhD thesis, University College Dublin, 2006; Armstrong, *Protestant War*. Other valuable contributions are E. Darcy, *The Irish Rebellion of 1641 and the Wars of the Three Kingdoms* (London 2013); C. McCoy, 'War and

revolution: County Fermanagh and its borders, *c.*1640–1666', PhD thesis, Trinity College Dublin, 2007.

48 For a general discussion of the importance of violence and violent reputations in understanding early modern Irish history and its historiography, see C. Tait, D. Edwards and P. Lenihan, 'Early Modern Ireland: a history of violence', in Edwards, Lenihan and Tait (eds), *Age of Atrocity*, pp. 9–32.

49 D. Hirst, *Dominion: England and Its Island Neighbours* (Oxford, 2012), pp. 197–215 provides an elegant recent synthesis of these developments; see also Forkan, 'The Ulster Scots and the Engagement'.

50 D. Stevenson, *King or Covenant? Voices from Civil War* (East Linton, 1996).

51 R.J. Hunter (ed.), *Men and Arms: The Ulster Settlers, c.1630* (Belfast, 2012).

1

Scottish officials and secular government in early Stuart Ireland[1]

DAVID EDWARDS

It is an established fact that the accession to the English throne in March 1603 of James Stuart, king of Scotland, was marked by the emergence of a new political rhetoric in the British Isles, one emphasising the communal bonds that existed between English and Scots. As historians have shown, in London and Edinburgh the air was filled with talk of Anglo-Scottish union.[2] Building on a shared language, English, and a common religious culture, Protestantism, senior figures in church and state were optimistic that English and Scots would soon enjoy a greater unity of hearts and minds, even a 'Union of Love'.[3] In his *Discourse* of 1604 Bishop Thornborough of Bristol wrote that as the inhabitants of England and Scotland now shared the ancient land of 'Albion' they must 'All be One'.[4] The term 'British', so long the preserve of humanistic discourse, became a catchword of the times. Leading from the front King James represented himself as the heir of Cadwallader and Edward the Confessor. Rather than 'delight in a long enumeration of [his] many Kingdoms and Seigniories' – king of England, king of Scotland, etc – he wished simply to be called 'King of Greate Britain', for 'Britain' was, he insisted, 'the true and ancient name … [of] this Isle'.[5]

There was, of course, rather more to such language than the mere matter of identifying an appropriate royal style for the multiple monarchy of the king. The union of crowns of 1603 had generated at least as much popular anxiety as state-proclaimed joy, especially in England. Many members of the English political nation (the lords, squires and gentry) were alarmed by the union, concerned that a flood of hungry, grasping Scots following James to London would devour their wealth by adding to the tax burden and consume their prospects for betterment by gobbling up all available rewards and offices that lay in the king's gift.[6] If James VI and I was ever to fulfil his desire to bring about a full political merger between England and Scotland – a union of institutions, laws and peoples – it was imperative that the fears of the English lords and gentry be allayed, and that they witness the benefits of closer association with the Scots. With this in mind James advanced a series of largely symbolic initiatives designed to promote the idea that rather than lose ground to the Scots, union would enhance the power and prestige of the English ruling class. Even before leaving Edinburgh for London in 1603 he had invited English noblemen and gentlemen to join the entourage of his chamber at the Scottish court.[7] Two years later, when he authorised his Edinburgh privy council to proceed with the reduction of the Western Isles to greater royal authority, he conceived the plan in a 'British' context, wishing to have Englishmen share the responsibility for this essentially Scottish policy.[8] For all his prompting, however, the notion of a new, distinctly 'British' elite emerging to serve the new 'British' monarchy, made precious little progress. The English had little regard for it and continued to see the union as a one-way street designed to give the king's Scottish clients access to the riches of England. Disinterested in becoming involved in Scotland, a relatively poor country that promised few opportunities for advancement, the English political nation instead looked to place limits on the prospects available to the Scots in England. Crucially, in successive sessions of the English parliament of 1604–10 the king saw his dream of British union smothered almost to the point of death by the obstructionist tactics employed by the house of commons, which used 'delay unto delay' to frustrate closer integration with Scotland. It is generally agreed that by 1612 he had abandoned all hope of a 'perfect union' and resigned himself to ruling his kingdoms separately.[9]

To date study of the union of crowns and its problems has focused almost exclusively on events in the 'dual monarchy' of England and Scotland, overlooking the fact that in 1603 King James succeeded to a 'triple monarchy' that also included the kingdom of Ireland. This chapter attempts to discover to what extent Anglo-Scottish union was achieved outside England and Scotland, in Ireland. In theory, Ireland was ideal for the king's purposes, providing a possible marriage bed in which to consummate the 'Union of Love' and beget a new British ruling class of English and Scottish servitors. If James's post-1603 experiences in London taught him anything it was that the creation of a new British order could not be achieved formally, through the enunciation of great royal programmes of action or the introduction of new political structures or institutions. However, although it might take much longer, it did remain a possibility that an Anglo-Scottish merger might be achieved informally, through the interconnection of the activities and interests of individual English and Scottish people: as the king put it in 1607, 'to bring it [Britain] to an accomplished union, it must have time and means'.[10] That is to say, if handled properly, maybe he and his successors might utilise Ireland to bring Englishmen and Scotsmen together, as partners in government service.

From the standpoint of English officials in Ireland there were, to put it mildly, some obvious objections to any arrangement requiring them to share power with the Scots. In constitutional terms, the kingdom of Ireland was a sister kingdom of England, not of Scotland, and like a sister it was held as a dependency.[11] It was for this reason, for instance, that the great seal of England was used in the allotment of Scottish grants in the Ulster Plantation.[12] Moreover, in 1603, following the Treaty of Mellifont and the end of Tyrone's rebellion, Ireland lay conquered at the feet of James VI and I because of the exertions of English soldiers, not Scots, prior to that date. English officials with long experience of Ireland expected the run of the country as something that was theirs by right. Their resentment of the king's decision in 1609 to grant a significant proportion of the escheated counties of Ulster to planters from the Scottish Lowlands is well known. As Nicholas Canny has observed, some of the English community in Ireland 'were opposed to giving any foothold [in the country] to any Scots'.[13] However, while Irish historians have afforded detailed examination of the extent of Scottish involvement in the Jacobean plantations,[14] until recently little has been said of the extent to which Scots also secured a share of government office in early Stuart Ireland. It is high time this lacuna was filled, not just because it is an important subject in its own right, but also because it should shed new light on the fate of the early Stuart experiment in 'British' state formation.

The first Scotsman to hold office in Ireland after the accession of James VI and I to the thrones of England and Ireland in March 1603 was Sir James Fullerton, younger brother of John, laird of Dreghorn in Ayrshire.[15] Fullerton was not new to Ireland, having served the interests of King James there since about 1587, when he is said to have first settled in Dublin.[16] A trusted royal servant, occasionally even a favourite, in August 1603 he was named muster-master general and clerk of the check of Ireland,[17] replacing Sir Ralph Lane, who had held both posts since 1592 but had fallen into poor health in recent years.[18] Usually unnoticed, passed over as a mere biographical detail, Fullerton's appointment was significant. It gave him, a dependable Scottish servant of the king, a measure of control over the English forces in Ireland at the very time that his royal master was trying to secure his new English and Irish kingdoms. Immediately on assuming office Fullerton set about demobilising the greater part of the army: according to his own reckoning in barely twelve months he oversaw its reduction from 12,000 foot and 1,000 horse to 3,000 foot and 400 horse.[19] For a number of years thereafter he continued to be closely involved in the conduct of government in Ireland. In 1606 he was made a member of the Irish privy council,[20] becoming the first Scotsman ever to serve on that body,[21] and he also sat on the committee established late in 1608 to draw up the original plans for the Plantation of Ulster.[22] Even when he left Ireland forever, in 1610, he did not lose touch with Irish affairs, in 1611 being appointed to the commission for Irish causes that held its proceedings in London, its only Scottish member.[23]

Other Scotsmen followed Fullerton into the ranks of Irish officialdom early in the reign of James VI and I. They became especially prominent in ecclesiastical office,[24] colonising the hierarchy of the established church after 1605 when George Montgomery arrived to take up the three northern bishoprics of Derry, Raphoe and Clogher. By 1612 there were three Scottish bishops holding down six bishoprics in the Church of Ireland: Montgomery himself, in Derry, Clogher, and, since 1609, the bishopric of Meath; Andrew Knox, who replaced Montgomery in Raphoe in 1610; and James Dundas, who had recently been appointed to the combined bishoprics of Down and Connor.[25] The Scots were also beginning to make their mark in secular office. By 1612 the first Scottish official had penetrated beyond the northern and eastern regions of Ulster and the Dublin Pale, appearing in the southern province of Munster, for it was in that year that Sir James Craig was appointed *custos rotulorum*, or keeper of the rolls, of the liberty of Tipperary by the lord of the liberty, the tenth earl of Ormond.[26]

These appointments, and others like them, have attracted the attention of Irish and British historians. In particular, in the course of a magisterial study of early Stuart government in Ireland Victor Treadwell has asserted that one of the methods used by *both* James VI and I (1603–25) and Charles I (1625–49) to integrate their Irish realm into the British composite monarchy was to grant official positions in the country to Scotsmen – a statement which carries an implicit suggestion that the procreative intent of the Union of Love continued to apply in the kingdom of Ireland long after its abandonment circa 1612 as a maxim of state in the kingdoms of England and Scotland: until the 1630s, in fact.[27] Going further, Treadwell has chastised other historians for having underestimated the extent of 'the Scottish penetration of the Irish bureaucracy'.[28] He claims that not only did the Scots secure 'a foothold in the council and central bureaucracy', they did so partly at the expense of English-born officials, for whom the government of Ireland had been hitherto 'a jealously guarded preserve'.

It should perhaps be noted that Treadwell's suggestion of Englishmen ceding power to Scotsmen fails to fit neatly with the findings of his fellow expert on the Stuart administration in Ireland, John McCavitt. Far from seeing the English losing ground, McCavitt has instead revealed them as gaining greater control of government positions in combination with the Scots, and all at the expense of the Anglo-Irish, or 'Old English', who effectively forfeited their age-old prominence in government after the accession of the Stuarts.[29] Yet McCavitt has provided support for Treadwell's thesis all the same, albeit quietly, without fanfare. In his fine study of the lord deputyship of Sir Arthur

Chichester, McCavitt has viewed the presence in Dublin of 'a group of Scottish privy councillors' as evidence of the Scots having emerged as a 'distinct category' in the Irish administration before the end of Chichester's term of office in 1616.[30] It seems, then, that recent historical scholarship is agreed that in Ireland at least the Union Of Love was able to enjoy a longer and more fruitful marriage than elsewhere, and that what John Morrill has suggested should be termed the 'briticization' of the ruling classes was indeed proceeding to some degree.[31] As Treadwell has put it, during the reign of James VI and I the government of Ireland was in the process of being converted into 'the crucible of British union'.[32]

But was this clearly the case? Were Scottish officials really so visible in early Stuart Ireland, an identifiable group? Not all Irish historians think so. In one of the most extensive investigations undertaken of 'British' policies in Ireland, Canny has asserted that 'at the official level "British" Ireland became very much "English" Ireland, with practically all senior positions held by English-born people (or their Irish-born children), with [just] a few appointments going to Scottish favourites [of King James]'.[33] Chiefly concerned with charting the impact of the plantations, he offers this observation only in passing, but his dissent from the emphasis on the 'briticization' of government made by his colleagues is unsettling, and surely requires more detailed consideration.

Treadwell, to support his argument, has given the briefest roll call of Scottish secular office-holders, selecting just three names for discussion: Sir James Fullerton, the muster-master general, already noted; Sir Archibald Acheson, a future secretary of state for Scotland who began his career in Dublin as master of the Irish chancery; and lastly, the poet Patrick Hanna, a Longford planter who was named clerk of the Irish privy council and master of chancery in the 1620s.[34] McCavitt likewise has supplied only a brief list of Scotsmen who became prominent in Ireland during the early seventeenth century, naming six who served as members of the Irish privy council: the ubiquitous Fullerton; Bishop Montgomery; Bishop Knox; Hugh Montgomery (future Viscount Ards); Sir James Hamilton (future Viscount Clandeboy); and Sir Claud Hamilton of Schawfield.[35] How representative were these men? Did they act in concert, as 'a group'? How many other Scots enjoyed official positions on the lower rungs of the Irish administration? It should be noted from the outset that certain assertions that have been made about the extent of Scottish promotion in Ireland are not supported by the facts. It has been stated, for instance, that between 1602 and 1611 'Scotsmen were lavishly endowed' with crown pensions in Ireland on the orders of King James.[36] Yet extant lists of pensions and other annuities for precisely those years record a negligible Scottish presence.[37] One document, a list of 77 pensions granted on the Irish establishment between March 1602–03 and September 1611, records not a single Scottish beneficiary.[38]

It is the purpose of this chapter to go beyond simple observation of Scottish involvement in the secular government of Ireland. Based upon a systematic search through extant records of central, provincial and county government, it attempts to present a more accurate picture of the extent to which the Scots were allowed to share power with English officials in early Stuart Ireland. It is usually assumed that insufficient documentary materials have survived in Ireland to facilitate a proper understanding of the history of the administration of the country, yet this is true only up to a point. Despite the appalling loss of documents that resulted from the 1922 explosion at the Dublin Public Record Office (PROI), sufficient materials have survived to identify most of those individuals who held office in central government. Accordingly, the findings presented here are chiefly derived from the published Irish Patent Rolls of James I and Charles I, and from the lists of government officials that were drawn up by antiquarians and clerks who worked in the PROI long before 1922. An especially valuable source, often neglected by historians, who have tended to dismiss it as a mere hand-list, was the catalogue and index of the Irish fiants of the early Stuart monarchs. Ideal for the present purposes of simply counting the names of Scotsmen who held office in Ireland between 1603 and *c.*1641, the catalogue and index survived the 1922 explosion and is now preserved in the Irish National Archives. Also useful were materials compiled by two keepers of the Irish public records from the pre-Independence period: first, John Lodge (d. 1774), whose work formed the basis of two important subsequent publications, *Liber Munerum Publicorum Hiberniae* (published 1852)[39] and *Patentee Officers of Ireland* (published 1960);[40] second, James Ferguson (d. 1855), whose notes taken mainly from the records of the Irish exchequer can be consulted in the Irish National Archives and the Royal Irish Academy.[41] Another important source was the various lists of the civil and military establishment that can be found scattered through the Irish state papers and other manuscript collections.[42] When brought together, these materials provide a solid foundation for any study of the central government in early Stuart Ireland, recording the names of hundreds of offices and office-holders from the period before 1641. As will be shown, however, they reveal relatively little about officials in local government, the records of which were among the chief casualties of the 1922 disaster at the PROI. Information about Scottish involvement on the Irish privy council has come mainly from the published Irish state papers.

Before outlining the facts and figures of Scottish participation in Irish officialdom, it is necessary to first determine something of the quality of those Scotsmen who were available for government service in Ireland after the Stuart succession of 1603. In the course of the last thirty years historians and historical geographers have revealed a great deal about the background of

Table 1: Scottish grantees in the Ulster Plantation scheme of 1610–11 who had previous experience of government

Planter's name	*Ulster estate*	*Government experience before 1610*
James Hamilton, earl of Abercorn	Co. Tyrone	Scottish Privy Councillor; Commissioner for the Union with England
Michael, Lord Balfour	Co. Fermanagh	Scottish Privy Councillor; Justice of the Peace
Andrew Stewart, Lord Ochiltree	Co. Tyrone	1st Lord of the Bedchamber
Sir James Douglas	Co. Armagh	Gentleman of the Privy Chamber
Sir Robert McClelland	Co. Donegal	Provost of Kirkcudbright
Sir Alexander Hamilton	Co. Cavan	Justice of the Peace
Sir Claud Hamilton	Co. Tyrone	Scottish Privy Councillor; Deputy sheriff of Lanarkshire
Sir James Craig	Co. Armagh	Clerk of the Wardrobe (England); Purveyor of the King's Mines (Scotland)
Sir Robert Hepburn	Co. Tyrone	Lieutenant of the King's Guard (Scotland); Justice of the Peace
Sir John Wishart	Co. Fermanagh	Justice of the Peace
John Achmutie	Co. Cavan	Groom of the Bedchamber
Bernard Lindsay	Co. Tyrone	Groom of the Bedchamber
George Murray	Co. Donegal	Groom of the Bedchamber
Patrick Vans	Co. Donegal	Gentleman of the Scottish Privy Chamber
James Gibb	Co. Fermanagh	Servant of King James
William Fowler	Co. Fermanagh	Servant of Queen Anne
James Clapam	Co. Tyrone	Servant of the Royal Household
Alexander Achmutie	Co. Cavan	Servant at the royal courtl
John Brown	Co. Cavan	Constable of the sheriffdom of Edinburgh

Source: M. Perceval-Maxwell, *The Scottish Migration to Ulster in the Reign of James I* (London, 1973; reprinted Belfast, 1999), pp. 323–61

those Scots who engaged in colonial enterprises in the northern parts of the country during the reign of James VI and I. In particular, the prosopographical approach pioneered by Michael Perceval-Maxwell has uncovered much about the extent to which the Scottish settlers possessed experience of government and administrative office in Scotland prior to their arrival as landowners in Ulster. His findings are presented in Table 1.

Clearly, had the senior Scottish settlers been political novices, not used to wielding power or carrying out royal orders, it would have been easy for hostile Englishmen among the king's advisers to have them excluded from office in Ireland, an unsettled country where, it might have been argued, inexperience among officials would produce further instability. But such an argument, if it was ever made, was not sustainable. Some of the settlers had extensive governmental experience, and had helped King James re-establish effective royal power in Scotland before 1603, and this without ever receiving much reward.[43] Three of the principal Scottish planters, James Hamilton, earl of Abercorn, Michael, Lord Balfour and Sir Claud Hamilton of Schawfield, had each served on the Scottish privy council in Edinburgh before receiving land in Ulster. What was there to stop them attaining a corresponding position on the Irish privy council in Dublin, where they might represent the interests of their countrymen, other than their own reluctance to get heavily involved in Ireland? Likewise, another group among the Scottish planters, numbering twelve in all, had served King James and his queen in various capacities at the Scottish and later the English royal court. If the determination really existed at Whitehall to forge ahead with Anglo-Scottish power-sharing in Ireland, might not these have performed useful services to the crown and added to their own wealth and power on the lower rungs of the Irish central administration?

To deal first with the principal landowners: no matter how well qualified the likes of Abercorn, Balfour, or Sir Claud Hamilton were to participate at the very highest levels of government in early Stuart Ireland, the stark reality was that they held very little power in the country. Throughout the entire period 1603–41 no Scottish lord or courtier was ever in contention for the great offices of state in Ireland, the lord deputyship (or chief governorship), the lord chancellorship, or the vice-treasurership. Without exception, these posts remained the preserve of Englishmen, as they had since the mid-sixteenth century.[44] It should probably be noted that this lack of prominence owed as much to Scottish preference for position in England as it did to any overt attempts by the English to keep them out of Ireland. No major Scottish lord seems to have put himself forward for the most senior government posts in Ireland.[45]

Nor was a Scot ever advanced to one of the five principal legal positions in Ireland below that of lord chancellor – there was no Scottish master of the rolls of chancery, baron of the exchequer, chancellor of the exchequer, chief justice of king's bench, or chief justice of common pleas. While it might be argued that they could not realistically aspire to senior judicial posts in Ireland given that, as Scots, they had no prior knowledge of English law, this did not affect their prospects in England, where King James appointed a Scottish master of the rolls, Edward, Lord Bruce, and chancellor of the exchequer, Sir George Home (future earl of Dunbar). Moreover, regarding chancery, Scots were as well suited as either English or Irish to command positions there, it being an equity jurisdiction and 'courte of conscience'. As will be shown in this chapter, Scotsmen did manage to penetrate the Irish chancery at a lower level.[46]

This general absence of Scots in senior posts only serves to underline the significance of the appointment to Irish office in 1603 of Sir James Fullerton. As muster-master general and clerk of the cheque he was the only Scotsman to possess personal authority over a major area of secular government in early Stuart Ireland (the army).

However, as the work of Treadwell and McCavitt has shown, other Scots did at least manage to attain positions of potentially considerable influence in the Irish executive, chiefly through membership of the Irish privy council. Some of the most successful Scotsmen in early seventeenth-century Ireland managed to secure a position on the Dublin council. In fact, more Scots were appointed to the council than either Treadwell or McCavitt have identified, as many as eleven in the reign of James VI and I: Sir James Fullerton (appointed 1606), Bishop George Montgomery (1607), Bishop Andrew Knox (1610), Sir James Hamilton, future Viscount Clandeboy (1613); Sir Claud Hamilton of Schawfield (1614); Michael, Lord Balfour of Burley (1617); Sir Hugh Montgomery, future Viscount Ards (1618); Sir James Balfour, future baron of Clanawley (1618); Sir James Erskine (1622); Richard Preston, earl of Desmond (1624); and Malcolm Hamilton, archbishop of Cashel (1624).

Although these appointments show that Scotsmen were able to penetrate Irish government office at a very high level after 1603, it does not necessarily support the contention that they represented a distinct group in the council chamber at Dublin Castle. Common membership of an institution is not the same as common behaviour or cooperation while participating. To prove the existence of an identifiable Scottish 'group' in the Irish council it is necessary to produce details of the council activities of the Scots. Therefore the first thing that must be determined about the Scottish privy councillors in Ireland is how many of them sat at the council table at the same time.

In this regard, surviving evidence seems to lend some credence to the notion of a Scottish group on the council, insofar as several of the Scottish appointees served simultaneously. Fullerton's period on the Irish privy council (1606–10) overlapped with the period of service of Bishop Montgomery (1607–18). In the wake of Fullerton's departure, Montgomery was not left as the only Scotsman in the council chamber, as Bishop Knox soon arrived to commence his council career (1610–15). Furthermore, a memorandum among the state papers drawn up in September 1611 to identify all the privy councillors in Ireland supplies the names of no less than five Scotsmen as serving in Dublin by that date – Fullerton, Bishops Montgomery and Knox, Sir James Hamilton, and Sir Claud Hamilton.[47] Here, it would appear, is irrefutable evidence of the Scots as a 'distinct category' of the Irish executive after 1603.

Yet appearances contrive to deceive. The 1611 list, written anonymously, owes its origin to the Carew Commission of that year, in which Sir George Carew, himself a former member of the Irish privy council, was required to report to James I on the general progress towards a new 'British' regime in Ireland.[48] On passing from its author into Carew's possession, the document was subsequently modified and corrected, so that only three Scottish privy councillors remained. Struck off the list by Carew were the two Hamiltons, Sir Claud of Schawfield and Sir James of Clandeboy, both of whom had subsequently to wait several more years before attaining a council seat. The 1611 memorandum does not, then, confirm the emergence of a readily identifiable and sizeable 'group' of Scottish privy councillors in Dublin. Instead it tends to suggest that although two of the most prominent Scottish landowners and men of affairs in Ireland by the time of the Ulster Plantation were considered of high enough status to serve on the council – so much, indeed, that the list's author thought they were Irish councillors already – yet for some unexplained reason their prominence had not been translated into official positions at the heart of government.[49] Significantly, and as McCavitt has observed, once he had completed his commission of inquiry, Carew presented a depressing report to the king on the tardy progress of British union in Ireland, merely confirming what Lord Deputy Chichester had stated earlier, that the Ulster Plantation was advancing at snail's pace, and that thus far a substantial Anglo-Scottish planter class had failed to materialise in the country.[50] The retarded development of Anglo-Scottish power-sharing in Dublin was but one symptom of a wider failure.

Far from improving as time went on, Scottish membership of the Irish council stagnated. The appearance of four new councillors in 1617–18 (Michael, Lord Balfour of Burley, Hugh Montgomery, Sir James Hamilton and Sir James Balfour) might have signalled a second chance for Anglo-Scottish power-sharing in Ireland, or 'briticization', but in the event it seems that two of the appointees (Montgomery and Hamilton) only took up their positions in order to ensure a favourable outcome to a royal inquiry into the boundaries of Iveagh in Co. Down.[51] As soon as the boundaries had been approved at meetings of the Irish council in May and June, first Montgomery and then Hamilton departed from Dublin;[52] thereafter Montgomery seems never to have returned to the council chamber before the death of King James, and Hamilton only fitfully. Their withdrawal became almost permanent after

1621–22, when the government investigated them both for their patronage of Presbyterian ministers in East Ulster.[53] Accordingly, the reign of James VI and I concluded with just two Scots occasionally serving on the Irish privy council, James Balfour (from November 1619 Lord Balfour of Clanawley),[54] and Sir James Erskine.

The reign of Charles I saw stagnation turn to decline. Unlike his father, King Charles did not have much of a Scottish following, and exhibited little interest in the extent of Scottish power in Ireland. Shortly after his accession the one Scotsman capable of procuring a wide-ranging executive position in the country, Buckingham's confidant Richard Preston, earl of Desmond, fell into disgrace over his efforts to advance an impostor to one of the great Anglo-Irish peerages, the earldom of Ormond. A servant of King James since before 1603, Preston had profited greatly from the union of crowns, becoming Lord Dingwall in the Scottish peerage (1609) and British diplomatic envoy to Venice (1609, 1616) before being made earl of Desmond in Ireland (1620) and a member of the Irish privy council (1624).[55] In late spring or early summer 1625 it was reported that, having earned King Charles's displeasure, he had left the British Isles and gone to the continent.[56] On his return in 1626 he managed to regain some of his former standing, but, crucially for the purposes of this study, he seems never to have sat on the Irish council before his sudden death, drowned in the Irish Sea, in October 1628.

Desmond was not replaced by anyone of similar stature. Sir William Stewart, who was appointed to the council in January 1628, was an experienced soldier and a prominent planter in Counties Donegal and Tyrone,[57] yet lacked the prestige and connections necessary to wield any influence in the council chamber.[58] Moreover, being fully engaged in developing his plantation estates, Stewart was at best an infrequent visitor to Dublin after 1629.[59] Hence, for the first five years of Charles I's reign only three Scots featured with any sort of regularity at council meetings, James, Lord Balfour; James Hamilton, Lord Clandeboy; and Malcolm Hamilton, archbishop of Cashel.[60] On the archbishop's death in 1629 Scottish involvement in the council nearly ceased completely, with Balfour retiring from affairs of state.[61] Indeed, following his third and final marriage, to Anne, daughter of Edward, Lord Blayney, in 1627, Balfour was apparently content to have his interests represented at council meetings by his father-in-law, an Englishman, before the latter's death in 1630. In 1633 Balfour procured a licence of absence and left Ireland, destined never to return, dying in London in October 1634.[62]

It was left to Lord Clandeboy to act as the sole Scottish privy councillor of note throughout the 1630s, with Sir James Erskine but a spectral figure.[63] For a time, while the earl of Cork and Lord Chancellor Loftus headed the government, Clandeboy found himself unusually close to the centre of power, in August 1631 even being considered as one of eleven possible candidates who might take charge of civil affairs in Leinster and Ulster during the absence of Cork and Loftus.[64] Following Sir Thomas Wentworth's arrival as the new lord deputy in 1633 Clandeboy managed to keep his Presbyterian sympathies concealed, and retained a degree of influence in Dublin as Wentworth and the Irish bishops commenced the persecution of Protestant nonconformists in Ulster.[65] Yet Clandeboy was getting old. Although he did enough to escape Wentworth's wrath, he seems not to have set foot in Dublin after the closure of parliament in 1635;[66] the same could be said of Erskine. When Wentworth's relations with the Ulster Scots turned from bad to worse, the deputy was not inclined to seek the appointment of new Scottish councillors. As he put it in 1638, 'the English ... are the [only] subiects that profit the crowne and safety of this kingdom'.[67] And so it was under his rule that Scottish involvement on the Irish privy council almost ended completely. With the sole exception of Henry Leslie, bishop of Down – the deputy's chief instrument against nonconformist Scots – extant records of Wentworth's regime between 1635 and 1640 reveal a negligible Scottish presence.

Examination of the documentary records of the Irish privy council held among the state papers reveals that, even during the reign of James VI and I, the council rarely had more than a single Scot actually serving on it at any one time. Attendance figures, derived from the sederunts subscribed to council letters in the state papers, demonstrate that royal appointments of Scotsmen to posts on the Irish privy council did not lead automatically to increased Scottish involvement in the government of Ireland. A typical Scottish privy councillor was an absent one – of 157 meetings known to have taken place under King James, Scottish councillors attended just 38, barely a quarter of all meetings (see Table 2). There is no record of the earl of Desmond ever having attended council, while Sir Claud Hamilton of Schawfield could not have attended a meeting, as he died four days after receiving his belated appointment, in October 1614. Bishop Andrew Knox may only have attended one meeting, in 1613; likewise Michael, Lord Balfour of Burley, in 1617, and Sir James Erskine, in 1623.[68]

It was hardly as though council membership was a great strain in Ireland. Lord Deputy Chichester preferred to rule with the assistance of only a handful of advisers, so that during the eleven years of his governorship (1605–16) the Irish privy council met not very frequently, perhaps ten times a year before 1613, and less often thereafter. His successor as deputy, Lord Grandison (1616–22), though marginally more demanding of his councillors, followed very closely in Chichester's footsteps. Under this relatively lax regime, Bishop Montgomery proved the most conscientious of the Scots after the departure of Fullerton in 1610. When Montgomery was away, however, the council had no Scottish representatives at all. The bishop was never adequately replaced. Between his death in 1618 and that of King James in 1625, there were at least

Table 2: Scottish involvement on the Irish Privy Council, 1603–25

Period	*Meetings*	*Scottish councillors in attendance*
1603, 6 Apr.–1606, 26 Sept.	23	None
1606, Oct.–1607, Jan.	9	Sir James Fullerton
1607, 20 Apr.	1	None
1607, 2–24 June	5	Bishop George Montgomery
1607, 2 Aug.	1	None
1607, 7–9 Sept.	2	Bishop George Montgomery
1607, 16 Oct.–21 Dec.	4	Sir James Fullerton
1608, 23 Apr.	1	Bishop George Montgomery
1608, 2 July–1609, 6 June.	13	None
1609, 3 Dec.	1	Bishop George Montgomery
1610, 19 Feb.	1	None
1610, 24 Feb.	1	Bishop George Montgomery
1610, 14 May–1612, 23 July	12	None
1612, 30 Dec.	1	[Unknown]
1613, 10 Feb.	1	Bishop George Montgomery
1613, 27 May	1	Bishop George Montgomery; Bishop Andrew Knox; Sir James Hamilton
1613, 16 Nov.	1	None
1613, 24 Nov.	1	Bishop George Montgomery
1613, 31 Dec.	1	None
1614, Aug.	1	[Unknown]
1615, 29 June	1	None
1616, 17 March	1	Bishop George Montgomery
1616, 25–28 Apr.	2	None

Period (cont.)	*Meetings*	*Scottish councillors in attendance*
1617, 21 Feb.	1	Michael, Lord Balfour of Burly; Hugh Montgomery
1617, 21 Aug.–1618, 27 Feb.	3	None
1618, 6 May	1	Hugh Montgomery
1618, 14–18 May	2	Bishop George Montgomery; Hugh Montgomery; Sir James Hamilton
1618, 18 May	2	Bishop George Montgomery
1618, 25 May	1	Bishop George Montgomery; Sir James Hamilton
1618, 8 June	1	Sir James Balfour; Sir James Hamilton
1618, 20 July–1622, 14 Oct.	53	None
1622, 16 Nov.	1	Viscount Clandeboy
1622, 19 Nov.	1	None
1622, 29 Nov.	1	Viscount Clandeboy
1623, 21 Jan.–12 Nov.	4	None
1623, 8 Dec.	1	James, Lord Balfour; Sir James Erskine
1623, 27 Dec.–1624, 24 Apr.	7	None
1624, 23–30 Oct.	2	James, Lord Balfour

Source: CSPI, 1603–06, pp. 11, 36, 68, 70, 95, 169, 259–60, 266, 283–4, 288, 289–90, 294, 323, 333, 358, 417, 449, 460, 480, 484, 487, 562; *ibid.*, 1606–8, pp. 9, 14, 33, 40, 42, 80, 86, 92, 141, 159, 190, 200, 208, 209, 235, 263, 268, 278, 306, 311, 363, 485, 597; *ibid.*, 1608–10, pp. 14, 20, 25, 40, 53, 67, 70, 103, 112, 138, 184, 213, 328, 390, 392, 445, 491, 546; *ibid.*, 1611–14, pp. 152–3, 167, 191–3, 355, 457; *ibid.*, 1615–25, pp. 124, 168, 193–4, 196–8, 204, 212, 219, 237, 240, 241–2, 243–5, 247, 249–50, 252, 254–8, 265–9, 277–9, 281–4, 286–8, 294–5, 297, 303–5, 315, 326, 328, 331–4, 336–40, 343, 345, 348, 358–9, 394–6, 399, 408, 423, 435, 438, 445–6, 457, 459–60, 463, 482, 484, 539, 541; *ibid., 1647–60 & Addenda, Charles I*, p. 44; R. Dudley Edwards, [N. Costello and E. Piatt] (eds), 'Chichester Letter-Book', *Analecta Hibernica* 8 (1938), pp. 37–42, 70–3, 80–1, 100–3, 143–9, 153–7, 166–8; *Cal. Carew MSS, 1603–24*, pp. 12, 42, 74–5, 92, 116, 164, 251, 329, 333, 425, 433; Historical Manuscripts Commission, *Hastings MSS*, iv (London, 1947), pp. 182–3; TCD, MS 672, fols 35v, 48v, 49r, 61r; *ibid.*, MS 853, fols 137–8.

70 council meetings in Ireland. Of these, more than 90 per cent (65 meetings) were held without a single Scottish councillor in attendance. Given these figures, it was impossible for a Scottish 'group' to emerge at the heart of the Irish executive.

Beneath the council, or executive, there were perhaps 70 other offices to be filled by the crown in the central government of Ireland at the start of the seventeenth century. Although lacking the sort of influence associated with council membership, involvement in the lower levels of the Dublin administration was nonetheless of considerable value, not least for the potential revenues that came with it, through graft. Indeed, for English officials the prospect of Scottish interlopers laying their hands on remunerative administrative positions was a source of considerable unease. However, as various extant lists of the civil establishment testify, the number of Scotsmen who gained such positions was very small – just five, in fact, between 1603 and 1641.

The earliest recorded appointment of a Scot to a position in the administration is that of Sir James Hamilton (future Lord Clandeboy), who was named a commissioner of the court of wards in 1613. His appointment was not all that it seemed. As Treadwell has revealed, the Irish court of wards was a court in name only before 1616, when efforts were finally put in place to bring the administration of wardships in the country into line with the work of the court of wards in England.[69] Instead of gaining entry to a formal administrative body, through his appointment as a commissioner Hamilton was in reality granted the right to act as an agent of the crown, scouting out wardships and unlicensed alienations in that one part of Ireland where hitherto feudal incidents had rarely been secured into royal hands – East Ulster. This is not to say that the appointment was insignificant. In personal terms Hamilton may have derived considerable material benefit from the speculative nature of the office, either by receiving a share of the profits of whatever wardships and alienations his investigations uncovered, or else by accepting gratuities from local landowners for failing to reveal their liability for fines to the authorities.[70] The appointment, however, did not lead to Hamilton's more formal involvement in central government. When subsequently the Irish court of wards was reconstituted between 1616 and 1622, he was not required to serve on the drafting committee.[71] Likewise, when the new court emerged squinting into the light he was not made one of its officials.

The unlikely figure of Ludovick Stuart, second duke of Lennox and first duke of Richmond, was the second Scot to feature in the Irish administration. On 26 July 1618 he was named aulnager of Ireland,[72] a position that entitled him to collect the subsidies on cloth. One of the great personages of the royal court, Lennox seems never to have set foot in Ireland, leasing his interest in the cloth revenues to others. As such it is perhaps not surprising that his name does not feature on either the 1618 or 1623 list of the Irish civil establishment.[73] As Victor Treadwell has shown, the nature of the office, and Lennox's use of it, attracted much criticism,[74] and it seems to have disappeared with his death in 1624.

The next Scotsman to feature in the administration was Sir Archebold Acheson, who was appointed as one of the two masters of chancery in Ireland in June 1621[75] and had arrived in Dublin to take up his place by the following November.[76] A member of a prominent East Lothian lineage, he was confirmed in his post in November 1625 following the succession of Charles I, when he was also named as one of the commissioners of the prerogative court.[77] It is possible that information about his work as master of chancery might be found among the salved chancery pleas in the Irish National Archives; otherwise precious little has survived about his activities. Whatever the case, Acheson at least remained in Ireland for a number of years, and was actively involved in government business, especially in Ulster, where, as 'agent for the escheated lands', he earned much praise for his scrutiny of plantation tenures in 1627.[78] However, he surrendered his post in the Dublin chancery sometime before June 1627, when he was replaced (see below),[79] and having left Ireland for the royal court, in March 1630 he became secretary of state for Scotland.[80]

The fourth Scottish member of the Irish administration to appear was Patrick Hanna (alias A'Hanna or Hannay), a poet and minor courtier who procured a grant in the plantation of Longford.[81] It has been claimed, erroneously, that he obtained the clerkship of the Irish privy council in 1624.[82] In fact what he obtained was a grant of the reversion of the office. Although King James gave instructions that Hanna be admitted to the exercise of the post, without fees or profits, the Anglo-Irish incumbent, Sir William Ussher, an old man who had occupied the clerkship since Elizabethan times, disputed the appointment. Eventually, a second royal grant, made on 10 December 1628, was needed to overcome the impasse, giving Hanna 'absolute' right to receive emoluments from the clerkship during Ussher's life for 'such things as should pass through his [Hanna's] hands', and to assume the post on the old man's death. However, he never actually occupied the clerkship, for the simple reason that he failed to outlive Ussher, dying at sea late in 1629.[83] Thus, instead of being the procurer of one of the most significant (and lucrative) posts in the Dublin administration, Hanna's place in the government of Ireland was decidedly less impressive. On 21 June 1627 – in succession to Acheson, possibly as his assignee – he was named a master of chancery, a position he obtained while in the throes of battle with Ussher over the clerkship.[84] Although he is recorded in the 1629 civil establishment list as claiming his chancery salary of £26 13s 4d per annum,[85] it seems clear that, before his death, he never physically assumed this position either.[86]

The frustration of Hanna's ambitions over the clerkship of the council deserves further comment, as it was more important than at first sight it might seem. It forced the royal authorities in London to confront the uncomfortable fact that attempts to forge a stronger Anglo-Scottish union in Ireland had utterly failed, and driven a wedge between English and Scots instead of bringing them closer together. Hanna's fellow Scottish settlers were enraged by the hostility shown to him in Dublin. From their perspective the treatment he received confirmed their darkest suspicions: that the English were determined to keep the best positions for themselves and their Anglo-Irish cronies, come what may. Hanna had done everything he could to secure the post, lobbying ministers and courtiers at Whitehall, and even obtaining the personal support of both James I and Charles I, who praised him as 'an able and deserving man'. When, shortly before King James's death, the monarch learned of the English opposition to Hanna in Dublin, he took the news 'in very evil part', and he asked Prince Charles to take up Hanna's case after he died.[87] Yet still Hanna was frustrated, his progress obstructed. Peculiarly, while he was absent in London, unable to represent himself, the royal patent for his appointment to the clerkship was examined and found wanting in the Dublin courts, and he had to wait a full three years before forcing his opponents to retreat. By the time of his own death his long struggle for office had become a source of serious political tension in Ireland between senior Scottish planters and the English government. In 1630 'a Scottish Lord of this kingdom' – unfortunately un-named – took up Hanna's cause and began scratching the itch of resentment felt by many of his countrymen. There should, the lord suggested, be two clerks of the Irish council, one of them 'a Scotchman', 'to attend the better to the affairs of that nation', for clearly the English had no intention of looking after their fellow 'Britons'. The idea, needless to say, was dismissed out of hand by English officials, who viewed it as a mere 'tear of envy' emitted by greedy Scottish settlers who would never be satisfied with their lot.[88] Presumably one of the underlying reasons of Hanna's frustration was the lack of any influence exerted on his behalf by the Scottish members of the Irish council; but then, given their low numbers and poor attendance at council meetings, this was hardly surprising.

The fifth and final Scottish member of the Irish central administration was Sir Robert Hanna (later baronet), appointed clerk of the nihels (alias nichells) in the court of exchequer on 11 December 1631, for life.[89] A relative of Patrick Hanna, and a minor figure about the royal court, Sir Robert's post was a new one, possibly created specially for him. Involving the collection of debts due on market licences, it promised to yield a generous income. Nonetheless Sir Robert at once leased it to an un-named deputy, content to receive a guaranteed return from his Irish office while remaining in London. Even after moving to Connaught to take up residence at Moyne Castle in Co. Sligo,[90] he left the clerkship in the hands of a deputy, who after 7 December 1635 was one Edward Daniel, a young Anglo-Irishman.[91]

The Scots failed also to materialise to any significant extent in provincial or local government. Here too the lead given by Sir James Fullerton early in the reign of James I was never exploited. In summer 1604, while serving as muster-master general and clerk of the cheque, Fullerton was granted a seat on the council of Munster. The appointment was necessary to help him carry out his principal task of beginning the demobilization of the army: he needed to ensure that that part of Ireland most vulnerable to foreign threat, the Munster coastline, had sufficient forces available for its defence.[92] Accordingly we find him in Co. Cork in August 1604 working with Sir Henry Brouncker to secure the agreement of the local lords to the army tax known as the composition,[93] and he was in Limerick during September.[94] Following his return from Munster a period of twenty years elapsed before another Scot replaced him: on 19 September 1624 Richard Preston, earl of Desmond, was named on a commission for the government of the province.[95] As with his membership of the Irish privy council, Desmond failed to make much of the appointment, and consequently the presidency and council of Munster remained a preserve of Englishmen, supported by a handful of Protestant Irishmen, right down to the outbreak of the Irish Catholic rebellion of 1641–42.[96] Less is known about the Connaught presidency, but it seems conditions on the council there were much the same. The one Scot definitely known to have obtained the rights to a position, Patrick Pitcairn of Pitlochry – granted the reversion of the clerkship of the council of Connaught in December 1603 – never in fact secured the post, and surrendered it a decade later, in March 1613.[97]

Given the high number of Scottish settlers that arrived in Ulster during the reign of James I, it might be expected that the Scots would have achieved a greater share of secular government at county level than they managed at national or provincial level. However, surviving documents indicate strongly that the Scots were rarely granted administrative power in the Ulster counties, or elsewhere. In the wake of the flight of the northern earls, in September 1607, Bishop George Montgomery was named as one of the governors of Counties Tyrone, Donegal and Armagh, but the appointment was just an emergency measure, and was not renewed once the north had been secured.[98] Prior to his death in 1618 the greatest Scottish lord to participate in the plantation, James Hamilton, earl of Abercorn, was named on commissions of inquiry for Co. Tyrone, but no formal position of authority was found for him or his representatives, perhaps because of his Catholicism. Indeed, it was not until the last regnal year of James I (1624–25) that senior posts in local government were found for the principal Scottish settlers in Ireland. In a belated attempt to create a new category of officials in Ireland, the county governors, the earl of Desmond (7 July 1624), Lord Balfour of Clanawley (3 December), and John Murray, earl of Annandale (7 March 1625) were named governors of Counties Kilkenny and Carlow, Co. Fermanagh, and Co. Donegal respectively.[99] In theory, as governors they enjoyed considerable authority over the counties under their jurisdiction. Responsible for the 'defence and safety of good and loyal subjects' and the 'punishment and reformation of … evil disposed persons', they were entitled to assume command of local military forces and levy men, and to convene parleys with disaffected natives and issue protections. In practice, however, their authority was tightly restricted. Unlike several of their English (and Irish) counterparts who were appointed to county governorships at about this time, the Scottish governors of Fermanagh and Donegal did not receive 'power of life and death' over their subjects 'according to the martial law'. Desmond, however, as a sidekick of the duke of Buckingham, was granted such power.[100]

At the accession of Charles I both Balfour and Annandale were soon reappointed to their positions;[101] Desmond, having fallen into disgrace, was not, and after just eight months in office was compelled to relinquish the rule of Kilkenny and Carlow. Not that his fellow Scottish governors exercised their positions all that much, or for very long. Balfour, as already noted, became less and less active in government business after 1627, and died in England in 1634. Annandale for his part was an important figure at the royal court, and took little interest in Ireland. A gentleman of the bedchamber and for a few years keeper of the privy purse, he had helped James I to manage Scottish affairs from London. Although his influence declined somewhat after King James's death, he remained a creature of the royal palace, and retained his place in the bedchamber under Charles I. He resided principally at Guildford Park in Surrey and otherwise took a keen interest in the development of his estates in South West Scotland.[102] In the words of one Irish scholar, '[Annandale's] presence in Donegal must at best have been no more than occasional'. An absentee landlord, he left the management of his interests there to his agent, Herbert Maxwell.[103] No evidence survives to suggest that he ever exercised the county governorship.

At least the Scots had been afforded the opportunity of heading up county government in Ireland, albeit in only four of the twenty or more counties in which they had settled. As for the remaining positions of importance in Irish local government, the provost marshalships, the martial law commissionerships and the county shrievalties, the Scots were remarkably under-represented. Between 1603 and 1641 there was not a single Scottish provost marshal appointed in Ireland.[104] Of commissioners of martial law there were but two, one appointed in 1604 (Sir James Fullerton), and the other in 1627 (Sir Frederick Hamilton). In neither case were the commissions issued for ordinary government use, against the civilian population, but rather for use against disobedient soldiers in the royal army.[105] As the experience of lords Balfour and Annandale had revealed with the county governorships, in early Stuart Ireland power of martial law was reserved for English (and some Irish) officials only.[106]

Table 3: Scottish sheriffs of Co. Antrim, 1606–38

Year	*Sheriff*	*Estate*
1628	William Houston	Craigscastle
1629	Alexander McDonnell	Glenarm
1630	Robert Adair	Ballymena
1632	Alexander Stewart	Ballintoy
1633	John Donaldson	Glenarm
1635	Edward Maxwell	Connor

Source: Anon, 'High Sheriffs of the County of Antrim', *Ulster Journal of Archaeology*, 2nd ser., xi (1905).

Regarding the shrievalties, records are scarce, but a published list of the sheriffs of Co. Antrim, compiled from documents held in the PROI before 1922 (Table 3), names not a single Scottish sheriff of the county during the reign of James I.[107] Belatedly, from 1628, Scots began to be appointed, but after Lord Deputy Wentworth began his attack on Protestant non-conformity in 1635 no more appear to have been selected. However, definite conclusions are hazardous. The compiler of the Co. Antrim material was unable to assemble anything resembling a complete annual list; nonetheless, comparison with a similar list for Co. Leitrim suggests, again, not a single Scottish sheriff during the early seventeenth century, and this although Leitrim contained a sizeable Scottish settlement under the leadership of Sir Frederick Hamilton and James Dunbar.[108] A great deal more work is needed before a reliable impression of the number of Scottish sheriffs can be determined.[109] It is perhaps worth noting that at least one Scot was appointed as a sheriff outside Ulster and North Connaught – Patrick Wemyss, a one-time client of the earl of Desmond, who served as sheriff of Co. Kilkenny on three occasions between 1633 and 1637.[110]

To end this chapter where it began, with Scottish involvement in the Irish army. Following Fullerton's overseeing of the demobilisation of crown forces in Ireland during 1603–04, English officials might have feared that the Scots at court would bring pressure to bear on King James to grant them positions of command in the new, Stuart, Irish military establishment. Given the scale of 'briticizing' rhetoric then in vogue at Whitehall, such a development would have made sense. Moreover, already in 1603 Fullerton's friend, Sir James Hamilton (future Lord Clandeboy) had acquired the constableship of Trim Castle, one of the key royal fortresses in the country,[111] and by 1605 Fullerton himself had procured the constableship of Sligo Castle.[112] Nevertheless, these appointments aside, financial pressure to reduce military expenditure in Ireland ensured that English officers were neither replaced with nor augmented by Scottish officers before the rebellion of Sir Cahir O'Dogherty and the ransacking of Derry in 1608.

Though it posed little military threat to royal power in Ireland,[113] O'Dogherty's rising was significant not just because it persuaded the government to broaden the scope of its projected Plantation of Ulster – a decision which, incidentally, enabled Scottish courtiers to muscle in on the Plantation scheme – but also because it witnessed the Stuart regime's first attempt at Anglo-Scottish military cooperation. According to a letter of Lord Deputy Chichester written in September 1608, on learning of the revolt James VI and I immediately recognised its potential for demonstrating 'British' unity: 'That the rebellious generation of Ireland might be the more discouraged and kept in awe by seeing a scourge so ready at hand, as well from Scotland as from England, and that thus the happy union might be demonstrated to the world'.[114]

Sadly for the king, the operations against O'Dogherty's followers revealed only too starkly the lack of real political substance underlying his dream of greater 'British' union. To begin with, in Scotland the local lords were disinclined to cooperate by volunteering for positions of command or raising forces on their lands for use in Ulster, objecting to what they saw as the measly rates of pay on offer for service.[115] Consequently, of the total emergency force of 1,000 men that was sent into Ulster to serve against O'Dogherty, the Scots contributed just 300, significantly short of the 500 envisaged by the crown. So disinterested were the Scottish lords in the enterprise that a third of this small force (100 men) were actually raised in Scotland by an English captain, Sir Ralph Bingley, and a Welsh one, Captain John Vaughan,[116] and the remainder by decidedly inferior Scottish commanders, Captain William Stewart (the future Irish privy councillor), an impoverished minor landowner from Wigtonshire, and Captain Patrick Crawford, an obscure figure, possibly from Ayrshire.[117] On mustering the Scottish forces the deputy muster-master, Fullerton's agent, Walter White, complained that 'the ablest men' were in short supply, and that by and large the companies that presented to him were comprised of 'lads and youths presented for soldiers', raw inexperienced peasant recruits who were without proper weapons, badly apparelled, malnourished and desperate for money.[118]

The row over pay rates threatened to embarrass the government by revealing the essentially loveless nature of the Anglo-Scottish marriage. Fearful that the Scots would dig their heels in for better pay and conditions, the London privy council instructed Chichester to discharge them, but to do so 'warily and discreetly, lest either the Irish should be led to think that these Scotch will not serve against them, or the Scots should conceive that they have a liberty to refuse the service at their pleasure'. To save the king's blushes the council further advised that the Scottish troops should be discharged 'in parcels', 'to wear the appearance that there is no further need of them'.[119] Eventually the matter was settled, with the Scots accepting the pay that was offered, and they did not have to be discharged, but they remained resentful of their English paymasters (and the English of them).

Moreover, there is no evidence that the company commanded by Stewart ever saw service in the field. Having been transported to Ireland at the expense of both the Scottish and Irish governments, it was stationed initially at Carrickfergus, then at Dundalk, far away from the action. It seems feasible, therefore, that the only Scottish casualty of the insurrection, one Lieutenant Gordon, must have belonged to Crawford's force, based at Lifford in Donegal. Yet even this was not the case. Crawford and his men only arrived in Ulster towards the end of June, and were sent first to Dungannon in Tyrone, where they remained until the end of July, and only entered Lifford some weeks later, long after the revolt had ended.[120] For the record, Gordon was killed at Derry on 19 April, i.e., at the time of his death he was most probably commanded by the Welsh servitor, Vaughan, whose Scottish recruits were housed in 'the city of Derrie'.[121]

It is perhaps not surprising that, given such an unpromising start, further attempts to integrate a Scottish military component into the army of Ireland were few and far between after 1608. Captain Crawford's company was kept on at Lifford until at least 1611, but it subsequently dispersed.[122] Captain Stewart, having stationed his followers at Strabane in 1610 as part of a military operation to prepare the ground for plantation, managed thereafter to convert his men from soldiers to planters with a fair decree of success, mainly on his plantation estate at Gortavaghie in Donegal, and later at Ramelton.[123] Although Stewart continued to draw pay as a captain of foot in the army for many years to come, his company may have existed on paper only; his position was abolished after the Irish Commission of 1622.[124]

Attempts to replace Crawford and Stewart with other Scots on the Irish military establishment were distinctly unsuccessful. In 1611 King James had written to Chichester recommending that command of an Irish company be given to one Captain John Meldrum, a client of the Scottish privy councillor, Lord Burley, but nothing came of the king's suggestion.[125] Indeed, it was not until 12 April 1619 that another Scottish officer at last appeared – Sir Claud Hamilton of Cochonogh, named constable of Toome Castle, Co. Antrim, a royal outpost or 'petty ward' of six soldiers on the River Bann, after purchasing the post from the previous incumbent, Sir Thomas Phillips.[126] In October 1620, as part of a scam devised by Sir Thomas Dutton, gentleman of the privy chamber, to make money out of military grantees in Ireland, Sir Claud faced losing the constableship unless he 'compounded' with Dutton for a grant in fee of the position within a year.[127] As he is known to have retained the constableship subsequently, it follows that he must have compounded.[128] No further appointments were made for several years, until 1625, when following the outbreak of hostilities with Spain, Scotsmen seeking military appointments in Ireland were excited by the prospect of new opportunities. In January 1625 the council of war for Ireland (which included no Scottish member)[129] was made aware of the petitions for army commissions of at least six Scots – the earl of Desmond, Ludovick Stuart, Robert Maxwell, and James Ramsay, who each sought a captaincy; and James Stewart and James Leslie, who each looked for a lieutenancy. Despite recommendations by close personal servants of the old king, only one of these – Buckingham's client, Desmond – secured a captaincy, while Ludovick Stuart and Maxwell had each to settle for a lieutenancy. James Stewart was made a lesser officer, called an 'ancient'. Neither Ramsay nor Leslie secured a place.[130] Not that the Scots' failure to gain better positions greatly mattered. When it transpired that the crown was unable to pay proper wages to many of the new companies or their officers, only Desmond took up his commission.[131] None of the other new Scottish officers seem ever to have appeared in Ireland; the positions dissolved in their absence. In consequence, the reign of James VI and I ended in March 1625 with the king served by the same number of Scottish military officials in Ireland as had served him in 1603 – just two (Desmond and Sir Claud Hamilton), both of whom held far less power in the army than his first appointee (Fullerton).

A third officer was appointed soon after the accession of Charles I, the Ulster planter Sir Robert McClelland (future Lord Kirkcudbright), who earned general praise for his commitment to security, raising a company in Scotland for the defence of Ulster at his own expense.[132] But it was only after the outbreak of war with France in 1626 that the number of Scottish captains in the Irish army increased substantially. At the insistence of King Charles, Sir William Stewart regained the captaincy he had lost by 1622, and Sir George Hamilton and Sir Frederick Hamilton also obtained commissions.[133] But thereafter the Scots made no further progress. On Desmond's demise in 1628 his captaincy passed to an Englishman. Likewise, when, in 1638, shortly before his death, Lord Kirkcudbright resigned his captaincy of a company of horse stationed at Ardnekillin in Co. Londonderry, the repeated efforts of his son-in-law, Robert Maxwell, to secure his command, proved futile, and it passed into the hands of an English lord.[134] Sir George Hamilton's company of foot, based at Roscrea in Co. Tipperary, disappeared from establishment lists after 1636;[135] it is not clear who obtained his command.

Consequently, before the outbreak of the Anglo-Scottish, or Bishops', War in 1638, out of a total of 43 positions available[136] there were but three Scotsmen serving on the Irish military establishment – Sir William Stewart, at Ramelton, Co. Donegal; Sir Frederick Hamilton, at Manorhamilton, Co. Leitrim; and Sir Robert Stewart, recently appointed constable of Culmore Castle, Co. Londonderry. The fact that they were each based in the North West may not have been a coincidence. Lord Deputy Wentworth was anxious to reduce Scottish power in the North East, for fear that the king's enemies in Scotland might combine with their kinsmen and co-religionists across the North Channel, in East Ulster. It was for this reason that he considered sending old Sir William Stewart further west, toying with the idea of banishing him to a command in Connaught in order to remove him from the vicinity of Lough Swilly, a possible point of Scottish invasion in Ulster.[137] In the event Sir William clung on to his Ramelton station, but he played little part in subsequent military events – nor did his fellow Scottish officers. By the time Wentworth moved to impose the 'Black Oath' on Scottish settlers in Ulster in 1639 the officers he authorised to implement his policy in the province were either English or Anglo-Irish. Indeed, the army commands of all three Scottish officers seem to have been frozen: although I can find no evidence to suggest that their positions were ever formally terminated, Sir William Stewart, Sir Frederick Hamilton and Sir Robert Stewart were omitted from the army lists after 1638.[138] The new army assembled on Wentworth's orders in Ireland between 1638 and 1640 had just one Scottish officer out of forty – a new appointment, Sir Henry Bruce, who was named as one of three brigade colonels and a colonel of foot.[139] As a result, when the Irish Catholics rebelled in October 1641 many of the 'British' Protestants of the Lagan Valley found themselves without properly authorised defenders. It was only through the personal involvement of King Charles that Sir Frederick Hamilton and Sir Robert Stewart were again able to act in a military capacity, issued with new commissions to raise and command local forces, a fact that suggests the real extent of 'British' political failure in early Stuart Ireland.[140]

As this chapter indicates, evidence of genuine power sharing between English and Scottish secular officers in early Stuart Ireland is only very slight. Although the Scots managed to obtain appointments at every level of government in Ireland, they did so to little effect. Certainly the extent of their power produced nothing that could accurately be defined as the 'briticization' of the Irish governmental elite. At practically no stage during the reigns of either James VI and I or Charles I could the Scots be said to have comprised a distinct category of the Irish government – apart, perhaps, from 'absent'. Indeed, it seems those Scots who pursued official positions in Ireland did so largely to make profit, not to exercise authority. Of eleven Scotsmen appointed to positions on the Irish privy council between 1606 and 1625, only two bothered to attend council meetings regularly, Sir James Fullerton and Bishop George Montgomery; even these missed more meetings than they attended, Fullerton missing 23 of 36 and Montgomery 34 of 53 council meetings that are known to have been held during their respective periods of service as councillors (see Table 2). As the first two Scots appointed to the Irish council, they were far more conscientious than those other Scots who followed them onto the council board, presumably because at the time of their appointments (1605–07) King James's desire for greater British union had yet to run aground on the rocks of political necessity. They may even have shared the king's enthusiasm for his great 'British' experiment. What is remarkable about the behaviour of other Scottish officials in Ireland is the extent to which they evinced no enthusiasm whatsoever for the work of Anglo-Scottish state building. Mostly, this merely reflected the fact that, in their eyes, involvement in Ireland afforded them a remarkable opportunity to get rich quick through the plantations, trade, land speculation and a raft of other wealth-producing schemes. To pursue office too eagerly might have limited the opportunities for profit by antagonising those who really controlled the country – the English.

NOTES

1 Research for this chapter was aided by the Higher Education Authority funding made available through the Department of History, University College, Cork. For helping me to locate and check certain sources cited here I wish to thank Kenneth Nicholls, Margaret Curtis, Brian Donovan and Professor Nicholas Canny.

2 B. Galloway, *The Union of England and Scotland, 1603–1608* (Edinburgh, 1986); B.P. Levack, *The Formation of the British State: England, Scotland and the Union, 1603–1707* (Oxford, 1987); C. Russell, 'The Anglo-Scottish union, 1603–43: a success', in A. Fletcher and P. Roberts (eds), *Religion, Culture and Society in Early Modern Britain: Essays in Honour of Patrick Collinson* (Cambridge, 1994), pp. 238–56; J. Wormald, 'James VI, James I and the identity of Britain', in B. Bradshaw and J. Morrill (eds), *The British Problem c.1534–1707: State Formation and the Atlantic Archipelago* (Basingstoke, 1996), pp. 148–71; and J. Wormald, '"Tis true I am a cradle king": the view from the throne', in J. Goodare and M. Lynch (eds), *The Reign of James VI* (East Linton, 2000), pp. 252–5.

3 J. Dawson, 'Anglo-Scottish Protestant culture and integration in sixteenth-century Britain', in S.G. Ellis and S. Barber (eds), *Conquest & Union: Fashioning a British State, 1485–1725* (London, 1995), pp. 87–114; R. Mason, 'The Scottish reformation and the origins of Anglo-Scottish imperialism', in R. Mason (ed.), *Scots and Britons: Scottish Political Thought and the Union of 1603* (Cambridge, 1994), pp. 161–86.

4 J. Thornborough, *A Discourse plainly proving the evident Utility and urgent Necessity of the desired happy Union of England and Scotland* (London, 1604). Though the *Discourse* was suppressed for antagonising anti-Union MPs in the English Parliament, his play on the name 'Albion' was soon in vogue: Historical Manuscripts Commission, *Report on the Manuscripts of the Late Reginald Rawdon Hastings, esq.* (4 vols, London, 1928–47), iv, p. 2.

5 J.F. Larkin and P.L. Hughes (eds), *Stuart Royal Proclamations* (2 vols, Oxford, 1973), i, pp. 96–7.

6 For anti-Scottish sentiment G.P.V. Akrigg, *Jacobean Pageant: The Court of King James I* (London, 1962), chapter 5, though dated, is still valuable.

7 N. Cuddy, 'Anglo-Scottish union and the court of James I, 1603–1625', *Transactions of the Royal Historical Society*, 39 (1989), 109.

8 J. Goodare and M. Lynch, 'James VI: universal king?', in J. Goodare and M. Lynch (eds), *The Reign of James VI* (East Linton, 2000), pp. 25–6.

9 Galloway, *The Union*, pp. 137–57, 161–75; R. Lockyer, *The Early Stuarts: A Political History of England, 1603–42* (London, 1989), pp. 158–68; T.K. Rabb, *Jacobean Gentleman: Sir Edwin Sandys, 1561–1629* (Princeton, NJ, 1998), pp. 76–88, 122–32.

10 *Journals of the House of Commons, 1547–1629* (London, 1742), p. 367.

11 J. Morrill, 'The fashioning of Britain', in S. Ellis and S. Barber (eds), *Conquest & Union: The Fashioning of a British State, 1485–1725* (London, 1995), p. 17.

12 J.H. Burton and D. Masson (eds), *Register of the Privy Council of Scotland* (*RPCS*), *1610–13* (14 vols, Edinburgh, 1877–98), p. lxxix. Likewise, as a recent reviewer has noted, 'Scottish settlers in Ulster were nominated not by the Scottish privy council but by the royal court [at Whitehall]': J. Goodare, book review in *Scottish Historical Review*, 80:2 (2001), 272.

13 N. Canny, *Making Ireland British, 1580–1650* (Oxford, 2001), pp. 196–7.

14 *Ibid.*, chapters 4 and 5; M. Perceval-Maxwell, *The Scottish Migration to Ulster in the Reign of James I* (Belfast, 1999); P. Robinson, *The Plantation of Ulster: British Settlement in an Irish Landscape, 1600–1670* (Belfast, 1984); R. Gillespie, *Colonial Ulster: The Settlement of East Ulster, 1600–41* (Cork, 1985); R.J. Hunter, 'The plantation in Donegal', in W. Nolan, L. Ronayne and M. Dunlevy (eds), *Donegal: History & Society* (Dublin, 1995); T.W. Moody, *The Londonderry Plantation* (Belfast, 1939); B. Mac Cuarta, 'The plantation of Leitrim, 1620–41', *Irish Historical Studies*, 32:127 (May 2001), 297–320.

15 J. Bain, W. Boyd, A. Cameron *et al.* (eds), *Calendar of State Papers Relating to Scotland and Mary, Queen of Scots* (*CSPSc*), *1593–5* (13 vols, Edinburgh, 1898–1969), xi, p. 627.

16 D. Edwards, 'Securing the Jacobean succession: the secret career of James Fullerton of Trinity College, Dublin', in S. Duffy (ed.), *The World of the Galloglass: Kings, Warlords and Warriors in Ireland and Scotland, 1200–1600* (Dublin 2007), pp. 188–219. He was bursar of Trinity College, Dublin, from 1596: Edinburgh University Library, Laing MSS, La. II. 646/24.

17 J. Hughes (ed.), *Patentee Officers of Ireland, 1173–1826* (Dublin, 1960); National Archives of Ireland (hereafter NAI), Catalogue of Fiants, James I, no. 1514.

18 Lane died the following October and was buried in St Patrick's Cathedral, Dublin. For his appointments, see *The Irish Fiants of the Tudor Sovereigns: During the reigns of Henry VII, Edward VI, Philip & Mary, and Elizabeth I* (4 vols, Dublin,1994), iii, nos. 5750, 5765.

19 H.C. Hamilton, E.G. Atkinson, R.P. Mahaffy *et al.* (eds), *Calendar of State Papers relating to Ireland* (*CSPI*), *1603–06* (24 vols, London, 1860–1911), p. 211; Edwards, 'Securing the Jacobean succession'. A fine recent study of military demobilization in Jacobean Ireland overlooks Fullerton's role in 1603–04, emphasising instead reductions in the military establishment carried out by Lord Deputy Chichester after 1605 and Sir John King (Fullerton's successor as muster-master) after 1609: J.M. McLaughlin, 'The making of the Irish leviathan, 1603–25: statebuilding in

Ireland during the reign of James VI and I', PhD dissertation, National University of Ireland, Galway, 1999, pp. 142–5 and chapter 11 *passim*.

20 Not 1608, as claimed in V. Treadwell, *Buckingham and Ireland, 1616–1628: A Study in Anglo-Irish relations* (Dublin, 1998), p. 320 n. 39. For his council activities in late 1606, see *CSPI, 1606–08*, pp. 9, 14, 33, 40, 42.

21 He was not, however, the first Scot to be nominated to the Irish council; that distinction belongs to Bishop George Montgomery, nominated by King James on 14 February 1605 (*CSPI, 1603–06*, p. 258).

22 McLaughlin, 'The making', p. 158 n. 82; J.S. Brewer and William Bullen (eds), *Calendar of Carew Manuscripts Preserved in the Archiepiscopal Library at Lambeth* (*Cal. Carew MSS*), *1603–24* (6 vols, London, 1867–73), pp. 13–22, 40.

23 *Ibid.*, p. 31. He had served in a similar capacity in June 1609: *CSPI, 1608–10*, p. 222. In 1612 he attended a series of meetings in London concerning the 'escheated lands' in Ulster: F. Devon (ed.), *Pell Records: Issues of the Exchequer During the Reign of King James I* (London, 1836), p. 153.

24 J.M. Barkley, 'Some Scottish bishops and ministers in the Irish church, 1603–35', in D. Shaw (ed.), *Reformation and Revolution* (Edinburgh, 1967); Perceval-Maxwell, *The Scottish Migration*, appendix F, pp. 363–5; A. Ford, *The Protestant Reformation in Ireland, 1590–1641* (Dublin, 1997), pp. 73–6, 90, 121–2.

25 Dundas died shortly after his appointment, but this did not diminish the Scottish grip on the church, as he was immediately replaced by Robert Echlin, his fellow countryman, who held Down and Connor until 1635.

26 National Library of Ireland (hereafter NLI), MS 11044 (23).

27 Treadwell, *Buckingham*, pp. 35–8.

28 His criticism is chiefly targeted at Michael Perceval-Maxwell (Treadwell, *Buckingham*, p. 320 n. 39).

29 J. McCavitt, *Sir Arthur Chichester, Lord Deputy of Ireland, 1605–16* (Belfast, 1998), pp. 53–110, but especially pp. 91–110.

30 McCavitt, *Sir Arthur Chichester*, p. 79.

31 Morrill, 'The fashioning', p. 26.

32 Treadwell, *Buckingham*, p. 36.

33 Canny, *Making Ireland British*, p. 301.

34 Treadwell, *Buckingham*, p. 37.

35 In fact, McCavitt claims there were seven Scotsmen on the Irish Council (McCavitt, *Sir Arthur Chichester*, p. 79).

36 McCavitt, *Sir Arthur Chichester*, p. 47.

37 The Irish state papers for 1605–06 contain no less than five lists of government pensioners drawn up as part of an extensive inquiry into the Irish finances, recording all pensions and annuities granted by the crown in Ireland since the accession of James I. Not a single Scottish pensioner is mentioned: *CSPI, 1603–06*, pp. 376–8, 420–9, 430–5, 441–2, 456.

38 *CSPI, 1611–14*, pp. 115–17. Similarly, another list dated 1611, giving 18 pensioners, contains no Scots (*Ibid.*, pp. 197–8). One pensioner, Archie Moore – nominated by the king in August 1604 – may have been Scottish, but corroborative evidence is lacking (*Cal. Carew MSS, 1603–24*, pp. 185–90).

39 R. Lascelles (ed.), *Liber Munerum Publicorum Hiberniae* (2 vols, London, 1852).

40 Hughes (ed.), *Patentee Officers*.

41 NAI, Ferguson MSS, 38 vols, especially vol. ix: Revenue Exchequer Orders, 1592–1657; vols xi–xii: Equity Exchequer Orders, 1604–18, and 1618–38; vol. xx: Reportory to Memoranda Rolls, James I – Cromwell. See also Royal Irish Academy (RIA), MS 12 S.1. Ferguson's other papers at the RIA comprise his notes taken from various sources held at the British Library, The National Archives, and Bodleian Library.

42 E.g., the library of Trinity College Dublin has civil establishment lists for 1618, 1623 and 1629 (Trinity College Dublin (hereafter TCD), MS 808, fols 59r–64r, 66r–72v, 92r–97r), and military establishment lists for 1616, 1618, 1622 and 1641 (*ibid.*; TCD, MS 672, fols 96r–100r, 116r–118r, and MS 808, fols 53r–58r, 148r–152r). A list for 1611 is in *Cal. Carew MSS, 1603–24*, pp. 179–90. Likewise, the Strafford Papers have army lists for 1628, 1636 and *c.*1638–39 (Sheffield City Library (hereafter SCL), MS Wentworth Woodhouse Muniments (hereafter WWM), Str. P. 24–25/236–40, 242–3, 250–3, 267, 273). For a discussion of the emergence of establishment lists as formal records of state after 1603, see McLaughlin, 'The making', chapters 5, 9, 10.

43 Galloway, *The Union*, p. 17.

44 The last non-English lord chancellor of Ireland had been Sir Thomas Cusack, 1550–55, with Andrew Wise, 1551–53, the last non-English vice-treasurer: S.G. Ellis, *Ireland in the Age of the Tudors, 1447–1603: English Expansion and the End of Gaelic Rule* (London, 1998), p. 331.

45 The only possible exception was Henry Carey, Viscount Falkland, the English courtier who was given a Scottish peerage before being named lord deputy of Ireland in 1622.

46 For the growth of chancery's equitable jurisdiction in Ireland from the fifteenth century, see S.G. Ellis, *Reform & Revival: English Government in Ireland, 1470–1534* (London, 1986), pp. 159–62. See also M. McGlynn, 'Equitable jurisdiction in the Irish Chancery Court', MPhil dissertation, University College Dublin, 1990.

47 *CSPI, 1611–14*, p. 102; *Cal. Carew MSS, 1603–24*, p. 92.

48 For the Carew Commission, see especially Perceval-Maxwell, *The Scottish Migration*, pp. 123–32, and McCavitt, *Sir Arthur Chichester*, pp. 32–5.

49 *Cal. Carew MSS, 1603–24*, p. 92.

50 McCavitt, *Sir Arthur Chichester*, p. 33

51 The 1618 perambulation of Iveagh is printed in Irish Manuscripts Commission (hereafter IMC), *Irish Patent Rolls of James I: Facsimile of the Irish Record Commissioners' Calendar Prepared Prior to 1830* (*Cal. Patent Rolls, Ire., James I*) (Dublin, 1966), pp. 304–5.

52 On 15 June 1617 Montgomery and Hamilton had been named on the royal commission to establish the bounds of the territory: *CSPI, 1615–25*, pp. 193–4, 197–9.

53 Further information on the introduction of Presbyterianism to Ulster can be found in Glasgow University Library, MS Murray 70, pp. 171–87, an anonymous account of the first generation of ministers written in Scotland in the mid-seventeenth century. I am presently preparing an edition of the manuscript for publication.

54 Balfour was an industrious recoverer of the crown estate in Ireland, and was granted fee farm rents worth £100 (stg) per annum for his troubles: James I to St John, 12 April 1619 (TCD, MS. 10724).
55 For an outline of his introduction to Irish political life after 1614, see D. Edwards, *The Ormond Lordship in County Kilkenny, 1515–1642: The Rise and Fall of Butler Feudal Power* (Dublin, 2003), pp. 111–19, 121–7.
56 B. Jennings (ed.), *Wadding Papers, 1614–38* (Dublin 1953), p. 103.
57 For his career, see Perceval-Maxwell, *The Scottish Migration*, pp. 360–1; for his appointment, Treadwell, *Buckingham*, p. 327 n. 53.
58 He was, however, a useful crown representative in Ulster and helped Lord Deputy Falkland to secure support for a government levy in the province in February 1630: NAI MS 2445, pp. 50, 56.
59 He attended council meetings in Dublin on 28 February (The National Archives, London (hereafter TNA), SP 63/248/32) and 17 June 1629 (SCL, MS WWM Str. P. 24–25/254). It might be noted that he only procured letters of denization on 26 July 1629: J. Morrin (ed.), *Calendar of the Patent and Close Rolls of Chancery in Ireland : of the reign of Charles the First. First to eighth year, inclusive* (hereafter *Cal. Patent Rolls Ire., Charles I)* (Dublin, 1863), pp. 476–7.
60 E.g., *CSPI, 1625–32*, pp. 225 and 245, for Balfour and Archbishop Hamilton; TNA, SP 63/249/6, for Clandeboy; SCL, MS WWM Str. P. 24–25/252, for all three in attendance at a meeting on 31 Oct. 1628.
61 Balfour was present at Irish council meetings on 9 March and 2 April 1629 (TNA, SP 63/248/39, 55), after which his name disappears from extant council sederunts.
62 *CSPI, 1633–47*, p. 55; G.E. Cockayne, *The Complete peerage of England, Scotland, Ireland, Great Britain and the United Kingdom, Extant, Extinct, or Dormant* (8 vols, London, 1887–98), sub 'Glenawley'.
63 Erskine attended the great meeting of the council held in Dublin on 23 May 1634, to discuss the upcoming parliament (SCL, MS WWM Str. P. 24–25/102); Clandeboy was absent.
64 *Cal. Patent Rolls, Ire., Charles I*, p. 581.
65 M. Perceval-Maxwell, 'Strafford, the Ulster Scots and the Covenanters', *Irish Historical Studies*, 18:72 (1973), 532, 547; W. Knowler (ed.), *Letters and Dispatches of the Earl of Strafford* (2 vols, London 1739), ii, pp. 382–3.
66 Clandeboy had supported Wentworth's policies in the House of Lords: H. Kearney, *Strafford in Ireland, 1633–41: A Study in Absolutism* (Manchester, 1959), p. 50.
67 T. Carte, *Life of James Butler, Duke of Ormond* (6 vols, Oxford, 1851), v, pp. 230–1.
68 Interestingly, Erskine's appointment on 30 October 1622 was made on the understanding that he would 'make his residence' in Ireland (*CSPI, 1615–25*, p. 395). However, soon after purchasing his estate – at Augher in Co. Tyrone – he faced a legal challenge by the government because he had bought the lands from English proprietors, a development which some officials took as contravening the terms of the Ulster plantation (*CSPI, 1625–32*, pp. 180–1). This dispute probably accounts for his poor record as a privy councillor. He was still experiencing difficulty in 1630 (NAI, MS 2445, p. 93).

69 V. Treadwell, 'The Irish Court of Wards under James I', *Irish Historical Studies*, 12:45 (1960), 6–12.

70 Although it is possible that he was responsible for uncovering the first wardship for the crown in Co. Antrim in the seventeenth century, Hamilton's performance as commissioner is not notable for its productivity. In the later 1620s new officials of the court of wards discovered hundreds of unreported alienations and other feudal incidents in Antrim and Down, dating back to the 1590s: Gillespie, *Colonial Ulster*, pp. 98–100, 229.

71 Once again, the only Scot involved was Hamilton's friend, Sir James Fullerton, who was named to the committee in 1615, but seems never to have taken part in its proceedings, and was gone by 1616: Treadwell, 'Irish Court of Wards', 11–13.

72 Hughes (ed.), *Patentee Officers*, p. 79; NAI, Catalogue of Fiants, James I, p. 796, no. 2168.

73 TCD, MS 808, fols 59r–64r, 66r–72v.

74 Treadwell, *Buckingham*, pp. 37, 211.

75 *Ibid.*, p. 37, states that Acheson was appointed master in 1618. However, Acheson's name features on the 1623 list of the civil establishment in Ireland (TCD, MS 808, fols 66r–72v), not the 1618 list (*ibid.*, fols 59r–64r). Hughes (ed.), *Patentee Officers*, p. 1 records the date of his appointment as 26 June 1621.

76 Acheson was admitted to the Irish Inns on 16 November 1621 as 'master of chancery' (E. Keane, P.B. Phair and T.U. Sadleir (eds), *King's Inns Admission Papers* (Dublin, 1982), p. 1).

77 Keane *et al.* (eds), *Kings Inns Admission Papers*; NAI, Catalogue & Index: Fiants, Charles I, no. 99.

78 *CSPI, 1625–32*, pp. 273, 281.

79 *Cal. Patent Rolls, Ire., Charles I*, pp. 235–6.

80 J. Maitland Thomson (ed.), *The Register of the Great Seal of Scotland, 1620–1633* (11 vols, Edinburgh, 1894), p. 523.

81 R. Gillespie, 'A question of survival: the O'Farrells and Longford in the seventeenth century', in R. Gillespie and G. Moran (eds), *Longford: Essays in County History* (Dublin, 1991), pp. 16–17, misidentifies Hanna as English, and as being already a government official at the time of the Longford plantation scheme in 1619.

82 Treadwell, *Buckingham*, p. 37.

83 For his efforts to secure the clerkship, see *CSPI, 1625–32*, pp. 26–7, 141, 576, 579, and especially *ibid., 1647–60 & Addenda, Charles I*, pp. 153–4. The latter reference is misdated in the calendar to *c.* September 1630, but internal evidence clearly shows that the document pre-dates Hanna's death. For his death, see NAI, MS 2445, p. 14. Further confirmation of Hanna's non-occupancy of the clerkship is provided by the fact that his name does not appear on any of the letters of the Irish council written between December 1628 and December 1629 (TNA, SP 63/248, *passim*; *ibid.*, SP 63/249, *passim*). Several of the council letters were drafted and signed by Ussher's deputy, Adam Loftus.

84 *Cal. Patent Rolls, Ire., Charles I*, pp. 235–6.

85 TCD, MS 808, fol. 93r.

86 The fact that he was not admitted to the Irish Inns strongly suggests non-occupancy of the mastership (Keane *et al.* (eds), *Kings Inns*, p. 212).

87 *Cal. Patent Rolls, Ire., Charles I*, p. 42.
88 *CSPI, 1625–32*, pp. 580–1.
89 Hughes (ed.), *Patentee Officers*, p. 62; NAI, Catalogue and Index: Fiants, Charles I, no. 1258d. This Sir Robert may be the same Sir Robert Hanna who served as a member of the council of the presidency of Connaught in 1661.
90 M. O'Dowd, *Power, Politics & Land: Sligo, 1568–1688* (Belfast, 1991), p. 115.
91 NAI, MS. 2448, pp. 212–15. As an indication of the potential profitability of the post it should be noted that Daniel secured the deputy clerkship from Hanna on a recognizance of £2,000.
92 British Library (hereafter BL), Harleian MS 697, ff 15r, 22v, 24r, 26v, 29v, 34v.
93 NLI, Sarsfield Papers, MS D 25963–4.
94 BL, Harleian MS 697, fols 24r, 26v, 29v
95 *Cal. Patent Rolls, Ire., James I*, p. 584; NAI, Catalogue of Fiants, James I, p. 811.
96 For the Munster council see especially D. Kennedy, 'The Presidency of Munster, 1570–1625', MA dissertation, University College Cork, 1973; L. Irwin, 'The Lord Presidency of Munster, 1625–1662', MA, University College Cork 1976; M.P. Curtis, 'Provincial government and administration in Jacobean Munster', 2 vols, PhD thesis, University College, Cork 2006.
97 TNA, E 214/358. In addition, Thomas Boswell, appointed clerk of the crown and peace for Connaught in 1627, was probably Scottish, but I have been unable to find corroborative evidence about him.
98 *CSPI, 1606–08*, p. 263.
99 NAI, Catalogue of Fiants, James I, pp. 811–12.
100 The terms of their appointments are outlined most fully for Annandale in *Cal. Patent Rolls, Ire., James I*, pp. 588–9; see also *ibid.*, pp. 574 (Desmond) and 591 (Balfour).
101 Balfour was reappointed on 20 June 1626, Annandale on 14 January 1627 (NAI, Catalogue & Index: Fiants, Charles I, nos. 184, 266).
102 K. Brown, 'Courtiers and cavaliers: service, anglicisation and loyalty among the royalist nobility', in J. Morrill (ed.), *The Scottish National Covenant in its British Context* (Edinburgh, 1990), p. 167; S. Adams, 'James VI and the politics of south west Scotland, 1603–25', in Goodare and Lynch (eds), *The Reign of James VI*, p. 233.
103 R.J. Hunter, 'Plantation in Donegal', in W. Nolan, L. Ronayne and M. Dunlevy (eds), *Donegal: History & Society* (Dublin, 1995), pp. 293–4.
104 McLaughlin, 'The making', pp. 348–9, provides a useful list of provosts marshal in Jacobean Ireland.
105 NAI, Catalogue of Fiants, James I, p. 689, no. 1055; *Cal. Patent Rolls, Ire., Charles I*, p. 244.
106 For the continuing importance of martial law in the government of Ireland after 1603, see D. Edwards, 'Two fools and a martial law commissioner: cultural conflict at the Limerick Assize of 1606', in Edwards (ed.), *Regions & Rulers: Essays for Kenneth Nicholls* (Dublin, 2004), pp. 237–5; D. Edwards, 'The plight of the Earls: Tyrone and Tyrconnell's "Grievances" and crown security policy in Ulster, 1603–7', in T. O'Connor and M.A. Lyons (eds), *The Ulster Earls and Baroque Europe* (Dublin 2010), pp. 53–76.

107 More recent work on the sheriffs of Antrim and Down makes no mention of Scots either (Gillespie, *Colonial Ulster*, pp. 101–2). The absence of Scottish local officials before 1625 might explain why Clandeboy sought the virtual exemption of his East Ulster lands from government jurisdiction (*ibid.*, p. 89).

108 J. Meehan, 'Catalogue of the High Sheriffs of County Leitrim, 1605–1800', *Journal of the Royal Society of Antiquaries of Ireland*, 18 (1908), 386; Mac Cuarta, 'The plantation', pp. 315–16. For Tyrone Sheriffs after 1625 see Roulston's Chapter 3 in this volume, p. 109.

109 Likewise the question of Scots who served as justices of the peace: I am aware of one Scottish JP in Leinster, a Mr Pont, who was murdered in Co. Wicklow in 1626: *CSPI, 1625–32*, p. 191.

110 Edwards, *The Ormond Lordship*, p. 353.

111 *CSPI, 1611–14*, p. 114. He seems still to have held the constableship in 1611 (*Cal. Carew MSS, 1603–24*, p. 183).

112 NAI, Catalogue of Fiants, James I, p. 690. Fullerton also acquired a crown grant of Ballymote Castle, Co. Sligo, which he subsequently sold to William Taaffe for £1,500 (O'Dowd, *Power, Politics & Land*, pp. 90, 95; *CSPI, 1603–06*, pp. 272–3).

113 J. McCavitt, 'The political background to the Ulster Plantation, 1607–1620', in B. Mac Cuarta (ed.), *Ulster 1641: Aspects of the Rising* (Belfast 1993), pp. 12–14; F.W. Harris, 'The state of the realm; English military, political and diplomatic responses to the Flight of the Earls, 1607–8', *Irish Sword*, 14 (1981), 47–64.

114 *CSPI, 1608–10*, pp. 22–3.

115 They were offered the same rates as English and Irish servitors (*ibid.*). See also *RPCS, 1607–10*, p. 109.

116 *CSPI, 1608–10*, p. 10. The speed of Bingley's response to the O'Dogherty threat played no small part in his political rehabilitation with the crown: R.J. Hunter, 'Sir Ralph Bingley, *c.*1570–1627: Ulster planter', in P. Roebuck (ed.), *Plantation to Partition: Essays in Ulster History in Honour of J.L. McCracken* (Belfast 1981), pp. 19–21.

117 Perceval-Maxwell, *The Scottish Migration*, appendix D, pp. 359–60.

118 *CSPI, 1608–10*, pp. 10–11. White's description was repeated, almost word for word, by Chichester in a letter to the Scottish council: *RPCS, 1607–10*, p. 519.

119 *CSPI, 1608–10*, pp. 22–3. For a slightly different view, see R. Gillespie, 'An army sent from God: Scots at war in Ireland, 1642–9', in N. MacDougall (ed.), *Scotland and War, AD 79–1918* (Edinburgh, 1991), pp. 114–15.

120 *Ibid.*, pp. 10, 32; *RPCS, 1607–10*, p. 519.

121 *CSPI, 1606–08*, pp. 505–7.

122 *CSPI, 1611–14*, pp. 8–9, 160; *ibid.*, *1615–25*, pp. 10–13.

123 Perceval-Maxwell, *The Scottish Migration*, p. 360.

124 TCD, MS 672, fol. 97r, 117v; *CSPI, 1615–25*, p. 343.

125 *Ibid.*, *1611–14*, p. 30.

126 Hughes (ed.), *Patentee Officers*, p. 36; TCD, MS 672, fol. 116r; *ibid.*, MS 808, p. 46.

127 *CSPI, 1615–25*, p. 292; *Cal. Patent Rolls, Ire., James I*, pp. 484–5.

128 *CSPI, 1615–25*, p. 406; *ibid.*, *1625–32*, p. 197.

129 *CSPI, 1615–25*, pp. 511, 541.

130 *CSPI, 1615–25*, pp. 555–7.

131 Commenting on Scottish involvement in the British army before 1638, one leading authority has characterised the Scots who served as 'mercenaries working for the English crown': K. Brown, 'From Scottish lords to British officers: statebuilding, elite integration and the army in the seventeenth century', in N. MacDougall (ed.), *Scotland and War, AD 79–1918* (Edinburgh, 1991), p. 137. For the problem of army pay, see A. Clarke, 'The army and politics in Ireland, 1625–30', *Studia Hibernica*, 4 (1964), 28–53; for Desmond conducting 250 men to Ireland from Milford Haven or Haverford West in February 1625, see J.R. Dasent (ed.), *Acts of the Privy Council, June 1623-March 1625* (46 vols, London, 1890–1964), pp. 440–1, 472–3, 474.

132 *CSPI, 1633–47*, p. 234; *ibid., 1647–60* and *Addenda, Charles I*, pp. 138–9.

133 *CSPI, 1625–32*, pp. 205, 275, 595.

134 *CSPI, 1633–47*, pp. 206, 209, 234.

135 SCL, MS WWM Str. P. 24–25/267. For Hamilton's arrival at Roscrea see C. Manning, 'The two Sir George Hamiltons and their connections with the castles of Roscrea and Nenagh', *Tipperary Historical Journal* (2001), 149–54.

136 SCL, MS WWM Str. P. 24–25/242–243.

137 Perceval-Maxwell, 'Strafford', p. 546.

138 They did not even receive a share of the officers' taffeta that was distributed in Ireland in 1639 (SCL, MS WWM Str. P. 24–25/273).

139 *CSPI, 1633–47*, p. 186; TCD, MS 808, fol. 150r. On 2 April 1640 Bruce was granted a pension of £300: NAI, Catalogue & Index: Fiants, Charles I, no. 3361.

140 D. Stevenson, *Scottish Covenanters and Irish Confederates* (Belfast, 1981), pp. 51–2, 98.

2

'Scottish peers' in seventeenth-century Ireland

JANE OHLMEYER

In 1625 when James VI and I, the Scottish king and sovereign of Great Britain and Ireland, died, six Scots held titles in the Irish peerage. There was one earl, two viscounts and three barons.[1] On the accession in 1685 of his son, James VII and II, there were five (three earls, a viscount and a baron). Forfeitures after 1690 reduced this number to three. The 'Scottish peers', 28 men spanning several generations, represented a small but distinctive group within the resident Irish peerage which in 1641 numbered 68 peers.[2] The Scots comprised 7 per cent of the resident peerage and represented the smallest ethnic group (the native Irish accounted for 10 per cent, the New English 32 per cent and the Old English 49 per cent). They also constituted a tiny proportion of the total Scottish population in Ireland which by 1641 probably numbered 30,000 people, living largely in Ulster and particularly in Counties Antrim and Down. During the early decades of the seventeenth century the 'Scottish peers', whose combined estates totalled by the mid-seventeenth century roughly 234,000 plantation acres (of a total acreage of *c.*9 million), played a key role in promoting 'civilization' as part of the plantation of Ulster.[3] Their dogged loyalty to the Stuart dynasty throughout the seventeenth century is striking. As landlords, politicians and military commanders, they served as the regional and national powerbrokers, exercising influence in Ireland and beyond.

None of the personal archives survive for the 'Scottish peers' who feature in this chapter.[4] A fire in 1664 destroyed the personal papers of the Montgomery family while the archive of Arthur Forbes, first earl of Granard, was lost 'owing to the dishonesty of my grandfather's agent'.[5] Instead the life stories of these men and their lineages need to be reconstructed by sifting through dry legal, estate, genealogical and testamentary records, isolated items of correspondence, together with land surveys (the Books of Survey and Distribution), the 1641 depositions, and pamphlets and family memoirs.[6] Rather than trying to patch together the political careers of 28 individuals – many of whom are worthy of study in their own right – this chapter takes a more structured approach and examines the 'Scottish peers' as a group.[7] It will look at the social, religious, political and military backgrounds of the 'Scottish peers', the extent of their estates, their marriage patterns, their networks and their survival strategies, especially their ability to secure their lineages. To what extent did these men (and their women and children) retain a sense of 'Scottishness' over the course of the century? At what point did they become fully assimilated into their host society?

The elevation of Scots to the Irish peerage needs to be viewed as part of James VI and I's 'civilizing' agenda for Ireland and his determination to create a truly 'British state' after the Union of the Crowns in 1603. Although the king concerned himself more with the union between England and Scotland and treated Ireland as a colony rather than a kingdom, his *Magna Britannia* undoubtedly included Ireland.[8] He genuinely hoped to unite his three kingdoms 'under one imperial crown' and to give his peoples the freedom 'to commerce and match together, that so they may grow into one nation'.[9] More particularly the king wanted to dilute the political dominance of the Old English, as the descendants of the Anglo-Normans were known, who had proved, from James's perspective, so obstructive. He also needed to reward those who had enthusiastically supported royal policies, especially that of plantation. These, together with his need for cash, resulted in a series of elevations after 1616. Of the new peers, five were Scots. In May 1617 James Hamilton, heir to the earl of Abercorn, was created baron of Strabane. Sir Randal MacDonnell was ennobled as Viscount Dunluce in May 1618, a privilege for which he paid a hefty £5,000.[10] The earldom of Antrim followed in December 1620. On 7 November 1619 Andrew Stewart, Lord Ochiltree, became Baron Castlestewart and the following day Sir James Balfour became baron of Glenawley. It was 3 May 1622 before Sir Hugh Montgomery became Viscount Montgomery of the Ards and 4 May before Sir James Hamilton was elevated to the viscountcy of Claneboy. These coincided with the real inflation of the Irish peerage, when between 1620 and 1629 some 34 titles were created, many of them to men who had little or no connection with Ireland and did not reside there.[11]

The quality of these new peers caused concern. Writing in 1652 Sir Edward Walker quipped 'many persons who could not procure titles of honour in England, for money and other reasons have with great ease gotten them … [in Ireland]; so as there is hardly a town of note, much less a county, but hath some earl, viscount or baron of it'.[12] He argued that rather than strengthening the crown with judicious elevations to the peerage, James and later Charles had debased it by bestowing honour on men without 'public merit'.[13] The social origins of many of the 'Scottish peers' were indeed modest and a number were clearly perceived to be grasping 'men on the make' but they were no less worthy than many of their English counterparts who secured favour from the king or his ministers during these years. Whether English or Scottish, the crown had created a 'service nobility', a new generation of ambitious and avaricious peers, who wanted either to consolidate their patrimonies and political influence or to make their fortunes in Ireland, and to secure public reward and social recognition. They were also determined to establish themselves in the community of honour and to demonstrate that they had been ennobled by merit, rather than the purse.

Parliament offered a public venue for the exercise of honour and, with the exception of Balfour of Glenawley, the 'Scottish peers' took their seats in the 1634 House of Lords, though none appear to have been particularly active. The new temporal creations had given the government full control of the upper house for the first time and thanks to the creation of 40 parliamentary boroughs out of the newly founded plantation towns the government also held a clear majority in the lower house. When parliament assembled again in 1640 four 'Scottish peers' took their seats but only the second earl of Antrim appears to have participated in the intense politicking that gripped the house as the political community plotted to secure the lord deputy's downfall.[14] Whether active or not, the 'Scottish peers' enjoyed strong links with members of the lower house. The Hamiltons and Montgomerys, for example, dominated the representation for Co. Down. Sir James Montgomery, the first viscount's second son, was returned for the county and his grandsons – Hugh, later earl of Mount Alexander, and George, his younger brother – for Newtown. The first Viscount Clandeboye's brother and agent, James Hamilton, was returned for Bangor, along with his nephew, John.[15] More concerned with the exercise of influence in their localities and in cultivating the king and influential courtiers in Whitehall, the 'Scottish peers' kept a relatively low political profile in Dublin. They did, however, ensure that the interests of the Scottish planters were adequately represented.

Unlike all of the other 'Scottish peers', the earl of Antrim's connections with East Ulster long pre-dated the formal plantations. A devout Catholic Randal MacDonnell, first earl of Antrim, was a descendant of Somerled, first Lord of the Isles. The MacDonnells, whose hereditary estates were in Kintyre and Jura, settled permanently in Co. Antrim and held much of the Route and Glynns of Antrim.[16] The Antrim estate, 'thirty miles of territory and vast estates with several castles', was bounded by the River Bann in the west, the Giant's Causeway and the coastal towns of Coleraine and Ballycastle in the north and the ports of Cushendall, Glenarm and Larne in the east.[17] Antrim's meteoric rise within the Irish peerage was largely due to his enthusiastic support for James VI and I's schemes for the plantation of Ulster. He would have been familiar with this concept because he had been fostered on the Scottish island of Arran (hence his name Randal Arranach) and thus exposed to James's unsuccessful attempts to 'plant' the troublesome Highlands with Scottish Lowlanders. In fact one recent scholar has suggested that the earl formed an important human link between the Irish and Scottish plantations.[18] Antrim recognized the economic advantages of the English system of landlord–tenant relations and of a commercial economy – both of which were introduced with the plantation. Between 1609 and 1626 he demised considerable amounts of land to Lowland Scots and within a relatively short period of time there was a thriving colony of Scottish Protestants living in the baronies of Dunluce and Glenarm.[19] Certainly the town of Dunluce consisted 'of many tenements, after the fashion of the Pale, peopled for the most part with Scotsmen'.[20] The earl's far-sighted policies soon paid off and in 1629 it was noted that he 'hath good tenants and is very well paid his rents'.[21] In addition to progressive economic and agrarian policies, Randal improved his property by building castles at Kilwaughter, Ballygalley, Glenarm and Ballycastle and refurbishing Dunluce.[22] On numerous occasions the king thanked him for 'his services in improving those barren and uncultivated parts of the country, and planting a colony there'.[23] His son and heir, Randal, second earl and first marquis, continued his father's improving policies and owned, by a very considerable margin, the largest estate of any 'Scottish peer' (see Table 4). His estimated wealth in 1635 was £10,000 in land and £3,077 in goods.[24] According to the Books of Survey and Distribution, in 1641 he held 149,353 plantation acres (108,915 of which were deemed to be profitable), spanning five baronies: Dunluce (40,293 acres), Cary (29,545 acres), Kilconway (40,334 acres), Glenarm (30,406 acres) and Toome (2,119 acres) in Co. Antrim together with 6,656 acres in Coleraine in neighbouring Co. Londonderry.[25] Patches of bogland littered his baronies which were in places barren, mountainous, wooded or inaccessible, but this was offset by fertile coastal plains suitable for tillage, especially along the north-east coast.[26] Despite the first earl's attempts to improve the roads and build bridges, internal communications remained poor and only two roads, one of which was impassable in winter, linked the Antrim estate with the outside world.[27] Nevertheless this sprawling, isolated territorial base on the periphery of Stuart Britain made its owner one of the greatest in Ireland, second to the duke of Ormond who, according to the Books of Survey and Distribution, held 191,629 acres (119,541 of which were profitable).[28]

The other great proponents of plantation in East Ulster were James Hamilton, first Viscount Claneboye, and James Montgomery, first Viscount Montgomery of the Ards, who both came from Ayrshire, the former the son of a minister and the latter the son of a local laird. Favourites of the king, they dominated the informal plantation of Co. Down where they were charged with 'civilizing the country people'.[29] In 1605 they carved up the estates of Con O'Neill, lord of Upper Claneboye and the Great Ards, in a tripartite agreement with O'Neill. Con's portion was in the north west at Castlereagh, while the newcomers settled in the north east of Co. Down, taking control of the sea coasts along the Ards peninsula and effectively creating a 'Scottish Pale'. The plantations quickly prospered and by 1630 their estates in north Down could muster 2,718 men, the majority of them Scots, 'or a settler population of 4,509'.[30] According to the Montgomery family chronicler Scottish colonists, including tradesmen, settled and within a short period of time:

> everybody minded their trades, and the spade, building, and setting fruit trees, &c, in orchards and gardens, and by ditching their grounds … Now the golden peaceable age renewed, no strife, contention, querulous lawyers, or Scottish or Irish feuds, between clans and families, and sirnames, disturbing the tranquillity of those times; and the towns and temples were erected, with other great works done.[31]

In 1611 plantation commissioners who visited the Claneboye estates commented on the 'fayre stone house' and the town of Bangor which 'consists of 80 newe houses, all inhabited with Scotyshmen and Englishmen'.[32] They also noted that Montgomery's town, Newtown, contained 100 houses, all inhabited by Scots. In 1625 Claneboye commissioned the cartographer, Thomas Raven, to draw maps of his estate. Raven's exquisitely detailed, coloured maps provide a vivid snapshot of the varied nature of the land (meadow, pasture, moor), how it was farmed and divided (the name of the holder is given) and show the location of roads, castles, deer parks, orchards, houses, cottages, mills, the harbours and the prospering towns of Bangor (with 70 houses), Killyleagh (with 75 houses) and Newtown, together with other natural features, especially bogs and woods. In 1635 Claneboy's estimated wealth was £3,750 in land and £1,154 in goods; Montgomery's was £2,000 in land and £615 in goods.[33] By 1641 Claneboye's estates in the baronies of Ards, Castlereagh and Dufferin totalled 44,569 plantation acres (nearly all of it was profitable). Montgomery held 16,001 plantation acres in the baronies of Ards and Castlereagh (15,495 of which were described as profitable). Greed for additional acres by both planters alienated the native population and ensured that the two neighbours quickly became embroiled in lengthy and expensive litigation, largely over boundaries.[34] Hostility reached such a pitch that Claneboye threatened to disinherit any of his heirs who 'shall marry with any of the posteritie of Sir Hugh Montgomery'.[35] Only a combination of high food prices, crop failures and disquiet in Scotland followed by the outbreak of rebellion in 1641 forced an uneasy reconciliation between the two families as they scrambled to resist the onslaught from local insurgents, many of whom had been dispossessed as a result of their plantations.[36]

The unregulated colonization of Antrim and Down, led by these three peers, proved hugely successful in attracting settlers to East Ulster and merits comparison with the informal colonization of Orkney and Shetland by planters from Fife which resulted in the extension of Lowland practices to the Northern Isles. Less successful was the colonization of the forfeited Isles of Lewis and Harris with adventurers from Fife (there were three attempts in 1595–1602, 1605, 1609) and this, together with experiences of the Munster plantation, influenced the king's attitude towards the formal plantation of the escheated Ulster counties. After 1610 land was allocated in relatively small parcels (ranging from 1,000 to 2,000 acres) to 100 Scottish and English 'undertakers' and *c.*50 'servitors' (largely English army officers who had settled at the end of the war) in the hope that they would create a British type of rural society. In his *Basilikon Doron*, James VI had expressed the hope that the Western Isles would be tamed by planting 'colonies among them of answerable inland subjects, that within short time may reform and civilize the best inclined among them: rooting out or transporting the barbarous and stubborn sort, and planting civility in their rooms'.[37] The same held true for Ulster, where the Scots – including some with direct experience of plantations at home – now migrated in their thousands.

Table 4: Land held (in plantation acres) by 'Scottish peers' in 1641 and after the Restoration

Peers	*1641 (total)*	*1641 (profitable)*	*1670+ (total)*	*1670+ (profitable)*
Balfour of Glenawley	8,275	7,520		
Forbes of Granard	3,149	1,778	9,466	7,573
Hamilton of Claneboye/ Clanbrassil	44,569	43,669	44,569	43,669
Hamilton of Strabane	**7,069**	**6,166**	**[7,069]**	**[6,166]**
MacDonnell of Antrim	**149,353**	**108,915**	**83,702**	**62,899**
Montgomery of Ards/ Mount Alexander	16,001	15,495	18,262	16,385
Stewarts of Castlestewart	2,116	1,756	2,116	1,756

Note: Names and data for Catholics indicated in bold type.
Source: I am grateful to Dr McKenny for allowing me access to his database and for his particular assistance in preparing figures for the peers. His database collates information from the Books of Survey and Distribution [Quit Rent set], the Civil Survey, transplantation lists and letters patent.

The largest planter in Co. Fermanagh was James Balfour, first baron Balfour of Glenawley, an adventurer from Fife. He was second son of Sir James of Pittendriech and brother of Michael, Lord Balfour of Burleigh, an undertaker who received lands in Co. Fermanagh, which he later sold to James. According to the Books of Survey and Distribution by 1641 the Balfour estates comprised 8,275 plantation acres, 7,520 of which were profitable, in the baronies of Knockninny and Magherastephana.[38] Development of the estate progressed slowly, partly because Balfour spent too much time in Dublin, and in 1619 'most' of his tenants were Irish (as opposed to 'British').[39] Nevertheless he oversaw the construction of Castle Balfour and the neighbouring village of Ballybalfour, which by 1622 had 40 mud houses, together with the town of Lisnaskea, which according to a 1622 report was inhabited by 'Britons'.[40] An inquisition held after the first baron's death highlights the extent to which the costs stemming from lengthy and acrimonious legal disputes, especially with Lord Blayney and the bishop of Clogher, and other liabilities associated with his three marriages had left his estates encumbered with debts.[41] Desperate for cash, he alienated in July 1634 much of this estate to his cousin, Sir William Balfour, for £3,328.[42]

One of the most successful and wealthiest planters of all was the royal favourite James Hamilton, first earl of Abercorn, from Renfrewshire, who in 1611 received estates in Co. Tyrone that lay along the River Foyle.[43] According to one courtier 'The Earl of Abercorn is discouraged because the land fallen to him in Ireland is not fitting his degree, although he took land to please the king and encourage others'.[44] Certainly he fulfilled his conditions as an undertaker by attracting roughly 180 Scottish settlers, he developed the market town of Strabane, which returned burgesses to the Irish parliament with Scottish surnames, and built there a castle, 100 houses, a mill, 'a sessions house and market cross', together with a gaol.[45] His early death in 1618 and a period of minority interrupted the pace of settlement. The year before, his son and heir, James, had been created first baron Strabane, but in 1633 James resigned his Irish peerage in favour of his brother, Claude, who became second baron. According to the Books of Survey and Distribution, his heir, James, third baron of Strabane, held 7,069 plantation acres in the barony of Strabane in 1641.

The other royal favourite who prospered thanks to the king's largesse was Andrew Stewart (1560–1628), first baron of Castlestewart and Lord Ochiltree, who hailed from Ayrshire. In 1610 James VI and I assigned him prime land bordering Lough Neagh in Mountjoy, Co. Tyrone, presumably as his reward for leading a 'fire and sword' expedition as part of the failed attempt to colonize the Western Isles in 1608. Despite being plagued by debts which forced him to sell in 1615 his Scottish estates and title, Castlestewart quickly introduced settlers to his estates, built a castle and developed an urban settlement at Stewartstown. According to a 1622 report 50 'British' families lived on his estates (*c.*100 males), along with 84 Irish.[46] By 1641, according to the Books of Survey and Distribution, the family had increased its holdings to include 2,116 plantation acres in the barony of Dungannon, as well as 3,000 plantation acres in Mountjoy. Stewartstown had become a proto-industrial settlement and home to 30 leaseholders who formed a diverse community that included three gentlemen, three butchers, eight tradesmen, two weavers, two carpenters, three tailors, a ditcher, quarrier, shoemaker, maltmaker, smith and schoolmaster.[47]

Planter towns, like Stewartstown or Ballybalfour or Strabane thus 'provided a focus for the diverse elements of rural society by means of regional gatherings, such as assizes and quarter sessions, and acted as engines of economic growth, centres of trade, and points from which new ideas and technology could be diffused'.[48] Many, however, never became fully integrated into an urban network and depended for their survival on the activities and connections of local lords like Castlestewart, Balfour or Abercorn.

In part because they supported the crown, albeit with varying degrees of enthusiasm, during the 1640s and 1650s, the 'Scottish peers' retained or were restored to at least portions of their pre-war estates after 1660. Antrim, who had been elevated to a marquisate in 1645, lost most and his holdings dropped by 44 per cent (or 65,651 acres) from 149,353 to 83,702 plantation acres (see Table 4).[49] Given his activities during the war years he was fortunate to secure even this. After initially supporting Charles I with enthusiasm he switched allegiance to the clerical party within the Confederation of Kilkenny before cutting a deal with the Cromwellians, who protected him from transplantation and provided him with a modest income during the 1650s. Thanks to an extraordinary combination of factors – especially the tenacity of his creditors (on the eve of war he owed at least £40,000), and the support and generosity of his family, the queen mother, and members of her court, combined with the fact that his enemies were disorganized, disunited and unprepared – he finally regained his estates. In July 1663 Charles II declared the marquis 'innocent of any malice or rebellious purpose towards the crown' and ordered Ormond to assist him to recover his estates by making known the king's wishes to the commissioners of the court of claims.[50] Adventurers and soldiers, led by Sir John Clotworthy, later Lord Massareene, who had acquired farms on the Antrim estate during the 1650s immediately protested and the publication of a pamphlet entitled *Murder Will Out* (August 1663) drew public attention to their grievances. But the marquis's tenacity was eventually rewarded and clause 173 of the Act of Explanation (December 1665) granted him a full pardon and restored him to his property in Co. Antrim. Those adventurers and soldiers who had actually settled on his estate were compensated with land elsewhere.[51] Antrim's losses were considerable but he remained one of the largest landowners in Ireland and second in rank to Ormond.

Though the details are obscure, royal favour also secured the estates of the Hamiltons of Strabane despite the fact that James, third baron, had joined the insurgents led by his father-in-law, Sir Phelim O'Neill. One of the 1641 depositions recorded how during their courtship over the winter of 1641 Sir Phelim boasted to Lady Strabane that he would continue to fight 'until mass should be sung or said in every church in Ireland'.[52] During the 1650s penury overtook the Strabanes but the restoration ushered in a revival of the family's fortunes.[53] The onset of war in 1641 divided loyalties amongst the Castlestewarts. Robert, the baron's brother who had married one of the earl of Tyrone's granddaughters, allegedly joined the insurgents while his brother offered refuge to English settlers before fleeing to Galway and from there to Dublin .[54] The family's fate during the 1640s and 1650s is unknown but at the restoration they were restored to their estates.

A decade of warfare left the other Protestant Scottish peers financially crippled. Viscounts Claneboye and Montgomery had led the anti-Catholic war effort in East Ulster and received earldoms for their loyalty. In June 1647 Claneboye became earl of Clanbrassil but adherence to the royal cause meant that he suffered at the hands of the Cromwellians who sequestered his estates (he was later allowed to compound on payment of a fine of £8,500), cut down his woods and parks. As a result he had been 'forced to contract debts of £30,000 at 20 per cent'.[55] Royal favour and the need to satisfy creditors and to honour two pre-war jointure agreements ensured that Clanbrassil retained intact his pre-war estates in Co. Down. Montgomery, who had to wait until July 1661 for the earldom of Mount Alexander, had similar experiences during the 1650s. The Cromwellians confiscated his estates but allowed him to compound by paying a hefty fine, which he could ill afford.[56] Plagued by chronic debts and continued poverty, he became depressed and took solace in alcohol.[57] Despite securing royal favour, Mount Alexander experienced mixed fortunes at the restoration. Unlike the other 'Scottish peers' his total holdings increased to 18,262 plantation acres. What is striking about these changes is not the modest increase of 2,200 acres but the fact that Mount Alexander lost his consolidated estate in the baronies of Ards and Castlereagh, where his holdings were reduced from 16,001 to 6,229 acres. To make matters worse the first earl died in 1663 leaving his relations to look after the interests of his young heir, Hugh. Eventually Ormond's intervention resulted in Charles II insisting that the family be compensated with lands elsewhere. These, combined with debentures that had been purchased, left the second earl of Mount Alexander with scattered pockets of lands in Counties Laois, Leitrim, Limerick, Roscommon, Tipperary, Wexford and Wicklow.[58] Mount Alexander's debts escalated and during the 1670s he sold (for roughly £20,000) most of his estates in Co. Down to the Colvills, a local gentry family determined to move up in the world. Shortly afterwards his avaricious English wife insisted that he move to England.[59]

The composition of the 'Scottish peers' changed over the course of the century. The Balfours of Glenawley failed to produce a male heir and as a result the line became extinct in 1636 only to be revived by Hugh Hamilton who in 1661 became first baron of Glenawley.[60] Hugh was born in Ireland, the younger son of Scottish parents (his father Malcolm, archbishop of Cashel, had originated in Lanarkshire). In 1624 he became a private soldier in Sweden, later rising to the rank of lieutenant colonel and spent most of his life in Northern Europe serving in Scottish regiments. During his years in Stockholm he married the daughters of high-profile Scots and secured a Swedish title (and lands as well) before returning to live in Ulster.[61] Also born in Ireland of Aberdeenshire parents was Arthur Forbes, who in 1675 became first viscount of Granard (he was elevated to the earldom in 1684). The Forbes family had settled in Ireland in 1620 having secured plantation lands first in Leitrim and later in Longford. A deposition dating from 1642 by Lady Jane Forbes provides a vivid snapshot of the family's prosperity. She claimed total losses of £3,774 8s 4d, which included 'beasts and cattle' worth £540 0s 8d, horses and mares worth £182, sheep and hogs worth £331 8s 0d and household goods worth £154 3s 0d, plus an annual rental income of £541.[62] In 1641 her son, Sir Arthur, held, according to the Books of Survey and Distribution, 3,149 plantation acres (only 1,778 of which was described as profitable) in the baronies of Longford and Granard in Co. Longford and in the barony of Mohill in Co. Leitrim.[63] By the late 1670s the estate had trebled in size to 9,466 plantation acres (7,573 of them profitable) and generated an annual income of £1,700.[64] Presumably Forbes helped to secure a title for William Stewart, his stepson, ward, and the grandson of a successful Scottish planter, Sir William Stewart (d. *c.*1647), who had amassed sizeable estates in Donegal and Tyrone. In 1683 Stewart requested a viscounty 'since viscounts are the men in fashion in Ireland … with the title of Mountjoy'.[65] When an objection was raised, Sir William retorted in a letter to Lord Lieutenant Ormond:

> My Lord, it is no new thing to assume an ancient title without having the land or place so called. Of near fifty Viscounts that I could number, hardly five enjoy the place of their honour, and I thought taking a name from a family so utterly extinct, that their lands, as this Mountjoy did, devolved to the Crown, would displease none.[66]

These later elevations to the peerage were all Protestant and Stewart of Mountjoy actively enforced laws against those who dissented from the Established Church of Ireland.[67] Yet his stepfather, Forbes of Granard, favoured Presbyterianism and secured for loyal Presbyterians royal favour. He also acted as the government's 'troubleshooter in the north of Ireland' especially during the 1670s when events in Scotland threatened to destabilize Ulster much as they had during the late 1630s.[68] Earlier in the century the Stewarts of Castlestewart had been active Presbyterians and Andrew, second baron, had been tutored in France by John Knox's son-in-law. Fellow Scots shared his Calvinist sympathies. In 1621 the archbishop of Armagh complained that Sir Hugh Montgomery had allowed 'certaine factious and irregular puritans … intertayning the Scottish discipline and litergie' to settle on his estates.[69] Though he may also have offered refuge to persecuted Presbyterian clergy, James, first Viscount Claneboy, conformed and in 1639 signed the 'Black Oath' which condemned the Scottish Covenanters. As the 1640s progressed and the Covenanters became established, the 'Scottish peers' came under considerable pressure to sign up for Presbyterianism. Hugh, second Viscount Montgomery and later earl of Mount Alexander, flatly refused and incurred the wrath of the local presbytery which excommunicated him having first instructed their people not to speak 'favourably of him, or pay contribution towards the maintenance of his army'.[70] At Mount Alexander's funeral in 1663 George Rust, dean of Connor, praised his 'zeal and cordial affection for the Church of England, which was a pledge of the ingenuity of his spirit, and greatness of his judgement, that his reason should prevail above the prejudice of his education'.[71] During the 1650s he insisted that his own children attend 'orthodox schools', not tainted by Presbyterian, Puritan or Anabaptist doctrines.[72] Despite his father's best efforts, Hugh, second earl, appears to have had Presbyterian sympathies and in 1704 secured £1,200 per annum for loyal Presbyterian ministers. In his will, which left his estate and title to his brother, Henry, the second earl insisted that any of his heirs who married Catholics should be disinherited.[73]

This would have precluded matches with offspring of leading Scottish houses like the Hamiltons of Abercorn or MacDonnells of Antrim who openly practised their Catholicism. In December 1629 the bishop of Derry reminded Claude, Master of Abercorn and later second baron of Strabane, that his responsibilities as a planter included the promotion of Protestantism. Instead, thanks to his influence, Strabane had become a magnet for Catholics, especially Scottish ones and Jesuits. 'The place is become', lamented the bishop, 'the sink into which all the corrupt humours purged out of Scotland run'.[74] The bishop threatened to arrest and prosecute those who openly celebrated the mass and warned Claude to embrace the reformed religion or to keep his own religion to himself and not to poison others with popery.[75] There is no evidence to suggest that Claude, his Hamilton kin or their successors heeded the bishop's advice.

Even though he encouraged Protestants to settle on his estates and built churches for them to worship in, the first earl of Antrim shared this devotion to Catholicism and in 1621 the king pardoned him for 'receiving Romish priests into his house'.[76] The same held true for his sons and the marquis of Antrim's commitment to Catholicism attracted particular praise. One Scottish chronicler described Antrim as 'a true and lawfull son of the church, a professor of true religion, and hater of superstition [Protestantism]'.[77] In the pre-war years he had been closely associated with Queen Henrietta Maria's Catholic court, at home he protected and nurtured the thriving Franciscan community at Bonamargy near Ballycastle (his illegitimate brother was a priest in the mission) and called for the preservation of St Patrick's Purgatory. He worshipped openly and according to his own admission he wanted to see 'the free exercise of the roman religion, which I am devoted to and am engaged to maintain in duty to God and [in] respect to my future happiness and salvation'.[78] His first wife, the duchess of Buckingham, shared his convictions, something that is so vividly captured in her extant 'Meditations'.[79]

On the whole the 'Scottish peers' married women of the same faith. The exceptions were the marquis of Antrim and his brother, the third earl. The marquis married as his second wife Rose, heir of Sir Henry O'Neill and to an estate at Edenduffcarrick in the barony of Toome, Co. Antrim.[80] Alexander, his brother and successor, married as his first wife Elizabeth Annesley, daughter of the staunchly protestant statesman, Arthur, first earl of Anglesey.[81] Political survival and economic necessity underpinned both matches.

Table 5: Marriages of resident peers

Never married	*Married once*	*Married twice*	*Married three times or more*	*Total sample*
20 (4)	241 (17)	73 (6)	14 (1)	348 (28)
6% (14%)	69% (61%)	20% (21%)	4% (4%)	

Note: 'Scottish peers' are in bold
Source: J. Ohlmeyer, *Making Ireland English: The Irish Aristocracy in the Seventeenth Century* (New Haven, CT, 2012), chapters 2, 4, 6.

A close examination of the marriage patterns of all 'Scottish peers' reveals some interesting trends. Of the 28 men analysed four (14%) peers never married, which is high when compared with other Irish resident peers (see Table 5). Of these men, John Stewart, fifth baron of Castlestewart, who died an old man in 1678, presumably chose not to marry. William Hamilton, second baron of Glenawley, died unmarried in 1681 following an accident. James, third baron of Strabane, drowned in 1655 – aged 22 – near Strabane. His nephew Claude (1659–91), fifth baron, who died aged 32, either chose not to marry or was delaying his wedding. The majority of 'Scottish peers', like their counterparts across Ireland, did marry. Seventeen (61%) married once, six (21%) twice and one married three times, figures which broadly reflect national trends (see Table 5). Though the evidence for the age of the groom at marriage is limited, it would seem that most men married for the first time in their early twenties. Subsequent marriages usually occurred a few years after the death of a wife. The exception was Alexander, third earl of Antrim, who was 50 when he married for the first time and 54 for the second. By this stage it was clear that his elder brother would not produce a legitimate male heir and this late marriage represented a last ditch, but fruitful, attempt to secure the line.

Table 6: The geographic origin of the wives of resident peers

	Scotland	*Ireland*	*England*	*Continent*	*Total*
pre-1649 marriages	17 (8)	114 (7)	74 (5)	3 (0)	208 (20)
post-1649 marriages	1 (1)	113 (11)	70 (2)	2 (0)	186 (14)

Note: 'Scottish peers' are indicated in bold
Source: J. Ohlmeyer, *Making Ireland English: The Irish Aristocracy in the Seventeenth Century* (New Haven, CT, 2012), chapters 2, 4, 6.

Selecting the right bride was essential for the continued success of the lineage. Whom did the 'Scottish peers' marry? Documentation that survives for 34 marriages where the geographic origin of the woman is known (see Table 6) suggests that Scottish women predominated as brides during the early decades of the seventeenth century but that Irish brides were also sought after, as were English women. What is so striking is the virtual absence of Scottish brides after 1649 and the marked preference for Irish ones over both Scottish and English ones. In other words the first generation of 'Scottish peers' who settled in Ireland either brought with them a Scottish spouse or actively sought one for themselves or their heir. Later generations did not, preferring to consolidate or create national alliances by matching with local women.[82]

Close scrutiny of 28 marriages where the rank of the bride's father is known, reveals that 19 women came from aristocratic backgrounds. Five fathers were Scottish lords (including Abercorn, Atholl, Huntly and Stirling) and three were English peers (Fitzharding, Monmouth and Rutland). The remaining 11 fathers were Irish lords. With the exception of the first earl of Antrim who married a daughter of the Catholic and Gaelic Irish, earl of Tyrone, these marriages were largely to New English Protestants (the Annesleys, Brabazons, Blayneys, Cootes, Jones, Masserenes and Moores). Two matched with the daughters of Protestant Old English peers (Dillons and St Lawrences). These upwardly mobile unions reflect the desire of 'Scottish peers', the majority of whom hailed from humble backgrounds, to secure recognition in the social hierarchy. Seven brides were the daughters of baronets and knights (the descendants of at least one of whom, Sir George Rawdon, later joined the Irish peerage as the earls of Moira). The remaining two were the daughters of wealthy gentlemen. One, Grisold, who was the first wife of James Balfour, first baron of Glenawley, was heir to Patrick Balfour of Pitcullo, Fife. Three other women were described as heiresses. Anne Stewart was co-heir to John Stewart, fifth earl of Atholl, and in 1604 married Andrew Stewart, second baron of Castlestewart. Their eldest son, Andrew, third baron, also married an heiress, Joyce Blundell, daughter of Sir Arthur of Blundellstown in King's County. The wealthiest by far was Katherine Manners, duchess of Buckingham, who in 1635 married the second earl and later marquis of Antrim. She was heir to her late husband, George Villiers, marquis (and later duke) of Buckingham and together with her sons she inherited an enormous fortune from Buckingham which included his London mansions – Wallingford House, Walsingham House and York House – nineteen more modest properties on the Strand, a mansion in Chelsea and another, New Hall, north of Chelmsford in Essex. The duchess was also extremely wealthy in her own right. She received an annual income of roughly £4,550 from the Irish customs and a state pension of £6,000; she was sole heir both to her mother's fortune and to extensive, unentailed portions of the Manners estates in Northamptonshire and Yorkshire; and she also owned estates near Winslow and Bletchley in Buckinghamshire and others in Leicestershire.[83]

The high profile that the duchess enjoyed has ensured that more is known about her than the other women who married 'Scottish peers'. Yet many were fascinating figures in their own right. Elizabeth Shaw from Greenock married in 1587 Hugh, first Viscount Montgomery, and played an active role in developing his Co. Down estates, overseeing the construction of watermills and the manufacture of linen and woollen cloth, supporting disorientated settlers and rearing her family of five.[84] Equally entrepreneurial was Jean, the eldest daughter of Sir William Alexander, Secretary for Scotland, who in 1620 married Hugh, second Viscount Montgomery. Like her mother-in-law, Jean was a loyal and devoted wife to Hugh (and after he died to her second husband, Lieutenant Colonel Robert Munro, the Scottish commander in Ulster), a dedicated mother and educator to her four children, and wily mistress of an extensive estate and large household. She also 'composed good godly verses'.[85] Rose O'Neill, Antrim's second wife, ran the estates for the duration of their 30-year marriage. Her funeral sermon recorded how her husband 'who being bred up in the delicacies of a court, and his genius not inclining to the fatigue of business, left the whole management of his estate and confused affairs to her prudence and discretion … few women (if any of our age ever attain'd to so great a dexterity in businesse, and yet without diminishing ought of her duty to God)'.[86]

Some women assumed a public role during the civil wars when they defended and managed the family estates or during the 1650s and early 1660s when they lobbied and importuned the authorities on behalf of their absent or disgraced spouses. Sir Arthur Forbes's mother, Jane, was a formidable Scottish woman who effectively reared her brood of four on her own (her husband died in 1632 in a duel in Hamburg).[87] She also oversaw the building of Castle Forbes, together with the farm, gardens and orchard, estimating in 1642 that the development had cost £1,000.[88] After the rebellion began her castle became a refuge for 220 'poor robbed and distressed British flying to her for succour and safety of their lives'. She defended it during a nine-month siege only surrendering on 2 August 1642, 'at which time she and they stooping to a most miserable and woeful want of victuals' were given quarter to leave for Trim and Dublin. The insurgents then burned the castle and her other property in Longford, Leitrim and Cavan.[89] Other women emerge from the shadows during periods of family crisis, particularly during a minority or disputed wardship, or when an estranged husband or grasping brother threatened to violate a marriage settlement which provided financial security for a woman and her offspring. For example, on his deathbed in June 1659 James Hamilton, first earl of Clanbrassil, appointed 'my beloved spouse, Anne' as his executor and left his two sons, Henry and Hans, 'to the education and instruction of my mother [Jane, d. 1662] and my wife during their minority, earnestly praying that they may be brought up in the true Protestant religion, and after the best form and manner of civil nurture used in any of the three nations'.[90] Anne did not hesitate to importune Charles II for the wardship of her young son and also enlisted the support of her influential parents. In 1663 she then dispatched the teenage earl to Oxford to be bred 'under the care and tuition of Dr. Fell, where he will be instructed in better principles than the place he now lives in usually affords'.[91]

Recovering relationships between wives and husbands is notoriously difficult in any era but particularly one where private records are so scarce. Wills highlight the extent to which husbands regarded their wives as trusted partners and increasingly women served as executors. An unexecuted will, dating from 1616, by James Hamilton, first Viscount Claneboy entrusted his wife Jean, daughter of Sir John Philips, with 'the breeding and keeping of my son, James Hamilton, unto his mother, the said Jean, during the tyme of his tender aige'. It was for Jean, together with two other trusted friends, to select a boarding school for young James and ensure 'that he be bred to all pietie and virtue, and be chieflie in the keeping of the said Jean, so long as he shall remain unmarried'.[92] It is clear from what has survived that the marquis of Antrim was devoted to his wife, the duchess of Buckingham, who throughout their relationship acted as his closest confidante and adviser, his deputy, secretary and watchdog. Particularly poignant is Antrim's appeal, in the preface to her spiritual meditations, to those 'that shall happen to looke upon this booke to be pleased to say three Aves for the soule of the Duchess of Buckingham'.[93] Antrim's second marriage to another heiress, Rose O'Neill, lasted 30 years. According to the minister who presided at her funeral:

> Her lord and she intirely loved each other, they in all things thought and spake the same thing, save in the manner of worshipping of God, and even in that, tho' they differed, they did not disagree, but each enjoyed their own way in which they had been educated in peace, content and happiness, without the least heats, or animosities, which are the usual consequents of differing opinions in the same heuse, betwixt man and wife, and not only betwixt themselves was all bitterness and rancour laid aside, but also their protestant tenants and neighbours enjoyed the favour and countenance of their lord; and never suffered by that furious zeal and bigotry, which too often byastes [besets?] the great men of that perswasion.[94]

Antrim's brother, Alexander, had a less happy marriage to Elizabeth Annesley, daughter of the earl of Anglesey. According to one account Elizabeth 'was most arrogantly rude with her husband, and he, of a pleasant humour, would onely and usually return in his Irish language, *how can it be otherwise with a man that has maryed the daughter of the devil*'.[95] Henry, second earl of Clanbrassil, fell for Alice Moore, a 'very handsome, witty and well bred' daughter of the first earl of Drogheda, whom he married in 1667.[96] His alleged involvement in the rape of Sarah Maverill in 1670 can only have alienated his wife.[97] That said, she was apparently more interested in 'giving too much opportunity and access to noblemen and gentlemen', including the king himself, in London and Dublin and failed to provide an heir.[98] To add insult to injury she persuaded her husband to sign over to her what remained of his estate shortly before he died in 1676.

Of course this was an age when marriages were carefully calculated political alliances aimed at securing social aggrandizement and economic gain, together with a male heir. Women often brought considerable marriage portions or dowries to the marriage.[99] Jointures, whereby land was enfeoffed to a wife for her life, afforded women some economic security – either in the form of income from a rental or a cash annuity – during their lifetime. In his will, the first earl of Antrim specified parcels of land 'for a joynture to my wife' and others that would provide marriage portions of £2,700 for each of his unmarried daughters.[100] In the 1620s James Balfour of Glenawley 'though an ancient man of great adge' married Anne, the fifteen-year-old daughter of Lord Blayney, who brought with her a portion of £1,200 on the understanding that she be granted jointure lands worth £300. After the wedding 'which was done one both sides with more haste than good speed', Balfour reneged on the marriage settlement on the grounds that another man 'had abused his wife both before his marriage with her and after'. Under duress, Anne confessed to her infidelities and a lengthy and very public lawsuit ensued that threatened to bankrupt her father, Lord Blayney (something that Balfour had fully intended).[101] The king wanted to know what were 'the causes that induced her to accuse herself in a matter of unchastity, to her own and her parent's dishonour'.[102] He then instructed the two peers to settle the 'unnatural' dispute without bringing further shame to all concerned and compromising his – and their – honour.[103]

As the century progressed the use of marriage or strict settlements became common. These provided for a wife's jointure and specified marriage portions, jointures and financial settlements for younger children.[104] In an attempt to secure sequestered estates during the 1650s Montgomery recited a deed that his father had executed in October 1639 which charged on his property with provisions for his wife, children, and for payment of his debts.[105] The Scottish peers whose wills are extant always provided for their children.[106] Under English law children were entitled on the death of their father to a third of his estate; a wife was entitled to a third (which increased to half if there were no children); and the remaining third was at the man's own disposal and was usually used for the payment of debts, to reward servants and friends, or to make religious or charitable bequests. Invariably the male heir inherited the estate and title. Provision for younger sons, which was sometimes by virtue of a marriage settlement or a mother's will, enabled them to live independently. Daughters were provided with marriage portions and these could either attract a husband or maintain a girl while single or under age. In his will, dating from 1689, William Stewart, first Viscount Mountjoy provided generously for his sons, daughters and sons-in-law and asked his son and heir, William, 'to treat his brothers and sisters with that tenderness that I have always shewed to him, and to pay that respect to his mother which I hope I have given him example for by my care not to offend mine'.[107] Typically women lived longer than their husbands and many estates – like those of the second earl of Mount Alexander, the second earl of Clanbrassil or the marquis of Antrim – were encumbered with at least two jointures.[108] In the short-term this represented a considerable drain on resources but in the medium and longer term these legal liabilities had the unexpected benefit of helping to secure estates for a specific family, particularly during the turbulent decades of the mid-seventeenth century.

The primary purpose of marriage was to produce a male heir (and ideally a 'spare') who reached majority prior to his father's death. Analysis of extant data for 16 'Scottish peers' who married suggests that they fathered, usually with their first wives, a total of 78 children, 48 of whom were boys and 30 girls. This figure includes six documented illegitimate children, a strikingly low number given the relatively high numbers of 'natural' children produced by aristocratic fathers elsewhere, but it does not include all children who died as infants.[109] Although the sample is small, these figures suggest that the average family size for the 'Scottish peers' was five, which falls slightly below the average in neighbouring Scotland and is surprisingly low given the apparently young age of brides at marriage (the evidence here is scant and impressionistic but brides appear to have been in their late teens when they married). That said, the number of sons – an average of 3 per peer – is impressive and compares favourably with their counterparts in Scotland.[110]

Of the 'Scottish peers' who did marry, four men did not father any children: the marquis of Antrim; Josias, fourth baron of Castlestewart; Henry Hamilton, second earl of Clanbrassil; and Hugh Montgomery, second earl of Mount Alexander. In the case of Antrim, the title passed to his younger brother, Alexander, and through him the line continued to the present day. As for the others, the lines became extinct. With the death of Josias Stewart the title passed to his unmarried uncle John, son of the first baron of Castlestewart, who had also inherited the Ochiltree title. When John died in 1678 the Castlestewart line passed to a minor and became dormant for nearly a century.[111] The houses of Mount Alexander and Clanbrassil became extinct for the want of male heirs.[112] The Hamiltons of Glenawley – like the Balfours of Glenawley during the early part of the century – died out after two generations. The Hamiltons of Strabane failed to produce male heirs and the title became extinct even though the Scottish earldom of Abercorn reverted to the issue of Sir George Hamilton of Donalong, the fourth son of the first earl of Abercorn and husband to Mary Butler, one of Ormond's sisters.[113] Thus within a century six of the Scottish houses (out of a total of nine) had become extinct. Even by early modern standards, where it was not unusual for a third of all lines to die out after four or five generations, this represents a very high rate of attrition.[114]

The premature death of a father left families vulnerable to external meddling. Andrew Stewart, third baron of Castlestewart, died in 1650 leaving a young daughter, Mary, as his heir. Her wardship passed to Roger, earl of Orrery, and it was presumably Orrery who arranged her marraige to Henry Howard, later earl of Suffolk, with the result that the family estate was 'carried away' to England.[115] Claude, second baron of Strabane, died in 1638 at the age of 32 leaving behind a young family of four. His eldest son and heir, James was only five and George, his second son, and heir to James, two years old. In 1657, nearly two decades after his father's demise, George was still deemed to be 'under age and very poor'.[116] The family's survival can – at least in part – be attributed to the resourcefulness of their mother, Jean Gordon, the youngest daughter of the marquis of Huntly, who took as her second husband, Sir Phelim O'Neill. Like his father before him, George, fourth baron, died at the age of 32 leaving four under age children. The Montgomerys suffered from similar bad luck. Hugh, second viscount, died in 1642 aged 36 and his son, Hugh, first earl of Mount Alexander, died in 1663 aged 38. Ormond became Hugh's guardian and, together with his mother Jean, watched over the family's affairs. At his death in 1663 Hugh left behind him two sons and a daughter by his first marriage and a son and daughter from his second. His pregnant wife, Catherine Jones, a daughter of Arthur, Lord Ranelagh, cared for the latter while William Montgomery of Rosemount, the earl's uncle, together with the Moores of Drogheda (his mother's family), looked after the young heir and his siblings.[117] Absence of evidence makes it difficult to reconstruct the nature of the relationship between parent and child or the dynamics of a given family. During his dark days living in Dublin during the 1650s Hugh, first earl of Mount Alexander, took great comfort in his 'dear children' who gave him the will to live, especially after the death in 1655 of his first wife and his own bouts of illness and depression. 'I had no desire to live', he wrote in 1657, 'butt the good of my poore children'.[118]

Of the children of 'Scottish peers' for whom data exists (75 in all), a remarkably high number, 67, achieved adulthood (42 boys and 25 girls). Of the eight who died under the age of 21, one was an infant boy and the remaining seven were children (four were under the age of 10).[119] The peerages record the career and marriages of the male heirs but less well documented are the life stories of the younger children of these 'Scottish peers'. An analysis of 61 marriages (for the children of 15 peers) reveals that a high proportion did marry (43 or 70 per cent). Of 37 male children, 21 married (nine to the daughters of fellow peers) and 16 opted not to marry; of the 24 female children, 22 married (seven to the sons of fellow peers) and only two opted not to marry. As a result of these unions Scottish blood flowed in the veins of many leading families across Ireland.

Consider for example, the matches negotiated by the first earl of Antrim for his six daughters, who were sought as spouses by some of Ireland's leading noblemen. Writing in 1629 Elizabeth Nugent, dowager countess of Kildare, reminded her kinsman, George, sixteenth earl of Kildare, that the earl of Antrim:

> hath at this present 4 daughters unmarried, 2 maidens under the age of 11 years old and 2 widows, the one at the age of 21 [Anne], the other at 18 [Mary], of which 4 he is please to give your Lordship choice … I would commend the eldest to you, whose virtue wisdom spirit and comeliness far surpasses the rest … by her former marriage she is my niece, being married to my nephew Delvin … Your difference in age is but 2 or 3 years which is nothing, and no question can be made but she will be a good mother of children, as having one goodly boy which is now Lord of Delvin and my brother of Westmeath's heir.[120]

In the event the eldest girl, Lady Anne, who had been married first to Christopher Nugent, Viscount Delvin and heir to the first earl of Westmeath, married as her second husband, William Flemming, baron of Slane. Lady Mary's first husband was Luke, second Viscount Dillon of Costelloe-Gallen, and her second was Oliver Plunkett, sixth Baron Louth. Lady Sarah was married three times: first to Neal Oge O'Neill of Killelagh, Co. Antrim; second, to Donough O'Connor of Sligo; and third, to Donal MacCarthy More. Lady Catherine wed Edward Plunkett, son of Patrick ninth Baron Dunsany, and Lady Rose married (in 1643) the Scotsman George Gordon (b. 1616), the posthumous third son of John, twelfth earl of Sutherland (d. 1615) and brother of John, thirteenth earl. Finally, Antrim's 'natural daughter', Lady Ellis, married first Neil O'Neill of Claneboy and then Tirlogh Oge O'Neill, brother of Sir Phelim O'Neill of Kinard.[121]

If daughters of the 'Scottish peers' were effectively destined for the altar, younger sons had alternative opportunities open to them. The bulk received some schooling and a few attended universities. Many undertook a grand tour of the continent usually with their elder brother. The life stories of the younger sons of Hugh Montgomery, first viscount, are particularly well documented. Sir James attended the University of St Andrews and then travelled throughout France, Germany, Italy and Holland before being sent to Gray's Inns to acquire legal training. From there he attended 'all his father's business which came before King James or King Charles' until 1627 when he returned home to serve as 'as his father's agent, both in the country and in Dublin, so that he became an expert solicitor, courtier and statesman, as before his travel he had been a pregnant scholar'.[122] His younger brother, George, attended school at Newtown and then travelled to Holland, 'ye school for warr', where he joined up with Scottish officers and learned to fight, drink, smoke and to talk like a Dutchman. On his return home in 1633 he married a Scottish woman from Ayrshire and led an undistinguished life as a country gentleman on family estates that yielded an annual income of £300.[123] Both James and George Montgomery were exposed to the exercise of arms during their continental sojourns; other younger sons opted for a military career abroad. During the early decades of the century the sons of Catholic peers served predominately with the Habsburgs, and the Protestants preferred securing commands in the German or Scandinavian armies. Maurice, a natural son of the first earl of Antrim, served as an infantry captain in Flanders.[124] According to the family chronicler the Forbes men folk were 'addicted to the profession of arms' and were 'bred as soldiers'. Arthur, first earl of Granard, and his wife, Catherine Newcomen, lost three (of their five) sons in battle, along with their son-in-law and their eldest grandson.[125] Though less popular than the army, the occasional younger son opted for a career in the church. An illegitimate son of the first earl of Antrim – Daniel (or Francis as he was later known) – became a Franciscan friar who, after being trained at St. Anthony's College in Louvain, returned to Co. Antrim and, using Bonamargy friary as his base, served in the Scottish mission in the Western Isles.[126]

Of the 28 'Scottish peers' analyzed here, the age of death for 18 of them is recorded. Eight died before reaching the age of 40, usually in their twenties and thirties as the result of an accident or as a result of war. Thus Hugh, second Viscount Montgomery, died shortly after a military encounter in November 1642. Claude, fifth baron of Strabane, survived the battle of the Boyne only to perish late in July 1690 en route to France, and William Stewart, Viscount Mountjoy, lost his life on the battlefield in William III's service. James Hamilton, third baron of Strabane, drowned while bathing and William Hamilton, second baron of Glenawley, also died in an accident. Equally unfortunate was Henry Hamilton, second earl of Clanbrassil, who was allegedly poisoned by his wife after she had prevailed upon him to bequeath to her his estates.[127] He was 28 years old. Described as 'corpulent, scorbutic, hydropsic', James Hamilton, first earl of Clanbrassil's premature death in 1659 presumably came as no surprise.[128] His contemporary, Hugh Montgomery, first earl of Mount Alexander, died 'suddenly' on 15 September 1663, aged 38. As a result of a childhood accident Mount Alexander had a 'large open space in his chest' which was covered by a metal plate. Charles I's physician, William Harvey, examined him as a young man and touched the 'apex of the heart'. His manservant washed the wound daily but over time his heart became, as an autopsy later revealed, 'wissened and shrivelled'. Shortly before Mount Alexander died he contracted dysentery which 'was very dangerous, his body being grown unwieldy and bulksome'. He recovered but became 'plethorick' and died soon after.[129] The longevity of the other 'Scottish peers' is striking. Seven died in their seventies and two – Alexander, third earl of Antrim, and James, first Viscount Claneboye – died in their mid-eighties. The cause of death for the longer-lived peers is rarely recorded and one must assume that they died of old age.

Those that died in Dublin, and many did, were buried there. Those who died on their estates tended to have elaborately choreographed funerals, usually after a lengthy period of public mourning. The marquis of Antrim's corpse, which must have been embalmed, lay in state from 3 February until 14 March 1683 when he was finally buried, after 'a great funeral', alongside many of his ancestors in the family vault at the Franciscan friary of Bonamargy near Ballycastle.[130] The grand funeral in 1636 of Hugh, first Viscount Montgomery, and of his son, the first earl of Mount Alexander, in 1663 served 'to demonstrate their new place in a mobile social order and to shake off all vestiges of their origins'.[131] Attended by hundreds of mourners who processed in order of social rank, these very public and dignified displays highlighted the status the family enjoyed in East Ulster and beyond. No expense was spared as the corpses were laid to rest in the family vault at Newtown and in the case of Mount Alexander 'the ordnance on the castle and custom-house [in Dublin] gave three peels'.[132] In his memoir Sir William Montgomery captured the hierarchical nature of the funeral and the 'great deference which the vulgar had for their late most loved landlord' which 'restrained their curiosity and rude behaviour' and led them to listen 'to the prayers (w[hi]ch was a novelty to them) and to the learned pious sermon (such being also rare among them)'.[133] Dr George Rust, later bishop of Dromore, gave the funeral sermon which the earl's 'sorrowful' countess later had printed.

The bishop concluded the oration by reminding his listeners that the late earl was 'a loyal subject to his prince: a dutiful son to the church, a worthy patriot to his country; a tender and affectionate husband to his excellent ladies, real and faithful to his friends; merciful and compassionate towards his tenants, free and charitable to the poor, courteous and obliging to all, in a word, just and righteous, noble and honourable in all his actions'.[134] Mount Alexander's sense of honour was a recurring motif in the sermon and in the 'Montgomery Manuscripts'. The same held true for the other 'Scottish peers' who were also determined to be represented as men of honour. Yet there was a hierarchy of honour. With the exception of the MacDonnells of Antrim and the Hamiltons of Abercorn, the majority were 'new men'. Thus the ancientness of the MacDonnell blood line was singled out for particular praise. Panegyric speeches dedicated to the marquis of Antrim which date from 1646 consistently portrayed him as a man of honour, virtue and decisive action, both in terms of his ancestry and his royal service: 'true nobleness inbred in their [i.e. Clan Donald] bloud is the true cause that thou art truly good and goodness causeth you to undertake heroick labours for king and countreys sake'. The author extolled the marquis's loyalty to Charles I and contrasted Antrim's constancy with the treachery of the king's 'false friends'.[135] Honour was the glue that bound together the Irish peerage irrespective of religious background or ethnic origin. The need to live a virtuous and honourable life determined how a peer interacted with his family, his servants and tenants, his neighbours and his social equals and betters. As the life stories of the 'Scottish peers' and particularly the Montogomerys and Hamiltons highlight, the acquisition of honour became an imperative for families, especially those of humble origins and they used every opportunity – birth, marriage, death and service to the monarch – to display their honour.

To what extent did the need to be accepted as part of this 'community of honour' override a sense of 'Scottishness'? How Scottish were the 'Scottish peers'? Some, especially first-generation settlers, retained a strong sense of Scottish identity. In his will James Hamilton, Viscount Claneboye, asked 'that land be taken in and disposed for the best advantag to Scottishment' and promoted 'Scottishmen' as the best tenants.[136] Despite being born and raised in Ireland, Hugh Hamilton, first baron of Glenawley, apparently spoke Scots.[137]

Hugh, first Viscount Montgomery, wrote in Scots (and presumably spoke it).[138] His third wife, Sarah Maxwell, disliked Ulster and continued to live in Scotland. In an attempt to lure her across the North Channel the viscount bought her a dwarf, 'the prettiest little man I ever beheld', but to little avail and his countess lived in Scotland, dying in Edinburgh with Montgomery at her side.[139] Lord Balfour of Glenawley advised a fellow Scot never to 'trust any English in that place' since they would deceive him by 'fair shows and protestation'.[140] In fact many of the early Scottish planters preferred to deal with Scottish merchants and to surround themselves with Scottish servants and friends.[141] Scottish builders and craftsmen gave a Scottish flavour to the architectural landscape of Ulster as they constructed square baronial tower houses or castles with a L- or T-shaped plan. Many had distinctive Scottish features – projecting turrets, crow-stepped gables, elaborate corbelling and canonical roofed turrets. Readily visible are the Scottish baronial influences at the seat of the MacDonnells of Antrim at Dunluce, the Hamilton castles at Killileagh and Bangor, Castle Balfour at Lisnaskea, at Mountcastle, home of the Hamiltons of Strabane, and at Stewartstown, seat of the Stewarts of Castlestewart.[142]

The fact that most of the 'Scottish peers' held lands in Ulster facilitated easy and regular exchange between the two kingdoms. The Montgomerys owned estates in Ayrshire until they were sold in the 1650s and regularly shuttled back and forth across the North Channel. The first viscount's market at Newtown was supplied directly from Scotland during the early years of the plantation.[143] It was 1678 before Arthur Forbes, earl of Granard, sold his Aberdeenshire estate.[144] Throughout the seventeenth century the MacDonnells of Antrim maintained a claim to lands that had traditionally been associated with Clan Donald South in the Western Highlands and Islands, especially Kintyre and Jura. In 1627 the first earl offered to purchase lands in Islay from Sir John Campbell of Calder for £5,000; early in 1633 and again in 1635 he attempted (again without success) to acquire Kintyre and Jura.[145] Between 1644 and 1647 an army loyal to the marquis of Antrim occupied much of the Western seaboard and again after the restoration the marquis made one final attempt to regain his Scottish patrimony and petitioned for the restoration of the:

> lordship of Kintyre and the lands of Caradle [sic] which is now fallen into the king's hands, by Argyll's forfeiture, paying the king £10,000 sterling, which is near the full value of it, or so much towards Argyll's debts unto his creditors as the rest of the estate is liable to.

Though he claimed, quite correctly, that the 'late king gave the now marquis of Antrim a grant of the said lands, which is ready to be produced, for his services in the last troubles of Scotland', the request was apparently denied.[146] Despite this the marquis continued to enjoy 'a great following in those islands' and cared for the inhabitants' spiritual welfare.[147] Throughout his life he supported the Franciscan mission at Bonamargy and in 1670 'at his own expense [he] sent three priests to these Isles in Lent to hear confessions and give Holy Communion'.[148]

Friendship networks within Ireland bound together the 'Scottish peers', especially in the early years. For example, James Hamilton, first earl of Abercorn, was an executor for the will of his cousin James, first Viscount Claneboye. He served as the arbitrator in Claneboye's disputes with Montgomery.[149] In 1613 the first earl of Antrim affianced his four-year-old son to Abercorn's daughter and requested that, in the event of his early death, Abercorn be awarded the wardship of his young son who was to be raised in Abercorn's household 'for the better education of his said son and heir'. James VI and I, eager to have the youth reared 'religiously and civilly', readily agreed.[150] Marriages with fellow Scots reinforced these alliances. If intermarriage is, as sociologists suggest, both as an index and a method of assimilation between ethnic groups, then it is particularly noteworthy that it was only the first generation of 'Scottish peers' who favoured Scottish spouses, with later ones preferring matches with the daughters of the New English elite (discussed above).[151] This suggests that the 'Scottish peers' who settled in Ireland did so with the intention of making a permanent commitment and from the outset wanted to become integrated with leading figures in their new communities and used marriage as a means of consolidating powerbases and enhancing political influence. In short, the 'Scottish peers' who settled in Ulster quickly saw Ireland as home and, despite the Presbyterianism of some, became assimilated. After spending only eight years living in Ulster one settler, Andrew, baron of Castlestewart (and formerly Lord Ochiltree), even described himself 'as it wer deade' in Scotland.[152]

Commitment to their new lives in Ireland helps to explain why so few returned, even temporarily. Even during times of crisis, the 1640s and after 1688, few saw Scotland as an obvious refuge. It is possible that Lady Forbes fled there after surrendering to the insurgents in 1642 but the other 'Scottish peers' and their kin remained on their estates to lead the local war effort.[153] Those that did fight in Scotland during the 1640s – the marquis of Antrim and Arthur Forbes, later earl of Granard, served the royalist cause – returned to Ireland. During times of peace, exchange was also limited. A number of the first generation 'Scottish peers' had attended university in Scotland, usually St Andrews or Glasgow, but only Forbes sent one of his younger sons, Patrick, to be educated in Glasgow (where the unfortunate youth succumbed to small pox).[154] Instead the 'Scottish peers' preferred to send their sons to English institutions, especially Oxford and the Inns of Court in London. Whether they attended university or not, nearly every 'Scottish peer', like their contemporaries throughout the Stuart kingdoms, sent their heirs to the continent as part of a grand tour. In the summer of 1639 Claneboy's son and heir, whom his father described as 'a hater of all vice and a Lover of Noble partes and of vertuous industries', retuned from 'his Travels having taken a generall Survey of Italie and France and seen the severall States and Courts there'. He immediately presented himself at court to avoid 'being found a Stranger in England'.[155] This did little to nurture a sense of 'Scottishness' in young men. The experiences of Hugh Montgomery, first earl of Mount Alexander were similar. He received a 'liberal education' at home and then travelled 'for his further improvement into foreign countries'. 'The civility he received in his travels in France', noted the family chronicler, 'had bred in him an inclination towards French servants' and he returned to Ireland in 1623 with a French valet 'to confirm his skill in that tongue'.[156] Little wonder then that an urbane papal envoy, Dionysius Massari, who met him during his incarceration after being taken prisoner at the battle of Benburb, described him as 'most gentlemanly, courteous and mild'.[157] Neither Massari nor George Rust, later bishop of Dromore, who delivered his funeral sermon, made mention of his Scottish origins, preferring to focus on his nobleness and honour. As for the family chronicler he simply noted that the earl had no love or hatred 'solely for country sake: English, Scotts and Irish were welcome to him, yet he liked and esteemed the English most (both his ladys being such)'.[158] Clearly, Mount Alexander was not alone and the extent to which it is appropriate even to label the descendants of the first generation of settlers as 'Scottish peers' is debatable. Like migrants throughout early modern Europe the Scottish lords who settled in Ireland often had problems in describing themselves. Instead of identifying with their place of birth they increasingly looked to their host nation, where they enjoyed rank and status, and to their monarch, as the source of honour and continued reward. The passage of time resulted in the bleaching out of the 'Scottishness' of Ireland's 'Scottish peers', much as it did for the Stuarts themselves.

NOTES

1 A number of influential Scottish figures, such as Sir George Hamilton, are not included because they were not peers.

2 Only seven of the 'Scottish peers' merit *Oxford Dictionary of National Biography* (*ODNB*) entries: S. Kelsey, 'Forbes, Arthur, first earl of Granard (1623–1695)', *ODNB*, www.oxforddnb.com/view/article/9816, accessed 14 September 2008; R.J. Hunter, 'Hamilton, James, first Viscount Claneboye (*c.*1560–1644)', *ODNB*, www.oxforddnb.com/view/article/12086, accessed 14 September 2008; H. McDonnell, 'MacDonnell, Randal, first earl of Antrim (*d.* 1636)', *ODNB*, www.oxforddnb.com/view/article/17461, accessed 14 September 2008; J. Ohlmeyer, 'MacDonnell, Randal, marquess of Antrim (1609–1683)', *ODNB*, www.oxforddnb.com/view/article/17462, accessed 14 September 2008; J. Ohlmeyer, 'MacDonnell, Alexander, third earl of Antrim (1615–1699)', *ODNB*, www.oxforddnb.com/view/article/17457, accessed 14 September 2008; P. Wauchope, 'Stewart, William,

first Viscount Mountjoy (*c*.1650–1692)', *ODNB*, www.oxforddnb.com/view/article/26519, accessed 14 September 2008; R.M. Armstrong, 'Montgomery, Hugh, first earl of Mount-Alexander (*b.* in or before 1626, *d.* 1663)', *ODNB*, www.oxforddnb.com/view/article/19068, accessed 14 September 2008. For a wider discussion of the Irish peerage see J. Ohlmeyer, *Making Ireland English: The Irish Aristocracy in the Seventeenth Century* (New Haven, CT, 2012).

3 K. McKenny, 'The restoration land settlement in Ireland: a statistical interpretation', in C. Dennehy (ed.), *Restoration Ireland. Always Settling and Never Settled* (Aldershot, 2008), pp. 35–52; R. Gillespie, *Colonial Ulster: The Settlement of East Ulster 1600–1641* (Cork, 1985); P. Robinson, *The Plantation of Ulster: British Settlement in an Irish Landscape, 1600–1670* (Belfast, 2000); M. Perceval-Maxwell, *The Scottish Migration to Ulster in the Reign of James I* (London, 1973).

4 Some estate papers have survived for the Castle Stewarts in the Public Record Office Northern Ireland (PRONI) 1618 and for the Balfours in PRONI, D 1939. For the dispersed papers of the MacDonnells of Antrim, see J. Ohlmeyer, *Civil War and the Restoration in the Three Stuart Kingdoms: The Career of Randal MacDonnell, Marquis of Antrim, 1609–1683* (Cambridge, 1993), pp. 290–3.

5 J. Forbes, *Memoirs of the Earls of Granard*, ed. G.A. Hastings (London, 1868), p. 5. Also see G. Hill (ed.), *The Montgomery Manuscripts (1603–1706). Compiled from the Family Papers by William Montgomery of Rosemount …* (Belfast, 1869), p. 173.

6 Forbes, *Memoirs* and Historical Manuscripts Commission (hereafter HMC), *Second Report. Appendix* (London, 1874), pp. 211–15 for a manuscript memoir written by his step-son, William Stewart, first Viscount Mountjoy; H. McDonnell, 'A fragment of an Irish manuscript history of the MacDonalds of Antrim', *Ulster Journal of Archaeology*, 64 (2005), 140–53; Hill (ed.), *Montgomery Manuscripts*; T.K. Lowry (ed.), *Hamilton Manuscripts: Containing Some Account of territories of Upper Clandeboye, Great Ardes, Dufferin in the County of Down, by Sir William Hamilton, afterward Viscount Clandeboye* (Belfast, 1867). For a fascinating analysis of these types of records, see R. Gillespie, 'The making of the Montgomery manuscripts', *Familia*, 2:2 (1980), 23–9.

7 In addition to the *ODNB* entries in note 2 above, see Ohlmeyer, *Civil War*.

8 J. Wormald, 'The creation of British multiple kingdoms or core and colonies?', *Transactions of the Royal Historical Scoiety*, 2 (1992), 175–94.

9 Francis Vesey (ed.), *The Statutes at Large Passed in the Parliaments held in Ireland* (21 vols; Dublin, 1786), i, pp. 443, 442.

10 G.R. Mayes, 'The Early Stuarts and the Irish peerage', *English Historical Review*, 73: 287 (1958), 227–51, 240.

11 The only non-resident Scottish peer was Richard Preston, Lord Dingwall, who in 1619 became baron of Dunmore and earl of Desmond.

12 E. Walker, *Historical Discourses* (London, 1705), p. 307; Mayes, 'Early Stuarts', p. 247.

13 Walker, *Historical Discourses*, p. 307; Mayes, 'Early Stuarts', p. 289.

14 Balfour was dead and Hamilton of Strabane a minor.

15 B. McGrath, 'A biographical dictionary of the membership of the Irish House of Commons 1640–1641', PhD dissertation, Trinity College Dublin, 1997, pp. 175, 218–21.

16 C. Maxwell (ed.), *Irish History from Contemporary Sources (1509–1610)* (London, 1923), pp. 300–1; Perceval-Maxwell, *The Scottish Migration*, pp. 3–10, 47–8, 60–4.

17 Plunkett to [Airoldi], 17/27 September 1671, J. Hanly (ed.), *The Letters of Saint Oliver Plunkett 1625–81: Archbishop of Armagh and Primate of all Ireland* (Dublin, 1979), p. 247.

18 M. Lee, *Great Britain's Solomon: James VI and I in his Three Kingdoms* (Urbana, IL, 1990), p. 212.

19 Perceval-Maxwell, *The Scottish Migration*, pp. 231–2.

20 'A report of the voluntary works done by servitors … within the counties of Downe, Antryme, and Monahan' (PRONI, T 811/3, f. 13); W.J. Smyth, 'Society and settlement in seventeenth century Ireland: the evidence of the "1659 census"', in W.J. Smyth and K. Whelan (eds), *Common Ground. Essays on the Historical Geography of Ireland Presented to T. Jones Hughes* (Cork, 1988), pp. 73–5.

21 Earl of Clanricard to earl of Essex, 14 November 1629 (British Library (hereafter BL), Add MSS 46188, fol. 120).

22 McDonnell, 'A fragment of an Irish MSS', pp. 278, 280.

23 Maxwell, *Irish History*, p. 301.

24 Gillespie, *Colonial Ulster*, p. 232.

25 Of the 2,200 acres he owned in Co. Londonderry 2,030 acres were described in the 'Civil survey' (of 1654) as 'profitable' and fit for both arable and pastoral farming while only the remaining 170 acres of 'red bog' were described as 'unprofitable and waste', C. Simington (ed.), *Civil Survey … Donegal, Londonderry and Tyrone* (Dublin, 1937), iii, pp. 155–7.

26 Gillespie, *Colonial Ulster*, pp. 11–13; Simington (ed.), *Civil Survey*, x, pp. 56–7, 60–1.

27 McDonnell, 'A fragment of an Irish MSS', 281. G. Hill, *An Historical Account of the MacDonnells of Antrim* (Belfast, 1873), pp. 377–89 and J. Irvine, 'Richard Dobbs' notes for his description of Co. Antrim, Written in 1683', *The Glynns*, 7 (1979), 43–4.

28 W. Smyth, 'Territorial, social and settlement hierarchies in seventeenth century Kilkenny', in W. Nolan and K. Whelan (eds), *Kilkenny: History and Society. Interdisciplinary Essays on the History of an Irish County* (Dublin, 1990), p. 156.

29 *CSPI, 1606–08*, p. 134.

30 Gillespie, *Colonial Ulster*, p. 56; Perceval-Maxwell, *The Scottish Migration*, pp. 56–60.

31 Hill (ed.), *Montgomery Manuscripts*, p. 66.

32 J. Stevenson, *Two Centuries of Life in Down, 1600–1800* (Belfast, 1920), p. 46.

33 Gillespie, *Colonial Ulster*, p. 232.

34 Perceval-Maxwell, *The Scottish Migration*, pp. 234–42.

35 Lowry (ed.), *Hamilton Manuscripts*, pp. 49–50.

36 *CSPI, 1633–47*, pp. 274, 468.

37 W.C. Dickinson and G. Donaldson (eds), *A Source Book of Scottish History* (3 vols, Edinburgh, 1961), iii, p. 261.

38 C. McCoy, 'War and revolution: County Fermanagh and its borders, c1640-c1666', PhD dissertation, Trinity College Dublin, 2008.

39 Perceval-Maxwell, *The Scottish Migration*, p. 201.

40 Perceval-Maxwell, *The Scottish Migration*, p. 324.

41 R. Gillespie, 'The trials of Bishop Spottiswood 1620–40', *Clogher Record*, 12:3 (1987), 320–33.

42 J.D. Johnston, 'The Plantation of County Fermanagh 1610–1641: an archaeological and historical study', MA dissertation, Queens' University Belfast, 1976, pp. 74–5; J. Hardiman (ed.), *Inquisitionum in officio rotulorum cancellariae Hiberniae asservatorum repertorium* (2 vols, Dublin, 1829), ii, Co. Fermanagh (45).

43 G. Hamilton, *A History of the House of Hamilton* (Edinburgh, 1933), p. 34; Perceval-Maxwell, *The Scottish Migration*, p. 326.

44 M.A. Everett Green (ed.), *Calendar of State Papers, Domestic Series of the Reign of James I, 1611–1618* (London, 1857–58) (hereafter *CSPD, James I*), p.113.

45 Robinson, *The Plantation of Ulster*, p. 148; Perceval-Maxwell, *The Scottish Migration*, p. 195.

46 Robinson, *The Plantation of Ulster*, pp. 118, 162; Perceval-Maxwell, *The Scottish Migration*, p. 329.

47 *Ibid.*, p. 277; N. Canny, *Making Ireland British, 1580–1650* (Oxford, 2001), p. 231.

48 R. Gillespie, 'The origins and development of an Ulster urban network, 1600–41', *Irish Historical Studies*, 24:93 (1984), 15–16. See also R. Hunter, 'Ulster plantation towns 1609–1641', in D. Harkness and M. O'Dowd (eds), *The Town in Ireland* (Belfast, 1991), pp. 55–80.

49 Antrim lost 29,545 acres in the barony of Cary. His share of the barony of Dunluce fell to 36,958 (from 40,293 acres), of Kilconway to 32,360 (from 40,334 acres), of Glenarm to 1,814 (from 30,406 acres) and of Coleraine in neighbouring Co. Londonderry to 6,031 (from 6,656 acres). He retained 2,119 acres in the barony of Toome and acquired, through his second wife, 4,420 in the barony of Co. Antrim.

50 Hill, *MacDonnells of Antrim*, pp. 467–8.

51 Clauses 172–80 of the act relate to Antrim, Rose and Alexander (who were all restored), Vesey (ed.), *Statutes at Large*, pp. 100–6; Charles II's patent for Antrim's restoration, 20 July 1666 (PRONI, D 2977); *CSPI, 1666–69*, pp. 179, 564; *ibid.*, p. 52.

52 M. Hickson (ed.), *Ireland in the Seventeenth Century* (2 vols, London, 1884), i, p.232.

53 *CSPI, 1663–1665*, pp. 91, 526.

54 TCD, MS 839, fols 1–2; J. Smyth, *The Memoirs and letters of Ulick, Marquis of Clanricarde and Earl of St Albans* (London, 1758), pp. 282, 329, 334.

55 *CSPI, 1663–65*, pp. 478–9 for the quote. Also see *CSPI, 1647–60*, pp. 597–9.

56 *CSPI, 1647–60*, pp. 673–4.

57 Hill (ed.), *Montgomery Manuscripts*, p. 204.

58 HMC, *Calendar of the Manuscripts of the Marquess of Ormonde, K.P. Preserved At Kilkenny Castle* (7 vols, London, 1911), iii, pp. 89–90, 92–3; *CSPI, 1663–65*, pp. 17, 19, 43, 235, 251; Hill (ed.), *Montgomery Manuscripts*, p. 235.

59 Quoted in Stevenson, *Two Centuries of Life in Down*, p. 103. In 1675 he sold part of the estate for £13,640 and in 1679 the remainder for a further £9780. A few staple deeds relating to some of these transactions have survived. For example, an indenture of defeazance lists the lands that Hugh, earl of Mount Alexander,

offered as security to Robert Colvill on a bond of £3,000 and dated 27 November 1675 (NAI, D 15,248). Also see NAI, D 15,245. Mount Alexander apparently defaulted on his repayment and the bond was registered into Chancery on 5 February 1676 (NAI, D 3210). In 1673 Mount Alexander also borrowed money from Colvill, NAI, C 3471 note 32. Also see the serialized article by J.M. Dickson, 'The Colville family in Ulster', *Ulster Journal of Archaeology*, 5:3 (1899), 139–45; 5:4 (1899), 202–10; 6:1 (1900), 12–16.

60 His wife, Susanna Balfour, was a daughter of Sir William Balfour, lieutenant of the Tower of London (National Library of Ireland Genealogical Office 73, p. 117) and not of Sir William Balfour of Pitcullo, as stated in A.N.L. Grosjean, 'Hamilton, Hugh , first Baron Hamilton of Glenawly (*c.*1607–1678)', *ODNB*, www.oxforddnb.com/view/article/12074, accessed 18 September 2008.

61 Interestingly, Glenawley's daughter by his first wife married a Swede, while his two younger daughters by his second spouse wed Irish peers, Hamilton, *House of Hamilton*, p. 1016; S. Murdoch,'Scotland, Scandinavia and northern Europe 1580–1707', www.st-andrews.ac.uk/history/ssne/index.php, accessed 3 January 2009, and Mary Elizabeth Ailes, *Military Migration and state formation: The British Military Community in Seventeenth-Century Sweden* (Lincoln, 2002), pp. 31, 52, 62, 65–6, 86–7, 127–8, 146 n. 59. On the Swedish estate see HMC, *Ormonde*, vi, p. 366.

62 TCD, MS 817, Depositions for Westmeath and Longford, fols 187-v.

63 Forbes (ed.), *Memoirs*, pp. 34, 36; A. Clarke, *Prelude to Restoration in Ireland: The End of the Commonwealth, 1659–1660* (Cambridge, 1999), p. 31.

64 M.A. Everett Green, F.H.B. Daniell and F. Bickley (eds), *Calendar of State Papers, Domestic Series, of the Reign of Charles II* (*CSPD, Charles II*), *March 1678 to Dec. 1678 with addenda 1674–79* (36 vols, 1860–1939), p. 165.

65 HMC, *Ormonde*, vi, p. 527.

66 HMC, *Ormonde*, vii, p. 5.

67 Wauchope, 'Stewart, William, first Viscount Mountjoy'.

68 Kelsey, 'Forbes, Arthur, first earl of Granard'; HMC, *Ormonde*, iv, p. 76.

69 Quoted in Perceval-Maxwell, *The Scottish Migration*, p. 270.

70 *A sermon preached at New-town the 29 of Octob. 1663. At the funeral of the right honourable Hugh Earl of Mount-Alexander, Lord Viscount Mountgomery of Ards, late master of the ordnance, and one of His Majesties most honourable Privy Council in Ireland. By George Rust D.D. and dean of Connor* (Dublin, 1664), pp. 36, 39.

71 *Ibid.*, pp. 37–8.

72 Hill (ed.), *Montgomery Manuscripts*, p. 206.

73 *Ibid.*, p. 299; HMC, *Seventh Report*, p. 771.

74 *CSPI, 1625–32*, p. 511.

75 *CSPI, 1625–32*, pp. 510–11.

76 *CSPI, 1615–1625*, p. 324.

77 H. McDonnell and J. Ohlmeyer (eds), 'New light on the marquis of Antrim and the "Wars of the Three Kingdoms"', *Analecta Hibernica*, 41 (2009), 11–66.

78 *A copie of a letter from the Lord Intrim* [sic] *in Ireland to the right honourable earle of Rutland, bearing date the 25 day of February* ... (London, 1642), pp. 3–4.

79 H. McDonnell and J. Ohlmeyer (eds), 'Meditations by Katherine Manners, duchess of Buckingham, 1646', *Analecta Hibernica*, 41 (2009), 67–82.
80 J. Ohlmeyer, 'MacDonnell, Rose, marchioness of Antrim (1631–1695)', *ODNB*, www.oxforddnb.com/view/article/69582, accessed 18 September 2008.
81 Hill, *MacDonnells of Antrim*, p. 361.
82 Very occasionally other members of the Irish peerage looked to Scotland for a spouse. Charles Coote, earl of Mountrath, took as his second wife Jane, daughter of Sir Robert Hannay of Scotland. Alice and Mary Moore, daughters of Henry, first earl of Drogheda, married as their first and second husbands Scottish lords.
83 R. Lockyer, *Buckingham: The Life and Political Career of George Villiers, First Duke of Buckingham 1592–1628* (London, 1981), pp. 26, 56–8, 60, 119–20, 212–16, 286, 412–13, 419, 460–2.
84 Perceval-Maxwell, *The Scottish Migration*, p. 60.
85 Hill (ed.), *Montgomery Manuscripts*, pp. 399–403.
86 H. Leslie, archdeacon of Down, *A sermon preached at the funeral of the most honourable Rose, Lady Marchioness of Antrim at Carrickfergus, the 4th of July 1695* (Dublin, 1695), p. 29.
87 Forbes (ed.), *Memoirs*, pp. 30, 31.
88 TCD, MS 817, Depositions for Westmeath and Longford, fol. 187.
89 TCD, MS 817, Depositions for Westmeath and Longford, fols 187-v.
90 Lowry (ed.) *Hamilton Manuscripts*, p. 84.
91 *CSPI, 1660–62*, p. 324; *CSPI, 1663–65*, pp. 92, 184, 478–9; quote at p. 92.
92 Lowry (ed.) *Hamilton Manuscripts*, pp. 48–59.
93 McDonnell and Ohlmeyer (eds), 'Meditations'.
94 Leslie, *A Sermon*, p. 29.
95 Hill, *MacDonnells of Antrim*, p. 361 (original emphasis).
96 Stevenson, *Two Centuries of Life in Down*, p. 97, through incompetence and extravagance he wasted his inheritance; as a youth 'very much drawn to idleness and low companionship'.
97 *CSPI, 1669–70*, pp. 195, 217.
98 Stevenson, *Two Centuries of Life in Down*, p. 96; Edward Berwick (ed.), *The Rawdon Papers* (London, 1819), p. 251.
99 M. Beckett, *Sir George Rawdon, a Sketch of his Life and Times* (Belfast, 1935), p. 95.
100 Hill, *MacDonnells of Antrim*, p. 435; Geraldine Talon (ed.), *Court of Claims: Submissions and Evidence, 1663* (Dublin, 2006), pp. 225, 357, 600, 601, 633.
101 J. Maidment, 'The Life of James Spottiswoode, Bishop of Clogher, my great-grand-father', in *The Spottiswoode Miscellany: A Collection of Original Papers and Tracts, Illustrative of the Civil and Ecclesiastical History of Scotland* (2 vols, Edinburgh, Spottiswoode Society, 1844), i, pp. 96–164; p. 103 and *CSPI, 1625–32*, pp. 18, 256, 291–2.
102 *CSPI, 1615–25*, p. 354.
103 *CSPI, 1625–32*, pp. 256, 291.
104 M. O'Dowd, *A History of Women in Ireland 1500–1800* (London, 2005), pp. 84, 100–3.
105 *CSPI, 1647–60*, pp. 673–4.

106 The following wills are extant: James Balfour, Lord Baron of Glenawley (d. 1634), TNA, 11/168/76; Randal MacDonnell, first earl of Antrim, Hill, *MacDonnells*, pp. 435–6; Hugh, first Viscount Montgomery of the Ards, extract in PRONI, D.552/B/1/1/30 and Hill (ed.), *Montgomery Manuscripts*, p. 130; first and second earls of Mount Alexander see Hill (ed.), *Montgomery Manuscripts*, pp. 226–30, 299; James Hamilton, first Viscount Claneboy, James, first earl and Henry, second earl of Clanbrassil see Lowry (ed.), *Hamilton Manuscripts*, pp. 48–59, 71, 89; and William Stewart, first Viscount Mountjoy (c.1650–1692), NAI, T/8725.

107 NAI, T/8725, will of Viscount Mountjoy, 12 January 1688/9.

108 *CSPI, 1663–65*, pp. 478–9.

109 Funeral entries often mention 'other children which died young' but their names are not given in the entry or in the peerages.

110 K.M. Brown, *Noble Society in Scotland. Wealth, Family and Culture, From Reformation to Revolution* (Edinburgh, 2000), pp. 36, 158.

111 *Case of the right honourable Andrew Thomas Lord Castlestewart ... asserting his right to the title ... Lord Ochiltree ...* (1793).

112 Hill (ed.), *Montgomery Manuscripts*, p. 295.

113 Hamilton, *House of Hamilton*, pp. 38, 42–3.

114 H. Scott, '"Acts of time and power": the consolidation of aristocracy in seventeenth-century Europe, c.1580–1720', *Bulletin of the German Historical Institute*, 30 (2008), 6.

115 *CSPI, 1660–62*, p. 104; *Case of the Right Honourable Andrew Thomas Lord Castlestewart*, p. 3.

116 *CSPI, 1647–60*, p. 628.

117 *CSPI, 1663–65*, p. 317.

118 Stevenson, *Two Centuries of Life in Down*, p. 93.

119 Hugh first earl Mount Alexander lost his infant son, John, on 4 June 1655 (John's mother, Mary, died two weeks later, presumably to a related complication) and in 1664 lost his two-year-old son by his second wife, Catherine. Andrew (d. 1639), second baron of Castlestewart and his wife, Anne, lost two daughters and a son.

120 PRONI, D 3078/3, 1/5, Letter-book of George, sixteenth earl of Kildare, pp. 24–5.

121 Hill, *MacDonnells of Antrim*, pp. 247–50; D. Jackson, *Intermarriage in Ireland 1550–1650* (Montreal, 1970), pp. 75–6; McDonnell, 'A fragment of an Irish MSS', pp. 278–80; J.J. Marshall, 'Sir Phelim O'Neill, 1604–1652 [–3]', *Ulster Journal of Archaeology*, 10 (1904), 146.

122 Hill (ed.), *Montgomery Manuscripts*, pp. 91, 93–4; W. MacIlwaine, 'Notice of hitherto unpublished portion of the "Montgomery Manuscripts"', *Ulster Journal of Archaeology*, 9 (1861–62), 154 and McGrath, 'A biographical dictionary', pp. 219–21.

123 Hill (ed.), *Montgomery Manuscripts*, pp. 94, 352–4.

124 *CSPI, 1625–32*, p. 81; McDonnell, 'A fragment of an Irish MSS', 278. It seems that James and Alasdair predeceased their father since they were not mentioned in his will.

125 Forbes (ed.), *Memoirs*, pp. 8, 10, 69.

126 It is not clear whether Francis died in 1636 as indicated in C. Giblin, 'Francis MacDonnell, OFM, son of the first earl of Antrim (d. 1636)', *Seanchas Ardmhacha*,

8:1 (1976–77), 44–54. Certainly a 'Francis MacDonnell' still served in the Franciscan mission in the Isles until 1684, C. Giblin, 'St. Oliver Plunkett, Francis MacDonnell OFM, and the mission to the Hebrides', *Collectanea Hibernica*, 17 (1974–75), 73–7, 81–2.

127 Marquis of Dufferin, 'A sketch of my mother', n.p., n.d. I owe this reference to the marchioness of Dufferin and am grateful to her for bringing it to my attention.

128 Stevenson, *Two Centuries of Life in Down*, p. 77.

129 Hill (ed.), *Montgomery Manuscripts*, pp. 238–41.

130 *CSPD, Charles II, January–June 1683*, p. 56; Hill, *MacDonnells of Antrim*, pp. 346–7; F. J. Bigger, *The Ancient Franciscan Friary of Bun-Na-Margie, Ballycastle, on the North Coast of Antrim* (Belfast, 1898), p. 36.

131 R. Gillespie, 'Funerals and society in early seventeenth century Ireland', *Journal of the Royal Society of Antiquaries of Ireland*, 115 (1985), 86–91.

132 Hill (ed.), *Montgomery Manuscripts*, p. 247.

133 *Ibid.*, p. 248.

134 *A sermon preached at New-town*, p. 38.

135 McDonnell and Ohlmeyer (eds), 'New light on the marquis of Antrim'.

136 Lowry (ed.), *Hamilton Manuscripts*, p. 55.

137 Grosjean, 'Hamilton, Hugh, first Baron Hamilton of Glenawly'.

138 Stevenson, *Two Centuries of Life in Down*, p. 39.

139 Hill (ed.), *Montgomery Manuscripts*, pp. 112–15.

140 Quoted in Canny, *Making Ireland British*, p. 235.

141 Quoted in *Ibid.*, p. 235 and accounts of Irish estates of Sir Claud Hamilton of Schawfield, Edinburgh University Library, Laing MSS Div 2 no 5.

142 E.M. Jope, 'Scottish influences in the North of Ireland: castles with Scottish features, 1580–1640', *Ulster Journal of Archaeology*, 14 (1951), 31–47. For detailed descriptions of Castle Balfour, see Johnston, 'The Plantation of County Fermanagh', pp. 110, 112, 117, 152–3.

143 Hill (ed.), *Montgomery Manuscripts*, pp. 3, 59.

144 Forbes (ed.), *Memoirs*, pp. 54–5.

145 A.J. MacDonald and A. MacDonald, *The Clan Donald* (3 vols, Inverness, 1896–1904), ii, pp. 714–17. He briefly leased lands in Islay in 1613, Lee, *Great Britain's Solomon*, pp. 217–18.

146 PRONI, T 473/1, p. 58. Charles I had promised that once Argyll's estates were forfeited Antrim could have possession of those lands which had formerly belonged to the MacDonalds.

147 Hanly (ed.), *Letters*, pp. 156–7.

148 *Ibid.*, p. 167.

149 *CSPI, 1647–60*, pp. 156–7.

150 *CSPI, 1625–32*, p. 325.

151 R.D. Alba, *Ethnic Identity: The Transformation of White America* (New Haven, CT, 1990), pp. 203–6, p. 6; M.A. Richard, *Ethnic Groups and Marital Choices: Ethnic History and Marital Assimilation in Canada 1871–1971* (VancoUver, 1991), pp. 16–39; and Stephen Thernstrom, Ann Orlov and Oscar Handlin (eds), *Harvard Encyclopaedia of American Ethnic Groups* (Cambridge MA, 1990), *sub* 'intermarriage'.

152 Quoted in Perceval-Maxwell, *The Scottish Migration*, p. 329.

153 J.R. Young, '"Escaping massacre": refugees in Scotland in the aftermath of the 1641 Ulster Rebellion', in D. Edwards, P. Lenihan and C. Tait (eds), *Age of Atrocity: Violence and Political Conflict in Early Modern Ireland* (Dublin, 2007), pp. 219–41.

154 *CSPD, January 1679 to August 1680*, pp. 306–7.

155 A.B. Grosart (ed.), *The Lismore Papers Viz. Selections from The Private And Public (Or State) Correspondence of Sir Richard Boyle, First And 'Great' Earl Of Cork* (second series, 5 vols, privately printed, 1888), iv, p. 80.

156 Hill (ed.), *Montgomery Manuscripts*, p. 257.

157 D. Massari, 'My Irish campaign', *The Catholic Bulletin*, 611 (1916), 620.

158 Hill (ed.), *Montgomery Manuscripts*, p. 255. In fact his wives were New English – one, Mary Moore, the daughter of the first earl of Drogheda and the other Catherine Jones, daughter of Arthur, Lord Ranelagh, and granddaughter of Richard Boyle, first earl of Cork.

3

Scottish settlement and society in Plantation Ulster, 1610–40

WILLIAM ROULSTON

In the early seventeenth century 20–30,000 Scots crossed the North Channel into Ireland. Their reasons for making the journey varied. A select few had received grants of land in Ulster. Others came as part of their entourage or were transplanted directly to the newly acquired estates. Many came independently in search of a better life. Together they formed part of one of the most significant movements of people in these islands. The background to Scottish involvement in the Plantation scheme has already been charted and the Scottish undertakers profiled, their land grants identified and their performances assessed. Likewise the processes of colonisation have also been studied and discussed.[1] Furthermore, it is now well established that the most significant migration of Scots to Ulster did not take place in the early seventeenth century, but in the 1690s, much of it fuelled by harvest crises in Scotland.[2] This chapter makes no claims to originality, but rather explores a number of aspects of Scottish settlement in Plantation Ulster – here referring to the escheated counties that formed part of the official Plantation scheme – in the early seventeenth century. In particular it focuses on the Scottish-owned estates in the escheated counties and in doing so seeks to make a contribution towards a better understanding of the society that emerged.

THE EVOLUTION OF A NETWORK OF SCOTTISH ESTATES

The Scots were just one of several groups who received lands in west Ulster in the early seventeenth century. In addition to their English counterparts, there were servitors, 'deserving' Irish, the church and institutions such as Trinity College. Nine precincts[3] were set aside for Scottish grantees: Boylagh and Bannagh, and Portlough in Co. Donegal, Strabane and Mountjoy in Co. Tyrone; Knockninny and Magheraboy in Co. Fermanagh; Clankee and

Tullyhunco in Co. Cavan; and Fews in Co. Armagh. There were originally 59 Scottish grantees, called undertakers, who between them owned 70 proportions, as the individual land units were known. Several undertakers, particularly the chief undertakers, owned two or, in one instance, three proportions, together comprising a single estate. The total plantation acreage granted to Scots came to 81,000, only 500 acres less than that granted to English undertakers.[4] The proportions allocated to the undertakers were of three sizes: small (1,000 acres), middle (1,500 acres) and great (2,000 acres). There was to be only one chief undertaker in each precinct and he was permitted to have lands totalling 3,000 acres, but the lesser undertakers were allowed to have estates of no more than 2,000 acres. Of all the different groups of grantees, the undertakers alone were expected to colonise. For every thousand acres that he was granted an undertaker was required to introduce ten families of British origin, comprising at least twenty-four adult males.[5]

Within a decade of the commencement of the Plantation scheme the network of Scottish estates had changed considerably from the original plan. By 1619 more than half of the Scottish estates – 33 out of 59 – had passed out of the ownership of the original grantees.[6] Several of the Scottish undertakers disengaged from the Plantation at a very early stage. A few never visited their estates at all, while others took possession in person, but sold out soon afterwards. Others attempted to develop their lands, and a few even made some progress, but for various reasons decided not to persevere. A consequence of the ready market in Plantation land was that it allowed several individuals, usually men who had not been among the original undertakers, to build up estates considerably greater than that originally permitted under the rules of the Plantation. For example, in Clankee, Co. Cavan, three Hamilton brothers, Sir James, John and William, who are more usually associated with settlements in Co. Down, acquired five of the six original proportions in the precinct before 1619. John Hamilton in addition acquired three proportions in the precinct of Fews in Co. Armagh.[7]

As far as territorial expansion was concerned, an even more successful Scot was Sir William Stewart who, from relatively unremarkable beginnings, was able to build up a large landed base extending to seven original proportions and spread over three precincts in Counties Donegal and Tyrone.[8] Inextricably linked to the consolidation of landownership in fewer hands was the amalgamation of two or more proportions to form a single manor which further altered the original network of estates. Changes in ownership in Strabane barony meant that on the eve of the 1641 rebellion the eleven original proportions had coalesced into seven manors and the number of owners had been reduced from the initial eight grantees to six.[9] There was no more dramatic departure from the initial scheme of landownership than in Co. Donegal where there was a complete overhaul of the network of Scottish-owned proportions in the precinct of Boylagh and Bannagh within eight years of the commencement of the Plantation scheme. Here in the largely mountainous and inhospitable terrain of west Donegal eight Scots were granted lands in 1610. Little progress was made and by 1618 all of the proportions were in the possession of one man, John Murray, a groom of the king's bedchamber and royal favourite, who controlled an area in excess of 200,000 statute acres.

Often Scottish-owned estates passed to another Scot, sometimes a close relative or neighbouring landowner. Some estates, however, passed out of Scottish control altogether. Four proportions granted to Scots in the Knockninny, Co. Fermanagh, were acquired by an Englishman, Sir Stephen Butler, by 1622 though one was later to revert to Scottish ownership.[10] Sir James Hamilton sold his 3,000 acres – half of the Plantation lands in Clankee – to Sir Henry Piers in September 1621.[11] In all some 10,000 acres, representing around 12.5 per cent of the Scottish precincts, ceased to be owned by Scots by the early 1630s.[12] The loss of Scottish land to Englishmen was partly, though not completely, compensated by the acquisition of previously English-owned estates by Scots. Scots were also able to extend their acreages through the acquisition of lands from English servitors and Irish landowners. In Co. Cavan, for example, Sir James Craig acquired 2,000 acres from the Irish family of McKiernan. The consequence of these changes was that a very different pattern of landownership emerged from the one that had been envisaged.

Much of the hard graft of assembling statistics on population and examining its spatial consequences in early seventeenth-century Ulster has already been carried out by Michael Perceval Maxwell and Philip Robinson. The former has calculated that there were some 3,740 Scottish men in the escheated counties by 1622 and a total Scottish population – based on there being three women for every four men – of just over 6,500.[13] Robinson's map based on the muster rolls of *c.*1630 serves as the best indicator of the distribution of Scots in early seventeenth-century Ulster.[14] From this several key areas of settlement in the escheated counties are identifiable. The most important area of settlement was the Foyle Valley straddling Counties Donegal and Tyrone where between Portlough and Strabane there were by 1619 over 1,000 Scottish men.[15] Other areas of significant Scottish settlement were the precincts of Mountjoy and Fews where there were, respectively, an estimated 210 and 220 Scottish families by 1622. Scottish settlement was, however, less impressive in counties Cavan and Fermanagh. In Co. Cavan there were probably no more than 100 Scottish families between the two precincts allocated to Scots in 1622. At the same time in Co. Fermanagh there may have been around 120 Scottish families on the proportions originally granted to Scots, most of them living close to Upper and Lower Lough Erne.

The figures calculated by Perceval Maxwell suggest that in 1622 some 40 per cent of Scottish settlers lived in areas that had not originally been allocated to Scottish undertakers. This in itself cautions against making the pattern of settlement too closely contingent on the original scheme of plantation.[16] While stability in landownership certainly contributed to creating an environment in which settlement could thrive, the passing of a proportion out of Scottish ownership did not necessarily mean that the numbers of Scottish settlers declined. For example, even after Sir William Cole acquired Jerome Lindsay's lands in Magheraboy Scots continued to outnumber English. Elsewhere, however, it did. From an estimated 40 families on the estate held by Sir James Hamilton in Clankee in 1618–19, there were only about half a dozen Scottish men left by 1630.[17] The 1622 commissioners found that many of the Scottish tenants on this estate had gone to Clandeboy – meaning Hamilton's lands in Co. Down – 'from whence they came'. It was also true that many Scots lived on English-owned estates or estates that had been acquired by Scots from English. As a precinct which changed from being English-owned to one where the majority of proportions were possessed by Scots, the evolution of Scottish settlement in Clogher is interesting. Here Scottish settlement predominated on a number of proportions even before those lands were acquired by Scots. In Clogher the presence of Scots is likely to have been associated with colonial spread from existing areas of Scottish settlement such as the Foyle Valley perhaps after being given some initial impetus by the acquisition of lands in the precinct by Sir William Stewart in 1616.[18]

One of the areas outside the precincts allocated to Scottish undertakers that was most heavily settled by Scots was north Co. Londonderry. Here on the estates owned by two of the London companies there were by 1622 some 200 Scottish men. This settlement was largely due to the efforts of one man. In 1616 Sir Robert McClelland, who had been the chief undertaker in Boylagh and Bannagh before selling out, received a lease of the lands of the Haberdashers' Company. Shortly after concluding the agreement with the Haberdashers, McClelland turned his attention to the neighbouring lands belonging to the Clothworkers' Company. Negotiations to lease this proportion were concluded early in 1618. The opportunity had now been created to introduce Scots to a county where, outside the towns at any rate, they had hitherto been few and far between, and where there had been some reticence by English agents acting on behalf of the London companies to accept Scottish tenants. George Canning, agent to the Ironmongers' Company, had noted that some Scots had expressed an interest in leasing lands and though they were willing to pay higher rents, Canning was of the opinion that they were not in as good a position to construct the necessary buildings.[19] The lack of drive that had characterised McClelland's involvement in Donegal was absent from his Londonderry venture and by the time of Pynnar's survey there were 80 British men on the estate, most of whom are likely to have been Scots. By 1622 there were 120 British settlers on the Haberdashers' proportion and another 86 on that owned by the Clothworkers.[20] These figures were higher than those for the other proportions in the county and meant that northern Co. Londonderry now had a distinctly Scottish tinge.

The presence of large numbers of Scots on lands owned by the church in the escheated counties, largely as a result of initiatives by Scottish bishops, must also be taken into consideration. George Montgomery, appointed bishop of Derry, Raphoe and Clogher in 1605, was praised by the chronicler of the family's history, writing at the end of the seventeenth century, for 'usefulness in advancing the British plantation in those three northern dioceses'.[21] Through offering land on good terms, he encouraged a significant number of Scots, among them many of his own kinsmen, to settle on church lands. His successor as bishop of Raphoe, Andrew Knox, claimed in 1632 to have introduced 300 British families to his see lands, the majority of which were almost certainly Scottish.[22] In the other escheated counties there may have been around 180 Scottish families living on church lands by 1630, mostly in Counties Fermanagh and Tyrone.[23]

On most of the Scottish-owned estates Scots made up the overwhelming majority of the settler population. For example, in the precinct of Portlough, Co. Donegal, Englishmen were almost unknown. Cavan, however, was different. What is very interesting about the population of the Scottish-owned estates in this county is that by 1630 the overall ratio of Scots to English was 2:1. In the barony of Tullyhunco it was even closer with three Englishmen for every four Scots. On Sir James Craig's estate there were actually more English settlers than Scots. Numerically, the largest number of English settlers on any estate was on that owned by Sir Francis Hamilton. Here 51, or nearly 40 per cent, of those mustered were English. From the inquisitions held during this period, it is clear that Englishmen were among the tenants on this estate almost from the start of the Plantation.[24] English tenants were certainly an attractive option where Scots may have been in short supply. At the same time, there is evidence in Craig's case that he deliberately set out to attract English settlers to his estate. When Bodley carried out his survey in 1613 Craig was in England looking for tenants.[25] It is also worth making the point that both Craig and Hamilton were married to the daughters of leading English settlers and it may have been through these contacts that they were able to attract English settlers to their estates.

What characterized virtually all Scottish-owned estates in the escheated counties was the fact that significant numbers of Irish families lived on them even though it had been originally intended that there should be no Irish tenants at all on the estates granted to the undertakers. Rare indeed was the comment, 'I saw not one Irish family on the land', made by Pynnar of the proportion of Ballyneagh in Portlough.[26] In practice, a shortage of British tenants and the willingness of the Irish to pay higher rents in order to hold on to their lands meant that significant numbers of Irish continued to live on the undertakers' proportions. Even on the better managed estates the numbers of Irish remained significant. In 1622 there were reportedly 120 Irish families on the three Abercorn proportions in Strabane. Some undertakers excused the presence of Irish on their lands on the grounds that they were not responsible for them being there. For example, in 1622 it was said of William Baillie's estate of Tonnergie that 'some of the undertenants do let lands to the Irish, whereof he complaineth'.[27]

In 1628 it was agreed that the undertakers would be allowed to lease up to one quarter of their lands to native Irish tenants, but only for twenty-one years or three lives, not in freehold. The way in which these measures worked out in practice varied from estate to estate. For example, it appears to have been possible for a landlord to combine two or more of his proportions when demarcating land suitable for leasing to native Irishmen. This can be seen on the estate owned by Sir George Hamilton of Greenlaw in Strabane where on his Derrywoon proportion some 44 per cent of the lands were reserved for Irish tenants, but on his Cloghogall proportion the figure was only 16 per cent. However, taken together these lands represented almost exactly one quarter (25.7 per cent) of the total acreage possessed by Sir George.[28] The segregation of British and Irish into clearly defined areas, with the latter on the townlands bordering the uplands, has also been observed in the Clogher Valley by Robinson who concludes that the effect of the agreement reached in 1628 was to 'institutionalise the economic segregation which had already taken place'.[29]

SCOTTISH SETTLER SOCIETY

If the top layer of Scottish landowning society in Ulster has been the subject of study and analysis, the same cannot be said for the bulk of the settlers who moved to the escheated counties in the early seventeenth century. Certainly we have the names of many of them, courtesy of the 1630 muster roll and other sources, and an idea of where they lived. However, aside from such basics, the minutiae of their everyday lives have still to be retrieved and there are still gaps in our understanding of the formation of Scottish colonial society in Plantation Ulster and the contribution of the ordinary settlers to that. There is as yet no equivalent to Gillespie's study of Antrim and Down with its exploration of rural and urban society for the escheated counties.[30] If the fact that large areas of Ulster became, as Gillespie suggests, 'an extension of south-west Scotland' is indisputable, the means by which this was accomplished at local level has only been investigated in detail in a few instances.[31] Using one of the few collections of estate papers relating to Ulster to survive from this period, Nicholas Canny has explored the way in which Sir Robert McClelland transformed the lands of the Haberdashers' Company in north Londonderry into an 'Ulster outpost of western Scottish rural society' in which Scottish culture dominated and Scottish practices as far as agriculture and estate management were concerned were the norm.[32]

For the most part the estate system provided a framework within which the Scottish communities functioned and defined the nature of the relationships within the settler population.[33] Not only was the estate the most important component in land organisation throughout the seventeenth century, it was also one of the key elements of social cohesion. This was particularly true for the Scots in Ulster in the early seventeenth century when kirk sessions along Scottish lines were unknown and parochial organisation in the form of vestries was in its infancy. The transformation of the Plantation proportions into manors has been highlighted as being of crucial importance to their success.[34] The manor courts created as a result played an important role in regulating the affairs of the estate and settling disputes between tenants. Unfortunately, this avenue of investigation is closed to us for very little of the workings of these courts has survived for any of the estates in Ulster, though the presence of seneschals on a number of manors suggest that courts were held.[35] Sir Robert McClelland claimed that on the lands he leased from the Haberdashers' Company a manor court was regularly held and the names of tenants and undertenants recorded in a roll.[36]

The conditions of the plantation laid down a specific landholding structure designed to prevent landlords from managing their estates as they pleased and to provide proper security to their tenants in the form of written leases. It also represented an attempt to fashion a social structure and social relationships in the escheated counties.[37] For each thousand acres the undertaker was to reserve for himself a demesne of 300 acres. The remaining 700 acres were to be divided up in the following manner: two fee-farmers or freeholders with 120 acres each; three leaseholders for three lives or twenty-one years with 100 acres each; and at least four families of husbandmen, artificers or cottagers on the final 160 acres. The structure of the tenancies required in the escheated counties contrasted with estates in east Ulster where such obligations were absent and where landlords exercised greater freedom in how they leased their estates. In some instances this meant that they were reluctant to grant farms on terms thought to be too generous. For example, it was said of Sir James Hamilton's estate in north-east Down that 'In managing of his estate he was careful and wary in giving inheritances or leases above three lives, and went that length but with very few'.[38]

For the most part, the usage of the term freeholder when applied to a tenant in the early seventeenth century equated with fee farmer, that is, someone who possessed a grant of land in perpetuity. In Scotland 'feuing' as a tenure had existed on church lands from the twelfth century and became much more widespread from the fifteenth century onwards.[39] It was therefore a tenure that the Scottish undertakers to Ulster would have been familiar with. The inclusion of fee farm grants among the required tenures in the Plantation scheme was viewed as a means of introducing substantial tenants to an estate who would form the backbone of rural society. The disadvantage was that having granted a fee farm the landowner lost all future economic potential in those lands since the rent remained the same no matter how much the lands in question increased in value.

Three of the fee farm deeds issued by the first earl of Abercorn survive for the manor of Dunnalong. These reveal that a cash payment was combined with requirements to provide livestock or other goods. For example, when Hugh Hamilton was granted the freehold of Moyagh in 1612 he was required to pay £8 in rent and also one bullock and two sheep.[40] More interesting was the deed issued to another Hugh Hamilton for Lisdivin in 1615 which stipulated that he was to pay either £6 in rent or a variety of luxury foodstuffs, including loaf sugar and marmalade.[41] The deed of 1614 transferring Cloghogle in fee farm to William Lynn shows that Lynn was required to build within four years a 'good and sufficient house of stone and lime or stone and clay with windows and chimneys after the form of Scottish buildings', a so far unique written example of the desire to transplant Scottish vernacular architecture to west Ulster. Defensive considerations can also be found in Lynn's fee farm deed, for under the terms of it he was required to have in readiness in his house one musket and two lances, and to keep two men armed with lances and muskets.[42]

While the deeds for Dunnalong fulfilled the requirements of the authorities, it is clear that not everyone claimed as a freeholder in the Plantation surveys fitted the correct criteria. Of the two fee farmers on the estate of George Home in Co. Fermanagh, both of whom possessed 100 acres, one held by lands by a deed, but it was only a grant 'during life', while the other held his lands 'only by promise, but no estate made'. Two of the three fee farmers on Sir John Dunbar's estate in the same county in 1622 held their lands by 'notes long since dated, but no deeds perfected, which is their own fault, for they have had the possession accordingly and may have deeds when they will, as [they] themselves confess'.[43] Among the observations presented by the 1622 commissioners was the complaint that some of the undertakers made their 'fee farmers not absolute but conditional, with provisoes of re-entry and forfeiture for non-payment of rents'. The commissioners also expressed concern over the fact that the absence of written deeds gave 'such, as are unconscionable, power to put poor men out of their holdings, when they have builded with confidence of settlement'.[44] There was also the problem of non-residence. In Co. Armagh the 1622 commissioners noted that Robert Montgomery, who was listed as a freeholder on the Clancarny estate of Archibald Acheson, 'lives not there, but at Clogher and sets the land to poor men'. Two of the other reputed freeholders on this estate were found to have returned to Scotland by

1622 and one of these, George Acheson, was 'never known to be a freeholder'. On the lands of Sir Claud Hamilton of Shawfield in Strabane barony, managed following his death in 1614 by his brother Sir George Hamilton of Greenlaw, it was said in 1622 that the freeholders 'dwell in other places'. There had been one resident Scot, but as he was a Protestant and Sir George 'an archpapist', the latter 'thrust him off with many injuries so that he is gone into Scotland'.[45]

The absence of written deeds conveying land in leasehold was even more prevalent and here too concerns were expressed about the validity of some of the leases issued. On the lands of John Murray in Boylagh and Bannagh, the agent, Herbert Maxwell, claimed to have made out over forty 'minutes purporting leases', each for 21 years.[46] On the estate of Sir John Home in Co. Fermanagh, the leaseholders held their lands on various different terms: by articles of agreement, during life, by promise, 'by notes of memoranda' and from year to year. The uncertainty that this created made some of the British tenants leave the estate.[47] Non-residence and the difficulties in reconciling the number of leaseholders claimed and those present were also problems. For example, in 1622 there were reputedly 21 leaseholders on the lands originally granted to Sir Alexander Hamilton in Tullyhunco, but only 13 appeared before the commissioners and some of these were non-resident.[48] Occasionally the undertakers or their agents were far from cooperative in their dealings with commissioners Carew, Bodley, *et al.* When asked by Pynnar to call together the tenants on the proportions of the duke of Lennox for which he was responsible, Sir John Stewart refused. Neither would Stewart reveal details of the nature of the tenancies held apart from showing Pynnar a counterpart of one lease and telling him 'that each of the tenants had the like'.[49]

Leasehold tenures varied considerably. Twenty-one years was popular, but leases for the life of the leaseholder or the lives of named individuals were also issued.[50] 'A particular of the leases' of several of the manors in south-west Donegal owned by John Murray in 1638 shows that leases of varying lengths were in use with nine and eleven years the most popular. This and a rental of the same year reveal that in addition to cash payments tenants typically provided livestock and agricultural produce as part of their rent.[51] For example, James Read and his mother Anne paid £4 9s 8d and provided '2 parte of a Scotch mutton' and four hens for their half of the quarter of Dromconner. Others paid part of their rent in butter. Payments in kind like this were also known on the Eden-Killeny estate in Strabane barony, where among the 'in kind' payments made by tenants were barley, sheep, pigs and hens.[52] Though perceived to be an infringement of the regulations, the absence of written leases on many of the Scottish-owned proportions in Ulster was not unusual in the context of contemporary agricultural practices in Scotland. The practice of issuing written leases only became widespread in Scotland in the early seventeenth century and in particular from the third decade of the 1600s onwards. In many parts of Scotland verbal agreements continued to be the norm until well into the seventeenth century. On the Cassillis estate in Wigtown, for example, less than a quarter of the holdings in 1622 were held by written leases with some 70 per cent of farms held on the basis of verbal agreements.[53]

The third principal category of tenant was the cottager. Typically a cottager had a house, garden and generally either a small quantity of land, usually not more than ten acres, or grazing rights. The holdings possessed by cottagers varied considerably. On the estate of William Baillie in Co. Cavan, one of the cottagers possessed ten acres, while another held only three, though he also was allowed grazing for three cows. On both of the estates of brothers John and William Hamilton in Cavan there were four cottagers each of whom possessed a house and garden with commons for four cows. On the estate of Sir John Hume in Fermanagh there were seven cottagers, each of whom had a house and a small holding of between two and twelve acres. These holdings were mostly held from year to year.[54] What is not always clear from the plantation surveys is whether the cottagers lived together in a nucleated settlement or whether their holdings were scattered across an estate.

Various factors were at work in creating the settler population in any one locality. Three main processes of colonisation have been identified by Philip Robinson: direct plantation, colonial spread and internal migration.[55] The first of these was especially observable in the earliest stages of the plantation. For example, Sir George Carew noted in 1611 that Lord Ochiltree, afterwards Lord Castlestewart, had travelled to his proportions in east Tyrone 'accompanied with 33 followers, gent. of sort, a minister, some tenants, freeholders, and artificers'.[56] Through surname analysis it is clear that many of the tenants on the Abercorn estate in Strabane barony came from Renfrewshire where he himself originated. Names commonly found there, such as Brisbane, Crawford, Hamilton, Houston, Maxwell, Pollock, Ralston and Shaw, all appear on the earl's Strabane lands.[57] What cannot be ruled out is the possibility that some of these settlers travelled to Strabane barony of their own accord, but were attracted to this destination because of kinsfolk already there.

In some instances what encouraged people to settle in Ulster was an opportunity to revive the family's economic fortunes and recover status lost in Scotland. For example, Alexander Cairns or Kearns was an impoverished Scottish laird who left his home country to seek a better life in west Donegal. He was the only son of John Cairns of Cults, Wigtownshire, who, through accumulating debts, was forced to sell most of the family's lands. In 1607 Alexander Cairns disposed of most of what was left.[58] In 1611 he appears as a 'general agent' for the Scottish undertakers in the precinct of Boylagh and Bannagh, to a number of whom he was related, including Sir Robert McClelland.[59] Here Cairns prospered, surviving the major overhaul of land-ownership, and building up a substantial leasehold, not only in Boylagh and

Bannagh, but also at Donaghmore in east Donegal.[60] In the 1630s his sons extended the family's landed interests into Co. Tyrone, through the acquisition of estates in Clogher barony.[61]

On many of the Scottish-owned estates, there is evidence that bonds of kinship existed between the landlord and his tenants. One of the freeholders on the proportion of Sir John Drummond in Strabane barony was his brother Malcolm who was to eventually succeed him as proprietor of this estate.[62] A freeholder on Lord Castlestewart's estate in the precinct of Mountjoy was his cousin William Stewart, one of a number of Stewarts among the tenantry on this landholding.[63] In 1622 it was noted that kinsmen of William Baillie lived on his Tonnergie estate in Co. Cavan, a statement corroborated by other information on the property in this period.[64] In another instance, several of the freeholders created by Sir Robert McClelland on the lands leased from the Haberdashers' Company in Co. Londonderry were his kinsman. In such instances one would imagine that these bonds would have been stronger than those created by written deed or verbal promise. At the same time, not all freeholds were granted on this basis, and occasionally outsiders acquired extensive freeholds on good terms. For instance, the largest freehold in the Scottish precincts in Cavan was one of 480 acres or ten polls granted by Sir James Hamilton to Richard Hadsor in 1616. Hadsor was a major figure in the Irish administration and was to become one of the commissioners of inquiry in 1622.[65] In this instance the granting of such a large block of land may have been in part payment of a debt or to curry favour with an influential figure. It may have been designed by Hamilton to recoup part of the money he had expended on purchasing the proportion from the original grantee.

Especially on the estates in Strabane barony granted to the three sons of Lord Claud Hamilton of Paisley – the first earl of Abercorn, Sir Claud Hamilton of Schawfield and Sir George Hamilton of Greenlaw – numerous Hamiltons were to be found among the tenants. Only one can be shown to have been a close blood relative – William Hamilton of Wedderhill. Sharing a common ancestor in the first earl of Arran, Hamilton was second cousin to the Paisley Hamiltons; their fathers had taken up arms in the cause of Mary, Queen of Scots, in the 1560s. Hamilton was also the brother-in-law of Sir John Drummond of Bordland, another of the Strabane undertakers.[66] Not long after his marriage in 1613, he moved to Co. Tyrone where he acquired a freehold of 240 acres in the manor of Strabane. Although a close relationship to the earl and his brothers cannot be shown for most of the Hamilton settlers in Strabane, there is evidence to link many of these tenants to the family in one way or another. For example, William Hamilton of Priestfield in Blantyre, and later of Ballyfatton in the manor of Strabane, was party to an instrument of sasine involving Sir Claud Hamilton of Shawfield in 1605.[67] The Hamiltons of Priestfield were also probably related to the Hamiltons of Easter Binning and with a member of this latter family, George Hamilton, having been briefly an undertaker in Strabane barony, there is a further possible reason for William Hamilton's appearance in Ulster. Hugh Hamilton, who possessed the freehold of Moyagh in the manor of Dunnalong was the son of James Hamilton of Blantyre. Once again, we can find a connection to the Paisley Hamiltons for his wife's uncle, the Rev. William Hamilton, had been presented to the parish of Rutherglen in 1604 by the future first earl of Abercorn.[68] However, such connections might appear tenuous and there may have been several different factors influencing the intentions of these settlers to emigrate to this particular part of the escheated counties.

Stronger links can be shown between the first Scot known to have been granted lands in the Eden-Killeny estate and his landlord, Sir Claud Hamilton of Shawfield. In the surviving rentals of this estate Dr Robert Hamilton appears in possession of the townland of Killycurry, but was not being charged with rent for it.[69] A major figure in Scottish medical history, in 1599 he established the Faculty of Physicians and Surgeons of Glasgow with Peter Lowe. He is likely to have been related to the Paisley Hamiltons, though precisely how has not been established. Significantly, his colleague Lowe dedicated the second edition of his work *Chirurgerie* to the first earl of Abercorn.[70] However he may have been related to Abercorn and his family, the connections between them remained strong. In 1628 Dr Hamilton was among those who granted a certificate of sickness to Marion Boyd, widow of the first earl of Abercorn, to excuse her from appearing before the Privy Council of Scotland to account for her Catholicism.[71] In some ways Dr Hamilton was a strange choice for a freeholder. There is no evidence that he ever visited his freehold in Strabane barony, or even intended to do so, and it may have been the case that he was granted Killycurry to cover a debt due to him by Sir Claud or simply as a favour.

Servants from the landlord's own household were occasionally among those who were granted tenancies. Matthew Crawford, who, when receiving a grant of denization in 1617 was identified as one of Abercorn's servants, turns up as a leaseholder in the manor of Strabane in 1622.[72] In the late 1630s Abercorn's son Claud, Lord Strabane, leased a townland in fee farm to his servant James Patton 'in consideration of good and faithful services'.[73] The practice of allocating lands to an employee was used by other Scottish landlords in Ulster. For example, it was noted in 1622 that the freeholders on Lord Balfour's lands around Lisnaskea in Co. Fermanagh were his own household servants.[74] In the 1630s Balfour's former cook, Donald Lennox, possessed a number of tenancies and also held the market rights for Lisnaskea.[75]

It becomes apparent through sorties into these shadowy worlds, that of the different categories of tenantry, the freeholders offer the greatest potential for detailed study. As what could justifiably be described as the second tier in settler society, they played an important role in local administration and leadership as well as economic development. Some observations on the characteristics of this category of tenant follow. In a number of instances, as has already been shown, we know something of their Scottish background and their connections to the undertakers.[76] Among those holding freehold tenancies was a sprinkling of lairds or those from lairdly families. William Hamilton of Wedderhill has already been mentioned and attention can also be drawn to David Barkley or Barclay, laird of Ladyland in Ayrshire, who was named as a freeholder on Sir William's Stewart's estate in Clogher barony in 1622.[77] In general, freeholders enjoyed higher social status than other categories of tenant, being usually denoted as 'gent.' or even 'esquire'. In part this reflected the position in society they enjoyed in Scotland, though it was reinforced through the terms on which they held land in Ulster.

Those who were involved in estate administration were often in possession of freehold tenancies. For example, the principal agent on the Abercorn lands in Strabane barony in the early years of the plantation was the aforementioned William Lynn, generally styled 'of Londonderry' where he possessed property, who, as noted earlier in this chapter, was the grantee of a freehold in the manor of Dunnalong in 1615. Other agents in possession of freeholds included Sir Robert Hepburn's agent in the precinct of Mountjoy, Thomas Goodlatt who possessed three and a half townlands in freehold.[78] Robert Algeo and David McGhee, successively agents to Sir George Hamilton of Greenlaw on his proportions in Strabane barony, both held freeholds under Sir George. In addition both shared his Catholicism. Algeo was from a Renfrewshire family and he, or at least members of his family, had been associated with Sir George's sister-in-law, the widow of the first earl of Abercorn, in Scotland.[79] By the early 1630s Algeo was also acting as agent to Sir William Hamilton, the owner of the neighbouring Manor Elieston estate in Strabane barony.[80] Appointed around 1625, McGhee served as agent to the Hamiltons for approximately fifty years.[81] By 1628 he had also been appointed the seneschal of the manor of Strabane.[82] Robert Hamill is an example of a Scottish freeholder who served as agent and seneschal on an English-owned estate in south Tyrone.[83]

Other freeholders, while perhaps not agents, contributed in a significant way to the development of the estates, and were involved in the creation of the manorial infrastructure. Rev. Patrick Hamilton, the possessor of the largest freehold in the manor of Dunnalong, is likely to have been the former minister in Abercorn's home town of Paisley.[84] He was instrumental in the construction of a castle and 'divers houses of cuples' in the manor prior to 1622.[85] Freeholders providing similar services to landowners can be found in other parts of the escheated counties. For example, in April 1614 Malcolm Campbell was authorised by his landlord, Cuthbert Cunningham, formerly the provost of the college kirk of Dumbarton, to oversee the building of a house on his proportion in the precinct of Portlough in east Donegal.[86]

A further characteristic shared by a number of the freeholders is that their propertied interests were not limited to the manor where they had initially received lands in fee farm. For example, William Lynn, whose fee farm of Cloghogle in the manor of Dunnalong has already been noted, was also by 1622 a freeholder in the neighbouring Eden-Killeny estate and the leaseholder of 400 acres in Sir Robert Newcomen's estate at Newtownstewart. He also had sufficient means to purchase two small properties in Kilmacrenan barony, Co. Donegal, originally allocated to a servitor, though he did nothing to develop these.[87] In the precinct of Mountjoy John Lifford held freeholds from two Scots, Sir Robert Hepburn and Alexander Sanderson.[88] William Cunningham, on the other hand, was a freeholder to Sir John Drummond in Strabane and a leaseholder to an English planter, Sir Henry Mervyn, in Omagh barony.[89] Also active in land acquisition was the abovementioned William Hamilton of Wedderhill. In 1622 he was not resident on his extensive freehold in the manor of Strabane, but lived in the castle on the Fentonagh estate owned by the Englishman Sir Henry Mervyn in Omagh barony, while he was also the leaseholder of 420 acres on another of Mervyn's proportions in that barony.[90] In addition he was the lessee of 1,000 acres of church lands in Omagh barony, for which fourteen men mustered in 1630–31.[91]

A few of those who possessed rural freeholds engaged in trade and commerce. For example, on the earl of Abercorn's estate several freeholders were also merchants in the embryonic town of Strabane, emphasizing the absence of a clear demarcation between an urban settlement and its rural hinterland. Strabane was the largest Scottish-founded town in the escheated counties. Among the reasons for the success of Strabane as an urban settlement was Abercorn's ability to attract to it merchants of some substance, who, as R.J. Hunter has explored, traded directly with ports in Scotland, England and the continent.[92] One of those who combined mercantile dealings with the acquisition of freehold land was William Hamilton (not to be confused with his namesake of Wedderhill). He was a burgess of Glasgow, where his son James was also admitted a burgess in 1616, and in 1620 both were party to an instrument of sasine involving property in the burgh of Linlithgow, for which the first earl of Abercorn had once been MP.[93] By this time he had been resident in Strabane for a number of years and by 1622 he had been granted a townland in fee farm near the town.[94] Another merchant based at Strabane, John Birsbane, was also granted a rural freehold near the town by 1622.[95] Birsbane was probably of the Bishopton branch of the family in Renfrewshire where the name was more commonly spelled Brisbane. By 1622 he had disposed of his freehold to his brother William, a man who was to play a much more significant role in the plantation in Co. Tyrone. John still retained a landed interest in Strabane barony for in 1622 he appears as a leaseholder on the estate owned by Sir Robert Newcomen.[96]

The Strabane merchant who was most successful in adding a landed portfolio to his business was Hugh Hamilton. A son of John Hamilton of Priestfield, following an apprenticeship in Edinburgh, he joined his brother William in Strabane barony in the early years of the plantation.[97] His business connections were extensive and he traded directly with France. Doubtless this explains how he was able to acquire the luxury items – 'one hogshead of Gascoign wine, one pound of good pepper, four pounds of loaf sugar and a box of marmalade containing at least two pounds of the preserve' – that provided the alternative to the cash rent he was to pay for the freehold in the manor of Dunnalong that he acquired from the earl of Abercorn in 1615.[98] He afterwards added to this property, several houses in Strabane, a fee farm in the manor of Cloghogall, and the former abbeylands of Grange, in all several hundred acres of good quality agricultural land.[99] By the time of his death in 1637 he would have been one of the wealthiest men in north-west Ulster.

Elsewhere in the escheated territories there are only a handful of examples of merchants who acquired freehold land. In part this was because, aside from Strabane, no commercial centre of real importance was under the control of a Scottish patron. One of the few to do so was Hugh Thomson. He was one of a number of successful Scottish merchants based in Derry, where he was also a burgess, and conducted an extensive trade with England, Scotland and beyond.[100] He acquired a fee farm in the precinct of Portlough in Donegal, while he also purchased a native freehold in the parish of Faughanvale in Co. Londonderry.[101] We also find him purchasing the lands of Garscadden in the parish of East Kilpatrick, near Glasgow, in 1620, evidence of continued links with the land of his birth.[102]

The tenantry, and specifically the freeholders, were expected to play their part in the administration of local justice through attendance at the assizes and through being called to serve in specific positions. This could be burdensome, especially to those tenants who felt that they did not have the means to give of their time at the court sittings. The many names that have survived in the summonisters' rolls, listing those who were fined for non-attendance at the assizes or for failing to serve on juries as and when required, indicate that many of the settlers opted out of active participation in the justice system probably because of the inconvenience it caused them.[103] Nonetheless, despite the difficulties that were associated with this, many of the Scottish tenants played their part in local governance. William Hamilton of Wedderhill was a justice of the peace by 1622, and in 1625 served as high sheriff of Co. Tyrone.[104] William Birsbane was another freeholder who served as high sheriff of Tyrone, in his case in 1628.[105] That Hamilton and Birsbane were chosen for these roles, which were normally the preserve of the landed elite, says much about their own status in the settler community, though to some extent it probably reflects the shortage of men considered qualified to fulfil the responsibilities required by them.

In a century of high mobility, the result of economic and social factors as well as war and its consequences, the freeholders often provided the vital link between the first half of the seventeenth century and the second. For example, in the manor of Dunnalong, Co. Tyrone, the four principal freeholds recorded in the Civil Survey of the mid-1650s were in possession of the same families who had been granted them in the early seventeenth century and were to continue in the ownership of these same families into the 1700s, and even in a couple of instances into the 1800s. This contrasts with the fact that only two of the surnames recorded in the 1630 muster roll for Dunnalong appear in the poll book just over 30 years later.[106]

Another area that requires further investigation is the way in which the Scottish tenantry interacted with the Irish. Although, as shown in this chapter, a degree of segregation existed between settler and native, there was still a considerable amount of interplay between the two groups. Freeholders whose lands were too large to be farmed entirely by their families needed Irishmen as undertenants.[107] Canny has found that most of the skilled work on Sir Robert McClelland's property in Co. Londonderry was done by Scots, while the Irish tended to be employed to carry out unskilled tasks.[108] At the same time, the relationship between the two was not necessarily always one where the Scot was the superior. In one instance a native Irishmen was given the responsibility for managing an entire Scottish-owned estate – Patrick Groom O'Devine, who in 1615 leased the entire Eden-Killeny estate from the heirs of Sir Claud Hamilton of Shawfield in Strabane barony.[109] Scots and Irishmen served together on chancery inquisition juries, while in 1628 William Hamilton of Wedderhill and Owen McEnemee jointly provided bail for John Tath of Tiremegan in Co. Tyrone.[110]

This discussion provides an insight into some aspects of Scottish settler society in early seventeenth-century Ulster, but mere glimpses of what could be achieved through more sustained study of some of the issues raised. More case studies, such as Canny's of McClelland's activities in north Londonderry, of individual or groups of Scottish manors are essential to understanding how these estates functioned and fitted into the overall settlement pattern. If the written record is well-worked terrain, from which new finds have to be extracted with effort and imagination, one alternative discipline that may be mentioned in closing that has the potential to contribute enormously to our understanding of Scottish settlement in plantation Ulster is archaeology. In particular, archaeology has the potential to show something of the revolutionary change that Ireland as a whole was experiencing in the early modern period, and of which the plantations were just part.[111] In recent years there has been a noticeable upsurge in interest in the archaeology of post-medieval Ireland, resulting in the formation of the Irish Post-Medieval Archaeology Group in 1999 and the publication of a number of important volumes.[112] The results of excavations already undertaken, such as the investigations into the location of the village on Sir John Hume's estate in Co. Fermanagh, have been mixed.[113] However, recent excavations at the 'lost town' at Dunluce have revealed much about its early seventeenth-century economy and society, and there are a number of sites in the escheated counties that offer potential for further investigation. If anything, this chapter has highlighted a number of areas in the history of Scottish settlement in the escheated counties that require further research. Only when these and other avenues have been explored will a fuller understanding of the contribution of the Scots to early seventeenth-century Ulster be realised.

NOTES

1 G. Hill, *An Historical Account of the Plantation in Ulster at the Commencement of the Seventeenth Century* (Belfast, 1877); M. Perceval-Maxwell, *The Scottish Migration to Ulster in the Reign of James I* (London, 1973); P.S. Robinson, *Plantation of Ulster* (Dublin, 1984), pp. 109–28; J. Ohlmeyer, '"Civilizinge of those Rude Partes": colonization within Britain and Ireland, 1580s–1640s', in N. Canny (ed.), *The Origins of Empire: British Overseas Enterprise to the Close of the Seventeenth Century* (Oxford, 1998), p. 139.

2 P. Fitzgerald, '"Black '97": reconsidering Scottish migration to Ireland in the seventeenth century and the Scotch-Irish in America', in W. Kelly and J.R. Young (eds), *Scotland and Ireland, 1600–2000: History, Language and Identity* (Dublin, 2004), pp. 71–84.

3 Precincts often equated with pre-existing baronies, but in some cases they represented only part of a barony or an amalgamation of parts of two or more baronies. For example, the barony of Raphoe was divided into two precincts, Lifford (granted to English) and Portlough (granted to Scots). The word barony will only be used in the text if the area denoted corresponded with a precinct, e.g. Strabane barony.

4 Robinson, *Plantation of Ulster*, p. 79.

5 T.W. Moody, 'The revised articles of the Ulster plantation', *Bulletin of the Institute of Historical Research*, 12 (1934–35), 178–83.

6 Robinson, *Plantation of Ulster*, p. 80.

7 Perceval-Maxwell, *The Scottish Migration*, pp. 219–20; Hill, *Plantation in Ulster*, p. 568 n. 288.

8 W.J. Roulston, 'Seventeenth-century manors in the barony of Strabane', in J. Lyttleton and T. O'Keeffe (eds), *The Manor in Medieval and Early Modern Ireland* (Dublin, 2005), pp. 164–5; Perceval-Maxwell, *The Scottish Migration*, pp. 360–1.

9 Roulston, 'Seventeenth-century manors', pp. 163–5.

10 J. Johnston, 'Settlement on a Plantation estate: the Balfour rentals of 1632 and 1636', *Clogher Record*, 12:1 (1985), 96.

11 Perceval-Maxwell, *The Scottish Migration*, p. 330; V. Treadwell, *The Irish Commission of 1622* (Dublin, 2006), p. 510.
12 This figure has been calculated using a range of sources including Pynnar's survey (Hill, *Plantation in Ulster*, pp. 451–590), the 1622 survey (Treadwell (ed.), *Irish Commission of 1622*, pp. 510–635); Hill's footnotes in *Plantation in Ulster* have proved invaluable.
13 Perceval-Maxwell, *The Scottish Migration*, p. 228.
14 Robinson, *Plantation of Ulster*, p. 94.
15 Perceval-Maxwell, *The Scottish Migration*, pp. 215, 225.
16 *Ibid.*, p. 228.
17 *Ibid.*, p. 222.
18 P.S. Robinson, 'Plantation and colonisation: the historical background', in F.W. Boal and J.N.H. Douglas (eds), *Integration and Division: Geographical Perspectives on the Northern Ireland Problem* (London and New York, 1982), p. 33.
19 N. Canny, *Making Ireland British, 1580–1650* (Oxford, 2001), p. 222.
20 Treadwell (ed.), *Irish Commission of 1622*, pp. 626–7.
21 G. Hill, *The Montgomery Manuscripts* (Belfast, 1869), p. 99.
22 Perceval-Maxwell, *The Scottish Migration*, p. 203.
23 *Ibid.*, p. 227.
24 Hill, *Plantation in Ulster*, p. 469 n. 58.
25 HMC, *Report on the manuscripts of the late Reginald Rawdon Hastings, esq.* (4 vols., London, 1928–47), iv, p. 164.
26 Hill, *Plantation in Ulster*, p. 511.
27 Treadwell (ed.), *Irish Commission of 1622*, pp. 512, 522.
28 PRONI, D 623/B 4/1; Roulston, 'Seventeenth-century manors in the barony of Strabane', p. 183.
29 Robinson, *Plantation of Ulster*, p. 102.
30 R. Gillespie, *Colonial Ulster: The Settlement of East Ulster, 1600–1641* (Cork, 1985).
31 Gillespie, *Colonial Ulster*, p. 195.
32 Canny, *Making Ireland British*, pp. 222–8.
33 R. Gillespie, *Seventeenth-Century Ireland* (Dublin, 2006), pp. 48–53.
34 W.H. Crawford, 'The significance of landed estates in Ulster, 1600–1820', *Irish Economic and Social History*, 17 (1990), 47; Gillespie, *Colonial Ulster*, p. 135; Roulston, 'Seventeenth-century manors', p. 161.
35 PRONI, T 1365/1.
36 Canny, *Making Ireland British*, p. 224.
37 Gillespie, *Seventeenth-Century Ireland*, p. 48.
38 T.K. Lowry (ed.), *The Hamilton Manuscripts* (Belfast, 1867), p. 36.
39 R.A. Dodgshon, *Land and Society in Early Scotland* (Oxford, 1981), pp. 101–2.
40 PRONI, LPC 1367.
41 PRONI, D 623/B/13/2A.
42 PRONI, D 623/B/13/1.
43 Treadwell (ed.), *Irish Commission of 1622*, p. 536.
44 *Ibid.*, p. 607.
45 *Ibid.*, p. 603.
46 *Ibid.*, pp. 610–13.

47 *Ibid.*, p. 535.
48 *Ibid.*, p. 520.
49 Hill, *Plantation in Ulster*, p. 513.
50 *Ibid.*, p. 452 n. 7; for a discussion of a lease from the Acheson estate in Co. Cavan, see C. Tait, 'Cavan in 1638: natives and newcomers', in B. Scott (ed.), *Culture and Society in Early Modern Breifne/Cavan* (Dublin 2009), pp. 188–99.
51 S. Elliott, 'Two early 17th century Co. Donegal rent rolls', *Donegal Annual*, 54 (2002), 61–75.
52 PRONI, T 544/1.
53 I. Whyte, *Agriculture and Society in Seventeenth-Century Scotland* (Edinburgh, 1979), pp. 154–7; Gillespie, *Seventeenth-Century Ireland*, p. 51.
54 Treadwell (ed.), *Irish Commission of 1622*, pp. 511, 535.
55 Robinson, *Plantation of Ulster*, pp. 109–28.
56 *Cal. Carew MSS, 1603–24*, p. 77.
57 *A General Description of the Shire of Renfrew* (Paisley, 1818); D. Dobson, *Scotland During the Plantation of Ulster: The People of Renfrewshire, 1600–1699* (Baltimore, MD, 2009).
58 National Records of Scotland (hereafter NRS), GD 455/3.
59 H.C. Lawlor, *A History of the Family of Cairnes or Cairns* (London, 1906), pp. 67, 73–4.
60 Elliott, 'Two early 17th century Co. Donegal rent rolls', pp. 61–75.
61 Lawlor, *Cairnes or Cairns* (London, 1906), p. 77.
62 Treadwell (ed.), *Irish Commission of 1622*, p. 571.
63 *Ibid.*, p. 581.
64 Hill, *Plantation in Ulster*, p. 456; R. J. Hunter and M. Perceval-Maxwell, 'The muster roll of *c.*1630: Co. Cavan', *Breifne*, 18 (1977–78), 218; W. Roulston, 'The Scots in Plantation Cavan, 1610–42', in Scott (ed.), *Culture and Society in Early Modern Breifne/Cavan*, p. 132.
65 Hill, *Plantation in Ulster*, p. 452 n. 6; Perceval-Maxwell, *The Scottish Migration*, p. 190.
66 Hamilton, *House of Hamilton*, pp. 150–5, 998.
67 *Ibid.*, p. 717.
68 *Ibid.*, pp. 158–9, 796–8.
69 PRONI, T 544.
70 J. Geyer-Kordesch and F. Macdonald, *Physicians and Surgeons in Glasgow: The History of the Royal College of Physicians and Surgeons of Glasgow, 1599–1858* (2 vols, London, 1999) i, pp. 37–9.
71 W.M. Metcalfe, *A History of Paisley, 600–1908* (Paisley, 1909), p. 239.
72 IMC, *Cal. Patent Rolls, Ire., James I*, p. 306; Cambridgeshire County Record Office (hereafter CCRO), Kimbolton MSS DD/M 70/35.
73 PRONI, D 1939/18/10/2.
74 Treadwell (ed.), *Irish Commission of 1622*, p. 524.
75 Johnston, 'Settlement on a Plantation estate', p. 106.
76 D. Dobson, *Searching for Scotch-Irish Roots in Scottish Records, 1600–1750* (Baltimore, MD, 2006) highlighted the potential that there is in this area.

77 Treadwell (ed.), *Irish Commission of 1622*, p. 578; G. Robertson, *A Genealogical Account of the Principal Families in Ayrshire, more particularly in Cunninghame* (3 vols, Irvine, 1823), i, pp. 72–4.
78 PRONI, T 808/15100; Goodlatt died in 1624 and his tombstone can still be seen in the churchyard of Killyman Church of Ireland church; W.J. Roulston, 'Memento mori: a study of seventeenth-century memorials to the dead in West Ulster', MA dissertation, Queens' University Belfast, 1996, pp. 137–8.
79 Metcalfe, *History of Paisley*, pp. 233–41; W.J. Roulston, 'The Algeo family of Strabane: a Scottish Catholic family in Plantation Ulster', *Due North*, 2:3 (Autumn/Winter 2009), 16–20.
80 NRS, E 661/142.
81 PRONI, D 1939/18/10/2.
82 PRONI, T 1365/1.
83 J.J. Marshall, *Annals of Aughnacloy* (Aughnacloy, 2009), p. 17; R.C. Simington (ed.), *Civil Survey ... Donegal, Londonderry and Tyrone* ed. (10 vols, Dublin, 1937), iii, p. 277.
84 Metcalfe, *History of Paisley*, p. 213.
85 CCRO, Kimbolton MSS, DDM 70/35; PRONI, T 808/6461; somewhat puzzlingly his will, which was not probated until 1635, states that he was entitled to the tithes of two parishes in 1629, though this could be a clerical error.
86 NRS, GD 220/6/1879(4).
87 W.J. Roulston, 'The Ulster Plantation in the manor of Dunnalong, 1610–70', in H. Jefferies and C. Dillon (eds), *Tyrone: History and Society* (Dublin, 2000), pp. 274–5.
88 Treadwell (ed.), *Irish Commission of 1622*, pp. 581, 594.
89 *Ibid.*, pp. 571, 573, 602.
90 *Ibid.*, pp. 573, 602–3.
91 BL, MS. 4770, fol. 101v.
92 R.J. Hunter, 'Ulster Plantation towns, 1609–41', in D. W. Harkness and M. O'Dowd (eds), *The Town in Ireland: Historical Studies XIII* (Belfast, 1981), pp. 71–4.
93 NRS, B 48/18/140; Hamilton, *House of Hamilton*, p. 375.
94 CCRO, Kimbolton MSS, DDM 70/35.
95 NRS, GD 86/405.
96 CCRO, Kimbolton MSS, DDM 70/35; Simington (ed.), *Civil Survey*, iii, p.385; National Library of Ireland (hereafter NLI), MS 8014/9.
97 Hamilton, *House of Hamilton*, pp. 716–17.
98 PRONI, D 623/B/13/2a.
99 PRONI, D 623/B/13/2B-C; T 808/6461.
100 TNA, SP 46/70/fol. 152.
101 Simington (ed.), *Civil Survey*, iii, pp. 30, 229.
102 W. Fraser, *The Chiefs of Colquhoun and their Country* (2 vols, Edinburgh, 1869), ii, p. 250.
103 PRONI, T 1365.
104 PRONI, T 1365.
105 PRONI, T 1365.

106 W.J. Roulston, *The Parishes of Leckpatrick and Dunnalong* (Letterkenny, 2000), pp. 31–48.

107 J. Hardiman (ed.), *Inquisitionum in officio rotulorum cancellariae Hiberniae asservatorum repertorium* (2 vols, Dublin, 1829), Co.Tyrone (31).

108 Canny, *Making Ireland British*, p. 225.

109 PRONI, T 544/1.

110 PRONI, T 1365.

111 N. Brannon, 'Archives and archaeology: the Ulster plantations in the landscape', in G. Egan and R.L. Michael (eds), *Old and New Worlds* (Oxford, 1999), pp. 97–105; R. Gillespie, 'Material culture and social change in early modern Ireland', in J. Lyttleton and C. Rynne (eds), *Plantation Ireland: Settlement and Material Culture, c.1550-c.1700* (Dublin, 2009), pp. 53–60.

112 A. Horning, R. O Baoill, C. Donnelly and P. Logue (eds), *The Post-Medieval Archaeology of Ireland, 1550–1850* (Dublin, 2007).

113 J.J. O Neill and B. Williams, '"Near unto the bawne": identifying Sir John Hume's village at Tully Castle, County Fermanagh', *Ulster Journal of Archaeology*, 61 (2002), 125–9. For an interesting archaeological study of a Highland Scottish village in east Ulster see A.J. Horning, 'Archaeological explorations of cultural identity and rural economy in the north of Ireland: Goodland, County Antrim', *International Journal of Historical Archaeology*, 8:3 (September 2004), 199–215.

4

Scottish Protestant clergy and the origins of dissent in Ireland

ALAN FORD

'The origins of dissent' is in many respects an old-fashioned title, redolent of the innumerable articles in Victorian Baptist journals with titles like 'Pioneers of Congregationalism'. Such scholarship is readily classifiable: it represents what has been labelled 'vertical history' – the history of a particular church, usually written by an 'insider' 'which has been all about origins, title-deeds, pedigree and descent'.[1] It is a notable feature of those religious traditions that dissented from the established church, since defining and tracing the origins of their distinctiveness and difference from the establishment was an essential part of their self-image. And indeed, this attempt to sort out the roots of Irish dissent, exhuming the names of obscure sectarians who briefly settled in remote places in Ireland in the period after the reformation, will have a whiff of that Victorian style of history.

But this chapter also has three wider, more 'modern' aims. First, to take a slightly perverse chronological perspective, looking not at the obvious ferment, political and religious, of the 1640s and 1650s which, granted, gave birth to Irish nonconformity, but an unfashionably early period in the history of Irish dissent, the later sixteenth and early seventeenth centuries, and the settlement of religion under Elizabeth and the opposition it aroused, prior to the Irish rebellion in 1641 – what might be termed the pre-history of Irish dissent.[2] Second, to place these developments in the context not just of Ireland, but of the three kingdoms and their interaction with Ireland. And finally, to place the origins of Irish dissent not within the pious confines of the vertical history of each sect, but in the horizontal setting of post-reformation piety and religion.

To begin with the broader geographical context: no one would argue that Irish Protestantism was home-grown. The primacy of the English model hardly needs stressing. The reformation was an English import, and remained such for much of its early history in Ireland. The Irish Acts of Uniformity and Supremacy of 1560 were based upon, indeed copied from is more accurate, the Elizabethan legislation in England. And not only the definition of the Protestant establishment, but dissent from it, was, as Miller has observed of the nineteenth century, closely linked to the process of immigration across the Irish sea, each sect focusing its efforts on distinct colonial communities.[3] The 'pre-history' of dissent in England, is, as a result, of primary importance in identifying the sources for dissent in late sixteenth-century and early seventeenth-century Ireland.[4]

Two groups, one tiny, one much larger, can be identified as the ancestors of the later dissenting tradition in England: the separatists and the puritans. The roots of English separatism can be traced back to the Marian martyrs and followed through the later sixteenth century as they rejected the Elizabethan settlement. Separatists' defining characteristics were, of course, a rejection of the all encompassing national Church of England, with its many compromises and contradictions, and a consequent determination to create purer congregations based upon believers and firm biblical principles. The puritan movement can similarly be dated to the early years of Elizabeth's reign, though it remained, by and large, within the confines of the established church, and, apart from those 'hasty' members who chose to separate, continued to advocate a national church. The attempt by English puritans to create Presbyterian structures within the Church of England ended in defeat in the late 1580s. Though Presbyterianism survived, English puritanism subsequently became less concerned with church government than with the creation of godly communities at a parochial level, often with the enthusiastic support of like-minded gentry or civic leaders.[5]

The translation of English dissent across the Irish Sea can be illustrated with apparent straightforwardness by tracing how individual English ministers settled in Ireland. The process of exporting English dissent began soon after the Elizabethan settlement, as puritan ministers, forced out of England, sought refuge in Ireland. The collapse of the English Presbyterian movement saw another influx after 1590, as distinguished English academics and preachers such as Walter Travers, Humphrey Fenn and Henry Alvey, sought to reconstruct their shattered careers in Ireland. Trinity College Dublin, safely tucked away from the gaze of the authorities in England, attracted a number of puritan students from England. The extensive movements of settlers from England to Ireland in the late sixteenth and early seventeenth centuries further facilitated the export not merely of puritan clergy, but also of a number of godly gentry.[6]

English separatists likewise sought refuge in Ireland, especially after the legislation against sectaries and the execution of John Penry and Henry Barrow in 1593. Meredith Hanmer, chancellor of Ossory and noted historian, when listing nonconformist activity in Dublin in the late 1590s distinguished between puritans and sectaries, and preserved a hostile list of separatist beliefs.[7] In 1594 an unnamed separatist in Ireland rejected the established church, 'its public worship, and its ministers, bishops, archbishops', declaring that it was 'in bondage and beareth the yoke of antichrist'.[8] It is possible that the anonymous writer might have been Henry Ainsworth, who, in the early 1590s came to Ireland before moving on to the Netherlands where he was to play such an important role in the exiled English congregation.[9] Colonisation provided further opportunities for dissenters. In 1598, a commentator on the Munster plantation complained at the lack of control over the religious outlook of the Munster settlers, which had resulted in 'Papists, Puritans, Brownists, atheists' settling in the province.[10] A further attempt to found a separatist community in Ireland came in the early 1620s, when a London dissenting minister, with his congregation, settled in Carrickfergus, Co. Antrim. When he died some two years later, however, they returned to England.[11] Another party of separatists from London settled in Antrim in the early 1630s.[12] There is even mention of an English Anabaptist finding refuge in Ireland.[13]

Yet, despite this exchange of personnel, and despite the clear evidence for its external origins, it would nevertheless be wrong to see Irish dissent as simply a mirror image of its English sister. The particular, not to mention peculiar, conditions of Ireland meant that the development of the reformation, after its early legislative plagiarism, subtly diverged from the English model. For a start there is the little matter of the failure of Irish Protestantism to win support. In the face of Catholic strength, Protestant unity became of prime importance. Nonconformists, far from threatening the established church, were welcomed as anti-Catholic evangelists. Sheer pragmatism suggested tolerance. The desperate shortage of protestant preachers in Ireland meant that the church would have been foolish to reject godly ministers who offered their services. There was, as a result, no Irish Whitgift, harrying puritans, driving them from their benefices.

Somewhat surprisingly, there is no evidence that English Presbyterians tried to establish their disciplinary system in Ireland. This was probably largely the result of the timing of their arrival, after the definitive collapse of the movement in England. Thus Walter Travers, when appointed provost of Trinity College, was specifically warned by Archbishop Loftus of Dublin of the dangers of innovation and the need to respect the existing church settlement. Where such immigrants did, however, influence the development of the Irish church was in its theological stance. For when the Irish church finally got round to preparing a detailed confession of faith in 1615, it differed in a number of important respects from the Thirty Nine Articles, with the inclusion of the Lambeth Articles and the identification of the pope as Antichrist marking the Church of Ireland as more clearly Calvinist and firmly anti-Catholic.[14]

The result was that the Irish church was more inclusive than the English. Though individual bishops and visitors, particularly those recently arrived from England, periodically complained about puritan practices, few steps were taken to limit comprehension: there was no subscription in Ireland – no tests to weed out nonconformist ministers at ordination or institution. Such tolerance may well explain the lack in the early seventeenth century of a continuous separatist tradition,[15] and the absence of puritan complaints and Presbyterian classes. English Puritans blended seamlessly into the Calvinist Irish church, resulting in a remarkably homogenous institution.[16]

So far we have only examined two parts of the geographical nexus that gave rise to the Church of Ireland and to Irish dissent, or to be more precise, the absence of Irish dissent. There was, however, a third, strikingly different, model for a reformation ecclesiastical settlement, that of Scotland. Knox and Melville's creation of a reformed kirk founded upon the Bible (as interpreted by Calvin) constituted a standing challenge to the cosy compromises of the Irish ecclesiastical polity. The very name given to the early constitution of the Scottish church – the Book of Discipline, points clearly to the determination to construct from the ground up a Presbyterian style of church government which the godly in England could only envy. At the same time, however, the form and structure of the Scottish church was far from simple or fixed. There was a continuous process of adaptation, development and challenge, as cautious but determined efforts were made by James to impose, on top of this structure, an episcopal system of government. The result was a curious compromise, never without its inherent tensions, with the true locus of authority being disputed both in the church and between church and state, as bishops sought to establish themselves within the system of presbyteries.[17]

The Scottish influence on the development of Protestantism in Ireland in the sixteenth century was largely confined to the presence in Ireland of individual Scots who chose to make their careers there. It is true that that Lord Deputy Sidney had suggested that Gaelic-speaking Scottish ministers should be recruited for work in Ireland, and that John Knox in the 1560s had contact with Archbishop Loftus, and was even invited to come to Ireland to further the reformation there, but generally the presence of Scots clerics in Ireland was much more concerned with the incestuous politics of the three kingdoms than with ecclesiological imperialism.[18] Thus both Denis Cambell, dean of Limerick and, at the time of his death in 1603, bishop-elect of Derry; another minister, Robert Maxwell; and two Scots schoolteachers in Dublin, James Fullerton and James Hamilton, acted as agents for Scottish and, in the case of Campbell, English interests.[19] Such individuals could nevertheless shape the development of institutions. Fullerton, like Hamilton a graduate of Glasgow University, was a friend of the Scottish Presbyterian leader, Andrew Melville, and played a key role in the early years of Trinity College Dublin. Indeed, both settled in Ireland

and Hamilton became a major landowner in Ulster in the early seventeenth century, being made Viscount Clandeboye in 1622.[20]

But the efforts of individual Scots were not backed up by any sizeable Scots Protestant presence in Ireland. For, though there was a significant number of Scots in north-east Ulster, they were predominantly from Highland, Catholic clans. Thus, at the death of Elizabeth, there were 8 English and 10 Irish or Anglo-Irish Church of Ireland bishops, but none from Scotland. What transformed the position of Scots in the Church of Ireland was the immigration of the early seventeenth century, both as part of the official Plantation of Ulster, and in the unofficial plantation of the two closest counties to Scotland, Down and Antrim. This produced a sizeable Scots population of about 14,000 adults, which, crucially, mostly consisted of Lowland Protestants.[21]

The size of the Scottish presence, and its concentration in several key Ulster dioceses, Down and Connor, Clogher and Raphoe, utterly changed the Scots relationship to and role within the Church of Ireland. By the early seventeenth century, it is no longer a matter of tracing the careers of scattered Scots adventurers. Whole parishes were now dominated by Scots settlers, who in turn brought with them Scots clergy. These, in turn, were appointed to benefices in, and served in the Church of Ireland. Thus by 1622, out of 18 clergy in the diocese of Down, 10 were from Scotland, while in Connor 13 out of 21 clergy were Scots. In the diocese of Raphoe on the west coast of Ireland, another centre of Scots settlement, 16 out of 26 clergy were Scottish.[22] Moreover, a Scots King, advised by Scottish courtiers, was much more willing to promote such ministers to positions of influence. The result was already evident by the beginning of Irish convocation in 1613, when there were three Scottish bishops, a number which doubled by the time of the next Convocation in 1634.[23] The impact was greatest where Scottish settlement was densest – in the east of Ulster, nearest to Scotland, particularly in the combined dioceses of Down and Connor. After 1612, three successive Scots were appointed to the see, and as many as two-thirds of the clergy known to be appointed to benefices between 1613 and 1635 were Scots.[24]

What impact did this Scots presence have upon the Church of Ireland? The answer to this is complicated, and far from straightforward, since it represents the confluence of two inherently ambiguous ecclesiastical settlements. The tensions of the Scottish church were exported to Ireland with its clergy and laity, where, in turn, they encountered, and tested to the full, the flexibility of Church of Ireland. The intricacy of this relationship can be seen most simply in terms of personalities and their attitudes. At one extreme were the enthusiastic supporters of episcopacy, men such as Robert Maxwell, appointed archdeacon of Down in 1628, or Henry Leslie, successively a prebendary in Connor in 1619, dean of Down in 1628 and finally bishop of Down and Connor in 1635.[25] The latter, an ally of that staunch Caroline bishop of Ross, John Maxwell, saw his role in Ireland in a similar light to Archbishop Spottiswood in Scotland, as an obedient and enthusiastic servant of his monarch in enforcing conformity.[26] At the other extreme were ministers for whom the changes James imposed upon the Scottish church, and the consequent pressure for their conformity, proved too much, leading them to seek refuge in the laxer climate of Ireland. Edward Brice, an Edinburgh graduate and minister at Dryburn in Stirlling, settled in Ireland in 1613 as curate of Templecorran in Down and Connor, having run foul of Archbishop Spottiswood.[27] Much more significant in the history of Irish dissent was the forceful and eloquent Robert Blair, who, because of his hostility to the Perth Articles of 1618 was forced to resign from his teaching post in Glasgow University, and found employment in Ireland as Vicar of Bangor. In 1624 two ministers in Scotland, George Dunbar and Richard Dickson, who, despite their deprivations for nonconformity had continued to preach, were banished to Ireland. There is no evidence that Dickson ever came to Ireland, but Dunbar became minister at Invermore in 1624 and remained there for ten years.[28] Soon after, Blair, on a visit to Scotland, persuaded Josias Welsh, grandson of John Knox, and firm opponent of prelacy, to join him in Ireland. Another principled emigrant was John Livingstone, educated at Glasgow University under, as he put it in his autobiography, 'the oversight of precious Mr Robert Blair'. Having been 'from my infancy bred with averseness from episcopacy and ceremonies', Livingstone found the Articles of Perth unacceptable.[29] Though called to several parishes, his efforts to secure an appointment were, he felt, blocked by the bishops. After a spell as an itinerant preacher in Scotland, he came to Ireland in 1630 to serve in the parish of Killinchy in the diocese of Down and Connor.[30]

What these ministers were exploiting was the liberality of the Irish church settlement on the issue of conformity which allowed puritans and conformists to co-exist, provided probing questions about issues such as discipline and ceremonies were studiously avoided. The compromises by which these ministers operated in Ireland were vividly described in their autobiographies, and depended upon a conscious exercise in ambiguity. Blair, on his arrival in Ireland, was assured by his patron that, despite his reluctance to submit to 'episcopal government … [or] any part of the English liturgy', there would be no difficulty in securing his admission to the ministry.[31] Indeed, according to Blair's own account he specifically warned the bishop of Down and Connor, Robert Echlin, of his reservations. 'Notwithstanding he was most willing I should be planted there'.[32] With regard to the crucial and sensitive issue of ordination, Echlin, as Blair recounted it, suggested a compromise:

> 'Whatever you account of episcopacy, yet I know you account a presbyter to have divine warrant; will you not receive ordination from Mr Cunningham and

> the adjacent brethren, and let me come in amongst them in no other relation than a presbyter.' This I could not refuse, and so that matter was performed.[33]

According to Livingstone's account, he was advised by his patron not to seek ordination from Bishop Robert Echlin of Down and Connor, who, it was thought, would by this stage require some commitment to conformity of him, but instead to obtain orders from Andrew Knox, the aged Scottish bishop of Raphoe. Knox, according to Livingstone's account, 'gave me the book of ordination, and desired that anything that I scrupled at I should draw a line over it in the margin … but I found that it had been so marked by some others before that I needed not mark anything'.[34]

He then required him to preach a sermon and afterwards joined with three or four other Scottish clergy in the laying on of hands.

The question of ordination is obviously a key one for the Scottish clergy who came over to Ireland. Two ministers, Edward Brice and George Dunbar, and, indeed, Bishop Echlin himself, are known to have been ordained by presbytery in Scotland, and the Irish church seems to have followed the example of the Scottish in accepting their orders as valid.[35] In the case of the vast majority of other ministers, because of their failure to secure a benefice in Scotland and possibly as a result of their concern that their ordination should be linked to their call to ministry, they were not ordained until after their arrival in Ireland.[36] Indeed, of 14 nonconformists in 1634 for whom details of ordination are available, two (Brice and Dunbar) were ordained in Scotland, one in England, while the remaining 11 were ordained by Ulster bishops, nine of them by Echlin.[37]

The vital point to note here, of course, is the possible ambiguity inherent in Blair's ordination. Viewed from the perspective of the bishop, his ordination was, arguably, thoroughly orthodox. It was perfectly normal in the Church of Ireland ordinal for ministers present to join with the bishop in the laying on of hands.[38] Thus the records of the Church of Ireland simply record that Blair was ordained deacon and priest on 10 July 1623 by Echlin.[39] The one piece of damning evidence in Blair's account – that the bishop knew when ordaining him that he was hostile to both episcopacy and the Book of Common Prayer – was flatly contradicted by Echlin in an account he gave of Blair's ordination in 1632.[40] It is therefore possible to claim that, while the ministers believed, with some justification, that they had been presbyterially ordained, Bishop Echlin had equal grounds for portraying his ordination of Blair as conforming to the rites of the established church.[41]

An even more uneasy compromise was arrived at in relation to ecclesiastical discipline. The general ineffectiveness and corruption of the ecclesiastical courts was a serious handicap for the Irish reformation.[42] The episcopal cession of authority to the canon lawyers, even, as in Down and Connor, to the widow of a local landowner, made it extremely difficult to fashion the courts into an effective instrument for moral control.[43] What the Scottish clergy offered was an alternative model, not the product of any overarching diocesan or even synodal authority, but firmly founded upon the parish, based not on canon law and a complex system of fees and fines, but upon the enforcement of a biblically based moral code by Calvinist pastors and locally appointed elders.[44] Livingstone gave a detailed account of the system and its operation in his parish of Killinchy:

> Not only had we the public worship free of any inventions of men, but we had also a tolerable discipline; for after I had been some while amongst them, by the advice of all the heads of families, some ablest for that charge were chosen elders to oversee the manners of the rest, and some deacons to gather and distribute the collection. We met every week, and such as fell in notorious public scandals were desired to come before us. Such as came we dealt with both in public and private, and prevailed with to confess their scandals before the congregation, at the Saturday sermon before the communion, which was twice in the year, and then were admitted to the communion. Such as after dealing either would not come before us, or coming would not be convinced to confess their fault before the congregation, their names, and scandals, and impenitency, was read out before the congregation, and they debarred from the communion, which proved such a terror, that we found very few of that sort.[45]

Given the fact that the Scottish ministers were attempting to create this alternative system like a Trojan horse within the framework of the Church of Ireland, a clash was almost inevitable. The catalyst in Blair's parish was a rich young heir who, resentful at being castigated by the ministers and elders for public scandal, appealed to the bishop 'whereby the order of that discipline was broken'.[46] Unsurprisingly, the effort to introduce Presbyterian discipline from below into the established church failed in Ireland in the 1620s, just as it had in England in the 1580s: without the combined support of the civil and ecclesiastical authorities discipline was just too easy to evade, as the 'young heir' demonstrated.

It will already be apparent that the crucial intermediaries, who enabled the Scots to be incorporated within the framework of the established church, were the local landlords and the Scottish bishops. Just as in England, where the gentry had been crucial in sustaining puritanism at a parish level, so too in Down and Connor, it was the Scots and English settlers that played a similar supporting role. Four distinct elements combined to enhance the ecclesiastical influence of the leading settlers. First, the distance of north-east Ulster from Dublin and London meant that, especially in the first two decades of the plantation, official interference, even interest, in the functioning of the church in Down and Connor was limited. Second, the power of patronage was concentrated in lay hands. In some Ulster dioceses, as, for example, in Kilmore, most of the benefices were collative – in the presentation of the bishop.[47] But in Down and Connor 65 out of the 75 livings listed in the 1634 visitation were in lay hands.[48] Moreover, as the settlers built up and consolidated their landholdings, by fair means and foul, they included in their predations church livings, swallowing up the income from benefices, replacing independently endowed vicars and rectors with dependent curates.[49] Finally, having acquired this influence over the church, a significant section of the landholders were not averse to using it to secure employment for nonconformist ministers. Here we again encounter James Hamilton, now Viscount Clandeboye. It was he, according to the ministers' own accounts, who actively sought out Blair and Livingstone in Scotland, invited them to serve in Ireland, secured the ordination of Blair by Echlin and pointed Livingstone in the direction of Knox.[50] Indeed, Clandeboye is known to have been the patron of at least seven nonconformist Scots clergy in Down and Connor, including his own nephew, James.[51] Other nonconformist clergy found similar support from the planters. James Montgomery presented his namesake (a relative by marriage of his wife) to Grey Abbey in 1633.[52] William Edmonston, another Scots planter, presented Edward Brice to Kilroot in 1613. And, as Scots settlers attracted Scots Presbyterian clergy, so English settlers were associated with English puritans: Sir Arthur Chichester, the former Lord Deputy, presented John Ridge to Antrim; Robert Langford presented Henry Calvert to Muckamore; and Josias Welsh was first employed in Ireland as a household chaplain to the Welsh settler, Humphrey Norton.[53] Nor were the ministers limited to local patrons. John Bole or Boyle, a blind Scots nonconformist cleric whom Clandeboye presented to four rectories in Down, also looked to the Earl of Cork, one of the lords justices, for support.[54]

One respected authority has suggested that there was a puritan network of prominent English settlers, including Chichester, the Clotworthys and Nortons, that was based upon Carrickfergus and S. Antrim.[55] There is no doubt that Carrickfergus had always been a bastion of Protestantism in Ulster, but it would be wrong make too firm a connection between the views of the clergy and those of their patrons. The Clotworthys were indeed firmly puritan, even Presbyterian, in their sympathies, but they possessed hardly any patronage in the diocese. Though Chichester and Clandeboye were clearly sympathetic to nonconformist clergy – quite possibly a product of their backgrounds– neither can be described themselves as nonconformist.[56]

There is, it is true, a more pragmatic approach to the landlords' support for such clergy. Bramhall in 1634 thought that patrons of nonconformist ministers were concerned solely with the plantation of their lands, 'and that work being done, are indifferent … what becomes of them'.[57] Though acknowledging that it might seem rather cynical, John McCafferty has followed this approach, suggesting that the émigré clergy were seen as cheap labour, a way to supply the cures while allowing the patrons to enjoy most of the benefices' income.[58] The reality was probably less simple and more mixed. Blair acknowledges that he had differences with his patron, who did not share his detestation of kneeling at communion, and Clandeboye in the later 1630s proved willing to cooperate with the authorities in weeding out non-conformity in Down and Connor.[59] At the same time, however, Clandeboye also proved willing to shelter non-conformist ministers from the authorities in his own home.[60] This Janus-like quality was passed on to his son, who succeeded in 1643, and was described by the family historian thus: 'His education and conversation inclined him to be episcopal; but he was therein very moderate, and paid a great respect to all good persons, and was in his practice Presbyterian'.[61]

At the centre of this network of ambivalence was, of course, the bishop, Robert Echlin. Early in his episcopate, safe from the gaze of the authorities in Dublin and London, he seems to have been prepared to go to considerable lengths to accommodate Scots ministers. When, in 1632, he had to explain to the Dublin authorities why he had allowed Blair, Livingstone, Dunbar and Welsh to minister in his diocese, he lamely and revealingly claimed that he had restricted them to curacies, had only permitted them to continue to preach because he had hope of their conformity, and that they were, besides, attracting considerable audiences.[62] Certainly the accounts of Echlin's personality by nonconformist clergy do not suggest that he was seen as strict by choice, but rather that he would take the easiest course open to him. In the eyes of John Ridge, the English puritan minister at Antrim, Echlin was 'not malicious, yet willing to strike all rather than to adventure himself to a blow'.[63] This judgement was shared by one of his episcopalian colleagues: though far from the nonconformists doctrinally, 'yet he is of so timorous a disposition that he is loath to take upon him the envy of the people'.[64]

Presiding over this curious compromise was James Ussher, the Irish-born archbishop of Armagh. Ussher's chief modern biographer has sought to dissociate the primate from any hint of collusion with the Presbyterian ordinations, determinedly showing that Ussher was a firm 'Anglican'.[65] Nonconformists, however, have repeatedly sought to enlist Ussher as a sympathetic supporter.[66] Thus Blair gives a pointed account of his amicable discussions with the primate in his palace at Drogheda.[67] Baxter nostalgically placed Ussher amongst the 'Old Episcopal Divines', who were flexible on the subject of ordination by presbyters rather than bishops, in marked contrast to the 'new episcopal divines', such as Bramhall and Laud who 'unchurch those churches that are not prelatical'.[68] Ussher's willingness in the early 1640s, when parliament was threatening the very basis of the English ecclesiastical settlement, to consider, in *The reduction of episcopacy,* a disciplinary system which merged bishops and ministers in a 'kind of presbyterial government' appears to lend support to Blair's and Baxter's judgements.[69] But John

McCafferty has warned against accepting Blair's and Livingstone's accounts as gospel: they were written many years after the events and, he argues, see Ireland in the 1630s through a warm retrospective glow with Ussher as a Calvinist saint. Ussher, he claims, was little different from an English Jacobean bishop, marking Blair's cards whilst espousing a minimal conformity.[70]

These views of Ussher, however, miss the key point–that he was the architect of a particularly Irish compromise which allowed Presbyterians such as Blair and Livingstone to operate within the confines of the Church of Ireland. Ussher was neither an Anglican–use of that term in relation to the English, let alone the Irish, church in the early seventeenth century is anachronistic–nor was he a Presbyterian fellow-traveller. He was instead a stout defender of the Church of Ireland's distinctive ecclesiastical settlement, including its reluctance to impose subscription on ministers, but was at the same time utterly loyal to its supreme governor and deeply respectful of the power of the king and his ministers.[71] So long as those ministers remained ignorant of the compromises practised in Down and Connor, Ussher felt no need to act against the Presbyterian clergy.

What forced Ussher and Echlin to confront the issue of nonconformity in the 1630s was the determination of Henry Leslie to bring the aberrations in the diocese to the attention of the king's ministers, not just in Dublin but in London, and the increasing desire of those authorities to abandon the ecclesiastical *modus vivendi* of the early seventeenth century in favour of much closer conformity with the English religious settlement. Leslie had shrewdly attached himself to the rising star of that 'new episcopal divine', William Laud, bishop of London.[72] In 1631 he formally complained about the activities of Blair and Livingstone to the lords justices in Dublin telling them how he had expostulated with Echlin and Clandeboye 'for winking at this disorder, protesting that I would complain to the state and procure a certificate of their irregularities to be transmitted unto England'. Leslie ensured that action was taken against the ministers through civil courts with the help of Sir Richard Bolton, Chief Baron of the Exchequer, and a firm opponent of nonconformity.[73] This finally forced Echlin's hand, and he suspended Blair, Livingstone, Welsh and George Dunbar.

The ministers, rather shocked at the sudden move after enjoying their 'full liberty' for so long, responded in two ways: first they looked at the possibility of compromise – faced with the traditional puritan dilemma of abandoning their principles or their flock, they hoped 'that some small thing (small in respect of the whole course of conformity) would, at least for a while, give content'.[74] Second, they sought to mobilize as much support as they could to press the authorities to let the matter drop. Appeal to Archbishop Ussher unsurprisingly secured a brief remission.[75] But Leslie kept up the pressure and in May 1632 the ministers were sentenced to be deprived.[76] At this point the focus shifted to the English court. The ministers could call on their considerable and powerful Scottish connections, and Blair himself went to court and secured a letter from the king which, while not favourable, was not hostile either, referring the dispute to the Irish lords justices for adjudication.[77]

The evil day was, by various shifts, postponed until 1634, but in that year the very nature of conformity, and the disciplinary framework of the Church of Ireland was fundamentally changed, as the new lord deputy, Thomas Wentworth, acting on the advice of his ally William Laud, Archbishop of Canterbury, imposed his will on the church. Sweeping aside the reservations of Ussher and other Irish churchmen, Wentworth ensured that Convocation in 1634 in effect replaced the Irish Articles by the English, and for the first time imposed a set of Canons, based upon those of 1604 in England, upon the Irish church. The result was that clergy had for the first time to subscribe to the Thirty-Nine Articles and the Book of Common Prayer.[78] Consequently the bishops of the Church of Ireland, urged on by Wentworth and Laud, finally were equipped with the essential weapons with which they could fight nonconformity. These weapons were indeed used in Down and Connor. Wentworth commanded the bishop to order the recalcitrant ministers to conform by 1 November, trying in the meantime to convince them by personal conference.[79] A regal visitation of the diocese in 1634, led by Bramhall, identified 20 nonconformist ministers, and five preaching schoolmasters. Some of these, Bramhall hoped, might submit, but others he categorised as 'desperate nonconformists'.[80] Over the next seven years the persistent nonconformists were deprived and even driven out from Ireland, most of them returning to Scotland.[81] Their chief persecutor was Henry Leslie, who, when Echlin died in 1635, was the obvious royal choice to succeed him.[82]

Recent analyses of Wentworth and Bramhall's Ulster policy have claimed that by the middle of 1637, they 'had been largely successful in their campaign against the ministers in Down and Connor, and were in a position to bring pressure to bear on nonconforming laymen'; and that the Church of Ireland succeeded in attracting back the mass of their parishioners following the expulsion of the ministers.[83] In institutional terms, this may be true. But looking beyond the institutional history of who was dismissed when, to the broader history of popular Protestant piety, there is little evidence that the established church quickly regained the loyalty of its nominal parishioners.

The Scots clergy, then, contributed something of major importance not just to the history of dissent in Ireland, but also to the broader tradition of Protestant religiosity, and, more specifically to the way in which reformed theology was related in Ireland to religious feeling and practice. Recent work on the impact of the reformation in England has resulted in a radical reappraisal of the power and coherence of pre-reformation piety. This has been a valuable corrective to the Foxean tradition of English religious history which, in the light of this research, now appears to have been overly dismissive of the popular appeal of Catholicism.[84] However, this reappraisal has been achieved at the expense of a certain imbalance. As the full richness of Catholic piety has emerged, with its fusion of sight and sound, this world and the next, the living and the dead in a warm, all-enveloping communal religion, Protestantism has tended to be defined antithetically, as a word-based, bibliocentric, iconoclastic individualistic piety associated with a cold self-analytical intellectualism. Taken to extremes, such an approach makes it difficult to explain the mass acceptance of Protestantism as anything other than an imposition by the state upon an unwilling populace.

The wider significance of the events in Down and Connor in the early seventeenth century is that they offer the first insight into the nature and development of popular Protestantism in Ireland. For one point which repeatedly emerges from the accounts of both conformists and their opponents in Down and Connor is that the Scots clergy won considerable local support and esteem, and created a powerful sense of shared communal piety. Blair records his ceaseless round of preaching, catechism, instruction and prayer and the positive response from the 1,200 adults in his parish.[85] When Livingstone arrived in 1630 he was initially worried about his lack of pastoral impact.[86] But he soon encountered the popular enthusiasm for the gospel, concluding that 'I do not think there were more lively and experienced Christians any where than were these at that time in Ireland, and that in good numbers'.[87]

Ridge, as an Englishman, viewed the matter from the perspective of a sympathetic outsider, yet, writing to a fellow puritan in Oxfordshire, he came to a similarly positive conclusion:

> Round about there are divers Scottish ministers that Scotland would not bear because of their nonconformity … These are such men for strict walking and abundant pains with their people Sabbath day, week days, in church and from house to house that I have never … known of any more heavenly in their conversation or more laborious in their ministry, and unto this they have a very sweet encouragement, for the Lord hath exceedingly blessed their labours for they have brought a great number of people for 20 miles about them to as great a measure of knowledge and zeal in every good duty, as, I think, is to be found again in any part of Christendom … Their congregations are some 7 or 800, some 1000, some 1,500, some more some less …

Moreover, the public efforts of the clergy had their effect within the community: Ridge specifically commented how 'the people have a notable commerce one with another, people with people, family with family, one private Christian with others, and being thus constant in their fervency and spiritual trading, the work comes on mightily among them'.[88]

These sources are, of course, self-serving, part of a familiar puritan genre, painting a heroic picture of the labours of the godly saints. But Leslie, not a friendly witness, also noted the boundless popular enthusiasm for the Scots ministers.[89] Indeed, even after their expulsion, he conceded that he was facing an uphill struggle in reclaiming his flock. He was, he confessed in 1636, amazed at their continued following amongst the people–'for every one of these presbyteriall dictators is more esteemed than the whole church of God'–and rather plaintively noted that, despite his efforts to root out their nonconformist zeal, 'as yet I have not found either my pains of my prayers to be so effectual.[90] Even in 1638 he was still complaining about 'both … the clergy and the laity, for their general non-conformity, and disobedience unto the orders of this church'.[91] A final confirmation of the depth and persistence of the community support for the Presbyterian clergy came in the early 1640s, when, after the fall of the Wentworth regime, the Scots in Ulster began sending plaintive petitions to their brethren in Scotland lamenting the loss of the 'fruitful and peaceable ministry of the gospel', 'chased into Scotland' by the 'tyranny of the prelates'. They asked for them to be sent back so that 'they might perfect what they had begun', since, despite the efforts of the prelates, 'our interest in them could not be taken away'.[92]

Indeed it is quite clear that the ministry of the Scots clergy gained more than support and esteem, it aroused mass enthusiasm. Their efforts created in 1626 the first recorded example of what was to become a notable feature of Scottish, Scots-Irish and, in due course, American religious culture–the popular revival, that organised movement of religious enthusiasm that culminated in the Great Awakening of the eighteenth century.[93] Blair and Livingstone give a meticulous account of the origins of the revival. Founded upon the two main marks of Calvin's church: the preaching of the gospel and the administration of the sacraments, it began in the valley of the Six Mile Water in southern Antrim, the initial impetus coming from James Glendinning, a Scots minister delicately poised on the boundary between enthusiasm and madness (he was convinced that those who turned in their sleep could not be faithful Christians, and eventually left Ireland to visit the seven churches of Asia).[94] Glendinning's approach was that of an Old Testament preacher–'having a great voice and vehement delivery, he roused up the people, and wakened them with terrors'.[95] His exclusive concentration upon the misery and sinfulness of the people, and his apparent inability to preach the gospel of salvation, aroused concern in his fellow ministers, who attempted to assuage the fears that Glendinning had aroused. John Ridge, the English minister at Antrim proposed that the ministers in the Six Mile Water valley combine to provide a monthly lecture at the main town, Antrim. The result was four sermons on a set day each month in summer, three in winter, preached by Ridge, Robert Cunningham, James Hamilton and Blair. Supported by the local landlord, Sir

Hugh Clotworthy, the monthly meetings were, Ridge claimed, 'constantly kept and greatly frequented'– with 1,000 or 1,500 people flocking there even from beyond Down and Connor.[96] In the early 1630s, 'the perpetual fear that the bishop would put away their ministers' merely heightened the people's 'great hunger' for such preaching.[97]

The essential appendage to the gospel was, of course the sacrament of the Lord's supper. In Down and Connor the popular impact of joint preaching was strengthened by the remarkable development of a form of cooperative communion. The ministers generally celebrated the Lord's supper but four times a year in their parish, a marked declension from Calvin's original vain hope of weekly communion in Geneva. But the concentration of Scottish settlers and ministers in southern Antrim and north Down enabled them to time each parish communion so that they could be jointly celebrated by all the surrounding parishes, thus increasing both frequency and attendance.[98] Such were the numbers attending that two sittings of communion had to be arranged in the church. Ridge spoke of 'seventeen or eighteen tables a day, each table taking about an hundred people'. Moreover, since people travelled such distances, they stayed overnight, thus offering the zealous clergy the opportunity of both preparing them for communion and further instructing them afterwards. People arrived on a Saturday to hear the evening sermon, spent much of the night in conference and prayer with the clergy attending, then heard another sermon together with communion on the Sunday, followed by a further sermon on Sunday evening, with time to take in a 'special exhortation' on the Monday before their departure. Livingstone, the ever-optimistic preacher, claims that they left untroubled by tiredness despite their having scarcely slept.[99]

This intense activity from 1625 to 1632, the first documented evangelical revival in Ireland, has many fascinating features. Theologically it represents a fusion of two elements of the reformation which are often seen as contradictory: word and sacrament. Ever since Weber pointed out that 'every consistent doctrine of predestined grace inevitably implied a radical and ultimate devaluation of all magical, sacramental and institutional distributions of grace', historians have tended to assume that the impact of Calvinism in Britain and Ireland was associated with a downgrading of the sacraments, in particular communion.[100] The grace of the word trumped that of the Lord's supper, leaving the latter as an occasional appendage to the centrepiece of the sermon. The revivalists' approach challenges this eminently challengeable assumption and shows that Calvinist piety, following Calvin's own preference for weekly communion, could accommodate, indeed integrate both preaching and the Lord's supper and enact the reformer's vision of the sacrament as an expression of ecclesial community.[101]

Ecclesiologically the revival was a product of complex fusion of Scottish, English and Irish influences, and represents in fascinating fashion the collision of the three different ecclesiastical polities. The way in which the Scottish church exported its inherent tensions to Ireland has already been mentioned, and it is impossible not to see the revival in terms of Scottish church politics. The Ulster ministers can be identified with the 'privy kirk' tradition, a dissenting group within Scottish Presbyterianism, and the revival in Ireland was linked to a similar one in the equally radical south-west of Scotland.[102] Support for the Ulster revival came overwhelmingly from Scots settlers and their Scots landlords. After Wentworth and Leslie suppressed it, the ministers, and even some of their congregations, moved back to Scotland, where they played prominent roles in the covenanting revolution.[103] At the same time, however, one must not forget the role of the English clergy and their parishioners. It was, after all, Ridge who had proposed the establishment of that typical English godly solution to a lack of preaching–the monthly lecture 'by combination'.[104] And as Ridge noted, there were tensions between the Scots and English ministers over the manner of receiving the Lord's supper.[105] Indeed so separate were the English clergy that Josias Welsh reported in triumph in 1632 when Ridge's congregation agreed to take communion sitting rather than kneeling.[106] Finally, one has to note again the capacity of the Irish church to absorb in the early seventeenth century the Scottish clergy, to provide a flexible enough framework for such an experiment to be conducted. Whether or not this ecclesiological structure offered a genuine alternative to those in Scotland and England is open to debate. On the one hand, as early as 1623, the archbishop of Armagh, Christopher Hampton, had complained about the Scots in Down 'entertaining the Scottish discipline and liturgy so strongly, that they offer wrong to the church government here established'.[107] On the other hand, his successor, James Ussher, showed little inclination to act against nonconformity.[108]

The revival also illustrated graphically the fundamental clash between enthusiasm and institutional structures. It broke free from the institutional restraints of the parish system and the liturgical, disciplinary and ceremonial requirements of the established church. The loosely structured Presbyterian church that transcended traditional boundaries was seen by the ministers themselves as a remarkable evangelical achievement, harnessing enthusiasm to a scripturally based vision of the unity of word and sacrament. It looked forward to the way in which the second wave of formally Presbyterian churches after 1642 would embed themselves in Ulster society through their powerful combination of 'a puritan vision to transform society with a voluntarist dynamic of participation'.[109]

Like all revivals, it was not without its challenges. By their own account, the clergy struggled repeatedly to ensure that popular enthusiasm did not slip into heresy or delusion, seeking to distinguish true from false faith, the work of the lord from the counterfeiting of the devil.[110] And, of course, for defenders of the structures of the Church of Ireland, however, the enthusiasm was simply out of control, crossing the border into fanaticism and mass hysteria. As Leslie reported in 1632, the popular frenzies had been excited by

> a new piece of divinity that no man can be converted unless he feels the pains of his new birth such as St Paul felt. So that every sermon, 40 or so people, for most part women, fall down in the church in a trance … grievously afflicted with convulsions, trembling … After they awake they confess that they have seen devils … [111]

Leslie, while bearing witness to the strength of the revival's hold on the people, repeatedly stressed its dangerous and unstable nature, as shown by the excessive support that the Scots ministers received from women 'in whom there is least ability of judgement'. It was, he noted, 'by this means the serpent overcame mankind'.[112] Hence his horrified cry, not untypical of establishments when faced with enthusiasm: 'If these things go on, God knows what shall become of our church'.[113]

The pre-history of dissent in Ireland is not, therefore, simple. There lurked within the Church of Ireland in the early seventeenth century multiple possibilities, the product of the interplay between the three kingdoms and their different but related religious settlements, and of the flexible way that the Irish church assimilated the English and Scots influences. Historians, as a result, have argued about the precise nature of the peculiar arrangements in eastern Ulster and the extent to which they represent the beginnings of Irish Presbyterianism. As far as most 'vertical' Presbyterian historians are concerned, Blair, Livingstone and their fellow Scots were indeed the first Presbyterian ministers in Ireland. At the other extreme, John McCafferty has warned against swallowing the retrospective special pleading of Blair and Livingstone in their memoirs, and assuming that the enthusiastic participants in the Six Mile Water revival were either Presbyterian or even proto-Presbyterian, and suggested that the toleration extended to them in Ireland was little different to the way in which bishops in England insisted on minimal conformity.[114] The reality probably lies somewhere in between these extremes. Though the Scots clergy clearly *sought* to exercise discipline, they, according to their own account, had to compromise, leading to the conclusion that 'properly', they 'were nonconformists rather than Presbyterians'.[115] Yet they were nonconformists decidedly within an established church. And they were accommodated in a very different way to puritans in England who ultimately always faced the legal threats of subscription and the 1604 canons. In Ireland there were no such requirements, and, so long as Ussher was in effective control of the Irish church, there was little enthusiasm for stricter discipline, as he sought rather to build up a Calvinist ministry united against the pervasive threat of Catholicism.

The intervention of Wentworth, Laud and Bramhall decisively ended the Irish attempt to develop the distinctive ecclesiology, as they drove out the Scots clergy and imposed English-style canons. When Bramhall set out to reconstruct the Church of Ireland after the restoration he was determined to ensure that there should be no repetition of the earlier flexibility and ambiguity. Presbyterian ministers as a result now had to be re-ordained if they wished to serve in the Church of Ireland.[116] The boundaries of conformity had been firmly and much more narrowly defined.

But the events of Down and Connor, and the quieter work of godly ministers elsewhere in Ireland, are of wider significance than just an abortive ecclesiological experiment. They provide us with the first clear evidence of Protestant religiosity in Ireland: the first time that we can look beyond the bounds of official formularies and examine the practical experience of Protestantism amongst the laity. We have in Down and Connor in the 1620s and 1630s the first example of Protestant religious enthusiasm. Given the rather austere picture of puritan piety, and, indeed, of Protestant piety that has recently been painted, it is important to note that this manifestation was far from individualistic and had, apparently made the transition from Calvinist theology into a popular religion, which, like Catholicism, appealed to a significant, though racially distinct, section of the population. Indeed, it is ironic that the revival's main feature, the three-day eucharistic festival, can be seen as a Protestant refashioning of key elements in traditional Catholic public piety–feasts, processions, and enthusiastic eucharistic religiosity–which were normally condemned by reformers.[117] As one perceptive commentator has put it: 'popular festivity centring on the sacrament was rehabilitated and maintained in reformed guise'.[118]

Whether this evidence of a vital popular piety was inevitably to be associated with dissent–whether, in short, such enthusiasm could only operate outside the bounds of the established church–is a difficult question to answer. One must be cautious about coming to judgements about the piety of moderate prayer-book Anglicanism within the Church of Ireland. By its very orthodoxy it removed itself from surviving records: few complain about moderation. Here too one needs to differentiate between the assumptions and approaches of the various national groups that we have identified within the Church of Ireland. As far as the English puritans in Ireland were concerned, it would probably be wrong to identify them as a 'fringe' group. They did not see themselves as separatists but as essential members of the national church: indeed, in their own eyes, and in the eyes of some historians, they constituted little less than the evangelical wing of the reformation. Ridge's image of the puritan's relationship to the rest of the Church of Ireland is conveyed in the story he tells approvingly about a conversation in which a leading Catholic told an Ulster Protestant that 'were I to change my religion and become a protestant, I should be of you puritans, for the rest among you are of no religion'.[119]

The position of the Scottish ministers is more difficult to define. Viewed proleptically, with the knowledge both of what they went on to do in Scotland, and of how Bramhall was to redefine conformity in the 1630s and at the restoration, they were beyond the pale of the Church of Ireland. Seen from this perspective, Edward Brice was indeed, as Adair claims, the first Presbyterian minister in Ireland. The vertical history of the dissenting churches thus begins in 1634, with the narrowing of the confines of the established church. But one must not forget the complex reality of the Irish context within which these various groups operated. Edward Brice was also, it must be remembered, collated in 1619 by Bishop Echlin to the prebend of Kilroot in the Church of Ireland, and served that church in all for 23 years, through repeated triennial visitations by an archbishop who had a principled commitment to the distinctive polity of the Church of Ireland. Looked at from this Irish perspective, the pre-history of Irish dissent consists, not of clear lines of descent that can be traced through from the Elizabethan settlement, as in England, but in a broadly based Church of Ireland which, partly through amnesia and carelessness, partly through the principled construction of a tolerant framework, managed the remarkable feat of holding together for two decades the disparate strands of Protestantism which it had imported from England and Scotland in a peculiarly Irish compromise.

NOTES

1 P. Collinson, 'The vertical and the horizontal in religious history: internal and external integration of the subject', in A. Ford, J. McGuire and K. Milne (eds), *As By Law Established. The Church of Ireland since the Reformation* (Dublin, 1995), p. 18; see also P. Collinson, 'Towards a broader understanding of the early dissenter tradition', in P. Collinson, *Godly People: Essays on English Protestantism and Puritanism* (London, 1983).

2 For the most recent and thorough treatment of the emergence of Ulster Presbyterianism in the 1640s, see R. Armstrong, 'Ireland's puritan revolution? The emergence of Ulster Presbyterianism reconsidered', *English Historical Review*, 121:493 (2006), 1048–74.

3 D.W. Miller, 'Presbyterianism and "modernization" in Ulster', *Past & Present*, 80 (1978), 73.

4 For the concept of pre-history see B.R. White, *The English Separatist Tradition: from the Marian Martyrs to the Pilgrim Fathers* (Oxford, 1971), p. xii; Collinson, 'Early dissenter tradition', pp. 527–8.

5 P. Collinson, *The Elizabethan Puritan Movement* (London, 1967); P.G. Lake, *Moderate Puritans and the Elizabethan Church* (Cambridge, 1982); for the survival

of Presbyterianism, see P. Ha, 'English Presbyteriansim, c. 1590–1640', PhD dissertation, University of Cambridge, 2006.

6 For a detailed treatment of English puritanism in Ireland, see A. Ford, 'The Church of Ireland, 1558–1634: a Puritan church?', in Ford, McGuire and Milne (eds), *As by Law Established*, pp. 52–68; A. Ford, *James Ussher: Theology, History, and Politics in Early-Modern Ireland and England* (Oxford, 2007), pp. 22–5, 41–55.

7 TNA, SP/214/36, fols 214r, 216r.

8 H. Barrow, *Mr. H. Barrows Platform. Which may serve as a preparation to purge away prelatism* ([London], [1611]), sig. [C6v].

9 M.E. Moody, 'Ainsworth, Henry (1569–1622)', *ONDB*, www.oxforddnb.com/view/article/240, accessed 27 August 2009; H.M. Dexter, *The Congregationalism of the Last Three Hundred Years, as seen in its Literature* (New York, 1880), pp. 270, 364; C. Burrage, *The Early English Dissenters in the Light of Recent Research (1550–1641)* (2 vols, Cambridge, 1912), i, p. 187; White, *English Separatist Tradition*, pp. 98–9, 113–15, 127–9, 142–55.

10 M. MacCarthy-Morrough, *The Munster Plantation: English Migration to Southern Ireland 1583–1641* (Oxford, 1986), p. 198.

11 J.S. Reid, *History of the Presbyterian Church in Ireland*, ed. W.D. Killen (3 vols, Belfast, 1867), i, p. 122; Samuel M'Skimin, *The History and Antiquities ... of Carrickfergus* (Belfast, 1823), p. 248; D. Neal, *The History of the Puritans* (5 vols, London, 1754), i, p. 474; Dexter, *Congregationalism*, p. 648 n. 97; Burrage, *Early English Dissenters*, i, p. 201, ii, pp. 305–6; M. Tolmie, *The Triumph of the Saints* (London, 1977), p. 37.

12 Reid, *Presbyterian church*, i, p. 128f.; W. Row (ed.), *The Life of Mr Robert Blair, Minister of St Andrews, Containing his Autobiography, from 1593 to 1636* (s.l., 1848), pp. 83–4.

13 A. Wood, *Athenae Oxoniensis*, ed. Philip Bliss (5 vols, London 1813–15), iii, 1067; A.G. Matthews (ed.), *Calamy revised* (Oxford, 1988), p.468; HMC, *Report on the Manuscripts of the Late Reginald Rawdon Hastings, esq.* (4 vols, London, 1928–47), iv, p. 73.

14 R.B. Knox, 'The ecclesiastical policy of James Ussher, Archbishop of Armagh', PhD dissertation, London University, 1956, pp. 69–95; R.B. Knox, *James Ussher Archbishop of Armagh* (Cardiff, 1967), pp. 16–19; A. Ford, *The Protestant Reformation in Ireland, 1590–1641* (Frankfurt, 1987), pp. 194–201; Ford, *Ussher: Theology, History, and Politics*, chapter 4.

15 It was in fact subsequently alleged that Ainsworth, while in Ireland, had conformed to the Church of Ireland: J. Paget, *An Arrow against the Separation of the Brownists* (Amsterdam, 1618), pp. 92–3.

16 Ford, *Ussher: Theology, History, and Politics*, pp. 52–5.

17 G. Donaldson, *The Faith of the Scots* (London, 1990); W.R. Foster, *The Church before the Covenants: The Church of Scotland 1596–1638* (Edinburgh, 1975); I.B. Cowan, *The Scottish Reformation: Church and Society in Sixteenth Century Scotland* (London, 1982).

18 A. Collins (ed.), *Letters and Memorials of State in the Reigns of Queen Mary, Part of the reign of King Charles the Second and Oliver's Usurpation* (2 vols, London, 1746), i, p. 113; J. Dawson and L.K.J. Glassey (eds), 'Some unpublished letters from

John Knox to Christopher Goodman', *Scottish Historical Review*, 84:218 (2005), 166–201.

19 HMC, *Salisbury MSS* (23 vols, London, 1888–1973), xv, p. 64; M. Perceval-Maxwell, *The Scottish Migration to Ulster in the Reign of James I* (London, 1990), p. 2; D. Edwards, 'Securing the Jacobean succession: the secret career of James Fullerton of Trinity College, Dublin', in S. Duffy (ed.), *The World of the Galloglass: Kings, Warlords and Warriors in Ireland and Scotland, 1200–1600* (Dublin 2007), pp. 188–219.

20 J. Durkan and J. Kirk, *The University of Glasgow 1451–1577* (Glasgow, 1977), pp. 304, 353, 381, 383.

21 Perceval-Maxwell, *The Scottish Migration*, pp. 289, 250f; R. Gillespie, *Colonial Ulster: the Settlement of East Ulster, 1600–1641* (Cork, 1985), pp. 50–3.

22 TCD, MSS 1067; Perceval-Maxwell, *The Scottish Migration*, app. F.

23 1613: Montgomery, Echlin, Knox; 1634: Spottiswood, Echlin, Leslie, Hamilton, Heygate, Adair; T.W. Moody, F.X. Martin and F.J. Byrne (eds), *A New History of Ireland: Maps, Genealogies, Lists.* (9 vols, Oxford, 1984), ix, pp. 393–438.

24 S.A. Millsop, 'The state of the church in the diocese of Down and Connor during the episcopate of Robert Echlin 1613–35', MA dissertation, Queens' University Belfast, 1979, pp. 275–6.

25 J. Leslie, *A Treatise of the Authority of the Church* (Dublin, 1637), sig. **4r.

26 C. Diamond, 'Leslie, Henry (1580–1661)', *ODNB* http://www.oxforddnb.com/view/article/16491, accessed 2 September 2009; TNA, SP 63/252/121 fols 235r–236r *CSPI, 1625–32*, p. 629; Row (ed.), *Life of Blair*, p. 90.

27 He was one of only two ministers to oppose Spottiswood's nomination as permanent moderator of the synod of Clydesdale, and subsequently was charged with adultery. He is rather inaccurately termed the 'first presbyterian minister in Ireland': P. Adair, *A True Narrative of the Rise and Progress of the Presbyterian Church in Ireland 1623–70*, ed. W.D. Killen (Belfast, 1866), p. 1; Representative Church Body Library, Dublin, J.B.Leslie, 'Connor clergy', p. 55; D. Laing (ed.), *Original Letters Relating to the Ecclesiastical Affairs of Scotland* (2 vols, Edinburgh, 1851), i, p. 105; Perceval-Maxwell, *The Scottish Migration*, p. 269.

28 Laing (ed.), *Original Letters*, ii, pp. 762, 766–7; Row (ed), *Life of Blair*, pp. 75f.; Adair, *A True Narrative*, p. 21; G.I.R. McMahon, 'The Scottish courts of High Commission 1610–38', *Records of the Scottish Church History Society*, 15 (1966), 200–1.

29 'The life of Mr John Livingstone, minister of the gospel', in W.K. Tweedie (ed.), *Select Biographies* (Edinburgh, 1847), pp. 129–33; McMahon, 'High Commmission', p. 200.

30 Tweedie (ed.), *Select Biographies*, pp. 134–5.

31 Row (ed.), *Life of Blair*, pp. 51, 54.

32 *Ibid.*, p. 58.

33 *Ibid.*, p. 59.

34 Tweedie (ed.), *Select Biographies*, p. 141.

35 TCD, MS 1067, p. 95; a further two ministers were probably ordained in Scotland: Andrew Stewart and James Glendinning: J.T. Barkley, *A Short History of the Presbyterian Church in Ireland* (Belfast, 1959), p. 4; J. M. Barkley, 'Some Scottish

bishops and ministers in the Irish church, 1605–35', in D. Shaw (ed.), *Reformation and Revolution: Essays Presented to … Hugh Watt* (Edinburgh, 1967), p. 143.
36 Ford, *Ussher: Theology, History, and Politics*, pp. 167–9.
37 Sheffield City Library (hereafter SCL), Wentworth Woodhouse Muniments (hereafter WWM) Str. P. 20/179; TCD, MS 1067, pp. 88–105.
38 Knox, *James Ussher*, p. 180.
39 TCD, MS 1034, pp. 100–1.
40 TNA, SP 63/253/2116 (*CSPI, 1625–32*, pp. 661–2).
41 The apparently crucial issue of whether or not the Prayer Book had been followed is not decisive: it was not until 1634 that the Church of Ireland had a canon which forbade adding to or subtracting from the prescribed liturgy.
42 A. Ford, 'The reformation in Kilmore to 1641', in Raymond Gillespie (ed.), *Cavan: an Irish County History* (Dublin, 1995), pp. 73–98.
43 TCD, MS 550, p. 244.
44 Gillespie, *Colonial Ulster*, p. 160.
45 Tweedie (ed.), *Select Biographies*, p. 142.
46 Adair, *True Narrative*, p. 12; Row (ed.), *Life of Blair*, pp. 68–9.
47 Ford, 'The reformation in Kilmore'.
48 Millsop, 'Diocese of Down and Connor', p. 245.
49 TCD, MS 550, pp. 244–61; TNA, SP 63/254/185 (*CSPI, 1633–47*, 87–8.); E.P. Shirley (ed.), *Papers Relating to the Church of Ireland (1631–9)* (London and Dublin, 1874), p. 41; SCL, WWM, Str. P. 20/179.
50 Row (ed.), *Life of Blair*, p. 51; Tweedie (ed.), *Select Biographies*, p. 141.
51 SCL, WWM, Str. P. 20/179; T.K. Lowry (ed.), *The Hamilton Manuscripts* (Belfast, 1867), pp. 33–4, 74–5; Row (ed.), *Life of Blair*, p. 64; Millsop, 'Diocese of Down and Connor', pp. 317–19, 321–3, 326; Blair (Bangor), Boyle (Killyleagh), Cunningham (Holywood), Hamilton (Ballywalter), Alexander Forbes (Blaris), Livingston (Killinchy), Porteous (Ballyhalbert).
52 Millsop, 'Diocese of Down and Connor', pp. 283–4.
53 TCD, MS. 1067, p. 96; A. Stewart, *The History of the Church in Ireland since the Scots were Naturalized*, ed. W.D. Killen, Belfast, 1866), p. 318.
54 TCD, MS. 1067, p. 88; NLI, MS 13237/26.
55 A.F.S. Pearson, *Puritan and Presbyterian Settlements in Ireland 1560–1660* (Typescript in The Presbyterian Historical Society of Ireland, Belfast), pp. 139, 174.
56 J. McCavitt, *Sir Arthur Chichester, Lord Deputy of Ireland 1605–1616* (Belfast, 1998), pp. 5–6; Lowry (ed.), *Hamilton Manuscripts*, pp. 31–2.
57 TNA, SP 63/254/185 (*CSPI, 1633–47*, pp. 87–88); Shirley (ed.), *Papers Relating to the Church of Ireland (1631–9)*, p. 41.
58 J. McCafferty, 'When reformations collide', A.I. MacInnes and J. Ohlmeyer (eds), *The Stuart Kingdoms in the Seventeenth Century* (Dublin, 2002), pp. 198–201.
59 Row (ed.), *Life of Blair*, p. 61; M. Perceval-Maxwell, 'Strafford, the Ulster Scots and the covenanters' , *Irish Historical Studies*, 18:72 (September 1973), 547.
60 Lowry (ed.), *Hamilton Manuscripts*, p. 35.
61 *Ibid.*, p. 71.
62 TNA, SP 63/253/2116 (*CSPI, 1625–32*, pp. 661–2).

63 NLI, MS 8014/i.
64 TNA, SP 63/252/121 fols 235v (*CSPI, 1625–32*, p. 629).
65 Knox, *James Ussher*, pp. 16–23, 167–89.
66 T.C. Barnard, *Cromwellian Ireland: English Government and Reform in Ireland 1649–1660* (Oxford, 1975), pp. 91–2.
67 Reid, *Presbyterian Church*, i, p. 136–7; Row (ed.), *Life of Blair*, p. 80–1.
68 R. Baxter, *Five Disputations of Church Government and Worship* (London, 1659), quoted in J.W. Packer, *The Transformation of Anglicanism 1643–1660 with Special Reference to Henry Hammond* (Manchester, 1969), pp. 197–8.
69 J. Ussher, *The Whole Works*, ed. C.R. Elrington and J.H. Todd (17 vols, Dublin, London, 1847–64), xii, p. 533.
70 Ussher's use of John Sprint's *Cassander Anglicanus* suggests that the Irish context was very different to the English: see Ford, *Ussher: Theology, History, and Politics*, pp. 167–70.
71 Ford, 'A puritan church', p. 67; W.M. Abbott, 'James Ussher and "Ussherian" episcopacy, 1640–1656: the primate and his *Reduction* manuscript', *Albion*, 22 (1990), 237–59.
72 TNA, SP 63/249/1485 (*CSPI, 1625–32*, p. 481); TNA, SP 63/252/121 fols 235r–236r (*CSPI, 1625–32*, p. 629).
73 SP, 63/252/121 fols 235r–236r (*CSPI, 1625–32*, p. 629); Row (ed), *Life of Blair*, p. 90; Tweedie (ed.), *Select Biographies*, p. 145; NLI, MS 8014/i.
74 NLI, MS 8014/i.
75 For a discussion of Ussher's attitude, see Ford, 'A puritan church?', pp. 65–6.
76 Row (ed.), *Life of Blair*, p. 91; Tweedie (ed.), *Select Biographies*, p. 145.
77 Perceval-Maxwell, 'Strafford, the Ulster Scots and the covenanters', p. 525; HMC, *The Manuscripts of the Earl Cowper, K.G: Preserved at Melbourne Hall, Derbyshire* (4 vols, London, 1888–89), i, p. 469.
78 Ford, *Ussher: Theology, History and Politics*, chapter 8.
79 SCL, WWM, Str. P. 8, p. 102.
80 SCL, WWM, Str. P. 20/179.
81 Reid, *Presbyterian Church*, i, chapter. 4.
82 For details of dates of deprivation see Millsop, 'Diocese of Down and Connor', pp. 316–18.
83 Perceval-Maxwell, 'Strafford, the Ulster Scots and the covenanters', p. 528; McCafferty, 'When reformations collide', p. 202.
84 J.J. Scarisbrick, *The Reformation and the English People* (Oxford, 1984); E. Duffy, *The Stripping of the Altars: Traditional Religion in England c.1400–c.1580* (New Haven, CT, 1992); C. Haigh, *English Reformations: Religion, Politics, And Society under the Tudors* (Oxford, 1993).
85 Row (ed.), *Life of Blair*, pp. 59, 63–4.
86 Tweedie (ed.), *Select Biographies*, pp. 141–2.
87 *Ibid.*, p. 144.
88 NLI, MS 8014/i.
89 TNA, SP 63/252/121 fol 235r (*CSPI, 1625–32*, p. 629).
90 Leslie, *Authority of the Church*, sig. *3v, *2v.

91 H. Leslie, *A speech delivered at the visitation of Downe and Conner: held in Lisnegarvy the 26th of September, 1638: wherein, for the convincing of the nonconformists, there is a full confutation of the covenant lately sworne and subscribed by many in Scotland* (London, 1639), p. 3.
92 *The humble petition of the Scottish, and many others the inhabitants of the Province of Ulster, in the Kingdome of Ireland. To the right reverend and right honorable the moderator, and remnant members of the Generall Assembly of Scotland, conveened at S. Andrews in July. 1642.* (London, 1642), sig. A2r–A3r
93 M.J. Westerkamp, *The Triumph of the Laity: Scots-Irish Piety and the Great Awakening, 1625–1760* (Oxford, 1988).
94 Row (ed.), *Life of Blair*, pp. 72, 74.
95 *Ibid.*, p. 70.
96 *Ibid.*, pp. 71, 84; Adair, *True Relation*, pp. 16f.; NLI, MS 8014/i.
97 Tweedie (ed.), *Select Biographies*, p. 144; HMC, *Reports on the Manuscripts of the Earl of Eglinton, Sir J. Stirling Maxwell, bart., C.S.H. Drummond Moray, esq., C.F. Weston Underwood, esq., and G. Wingfield Digby, esq.*, (London, 1885), p. 46.
98 Row (ed.), *Life of Blair*, p. 64.
99 *Ibid.*, pp. 84–6; Tweedie (ed.), *Select Biographies*, p. 144; NLI MS 8014/i; they were clearly following the Scottish model of communion: see M. Todd, *The Culture of Protestantism in Early-Modern Scotland* (New Haven, CT, 2002), pp. 91–4.
100 A. Hunt, 'The Lord's supper in early modern England', *Past & Present*, 161 (1998), 39; N. Tyacke, *Anti-Calvinists: The Rise of English Arminianism, c.1590–1640* (Oxford, 1987), p. 10.
101 B.A. Gerrish, *Grace and Gratitude: The Eucharistic Theology of John Calvin* (Edinburgh, 1993), p. 151; Hunt, 'Lord's supper', pp. 69–83.
102 P. Brooke, *Ulster Presbyterianism: The Historical Perspective 1610–1970* (Dublin, 1987), p. 17; D. Stevenson, 'Conventicles in the Kirk, 1619–37: the emergence of a radical party', *Records of the Scottish Church History Society*, 18 (1972–74), 99–114; Armstrong, 'Ireland's puritan revolution?', p. 1054.
103 Row (ed.), *Life of Blair*, pp. 148ff.; Tweedie, *Select Biographies*, pp. 160–2.
104 On combination lectures, see P. Collinson, *Godly People: Essays on English Protestantism and Puritanism* (London, 1983), pp. 468–9.
105 NLI, MS 8014/i.
106 HMC, *Eglinton MSS*, 10th Report, app. 1, p. 46.
107 Bodleian Library, MS Carte 30, fol. 110r.
108 See p. 126.
109 Armstrong, 'Ireland's puritan revolution?', p. 1050; Raymond Gillespie, 'The Presbyterian revolution in Ulster, 1660–1690', W.J. Shiels and D. Wood (eds), *The Churches, Ireland and the Irish* (Oxford, 1989), pp. 159–70.
110 Row (ed), *Life of Blair*, pp. 74, 89.
111 TNA, SP 63/252/121 fol 235v (*CSPI 1625–32*, p. 629).
112 Leslie, *Authority of the church*, sig. **2r.
113 TNA, SP 63/252/121 fol 235v (*CSPI, 1625–32*, p. 629).
114 McCafferty, 'When reformations collide', pp. 201–3.
115 R.L. Greaves, *God's Other Children. Protestant Nonconformists and the Emergence of Denominational Churches in Ireland, 1660–1700* (Stanford, CA, 1997), p. 14.

116 Brooke, *Ulster Presbyterianism*, pp. 47–8.
117 L.E. Schmidt, *Holy Fairs: Scottish Communions and American Revivals in the Early Modern Period* (Princeton, NJ, 1989), p. 200.
118 *Ibid.*, p. 213.
119 NLI, MS 8014/i.

5

Scots Catholics in Ulster, 1603–41

BRIAN MAC CUARTA SJ

Scottish migration to Ulster in the early seventeenth century has generally been considered in terms of the arrival of settlers marked in varying degrees by that strand of Protestantism prevalent in their native land.[1] The smaller Scots Catholic influx by contrast has been little noted, yet it was of significance both for the Catholic community in Scotland, and for Catholicism in Ulster. Although the Catholic dimension to Scottish immigration is not easily or comprehensively traceable, several strands may be identified. The first encompasses the movement of islanders from the broader MacDonnell lordship across the North Channel to the lands of their kinsman in north Antrim, Sir Randall MacDonnell, first earl of Antrim. Their migration occurred within the traditional context of Gaelic lordship. In the 1610s these *Scoti Hibernici* were the subject of Jesuit pastoral attention.[2]

A parallel and more novel exodus, where religious motivation was more explicit, was that of Catholic refugees from Scotland, generally Lowlanders. Starting in the first decade of the Plantation, some areas in Ulster which were under Catholic landlords became a haven for those avoiding religious pressure at home. While the earls of Antrim were noted patrons of Catholicism in their territory, the most striking (and best documented) concentration of Scots Catholics in Ulster was on the estates of the Hamilton family, earls of Abercorn, in Strabane, Co. Tyrone, from the late 1610s. Their vigorous promotion of Catholicism may be traced both in their patrimony of Paisley, in Renfrewshire, and on their Ulster plantation lands. The denominational stance of this landlord family, together with Catholic influence on adjacent plantation estates contributed much to the flourishing condition of the Catholic diocese of Derry by the late 1620s. It was the patronage afforded by these peers of Scottish background which placed Derry, and Down and Connor, among the better-resourced Catholic dioceses of Ulster in this era.

The Scots Catholic profile of Ulster in the early seventeenth century must be considered in the context of its Scottish recusant origins, and in particular in the experience of religious coercion there. Based on the registers of the privy council in Edinburgh, and on the records of the Glasgow presbytery, developments in Scottish recusancy which contributed to migration to Ulster will be outlined. While evidence on Catholic life in plantation Ulster is particularly scarce, reports of missionary activity in north Ulster and the Scottish isles, contained in the annual letters of the Jesuit mission superior in Ireland, allow us to adumbrate the emergence of Scots Catholic communities in Ulster. Correspondence arising from efforts to impose religious uniformity, associated with the Dublin administration's campaign of 1629–30, throws light on the growth of Scots Catholicism under lordly patronage in Strabane in the 1620s. In these ways it is possible to locate the Catholic strand of migration within its Scottish context, and to trace its diffusion and evolution in Ulster until the cataclysm of 1641–42.

In contrast to the openness to Protestantism discernible in the Lowlands from the 1560s onwards, recusancy – the refusal to attend the services of the established church – became strong in the north and north-east of Scotland, while in large swathes of the Gaelic west the old faith remained dominant into the seventeenth century.[3] By the mid-1580s a number of leading aristocratic families were becoming recusant. These magnates were located largely in the northern periphery, and in the south-west: they included the Gordon earls of Huntly, based in the north-west of Aberdeenshire, the Sinclair earls of Caithness, on the northern coast, together with the Hay earls of Erroll, in Perthshire, and the Maxwells based in Kirkcudbrightshire and Dumfriesshire. Marriage ties among these families reinforced this Catholic stance: in 1585, George Sinclair, fifth earl of Caithness, married Jean Gordon, only daughter of the fifth earl of Huntly, and in a subsequent generation, in 1632 Claud Hamilton, Lord Strabane married a daughter of the sixth earl.[4] This emerging recusancy coincided with the start of the small Jesuit mission in Scotland in 1584 comprising no more than a handful of fathers, directed to the conversion of the nobility and the king. It was a seigneurial Catholicism, based on the active promotion of the old faith among family, servants and tenants by a number of magnates in their localities.[5] From the mid-1580s until the early 1590s the Catholic nobles became involved in a movement of opposition to the government in Edinburgh, focusing on hopes for a restoration of Catholicism in Scotland with Spanish help.[6] Thereafter they disavowed foreign involvement in national politics, and focused rather on building up influence in their localities, a dimension of which was the promotion of Catholicism. Until the 1630s the heads of these families were Catholic.

In the early seventeenth century, the civil and ecclesiastical authorities resented the continuing local influence of the recusant magnates, which they exercised in protecting the Catholic community from the coercive religious powers of the state. As the Scottish privy council noted in November 1626: 'in some parts of the country the papists are so strong in kindred, alliance and friendship that none of the boundis dare or can execute any commission against them'.[7] Vigorous, indeed aggressive prosletizing characterized aristocratic recusants, whose high social standing enabled them to exercise considerable influence on the denominational adherence of their dependants, a fact which made them particularly irksome to the authorities. This was exemplified in an order issued in July 1616 for the earl and countess of Caithness to appear before the privy council in Edinburgh on grounds of refusing 'to give satisfaction to the kirk in matters of religion'. Their homes were centres of recusancy where they entertained 'professed papists' and kept Catholics on their staff. Through their influence in the locality they helped the spread of recusancy, for they were responsible for the 'perverting of numbers of his majesty's good subjects' and the consequent growth of Catholicism in Caithness.[8] As well as their personal example, vital to the peers' role as patrons of Catholicism was their protection of priests, a situation which in November 1626 necessitated a commission for the pursuit and apprehension of Jesuits and priests in Caithness, especially

> benorth the hill of the Ord where they ordinarily frequent and busy themselves by dispersing of books and by public and private reasoning and discourses to divert the simple and ignorant people … from the true religion professed and by law established … and to embrace their popish errors and superstitions.[9]

Government efforts at enforcing religious conformity, while gaining in severity in the mid-1610s, met with little success. Already in 1610 a court of high commission had been established for each of the two church provinces; among its functions was to proceed against what was considered to be the significant number of papists.[10] Even in Glasgow, residual Catholic sentiment was strong into the 1610s, expressed in 'superstitious behaviour' at Christmas (which had been proscribed), and in the presence of three artists engaged in painting crucifixes in many homes in the city.[11] The campaign affected recusants among both the nobility and the professional class, milieux where Jesuits were active. A series of prosecutions for attending mass, and 'reset' (shelter) of Jesuits, characterized a frenetic three-year period beginning in 1613. The high point of this militancy against recusancy was the capture of John Ogilvie SJ in Glasgow in October 1614, and his subsequent interrogation, trial and execution on a charge of treason.[12] Also in the early 1610s the earls of Huntly and Errol, the leading Catholic peers, were excommunicated, and after a short spell of confinement each had been restricted to his own estates, repeating a pattern established in earlier decades. No weakening of recusancy ensued: in 1619, commissions were issued to the bishops of the north (in the dioceses of Moray, Ross and Aberdeen) to enforce the 1581 act against various communal activities associated with the old faith – pilgrimages to chapels and wells, bonfires, and the singing of carols in churches.[13]

By 1619, however, government pressure on Catholicism was becoming less consistent, as negotiations for a match between Prince Charles and the Spanish infanta intensified. Toleration for Catholics was a crucial but controversial element in the proposed marriage treaty. As a result of these discussions, the early 1620s was a time of confusion with regard to Catholicism among authorities in church and state, in Scotland as elsewhere in the Stuart monarchy, as the prospect of official toleration loomed. In 1622 it was reported that Catholics imprisoned for religion were then being released. That the king felt it necessary in August 1624 to write to the privy council urging a strict implementation of conformity measures in Scotland suggests that enforcement of these had become slack.[14] Nevertheless action against individuals whom the kirk had excommunicated for apostasy continued into the 1620s, and in 1620 a Jesuit was arrested, while a man was apprehended for importing a 'chest of popish books' through Leith.[15]

The persistence of recusancy in the south-west, in Dumfries and Galloway, was significant. As was the case with Catholic peers elsewhere, the influence exercised by the Maxwell earls of Nithisdale undermined efforts against recusancy there, all the more so since in July 1626 the earl had acquired royal protection from official harassment for his religion. In that year the sheriff of Dumfries, Sir John Maxwell, was reprimanded for dilatory efforts in pursuit of a minister who had become Catholic. A priest who had made many conversions among the rural population was saved from arrest by the help of several 'excommunicate papists' in his company. They were not fully successful in protecting the cleric, for the ministers pursuing him managed to capture his horse, together with his cloak bag, containing 'hosts, superstitious pictures, priests' vestments, altar, chalice, plate boxes, with oils and ointments, with such other trash as priests carry about with them for popish uses'; these were to be publicly burnt at the market cross in Dumfries.[16] Thus by the late 1610s vibrant recusant communities had emerged under aristocratic patronage, especially in the north and east, and the south-west. In this denominational change the tiny number of Jesuits active in Scotland played a significant role.

Obdurate papists were to be excommunicated and were classed as rebels. In addition to legislation against Jesuits and massing-priests, measures affecting laity were strengthened in acts of the Scottish parliament in 1594. There was an act against the wilful hearing of mass. In a further enactment, responsibility for dealing with papists and suspected papists was given to the presbyteries, who were to summon these, and seek their conversion. If they refused to attend, or were otherwise disobedient, they were to be reported to the privy council.

They were to be penalized by the confiscation of their property.[17] By the second decade of the seventeenth century banishment was a recognized penalty for recusancy, as a result of which some individuals migrated to Ulster; and a licence was needed to protect the returnee from penalty.

In the vagaries of government religious policy, measures against recusants continued to be implemented in the 1620s and into the 1630s. For those experiencing religious coercion in Dumfries, its location facilitated migration across the sea to the more hospitable environment of the Co. Antrim estates of Randal MacDonnell, earl of Antrim. In July 1622 Herbert Brown was one of a number of people 'suspect of papistry, resetters of Jesuits and mass-priests, recusants, and altogether disobedient to the order and discipline of the kirk' who were summoned before the presbytery.[18] As was customary in the wake of non-appearance before the church authorities, the case was referred to the privy council; Brown was excommunicated and denounced as a rebel. Thereafter he was banished from Scotland for his religion and fled to Antrim. Such migration was provisional, for he was apparently moving to and fro between Antrim and Dumfries until he was imprisoned in Edinburgh in December 1628.[19] Thus for some Scots recusants a sojourn in a Catholic area in Ulster was a temporary expedient. Under pressure of legal processes, there were those who conformed while others left Scotland. Among these were some from the Glasgow area (discussed later in the chapter) and the south-west who took refuge on Catholic estates in Ulster. It was in the context of religious pressure, as this affected recusants chiefly in Renfrewshire and in the south-west, that a small number moved to the lands of their co-religionists across the narrow sea.

The proximity of the extensive estates of the MacDonnells in north Co. Antrim, a recusant family, facilitated the emergence of this part of Ulster as a place of refuge for some Scottish Catholics. Sir Randall MacDonnell (d. 1636), created viscount Dunluce in 1618, and earl of Antrim in 1620, became the largest landowner in Co. Antrim in the early seventeenth century. The earl was descended from the MacDonald lords of the Isles. While settled in north Antrim since the early fifteenth century, and expanding their landholding there from that time, the family retained their Scottish orientation, seeking to recover their lost lands in the isles until the 1630s. Thus this common Gaelic world linking north-east Ulster and the Western Isles provided the setting for Catholic life at this time, facilitating the movement of people and priests across the short channel. Thanks to a royal grant in 1603, MacDonnell extended his landholding to include most of north Antrim, extending to almost 340,000 acres. As powerful and extensive landlords, they exercised their local influence to encourage Catholic life on both sides of the water, by supporting priests on their own estates in Ulster and by fostering missionary activity in the western isles.[20] While the first earl was prominent among those Catholic landowners who promoted the activities of Catholic clergy, such as the Franciscans and the Jesuits, he did not let his Catholicism inhibit his economic advantage. As well as having Irish and Highland Scots as tenants, in the 1620s he also sought English and Lowland Scottish settlers, who were Protestant.[21] Nevertheless Scots Catholics, seeking refuge from religious pressure, were doubtless among those who settled on the earl's estates.

A significant agency of Catholic renewal in this area was the engagement of religious orders. Irish Franciscan ministry among the Gaelic-speaking Scots islanders in the 1620s and 1630s is well known.[22] While a few Franciscans fluent in English ministered on occasion to Catholic converts among the settlers in plantation Ulster, the chief form of this ministry was the series of missions undertaken by individual Jesuits from 1611 onwards.[23] As a group drawn largely from the Pale and the southern towns, Jesuits spoke English, which facilitated contact with the Lowland Scots in Ulster; in addition, men sent to the north and the isles could also operate in an Irish-speaking environment. Thus the small number of missioners involved could work both with islanders and Lowlanders. Their missions generally lasted about a month, and were often undertaken in the Lenten season. While Jesuits were active in different areas of Ulster (as among the O'Kanes in Co. Londonderry in 1615), references to the *Scoti Hibernici* and the islanders in the Jesuit letters suggest that north Co. Antrim was a particular focus of their activity. The protection and support afforded by Sir Randall MacDonnell facilitated the Jesuit presence in his territory. The arrival of the Jesuit missioners coincided with an increase in migration from Kintyre and Islay to Antrim, arising from political and military pressure on those areas from the Edinburgh government, and the Campbells in particular, from the end of the 1590s.[24]

The fathers laboured among the Scots in various years in the course of the 1610s, sometimes in Antrim and sometimes on the islands. Annual reports prepared by Jesuits in Ireland for perusal by their superiors in Rome throw light on their activities. Depending on the religious situation they encountered, their work entailed fostering spiritual renewal, strengthening adherence to the Catholic Church, and seeking conversions from Protestantism. These missions were launched from Co. Antrim and, on their way to and from the isles, missioners worked among the Scots living in north-east Ulster. Thus in 1613, arising from opposition in one Ulster locality, the missioner who had returned from the isles withdrew to another place, where he converted more than sixteen Scots, and some English, among whom was the son of a minister. As a result of his missionary efforts there, the Jesuit was in a position to ensure that Protestant books used in the teaching of the young were burned.[25] One father who operated in this area was David Galway, Irish Jesuit and native of

Cork, who ministered on the western islands of Scotland at various times over several years in the late 1610s and early 1620s.[26]

Missioners would return to visit the converts they had made in previous years and in this way sought to offer support to those living in a hostile religious environment, suggestive of the large Lowland Scots presence in east Ulster. Thus in 1615 a Jesuit visited a small group of converts he had gathered in a Scots village while on a missionary tour two years earlier. To avoid detection he arrived by night, heard confessions and, indicative of the precarious standing of this community, very early the following morning he celebrated mass with the little group about two miles from the settlement, at which the missioner preached. Five further converts were made in that area, including a schoolmaster who promised that henceforth he would teach only the Catholic catechism to his pupils.

On another occasion, thirty men (denoted 'Scoti Hibernici' – Scots-Irish – in the contemporary Jesuit reports) called on the visiting father and asked for baptism, saying that some Catholics had told them that this sacrament was necessary for salvation but that they had neither priest nor minister to baptise recently born infants. The priest knew that what they said regarding their lack of pastors was true and, after instructing them in the basics of the faith, he baptised them and sent them back to their people. As was customary, when the time allotted for the mission by the Jesuit superior elapsed, the missioner set off and travelled back to his base in the Pale. On the way, he secretly visited a group of Catholics living in an area where they were surrounded by Protestants.[27]

In ministering to the Scots Catholics, Jesuits faced the risk of harassment from some local officials. About the beginning of March 1617, a father was travelling on horseback to the north, and stayed overnight in a certain village, probably in south Antrim. His arrival was noted, for that evening the steward of Sir Arthur Chichester (whose residence was in Carrickfergus) together with a provost marshal were plotting his capture, as the pair were drinking together. The steward's wife (a Protestant) overheard the conversation, and warned the Jesuit accordingly. He escaped the following morning, and reached his destination, where he made four converts, heard many confessions, and preached every day for almost three weeks. Thereafter he travelled to other places, where he heard the confessions of some English settlers, before returning to his base in Co. Meath.[28]

It was often arising from the invitation of Catholic notables that Jesuits came to minister in specific localities. Moved by the pastoral neglect of the people in his area in Ulster, one landholder (it is not clear if he were Scottish or English) called on the help of the Jesuits, giving rise to a mission by an individual father at the beginning of Lent 1618. The priest preached almost every day, and converted seven Protestants, among them the brother of a knight and the brother of a minister. It is not possible to identify with precision the landholder in question; but Sir George Hamilton in Strabane, Co. Tyrone, who enjoyed a reputation for seeking conversions among the Scots, and for maintaining Catholic clergy, and who used the services of Jesuits in the 1620s, fits the profile offered. In addition, Catholics were prominent on the lands of Mervin Touchet, the English recusant second earl of Castlehaven, whose family by 1619 controlled most of the proportions in Omagh barony, Co. Tyrone.[29]

The apostolate in this locality was given priority by the Jesuit superior in Ireland, for when the missioner returned to his base, another father replaced him who had greater experience in ministering in those northern parts. Local priests, poorly trained, few in number and lacking English, were in no position to minister to the newcomers, lending urgency to Jesuit involvement in this task. The preacher who was more familiar with the territory adopted the stratagem of dressing in Irish, Scottish or English style in order to move among the various settlements more easily. In this way he perceived that Catholic practices remained among those living in the midst of the Protestant settlers, and he revived these isolated Catholic communities as occasion presented by preaching and administering the sacraments. The same man also ministered to several seriously ill Scottish heads of households, who, according to the missioner, after receiving the sacraments were restored to the fullness of health. Jesuits working in Ulster in that year reported making about fifty converts from Protestantism, though it is not clear if these were Catholics who had lapsed under religious coercion, or British settlers; the two doctors mentioned, however, were probably English or Scottish.[30]

Further light on Catholic migration to Ulster, and on the earl of Antrim's role in providing refuge, comes from the exile of Patrick Anderson SJ. In the 1610s, Anderson was one of the leading Catholic apologists in Scotland. Appointed in 1615 first rector of the Scots College, Rome, on his return to Scotland he followed the Jesuit apostolate of ministering in various upper-class households, and he was arrested in May 1620, en route to saying mass. Reflective of his high standing, he was examined some days later by the archbishops of Glasgow and St Andrews, together with the civic officials of Edinburgh, and some ministers. He was then imprisoned in the toll booth in Edinburgh. Thanks to Anderson's connections, the recent French ambassador to King James made representations on his behalf. As a result, on 31 January 1621 the king decreed his release. As sometimes happened in cases involving Catholics, the priest was ordered into exile, the authorities were enjoined to 'see him put on some ship for France or Flanders', and he was to face execution if he returned without the king's leave. On his departure he was to receive 'honest apparell', and one hundred pounds.[31]

It was illustrative of the place of Ulster in the social network of a prominent Catholic cleric such as Anderson that he sought exile there. By spring 1621 he was moving between the households of some of the leading Scots in east Ulster. Such sojourns typically afforded opportunities for conversions to Catholicism, especially among women and servants. He was a guest of Sir James Hamilton, of Killyleagh, in north-east Co. Down. The Jesuit's stay with this prominent Scottish settler reflected their common social and cultural background; Anderson's reputation and family connections in Scotland, transcending the denominational divide, may have accounted for his welcome in Killyleagh, while Sir James's intellectual interests led him to cultivate the company of the learned, which could also explain the Scottish father's visit.[32] Patrick Anderson's presence as a guest in the earl of Antrim's home (presumably Dunluce castle, his chief residence) was doubtless facilitated by the engagement of individual Irish Jesuits with the Scots Catholics on the earl's lands since the early 1610s.

It was while staying with the earl that Anderson was denounced to the authorities by one Alexander Boyd.[33] Boyd's interest in delating seminary priests was sharpened by the proclamation issued by lord deputy St John in 1617: the informer against people harbouring priests, if these householders were found guilty, was to receive half of the fine imposed. Boyd was involved in protracted wrangling in his attempt to make good this claim against Antrim and Sir James Hamilton.[34] It would appear that Fr Anderson returned to France shortly afterwards. According to a Jesuit source, the apparitor (presumably Boyd) who notified the authorities in Scotland about Anderson also tracked him while in Ulster. As a result the householders who sheltered him there faced raids and interrogations by officials. By this means an important part of the Catholic infrastructure of north Down and Co. Antrim was temporarily undermined. An indication of the damage inflicted was given by the Irish Jesuit who was in the habit of making a regular (perhaps annual) excursion in that area. He reported that these households were severely disrupted thanks to official searches and inquiries, so much so that the owners were terrified of sheltering priests again. Thus in the wake of this campaign, the whole network of gentry houses used by the Jesuit in the north-east was closed to him, and on this occasion he was forced to abandon his missionary tour.[35]

The Jesuit approach, focused yet flexible, was suited to the unsettled and inimical climate for Catholicism in Ulster prevalent in the plantation decade of the 1610s. While individual men were missioned by the superior to excursions of limited duration to specific communities, these had the freedom to visit other groupings of Catholics, as occasion presented. The Scots Catholics were a group at risk of denominational change, given the Protestant preponderance among the settlers, thus meriting the Jesuits' attention. The fathers were known and valued by some in aristocratic circles in Scotland, which facilitated their welcome on the Ulster estates of these families; further, fluency in

English made them apt missioners for migrants from the Scottish Lowlands, and England.

While the *Scoti Hibernici* of the west of Scotland, with contacts principally to the territories of the earl of Antrim, represented one strand of Catholic migration to Ulster, a Scottish Catholic community was also emerging in areas subject to the major Plantation scheme. Although achieving official notoriety in the government's attempted clampdown on Catholicism in 1629–30, the genesis of this community may be discerned in the previous decade. The period of severe coercion against recusants in Scotland coincided with the surge in departures to Ulster in the mid-1610s, and thus it was probable that some were migrating in these years because of religious pressure. Under the plantation conditions, it was a requirement that undertakers and servitors were to take the oath of supremacy. However, not all did so – the authorities may have been lax, or felt powerless, in insisting on this requirement. It was noted in 1622 that some grantees in Counties Tyrone and Armagh 'who have servitors' proportions are recusants and will not take the oath of supremacy'.[36] Several Scots were among those who refused to take the oath, yet did not forfeit their lands. Thus from the beginning of the Plantation there were recusants among the undertakers and servitors. Some, most notably Sir George Hamilton, were exploiting their social position to draw their British dependants to the old faith. In addition, by June 1614 several Scots undertakers were marrying Irish wives; given the influence of their Irish kin, and the leading role of women in the religious upbringing of children, it was probable that their offspring, if not the planters themselves, were coming under Catholic influence.[37]

As with developments on the lands of the earl of Antrim, lordly patronage also facilitated the other major settlement of Scots Catholics in Ulster. This was based on the plantation estates of the Hamilton family in the precinct of Strabane (granted to Scots) in Co. Tyrone: James Hamilton, first earl of Abercorn, was granted 3,000 acres, his brother Sir Claud Hamilton (d. 1614) was granted 2,000 acres, and another brother, Sir George, was granted 1,500 acres. By 1622 it has been estimated that the barony of Strabane contained about 280 Scottish families. The Hamilton estates comprised one of the most successful Scottish settlements in plantation Ulster, centred on the town of Strabane, with a stone castle, a mill, a bridge and about 100 houses.[38]

By the late 1610s, they had become one of the leading recusant families of Scotland. Indeed their espousal of the old faith in Strabane was an extension to Ulster of their particular brand of lordly Scottish Catholicism. Thanks in part to their large entourage of kin and clients, together with their extensive properties, recusancy survived in those localities where they held sway, sharing in the signs of Catholic growth which characterized other lordly estates by the 1620s. The Hamiltons' centre of influence was their estates around the town of

Paisley, in Renfrewshire, just west of Glasgow. Prominent in Scottish national life, especially in the mid-sixteenth century, the family had a chequered denominational history. Lord Claud Hamilton (*c.*1545–1621) was a younger son of James Hamilton, earl of Arran, duke of Chatelherault; the duke had served as lord governor for a time during the minority of Mary Queen of Scots, and his Catholic half-brother John was archbishop of St Andrews. Lord Claud was believed to have been a Catholic.[39] This recusant stance was maintained by Sir George (discussed further later in this chapter), one of Claud's younger sons. Claud's eldest son, James Hamilton (1575–1618), the head of the family in the early seventeenth century, adhered to the established church, a strategy which facilitated the Hamiltons' social and political survival. James played a prominent role in political life as a privy councillor, and was a member of the commission to examine the proposed union between Scotland and England in 1604. Created earl of Abercorn in 1606, James (like his brother Sir Frederick) was a staunch Protestant, and served on various church commissions.[40]

The death of the first earl in 1618 marks a turning point in the family's denominational adherence; thereafter their recusancy became notorious, in both Scotland and Ulster. The demise of the earl facilitated the emergence of Catholic sympathies in his immediate family which had been latent for some time. Typical of the prominent role of noblewomen in the survival of Catholicism in this era, Marion Boyd, the earl's widow, became noted as a resolute papist in the 1620s; the guardian of his sons was Sir George Hamilton, the earl's staunchly Catholic brother, and the boys too were Catholic.[41] The Hamiltons' muscular Catholicism was displayed in the expulsion of the minister of Paisley, some time before June 1626, when the countess was in charge, in the absence of the young earl. Robert Boyd, the cleric in question, had been principal of Edinburgh University, but arising from his opposition to the Articles of Perth (1617), he was removed from that post at the king's insistence; he had recently been appointed by the archbishop of Glasgow to the vacant ministry of Paisley.

The opposition of the countess was expressed in delaying tactics in providing the new minister with accommodation. When finally he had been granted rooms in the Abbey of Paisley, the earl's brother arrived with some companions, who scattered the cleric's books on the ground, and locked the doors. The two bailiffs of Paisley were directed to install Boyd in his manse; the officials failed in their charge, for a group of irate women arrived and castigated the pastor with vehement speeches, shouting and booing him, and throwing dirt and stones at him, so that he was forced to leave the town.[42] The bailiffs were summoned before the privy council accordingly. Similarly Claud Hamilton, the earl's brother, was ordered to remain in Edinburgh until the council received a report on his mother's cooperation in giving the minister repossession of these premises. Abercorn antipathy to the cleric prevailed, however, for after his expulsion, Boyd moved to Glasgow and thence to Edinburgh, where he died in January 1627.[43]

The countess and her servant Thomas Algeo were among those who refused to appear before their local presbytery. After many years of waiting for her conversion, the presbytery of Paisley finally initiated excommunication proceedings against her in September 1627, and as an unyielding recusant she was cited to appear before the privy council. She did not attend, but sent her son William, with a letter signed by the minister and some elders of the kirk of Kilbarchan, including a medical doctor. These testified that 'through weakness and infirmity' the countess was unable to travel. The privy council excused her absence, and deferred her appearance.[44] Lady Abercorn was excommunicated in January 1628, and was subsequently imprisoned in Edinburgh. Weakened by conditions during her captivity, she died in 1632.

The treatment of the countess was undoubtedly exceptional in its severity. However, in this context of widespread implementation of measures against recusancy, flight to Ulster was one means of avoiding the legal censures attendant on persistent recusancy.[45] This trend was illustrated from the late 1610s in members of the broad Hamilton connection of Paisley. The family of one John Hamilton were recusants: his father, Alan, together with his sister Grisell were excommunicated by 1619 because of their apostasy from the established church. Probably arising from a period spent in France, John was living with Jacqueline Quenlie, a Frenchwoman. Presumably due to the inimical religious climate in Scotland, the pair settled in Ulster, in Ballirobert, Co. Down. By August 1619 Hamilton had abandoned her, and married Margaret Stewart, daughter of Hercules Stewart, a local settler. The estranged couple's Catholicism was reflected in the picture of the Blessed Virgin Mary which was part of the contents of two coffers in dispute between them.[46]

Because of the firm espousal of recusancy by the Hamilton family both in their native Paisley, and on their Ulster estates, from about 1620 Scots Catholics began to settle in Strabane in significant numbers. The earl of Abercorn's colony in Co. Tyrone provided a safe haven, easily accessible by sea, for family and retainers threatened by anti-recusancy measures in Scotland. Strabane lay not far south of the port of Derry, on the banks of the River Foyle, which was navigable that far upstream, at least in suitable craft. Among these was Sir William Hamilton of Elistoun (or Eliestown), eldest son and heir of Sir Claud Hamilton, who shared the vigorous Catholicism espoused by his guardian, Sir George Hamilton. After returning to Scotland from a sojourn in France (considered part of a Catholic upbringing in that milieu), he 'avowed himself to be of the Roman religion' and 'at diverse times and in diverse places reasoned openly against the religion presently professed and established', and as a result by May 1626 was summoned to appear before the presbytery of Glasgow.[47] In search of refuge, Sir William spent some time on the family's estates in Strabane in the late 1620s, and by 1630, as heir to his father, he was owner of a plantation estate of almost 2,800 acres, with 43 British tenants mustered on his lands. With the support of Michael Chamberlain (the Jesuit residing in Strabane), Sir William gained his wife's conversion to Catholicism, and also secured that of her maid. His wife, who had been a staunch Protestant, was the widow of a son of Sir Hugh Montgomery, viscount Ards, originally from Ayrshire, another leading Scots settler. Perhaps because he left without licence, on his return to Scotland Sir William was forced to attend services of the established church.[48]

The Algeos (also Algie, Anger) were a well-established family of the middling sort in Renfrewshire; one John Algie was a burgess of Paisley in the mid-1610s. They were trusted servants of the Abercorn family, and by the late 1610s they shared in the recusancy of their masters: Thomas Algeo, servant to the countess, was excommunicated for apostasy by the Paisley kirk in 1627.[49] As a result of these pressures, some of the family migrated to the earl's plantation in Co. Tyrone in the 1620s. Already in 1614, Robert Algeo was involved in the administration of the Strabane estate of Sir Claud Hamilton of Schawfield. Given the settlers' practice of travelling to and fro between Ulster and their homes in Scotland, it was probable that this man was the Robert Algeo, of Scairhill (or Saterhill) in Renfrewshire who, in October 1619, was denounced (with others) as a rebel by virtue of excommunication 'for their not giving obedience and satisfaction in the kirk and presbytery where they dwell[,] for their apostasy from the true religion, disobedience and contumacy'.[50] In February 1620 a commission for his arrest was issued to the archbishop of Glasgow and others. By August 1622 Robert was the agent on the estate of Sir George Hamilton, in Cloghogenall, in Strabane barony. The Catholicism of these Scots exiles was expressed in the crucifixion plaque created in 1625, bearing Robert Algeo's name, and preserved in the locality.[51] Scots Catholics who returned home from Ulster faced continuing pressure; thus in September 1626 a commission was issued to the authorities in Renfrewshire to arrest Robert Anger (together with Alan and Grizell Hamilton).[52]

Sure of the protection afforded them by the family connection, Hamilton retainers on occasion acted violently in assertion of their recusancy against the representatives of the kirk. Claud Algeo (presumably a relative of Robert's) was a native of the Glasgow area who had also settled in Strabane by the late 1620s; he may have been the man of that name who in autumn 1624 was due to appear before the kirk or presbytery of Glasgow on a charge of scandal arising from an affair with the wife of William Gilleis, burgess of that city.[53] Resident in Paisley, Claud Algeo was a retainer of Claud Hamilton, known as the Master of Abercorn (he was brother of the second earl) who was one of the leading planters in Strabane. This Algeo, too, was a convert to Catholicism. Adamant in seeking to propagate his new denomination, Claud Algeo 'by his professed avowing of popery in reasoning against the true religion, he being become very offensive and scandalous within the town of Paisley'. What precipitated Claud's departure for Ulster was his attack on George Ramsay, the kirk officer of the local presbytery sent to serve Algeo with a summons on 15 May 1628. As Ramsay recounted the event, Algeo 'punched me with his hands and feet', as a result of which the delegate fainted; the attacker left him for dead, and went off to Claud Hamilton, his master. In a few hours Ramsay came round, and went to complain to Hamilton. Algeo was present, and began to beat Ramsay once again. At the request of the injured man, the bailiffs of Paisley proceeded against Algeo; Hamilton, however, threatened them, and for fear of their lives the officials felt obliged to desist from seizing Algeo. The archbishop of Glasgow and the presbytery of Paisley, together with George Ramsay, were granted an order from the privy council against Hamilton and his violent servant.[54] Algeo fled; and by autumn 1629 he too was part of the Hamiltons' Catholic colony in Strabane, where his master was also resident at that time.

Another troublesome recusant was Andrew Hadaway (or Haddiwayes), who 'was driven out of Scotland for religion'.[55] Married to a Hamilton, which may account for his migration to Strabane, he and his wife regularly sheltered priests in their Glasgow home. In early 1622, a Jesuit, George Mortimer, was captured there. The householder was arrested, imprisoned and sent for trial; in May 1622 the provost and bailiffs of Glasgow were ordered to arrest his wife. By 1629, and possibly earlier, Hadaway had settled on the Hamilton lands in Strabane.[56] As a result of such incidents, the archbishop of Glasgow wrote to the bishop of Derry complaining that the latter's diocese was a refuge for those fleeing from justice in Scotland.[57] These episodes contributed to the flow of Catholics to the lands of their Scots co-religionists in Ulster.

Because of the influence they could exert arising from their education, and their professional role in the care of the dying, medical doctors were a particular focus of missioners seeking to promote the old faith; in Scotland in the mid-1610s, the physician Clement King was involved with the Jesuits Ogilvie and Moffett.[58] Jesuit attentiveness to these individuals was well-placed, for medical practitioners who became converts were vigorous promoters of recusancy. Thus in 1622 in Dumfries, Robert Honnyman, 'doctor of phisick', was one of a number of people who were referred to the privy council as papists by the presbytery there; 'by public and private reasoning [he] does what in him lies to pervert and corrupt his majesty's good subjects in their religion'.[59] A similar stance was taken by Dr Barclay, exiled from Scotland for recusancy, who together with his wife and family was established in Strabane by the end of the 1620s.[60]

While trends within Scottish society encouraged some Catholics to contemplate leaving their homeland, it was the recusant leadership on the

Abercorn estates in Ulster which drew them to Co. Tyrone. That the Strabane barony became a Catholic haven was due to the emergence of Sir George Hamilton as the dominant influence there on the deaths of his two brothers, Sir Claud of Shawfield, in 1614, and James, first earl of Abercorn, in 1618: writing in 1630, the Church of Ireland bishop of Derry asserted that Sir George was 'the first and chief planter of popery in the barony of Strabane'.[61] Son of Lord Claud Hamilton, he was an active planter in Killybegs, Co. Donegal, an area granted to Scots under the Plantation, before settling on his proportion of Dirrione in Strabane barony. By 1622, Sir George was the leading figure in this precinct, for in addition to his own grant of two proportions totalling 2,500 acres, he had also acquired half of the proportion originally granted to James Haig. Further, he also managed the 2,000 acre proportion of his brother Sir Claud after the latter's death, and he was guardian to the earl's heir, a minor. In all, the holdings which Sir George either owned or controlled amounted to over 8,000 acres. Committed to developing the Strabane lands, by 1613 he and his wife were living on his main proportion of Cloghogenall, where by 1622 the family had a small slated stone house built within the bawn there; at this time he was building a large four-storey house, which took up most of the area of the bawn, on his other proportion, Dirrione.[62] Indicative of this undertaker's energetic and effective estate management, his tenants gave up the Irish practice of using short ploughs, as part of a government campaign in the 1610s.[63]

Sir George's role as promoter of the old faith must be viewed within this context of a career as an active and successful planter on several proportions in Donegal and Tyrone. Early in the Plantation his denominational credentials came to notice, for, as already noted, he refused the oath of supremacy; his wife, Dame Isabell Leslie, was herself a staunch recusant.[64] Landlords could advance Catholicism in two main ways, by facilitating and supporting clergy on their estates, and by favouring Catholics as tenants. Sir George practised both, and in addition he placed recusants on the payroll of his company of foot soldiers, where two servants of the Strabane-based Jesuit were employed. In Killybegs and in Strabane he was a patron and protector of the clergy; his generosity to priests was illustrated while returning to Scotland some time before December 1614, when he visited Gilbert Kennedy, a priest in Ayr, 'and comforted him and gave him one hundred marks'.[65] This role was of particular benefit to the Catholic community in Ulster in the 1610s, given the precarious state of church organization, together with the active religious coercion then practised by the government. Keen to make converts among his fellow Scots, and given the presence of a Jesuit in his household by the late 1620s, Hamilton doubtless enlisted the services of the Jesuits on their missionary tours in Ulster in the course of the 1610s. Further, his own prosletyzing activities illustrate the denominational pressure which leading planters could exert on their tenants. There was only one British family resident on the proportion of Sir Claud Hamilton (the first earl's brother); in 1622 it was reported that because they belonged to the established church, Sir George 'thrust [this tenant] off with many injuries so that he is gone into Scotland'.[66] Presumably other Scots families proved more docile to the landlord's denominational directives. By such means Sir George gained many converts both in Killybegs and Strabane.

This trend grew in the course of the 1620s, as the next generation of the seigneurial family, by now once more staunchly recusant, took charge: Catholic predominance in Strabane barony was likely to be maintained.[67] By 1630, four strongly recusant Hamiltons were the major landlords: Sir George, brother of the first earl; Claud (the Master of Abercorn), brother of the second earl; Sir William, heir to Sir Claud of Shawfield; and the dowager countess of Abercorn, each holding an average of 2,500 acres, with a total of almost 190 tenants named on the muster roll for that year; in addition, just over 200 men were listed for the town of Strabane, including Robert and Claud Algeo.[68] It was from among these families that the Scots Catholic community was drawn. The denominational tenor of the Hamilton estates was strengthened by marriage ties with other recusant nobles. In 1613 there had been abortive negotiations for an alliance between the families of Sir Randall MacDonnell of Antrim, and of the earl of Abercorn; in 1632, Claud Hamilton, Lord Strabane, brother of the second earl of Abercorn, married Lady Jean Gordon, daughter of the marquis of Huntly, thus forging an alliance with the leading recusant peer of Scotland.[69] Family links facilitated the movement of clergy between the various estates; Jesuits visiting the Scots on the Antrim lands also ministered to those residing elsewhere, as in Strabane.

Official dread of Catholic hegemony in the area was increased, at the end of the 1620s, by a rumour that the house and lands of Sir John Steward were to be conveyed to another Scot, a brother-in-law of Sir George Hamilton, who was following the Catholic migrant trail to Co. Tyrone. Such a development would mark a significant consolidation of the Hamilton landed interest, for Sir John's lands were located in Portlough barony, Co. Donegal, just across the River Foyle from Strabane. Similarly, it was feared that lands of John Murray, earl of Annandale (who owned several proportions in south Donegal) would pass into the hands of Sir William Hamilton.[70] Thus observers were apprehensive that, faced with the combined religious pressure of these landlords and other worthies, the Scottish colony in Strabane would become overwhelmingly Catholic.[71] The fact that a congregation of forty Scots was attending mass regularly at one venue in the town, together with an unspecified number at another rural venue within the 3,000-acre proportion granted to the earl of Abercorn, gives some indication of the spread of Catholicism in the settler population by the late 1620s.[72]

Landlord influence on tenants was exercised through their agents. By the end of the 1620s it was alleged that Strabane undertakers were preferring Catholics as tenants at the expense of Protestants. In the case of the Hamilton estates, the agents were Catholic. All Sir George's servants were papists. Robert Algee (or Anger), his agent, was one of three men (along with William Gembill and John Browne), who each lived in a newly built stone house in the village of twenty houses which had emerged on Sir George's proportion of Cloghogenall by 1622. These were Scots households, and it was probable that they were mostly Catholic, as was the agent on the countess of Abercorn's estate, James Crawford.[73] In neighbouring Omagh barony, Co. Tyrone, in the early 1620s the agent managing a proportion of 3,000 acres for the Castlehaven family was one Francis Lucas, 'an archpapist … [who] served the king of Spain and the archduke in his wars a long time'. Catholic influence on planter society was less than in Strabane, because the Castlehaven lands were sparsely settled.[74]

In addition to landlords and agents, pressure on settlers to become Catholic came from other influential figures within the colony. Chief among these was the physician Dr Barclay (and his wife), 'an apostate from the true religion'. As was the case with other Scots Catholic exiles, he actively promoted the old faith in the barony, with regular masses and clergy meetings in his house. Exploiting his professional contacts, Barclay sought deathbed conversions. As an educated layman, he was a vigorous and articulate opponent of the reformed faith, to the distress of Protestants, 'railing at them and their religion'.[75] Another leader of the community was the merchant, James Ferrall (or Ferrell), who presumably arrived in Strabane some time before his excommunication in 1620–21. By the late 1620s it was in his house that mass was most regularly said, and there too priests generally stayed; as a merchant his wealth was greater than most settlers, which enabled him to keep a spacious home, able to accommodate a congregation of over forty (though these may merely have sheltered under a lean-to or other rough shelter attached to the premises), and provide hospitality for visiting clergy.[76] Further he was in a position to exercise influence locally in favour of his co-religionists through the provision of credit.

In this shifting denominational situation, Jesuit involvement was crucial. Their role evolved from the short-term missionary tour in Ulster in the 1610s, which included visits to Scottish settlements such as that of Sir George Hamilton in Strabane. By the late 1620s the superior of the Irish mission considered the Catholic community there of such significance that a father was assigned to Strabane on a more continuous basis. The background of Michael Chamberlain (alias Blackney) was typical of Irish Jesuits of the early seventeenth century. A townsman (in his case, a native of Drogheda), and of a merchant family, in his mid-teens Chamberlain was a student in Paris before joining the Jesuits in Rome in 1610. After studies in Douai and ordination there in 1618, he returned to minister in Leinster, and was staying in the home of Lord Dillon at Moymeth, in Meath diocese in 1622.[77] By the late 1620s however Chamberlain was moving between the households of Sir George Hamilton and the Master of Abercorn on their Strabane estates.

The option for a Jesuit chaplain was based partly on the Hamiltons' earlier connections with Jesuits in Scotland, a link going back to about 1580, and the presence of the fathers in Ulster in the 1610s, and partly on the need for clergy able to minister both to landlords and tenants, English-speaking Lowland Scots. The reputation of the Society of Jesus for effecting conversions also matched Sir George's own proslytizing agenda. The fathers for their part saw the potential for Catholic expansion in the Strabane situation, based on links with the leading figures in the colony, and so were happy to assign a suitable man to this area. According to George Downham, bishop of Derry, Chamberlain was 'a pernicious Jesuit who has perverted many'; as noted above, he assisted Sir William Hamilton in securing the conversion of Hamilton's wife.[78] In the absence of functioning chapels, it was customary in areas with Catholic landlords for mass to be celebrated in the hall of the local gentry's residence. Thus on Sundays Chamberlain said mass in Sir George Hamilton's home, and in or about the town of Strabane, at the house of either James Ferrell or Robert Anger, leading members of the Scots community.[79] The Jesuit presence among the Strabane Scots apparently continued until 1641, thanks to the Hamiltons, for in that year a Scots father was residing as chaplain to Jean Gordon, widow of Lord Strabane, in the castle there.[80]

The Scottish colony contributed to the flourishing condition of Catholicism within Derry diocese in the 1620s and 1630s. Attracted by the security afforded by the Hamiltons, Strabane barony served as a centre for recusant clergy. In the early 1620s, the cleric in charge of the Catholic diocese of Derry (known as a vicar-apostolic), Patrick Matthews, was based in the Pale (as was the case with other northern prelates), in view of the hazards facing Catholic ecclesiastics in Ulster. However, indicative of the flowering of Catholic life under Sir George's leadership, by the late 1620s the then vicar-apostolic, Eugene MacSweeney, was living among the Scots in Strabane, where he used to celebrate mass at the homes of Andrew Haddiways, Dr Barclay, James Ferrell and Robert Anger. Congregations were ethnically mixed, for both Irish and Scots attended mass held in the homes of Scots residents of the town of Strabane. Both MacSweeney and, later, his successor Tirlogh O'Kelly, lived at the house of the merchant James Ferrall, which served as a chapel, for there daily mass was celebrated. During the religious coercion of 1629–30 the Master of Abercorn sheltered MacSweeney, together with the Jesuit Chamberlain.

In a further sign of the Hamiltons' role in fostering Catholic normality, regular assemblies of the Derry clergy were taking place in Strabane barony by the late 1620s, perhaps as often as twice a year. Between sixty and eighty priests used to attend, as in May 1628, where many stayed at the home of James Ferrell, and others were lodged about the town. Similarly a large convocation of local priests took place in November 1629, at which Tirlogh O'Kelly, just returned from studies at the recently established Irish college, Rome, was installed as vicar-apostolic of the diocese.[81] Until 1641, in addition to maintenance, the Hamiltons afforded Catholic prelates in Derry diocese protection both from Protestants, and from discontented Catholic clergy. Thus the diocese was the envy of ecclesiastics elsewhere in Ulster.[82]

Hamilton protection of Catholicism was further highlighted in local disregard of the government's anti-Catholic measures. Already about 1620, the more coercive measures were effectively in abeyance in Derry diocese, as exemplified in the sheriffs' failure to prosecute the excommunicate James Ferrall. The family's ability to vitiate measures against both clergy and laity was further demonstrated during the government's campaign of 1629–30, covering the entire kingdom. In the bishop's visitation of November 1629, presentments were made of many British recusants, and of the Master of Abercorn as their leader. In theory the civil authorities were to pursue the recalcitrant. Those called to appear before the bishop merely ignored the summons, yet no action was taken. Arising from the proclamation against Catholic clergy (April 1629), Lord Deputy Falkland had instructed Bishop Downham to have the then vicar-apostolic, MacSweeney, together with Chamberlain, the Jesuit resident in Strabane, arrested. When the bishop, through the provost of Strabane, sought to arrest the clerics, they were taking refuge with the Master of Abercorn.[83]

At times of attempted religious coercion in the localities, noble access to the court could mitigate if not undermine efforts to proceed against the old faith, illustrating the protective power of seigneurial Catholicism. Thus the earl of Antrim appealed to the king against the charge of keeping priests in his home in 1621. Similarly in Strabane in 1629–30, the security of Catholicism there rested ultimately on the court connections of the Abercorns, a consideration recognized by the different parties to the struggle. Leading local recusants argued that, as Catholics were tolerated at court, those in remote areas, such as themselves, should not be questioned. Bishop Downham, and even Lord Justice Cork, not to mention the provost of Strabane (to whom the implementation of anti-Catholic measures fell), recognized the threat which the royal connections of the Hamiltons represented, especially for those seeking to enforce the anti-recusancy measures in the family's Ulster territories.[84] Nevertheless Sir George Hamilton was detained in Dublin, about Christmas 1629, probably at the instigation of Bishop Downham. It was believed locally that the Master of Abercorn had been speedily alerted from Dublin about the crackdown on priests in his locality, and was hurrying to court to seek a stay of execution.[85] The campaign ceased, however, towards the end of 1632 with the appointment of Wentworth as lord deputy.

Renewed pressure against Catholics in Scotland in the late 1620s and into the early 1630s contributed to a steady flow of migrants to Ulster. In 1629 government measures against recusants were intensified: the court of high commission was specifically charged with proceeding against those who sheltered priests, and the privy council, now better equipped to implement decisions, set up a committee for 'Suppression of Papists'.[86] While not limited to Derry diocese, the benevolent climate there served to attract Catholic exiles. These tended to be converts drawn from the upper social level. In 1633, three gentry converts, together with the missioner Fr Patrick Hegarty OFM, fled from Scotland and were staying in Drogheda, at the southernmost part of the Armagh province. About the same time 34 Scots converts were visiting their co-religionists in Co. Donegal. Political uncertainty in Scotland in the late 1630s may have contributed to further Catholic migration to Ulster.[87]

The Scottish Catholic community persisted in Strabane until 1641. Jesuit ministry continued, based in the home of the leading planter, Claud Hamilton, baron of Strabane, and Hamilton protection, support and maintenance facilitated the vicar-apostolic in supervising the Catholic diocese of Derry. The Scots planter family's stance complemented that of the Londoners on their plantation, whose agents favoured the Catholic clergy in leases and lawsuits, and where by the early 1630s a mass-house had been erected on each proportion. Contemporaries recognized that an exceptionally benevolent climate for Catholicism reigned in Derry diocese: in 1636 both the prelate in charge of Kilmore diocese and the Catholic bishop of Raphoe were seeking a transfer to the vacant see of Derry.[88]

Stresses – economic, ethnic, religious – unleashed by developments in the winter of 1641 brought the Scottish Catholic colony under the Hamiltons to an end. Sir Phelim O'Neill, leader of the Ulster Irish insurgents, was then suitor to Jean Gordon (widow of Claud Hamilton, Lord Strabane); they married shortly afterwards, and O'Neill took her to live at his house in Kinnard, Co. Tyrone. She allegedly invited him to take over the town of Strabane. The collapse of the colony was graphically marked by the taking of Strabane in December 1641. As part of an offensive against the Scots by Sir Phelim's forces, Irish bands torched buildings and looted British property, and seized the fortified residence on the lands of Sir William Hamilton.[89]

Within the broad flow of Scottish migration to Ulster in the early seventeenth century, Catholics represented a small but significant strand. Until the 1620s a growth in recusancy in Scotland occurred at a time when religious coercion was an ongoing feature of Catholic life. Viewed from an English or Scottish perspective, the civil climate for the practice of Catholicism was more relaxed in Ireland. From the late sixteenth century, some in the English Catholic community were seeking refuge from pressure at home by moving to the less threatening environment of Ireland.[90] With the transforming of conditions in Ulster in the wake of peace in 1603, extended and consolidated with the Plantation, Scots Catholics, too, could look to the neighbouring isle to provide a haven from prosecution on religious grounds. Such motivation co-existed with a more traditional movement of islanders to north Antrim, within the context of the residual framework of the MacDonnell Gaelic lordship.

In both strands, however, seigneurial support for Catholicism was crucial in ensuring the presence of Scots Catholic communities on their Ulster estates. The earl of Antrim's patronage of Catholicism was well-attested, while the family of the first earl of Abercorn (in particular, Sir George Hamilton, the earl's brother) ensured that their precinct of Strabane became 'a plantation of popery among the British' in Ulster.[91] Not alone did the Hamiltons favour Scots Catholics as tenants, but they used their position to seek conversions from among the settlers. In addition, both the earl of Antrim and the Hamiltons facilitated the ministry of Irish Jesuits among their Scottish tenants, thereby consolidating the adherence of those already Catholic, and gaining new converts. Lordly support for the Catholic presence among the Scots in Strabane strengthened Catholicism in Derry diocese, providing maintenance and security for the vicar-apostolic and other clergy. Thus until the 1641 rising Scots Catholics, concentrated in Strabane and in north Antrim, represented a distinctive feature in the cultural and denominational landscape of plantation Ulster. The Scottish Catholic community in Ulster highlights the role of religious coercion in migration between the Stuart kingdoms, and points to a Scottish dimension in the story of Ulster Catholicism in the plantation era.[92]

NOTES

1 For a contemporary account of Scots migration to Ulster arising from Protestant commitment see Robert Blair, *Memoirs of the Life of Mr Robert Blair* (Edinburgh, 1754), pp. 51–70.

2 The term features in contemporary Jesuit annual reports, which were composed in Latin; see n. 26.

3 On the implementation of measures against recusancy, see M. Sanderson, 'Catholic recusancy in Scotland in the sixteenth century', *Innes Review*, 21:2 (1970), 87–107; on religious developments in Gaelic Scotland in the sixteenth century, see M. Mac Craith, 'The Gaelic reaction to the Reformation', in S. Ellis and S. Barber (eds), *Conquest and Union: Fashioning a British State, 1485–1725* (London and New York, 1995), pp. 139–61; on the early conversion of the Campbells of Argyll to Protestantism, see J. Dawson, 'Calvinism and the Gaidhealtachd in Scotland', in A. Duke, G. Lewis and A. Pettegrew (eds), *Calvinism in Europe, 1560–1620* (Cambridge, 1994), pp. 231–53.

4 J.B. Paul (ed.), *The Scots Peerage: Founded on Wood's Edition of Sir Robert Douglas's Peerage of Scotland; Containing an Historical and Genealogical Account of the*

Nobility of that Kingdom (9 vols, Edinburgh, 1904–14), iv, pp. 541–5; ii (Edinburgh, 1905), pp. 342–3; iii (Edinburgh, 1906), pp. 574–7; Claud Hamilton, second son of first earl of Abercorn (succeeded as Lord Strabane in 1633), married Jean Gordon, daughter of the first marquis of Huntly, November 1632, G. Hamilton, *A History of the House of Hamilton* (Edinburgh, 1933), pp. 37–8; on the recusancy of these families as a badge of opposition to centralizing tendencies in the Scottish polity, see R. Scott Spurlock, 'The laity and the structure of the Catholic Church in early modern Scotland', in R. Armstrong and T. Ó hAnnracháin (eds), *Insular Christianity: Alternative Models of the Church in Britain and Ireland, c.1570–c.1700* (Manchester, 2013), pp. 231–51.

5 T. McCoog, '"Pray to the Lord of the harvest": Jesuit missions to Scotland in the sixteenth century', *Innes Review*, 53:2 (2002), 127–88: 144–59; on seigneurial Catholicism, see J. Bossy, 'The character of Elizabethan Catholicism', *Past and Present*, 21 (1962), 39–59.

6 On the problem of faction centring on these northern earls in the early 1590s, see J. Brown, 'Scottish politics 1567–1625', in A. Smith (ed.), *The Reign of James VI and I* (London, 1973), pp. 22–39: pp. 27–8; on the varied motives within this movement, see R. Grant, 'The Brig o' Dee affair, the sixth earl of Huntly and the politics of the Counter-Reformation', in J. Goodare and M. Lynch (eds), *The Reign of James VI* (East Linton, 2000), pp. 93–109, and K. Brown, 'The making of a *politique*: the counter-reformation and the regional politics of John, eight Lord Maxwell', *Scottish Historical Review*, 67:182 (1987), 152–75.

7 J.H. Burton and D. Masson (eds), *Register of the Privy Council of Scotland (RPCS), 1625–27* (14 vols, Edinburgh, 1877–98), p. 456.

8 *RPCS, 1613–16*, pp. 584–5.

9 *RPCS, 1625–27*, p. 449; for an overview of priestly activity in the 1620s and 1630s, see P. Anson, *Underground Catholicism in Scotland 1622–1878* (Montrose, 1970), pp. 8–43.

10 G.I.R. McMahon, 'The Scottish courts of high commission, 1610–38', *Records of Scottish Church History Society*, 15 (1965), 193–209.

11 The presbytery charged several men with 'superstitious behaviour' at Christmas: Glasgow presbytery records (hereafter GPR), transcript, 3 January 1610, Glasgow City Archives, CH 2/171/35, p. 130; crucifixes, 8 July 1612, *ibid.*, pp. 248–9; the painters returned, and the kirk was unable to stop their activities, 20 Apr. 1617, *ibid.*, pp. 317–18.

12 Details of this campaign are summarized in *RPCS, 1613–16*, pp. xcvii-cii; John Ogilvie (*c.*1578/9–1615), M. Dilworth, 'John Ogilvie (*c.*1578/9–1615)', *ODNB* (61 vols, Oxford, 2004), xxxxi, pp. 570-1: on pressure on recusants in the period 1603-*c.*1640, see A. Macinnes, 'Catholic recusancy and the penal laws, 1603–1707', *Records of the Scottish Church History Society*, 23 (1989), 27–63: 27–47.

13 *RPCS, 1619–22*, pp. 47, 293, 343–4.

14 *RPCS, 1622–5*, pp. 598–9; on the Spanish match and toleration for Catholics, see G. Redworth, *The Prince and the Infanta: The Cultural Politics of the Spanish Match* (New Haven, CT and London, 2003), pp. 10–11; on this development in Ireland, see B. Mac Cuarta, *Catholic Revival in the North of Ireland 1603–41* (Dublin, 2007), pp. 203–10.

15 *RPCS, 1619–22*, pp. 226, 419–20.

16 *RPCS, 1625–27*, pp. 346, 406–8.

17 J.A. Fleming and J.H. Millar (eds), *The Acts of the Parliament of Scotland, 1424–1707* (12 vols, Edinburgh, 1814–1875), iv, pp. 62–3.

18 *RPCS, 1622–25*, pp. 15–16.

19 *RPCS, 1625–27*, pp. 413–14; *1627–28*, p. 535.

20 On the role of the MacDonnells in straddling Gaelic Scotland and Ulster, see J. Ohlmeyer, *Civil War and Restoration in the Three Stuart Kingdoms* (Dublin, 2001), pp. 18–23; R. Gillespie, *Colonial Ulster: The Settlement of East Ulster, 1600–41* (Cork, 1985), p. 144; on political developments in the isles in the early seventeenth century, see D. Stevenson, *Alasdair Maccolla* (Edinburgh, 1980), pp. 34–61.

21 On Antrim's estate management, see Ohlmeyer, *Civil War and Restoration*, pp. 36–42.

22 C. Giblin (ed.), *The Irish Franciscan Mission to Scotland, 1619–46* (Dublin, 1964); F. Macdonald, *Missions to the Gaels: Reformation and Counter-Reformation in Ulster and the Highlands and Islands of Scotland* (Edinburgh, 2006), pp. 55–96; on the Scottish political context of the Franciscan mission, see R. Scott Spurlock's Chapter 6 in this volume, pp. 169–202.

23 B. Jennings (ed.), *Wadding Papers 1614–38* (Dublin, 1953), p. 40.

24 On migration from Gaelic Scotland to Antrim in the early seventeenth century, see B. Turner, 'Distributional aspects of family name study illustrated in the glens of Antrim', PhD dissertation, Queen's University Belfast, 1974, pp. 51–63, 86–7, 113–38 (I am grateful to Raymond Gillespie for this reference); on the political background to this migration, see E. Cowan, 'Clanship, kinship and the Campbell acquisition of Islay', *Scottish Historical Review*, 58:166 (1979), 132–57.

25 Jesuit annual letter 1613, Rome, Archivum Romanum Societatis Iesu (hereafter ARSI), Anglia 41, fol. 66v.

26 On Irish Jesuit ministry in the western isles, see Jesuit annual letter 1611 (ARSI, Anglia 41, fol. 48r–v), annual letter 1613, and the 'Excursio Scotica' in annual letter 1619, Dublin, Irish Jesuit Archives (hereafter IJA), MacErlean Transcripts, pp. 19–28, where the term 'Scoti Hibernici' appears; it would appear that the Jesuits used this term to denote the Gaelic-speaking islanders they encountered; F. Macdonald, *Missions to the Gaels*, pp. 48–53.

27 'ex iis qui Scoti Hibernici vocantur', Jesuit annual letter 1615, ARSI, Anglia 41, fol. 92r

28 Jesuit annual letter 1617, IJA, MacErlean Transcripts, p.13; the marshal in question may have been Sir Moses Hill, Ulster provost marshal from 1603 until his death in 1629, who was notorious in implementing anti-Catholic measures, Mac Cuarta, *Catholic Revival in the North of Ireland, 1603–41*, pp. 20, 177.

29 On the Touchets as plantation grantees, see P. Robinson, *The Plantation of Ulster* (Belfast, 2000), pp. 204–5; by the early 1620s the earl and his wife were Catholic: C.B. Herrup, 'Mervin Touchet (1591-1631)', *ODNB*, lv, p. 79.

30 Jesuit annual letter 1618, ARSI, Anglia 41, fols 112v–113r.

31 M. Dilworth, 'Patrick Anderson (1574/5-1624)', *ODNB*, ii, pp. 68-9; J. Durkan, 'Two Jesuits: Patrick Anderson and John Ogilvie', *Innes Review*, 21:2 (1970), 157–61; *RPCS, 1619–22*, pp. 277, 419–20.

32 Sir James Hamilton welcomed strangers and scholars at Killyleagh, T. Lowry (ed.), *The Hamilton Manuscripts* (Belfast, 1867), p. 31; Killyleagh castle, G. Hill, *An Historical Account of the Plantation in Ulster* (Belfast, 1877), p. 452.

33 King to lord deputy Grandison, 22 May 1621, Acta Regia Hibernica, NAI, RC2/7, pp. 7–8; King to lord deputy, 6 October 1621, *CSPI, 1615–25*, p. 337; it is possible that this Alexander Boyd was the Glasgow minister of the same name, Glasgow presbytery records, CH2/171/35, pp. 400, 404.

34 Text of proclamation: 'Coppie veritable ... du dernier edict ... imprime dans la ville de Dublin ... le 15 Octobre 1617', [1619], TNA, SP 63/234/11; for another incident arising from this measure, see B. Mac Cuarta (ed.), 'A Catholic funeral in County Down, 1617', *Archivium Hibernicum*, 60 (2006–07), 320–5; King to lord deputy Grandison, 6 October 1621, *CSPI, 1615–25*, p. 337.

35 In the years 1621–23 Anderson was assigned to the Jesuit house in Bourges, France, 'Catalogue of Scottish Jesuits in the sixteenth century', in T. McCoog, '"Pray to the Lord of the harvest"', p. 163; Jesuit annual letter 1620, IJA, MacErlean Transcripts, p. 7.

36 V. Treadwell (ed.), *The Irish Commission of 1622* (Dublin, 2006), p. 608; chief of these was the family of the Englishman, Mervin Touchet, second earl of Castlehaven, who as already noted was the dominant landholder in Omagh barony, Co. Tyrone; in addition, Lord Audley (the first earl of Castlehaven) had received a servitor's grant in Co. Armagh: Robinson, *The Plantation of Ulster*, pp. 78, 204–5.

37 Robert Stuart 'hath refused the oath of supremacy', and Sir George Hamilton is 'a recusant papist', 'Instructions for Sir Arthur Chichester ... ', 5 June 1614, TNA, SP 63/232/8 (*CSPI, 1611–14*, pp. 482–3).

38 Estimates of Scottish families for various areas within plantation Ulster, 1622, M. Perceval-Maxwell, *The Scottish Migration to Ulster in the Reign of James I* (London, 1973), pp. 215–24; for an assessment of settlement and building in Strabane barony in 1622, see *ibid.*, pp. 194–5.

39 J. Cameron Lees, *The Abbey of Paisley from its Foundation till its Dissolution* (Paisley, 1878), p. 237; on the various networks of the Hamiltons until the 1580s, see E. Finnie, 'The house of Hamilton: patronage, politics and the Church in the Reformation period', *Innes Review*, 36:1 (1985), 3–28; for a study of a Catholic aristocratic entourage in early modern England, see M. Questier, *Catholicism and Community in Early Modern England: Politics, Aristocratic Patronage and Religion, c.1550–1640* (Cambridge, 2006).

40 M. Wasser, 'James Hamilton, 1st earl of Abercorn (1575-1618)', *ODNB*, xxiv, pp. 837-8; on the family of the earl of Abercorn until 1641, see G. Hamilton, *A History of the House of Hamilton* (Edinburgh, 1933), pp. 31–7; on the survival of recusancy in Ayr, and Hamilton influence in making Paisley a recusant centre in the 1560s, see M. Saunderson, *Ayrshire and the Reformation: People and Change 1490–1600* (East Linton, 1997), pp. 120–6.

41 Dame Margaret Hamilton, countess of Angus, was charged with recusancy, and was served with an injunction from the archbishop of Glasgow 'to proceed against all the rest of her family who will not give obedience', 28 June 1615, Glasgow presbytery records, transcript, Glasgow City Archives (GCA), CH2/171/35, p. 384; wife of Sir James Kneeland facilitating visit of John Ogilvie SJ to their home, *ibid.*, 25 January 1615, pp. 358–9; on women in Scottish Catholicism in the 1630s and 1640s, see A. Roberts, 'The role of women in Scottish Catholic survival', *Scottish Historical Review*, 70:190 (1991), 129–50 (the 1630s and 1640s are treated on 129–37).

42 Cameron Lees, *The Abbey of Paisley*, p. 266; for this episode, the author drew on the records of the presbytery of Paisley.

43 *RPCS, 1625–27*, pp. 309, 379–80, 397–8, 421–2 (note).

44 *RPCS, 1627–28*, p. 344.

45 The minutes of the presbytery of Paisley (a series housed in the National Archives of Scotland) are not extant for the years 1608–25, and thus a major source for anti-recusancy measures in the Abercorns' home area is missing; on the recusancy of Marion countess of Abercorn, see Cameron Lees, *The Abbey of Paisley*, pp. 262–82. For pressure on individual recusants in the Glasgow area in the years 1615–20, see Glasgow presbytery records, CH2/171/35: Sir George Hamilton and his wife, p. 352; those present at mass celebrated by John Ogilvie, pp. 357, 363–4; CH2/171/36: Matthew Adam, William Menteith, p. 4; Sir James Kincaid and his wife, p. 28; James Stewart, pp. 142–3; George Anderson, accused of sheltering Patrick Anderson SJ, p. 158; Robert Campbell, who received a consignment of Catholic objects from William Heygate in Bordeaux, pp. 192–3, John Scheilis and Adam Colquhoune 'suspect of papistry', p. 231. On the social profile of some Glasgow Catholics at this time, see J. Durkan, 'John Ogilvie's Glasgow associates', *Innes Review*, 21:2 (1970), 153–6.

46 The archbishop of Glasgow gave power to presbytery of Paisley to excommunicate Grizell Hamilton 'as an obstinate papist', 28 June 1615, GPR, CH2/171/35, p. 385; Jacqueline followed Hamilton to Scotland, and claimed they had been married, until she gained possession of the disputed goods, whereupon she admitted they had not in fact been married, *RPCS, 1616–19*, pp. 639–41; *1619–22*, pp. 201–2, 207–9, 759–62.

47 GPR, transcript, 17 May 1626, GCA, CH2/171/36, pp. 339–40.

48 J. Balfour Paul, *The Scots Peerage*, i (Edinburgh, 1904), pp. 40–1; 'Informations concerning the Scottish recusants in the barony of Strabane', 9 Jan 1629–30, TNA SP63/250/22 VI; 1630 muster roll, Strabane barony, Co. Tyrone, BL, Add Ms 4770, fols 90r–104v.

49 *RPCS, 1627–28*, pp. 343–4.

50 *RPCS, 1619–22*, pp. 201–2.

51 On Robert Algeo's career, and on the political and religious context of this image, see R. Hunter, 'Style and form in gravestone and monumental sculpture in Co. Tyrone in the seventeenth and eighteenth centuries', in C. Dillon and H. Jefferies (eds), *Tyrone History and Society* (Dublin, 2000), pp. 291–326: 294–8.

52 *RPCS, 1619–22*, pp. 201–2; Treadwell (ed.), *The Irish Commission of 1622*, pp. 569–70; *RPCS, 1625–27*, p. 426; 'Informations … Scottish recusants'.

53 *RPCS, 1622–25*, pp. 610–11; the bishop of Derry referred to the Strabane settler of that name as 'a lewd pseudo-catholic', 'Informations ... Scottish recusants'.
54 *RPCS, 1627–28*, pp. 596–7.
55 'Informations ... Scottish recusants'.
56 Treadwell (ed.), *Irish Commission*, p. 569; *RPCS, 1619–22*, pp. 721–3.
57 'Informations ... Scottish recusants'.
58 *RPCS, 1613–16*, pp. 459–60.
59 *RPCS, 1622–25*, pp. 15–16.
60 'Informations ... Scottish recusants'; William Barclay the younger (probably their son) was of military age in 1630, for he was mustered in Strabane barony, BL Add Ms 4770, fol.76v–77r.
61 'Informations ... Scottish recusants'.
62 Perceval-Maxwell, *The Scottish Migration*, p. 346; Treadwell (ed.), *The Irish Commission of 1622*, pp. 569–70; he was probably also managing the two proportions of Sir Claud in Co. Cavan, totalling 2,500 acres, *ibid.*, pp. 520–1; on the Hamilton lands in Strabane, see W. Roulston, 'The evolution of the Abercorn estate in north west Ulster, 1610–1703', *Familia*, 15 (1999), pp. 54–67.
63 Treadwell (ed.), *Irish Commission*, p. 248.
64 While living in Glasgow in 1622–23, she refused to attend church, 'being oftentimes admonished, exhorted and required by the ministers of the city to that effect', pleading that she be spared censure pending her husband's return; the presbytery saw little hope of her conversion, GPR, transcript, 16 October 1622 et seq., CH2/171/36, pp. 278 (quote), 280, 284, 287; on the recusancy of the Leslies (including several priests), see *RPCS, 1629–30*, index, sub Leslie.
65 Bishop Cullenan of Raphoe, 25 July 1639, in P. Moran (ed.), *Spicilegium Ossoriense* (3 vols, Dublin, 1874) i, p. 240; 'Informations ... Scottish recusants'; quote, GPR, transcript, 7 December 1614, *ibid.*, CH 2/171/35, p. 352.
66 Quote, Treadwell (ed.), *Irish Commission*, p. 603.
67 Sir George, as guardian, was raising the heir of Sir Claud Hamilton in that faith; as Sir George had no children, this heir was likely to succeed to his properties too, Treadwell (ed.), *Irish Commission*, p. 603.
68 1630 muster roll for Ulster, BL Add Ms 4770, fols 90r–104v.
69 Ohlmeyer, *Civil War and Restoration*, p. 26; *Burke's Peerage and Baronetage* (London, 1956), sub Abercorn.
70 Bishop of Derry to Lord Justice Loftus, 2 December 1629, TNA, SP63/250/22 I; Sir George's wife in 1609 was Isobel Leslie, daughter of James, Master of Rothes; presumably the rumour referred to one of these Leslies: Hamilton, *House of Hamilton*, p. 33; on Sir John Stewart and the earl of Annandale as Ulster landowners, see Perceval-Maxwell, *The Scottish Migration*, pp. 351–2, 354–7; for the Annandale rumour, see earl of Cork to Lord Dorchester, January 1629–30, TNA, SP63/250/21/ II.
71 Bishop of Derry to viscount Loftus, 2 December 1629, TNA, SP63/250/22 II; Cork to Dorchester, January 1630, TNA, SP63/250/22; 'Informations ... Scottish recusants'.
72 Testimony of Thomas Plunkett, examined by bishop of Derry, [January 1630], TNA, SP63/250/22 V.

73 Treadwell (ed.), *Irish Commission*, p. 569.
74 Robinson, *The Plantation of Ulster*, p. 78; Sir Piers Crosby acquired a joint interest in these lands through marriage in 1619 to the widow of the earl of Castlehaven, Treadwell (ed.), *Irish Commission*, pp. 572–3, 604 (quote); A. Clarke, 'Sir Piers Crosby, 1590–1646: Wentworth's "tawney ribbon"', *Irish Historical Studies*, 26 (1988), 142–60: 150–1, 153.
75 This and the previous quotation, bishop of Derry, 'Informations ... Scottish recusants'.
76 Bishop of Derry, 'Informations ... Scottish recusants'.
77 F. Finegan, 'Biographical dictionary of Irish Jesuits', IJA, sub Chamberlain; M. Chamberlain to William Dease, 28 October 1608, TNA, SP63/225/252; R. Hunter (ed.), 'Catholicism in Meath *c.*1622', *Collectanea Hibernica*, 14 (1971), 9.
78 'Informations ... Scottish recusants'.
79 On gentry homes as venues for mass in the Pale, see C. Lennon, 'Mass in the manor-house: the counter-reformation in Dublin, 1560–1630', in J. Kelly and D. Keogh (eds), *History of the Catholic Diocese of Dublin* (Dublin, 2000), pp. 112–26; for this trend in Ulster, see Mac Cuarta, *Catholic Revival in the North of Ireland 1603–41*, pp. 114–17.
80 Deposition of Robert Maxwell, 22 August 1642, M. Hickson, *Ireland in the Seventeenth century: or, the Irish Massacres of 1641–2, their Causes and Results* (2 vols, 1884), i, p. 332; Chamberlain may have served in Strabane until the late 1630s: arising from his experience in Tyrone, by autumn 1640 he was one of three Irish Jesuits assigned as chaplains to the royal army against the Scots, P. Moran (ed.), *Spicilegium Ossoriense* (Dublin, 1874), i, p. 237; on the role of a chaplain in a Scottish lordly family in the 1630s and 1640s, see Roberts, 'The role of women in Scottish Catholic survival', 133–6.
81 Testimony of Thomas Plunkett [January 1629–30], TNA, SP63/250/22 V; viaticum for Tirlogh O'Kelly, alumnus of Irish college, Rome, 8 May 1628, B. Jennings (ed.), 'Acta Sacrae Congregationis De Propaganda Fide, 1622–50', *Archivium Hibernicum*, 22 (1959), 47.
82 Bishop Cullenan of Raphoe, 25 July 1639, in Moran (ed.), *Spicilegium Ossoriense*, i, p. 240.
83 Bishop of Derry to viscount Loftus, 2 December 1629, TNA, SP63/250/22 II; in the absence of a letter from the lords justice, such as the bishop had previously from the lord deputy, 'scarce any of the natives, or any of the British recusants will appear at my court', bishop of Derry to lords justice, 9 January 1629–30, TNA, SP63/250/22 IV.
84 Bishop of Derry to viscount Loftus, 2 December 1629; earl of Cork to Dorchester, January 1630, TNA, SP63/250/22.
85 [William Bellew] to [Wadding], 4 January 1630, Jennings (ed.), *Wadding Papers*, p. 331; bishop of Derry to lord chancellor of Ireland, 2 December 1629, same to lords justice, 9 January 1630, TNA, SP63/250/22; for another example of contemporary anti-recusancy proceedings, see B. Mac Cuarta (ed.), 'A presentment of recusants, east Galway, 1632', *Journal of Galway Archaeological and Historical Society*, 61 (2009), 74–8.
86 McMahon, 'The Scottish courts of high commission, 1610–38', 202–3.

87 In August 1631, Sir Alexander Gordon (brother of the twelfth earl of Sutherland), together with his family, moved to Ulster in search of religious freedom; with his tenants and servants the family was living in Co. Cavan in the late 1630s, Macdonald, *Missions to the Gaels*, pp. 65, 79; B. Mac Cuarta, 'Catholic revival in Kilmore diocese, 1603–41', in B. Scott (ed.), *Culture and Society in Early Modern Breifne/Cavan* (Dublin, 2009), pp 147–72: p. 168.

88 W. Burke (ed.), 'The diocese of Derry in 1631', *Archivium Hibernicum*, 5 (1916), 5–6; B. Jennings (ed.), 'Acta Sacrae Congregationis De Propaganda Fide 1622–50', *Archivium Hibernicum*, 22 (1959), 102; R. Nugent to Jesuit general, 15 September 1636, ARSI, Anglia 6a, fol. 1.

89 Examination of Robert Maxwell, 22 August 1642, Hickson, *Ireland in the Seventeenth Century*, i, p. 332; examination of Michael Harrison, 11 February 1652–3, *ibid.*, pp. 229, 232; there was little trace of a Scots Catholic community in Strabane by the Restoration, W. Roulston, *Restoration Strabane, 1660–1714: Economy and Society in Provincial Ireland* (Dublin, 2007), p. 54.

90 On this trend, see D. Edwards, 'A haven of popery: English Catholic migration to Ireland in the age of plantations', in A. Ford and J. McCafferty (eds), *The Origins of Sectarianism in Early Modern Ireland* (Cambridge, 2005), pp. 95–126.

91 Bishop of Derry, 'Informations ... Scottish recusants'.

92 The author wishes to thank Dr Robert Armstrong for kindly commenting on an earlier draft of this chapter.

6

Confessionalization and clan cohesion: Ireland's contribution to Scottish Catholic renewal in the seventeenth century*

R. SCOTT SPURLOCK

Post-Tridentine Roman Catholicism has traditionally been understood to have made a minimal impact on the Gaelic-speaking west of Scotland during the seventeenth century. Having been chronically understaffed, the Catholic Church in the Western Isles was in a dire state by the reformation. Subsequently, it entered into a period between 1560 and 1620 labelled by Allan MacInnes and John L. Campbell as 'moribund'.[1] While Catholic Scots colleges began to appear on the continent from as early as 1580, they preferred Lowland, English-speaking students to Gaelic-speaking ones, which resulted in a dearth of Gaelic speaking Scots priests available in the generations after the reformation and through most of the following century.[2] Macinnes thus argues for negligible Scottish efforts to proselytise Scottish Gaeldom and an overall minimal legacy for missionary endeavours.[3] Yet Scottish-based attempts were not the only ones made. Beginning in 1619 a mission staffed by Irish Franciscans began to operate in the *Gaidhealtachd*, the Gaelic-speaking regions of Scotland.[4] This too met challenges. According to many historians, a severe lack of enthusiasm from the Irish colleges requested to provide Gaelic speaking missionaries blighted the mission, and has led to a prevailing interpretation that the mission was directed from Propaganda Fide, staffed by Irish Franciscans from hesitant continental Irish colleges, and took place outside the direct jurisdiction of the missioners' superiors under the nominal oversight of the nuncio in Brussels. However, such emphasis on continental interests and disinterests has served to cloud the mission's *modus operendi* and minimized its lasting significance to the overall heritage of the *Gaidhealtachd*.[5]

Traditional Catholic accounts of the period do not vary from this account to any great extent, other than emphasizing the noble individual efforts of the missioners to work in incredibly difficult conditions while being constantly underfunded and facing cultural practices, particularly relating to marriage, that necessitated specially assigned powers Rome was hesitant to dispense.[6] Additionally these accounts have shown particular interest in interpreting claims within the missionaries' own reports that during the first decade of the mission (between 1619 and 1628) they 'converted' over 10,000 people in the Western Isles.[7] These attempts have so far proved somewhat unsatisfactory, particularly because the large numbers of conversions were vigorously defended by the priests despite the fact that they heightened concerns in Rome. Propaganda Fide, encouraged by Lowland Scots clergy residing on the continent, scrutinized the reports as being unbelievable and threatened to terminate the mission.[8] Upon demands for clarification and precise lists, Cornelius Ward, a leading figure on the mission, produced a more precise tally of 12,269.[9] Rather than modifying reports to appease criticism, the missionaries responded by doing their best to provide evidence for the harvest that they themselves perceived as remarkable. Yet rather than seeking out what was distinctive about the mission to the *Gaidhealtachd*, the historiography has tended to interpret it through the monolithic prism of the institutional models proposed by Propaganda which mirrored the ideal patterns of work carried out in other regions of the world. What is crucial for understanding the resurgence of Catholicism in Gaelic-speaking Scotland is that it was not primarily driven by Rome, nor did it reflect models of counter-reformation from elsewhere in Europe.

Jason Harris in Chapter 7 identifies much more clearly the continental politics that were so fundamental to the formulation of the mission in Rome and the factors which caused support for the mission to the *Gaidhealtachd* to ebb and flow, which include: Papal and Spanish politics; the priorities of Propaganda and the demands for appropriating funds in North America, Asia Minor, the Far East and Africa; and, the sometimes vicious politics of the Irish and Scots colleges in Europe.[10] Harris's work is important and very illuminating in relation to clarifying how continental funds were allocated for mission and how policies were formulated; and as such, it enriches the explanations in earlier Catholic historiography which place too much emphasis on the role of Propaganda and too little on the real impetus behind the missions. Although Harris notes from the institutional side of the endeavour that 'poor planning and inflexible structures combined with ecclesiastical rivalries to scupper the enterprise' and therefore 'when the papacy was faced with a number of prominent Catholic Scots, hostile to the mission … they were happy to sacrifice the friars to the greater good',[11] the work in Gaelic speaking Scotland carried on regardless. This demands that further attention be given to the Scottish end of the endeavour.

Two recent works by Fiona Macdonald and Lisa Curry have made significant strides in highlighting the important sociological role of

Catholicism in Gaelic-speaking Scotland. However, just like the historiography they have inherited, they persist in viewing continental Catholic structures as the brokers in the missionary endeavours. As a result, the two traditional interpretations outlined above (minimal impact and continental dependence) persist.[12] However, whereas Macdonald argues the Franciscans, 'following the Jesuit guidelines taken up by most Catholic missionaries … paid considerable attention to the social hierarchy in the hope of influencing the general population', a process she refers to as 'cultivating the Scottish *Fine*' or 'clan elite', the evidence supports a much more proactive lay participation.[13] For this reason, despite the great steps taken forward by Curry and Macdonald, the primary question remains: what really prompted the return of a resident Catholic clerical presence in Gaelic-speaking Scotland after a 60-year absence and why? The answer is that at the behest of some clan elites in Scotland, and with their financial provision, a process of confessionalization among clans took place. From as early as the late 1560s appeals arrived in Rome for missionaries to be sent to Scotland. After repeated requests in 1611, the Scots Franciscan John Ogilvie carried out an initial reconnaissance mission in 1612.[14] What is important to note here is that initial contact seems to have been initiated from Scotland rather than from Rome.

Contrary to models of confessionalization implemented in processes of state formation, either on the continent or in the formation of Protestant Scotland, the process in Gaelic-speaking Scotland, like Ute Lotz-Heumann's interpretation of the process in Catholic Ireland, served to consolidate resistance to the government's systematic encroachments on traditional Gaelic language, culture and hegemonies.[15] These elements of Gaeldom were viewed as incompatible with both the formation of a Protestant state and James VI's ambitions for a centralized absolute, personal monarchy in Scotland.[16] However, it would be inaccurate to simply classify the process of Catholic confessionalization in the *Gaidhealtachd* with the traditional continental interpretations as being driven from 'above' or 'below', or even wholly summarized by Lotz-Heumann's definition of 'double confessionalization', because the *Gaidhealtachd* lacked the essentials of a diocesan or parochial system through which an institutional process of confessionalization could be implemented.[17] The lack of any functioning Catholic ecclesiastical structure in Scotland required a different structural framework that was provided by kin and clan connections. Therefore, this process was not primarily determined by continental ecclesiastical agendas as was the case in Ireland. In this regard the model in Scotland contravenes the dominant continental models of confessionalization.[18] According to Lisa Curry, writing in relation to the MacDonnells of Glengarry in the second half of the century, 'the strongly protestant-based authority in Scotland was at times unsympathetic and on occasion openly hostile to [their] society, language and culture and was consistently opposed to their Catholic religion'.[19] Her arguments have led at least one commentator to conclude that 'the clans' "real opponent" was Calvinism, rather than a "British" state, per se'.[20] However, this reverses the order of conflicting interests. Catholic missions to the *Gaidhealtachd* did not begin as a rapid counter-reformation response to the Protestant reformation, they began sixty years later. Neither were they primarily the result of Propaganda's policies. In fact, Catholic missionaries only returned to Scotland in the wake of systematic policies by the Scottish government to dismantle traditional Gaelic hegemonies and were predicated by Gaelic requests for priests.

The missions to the Western Isles can be broadly defined in three separate phases. The first took place between 1619 and 1647 under a crew of Irish Franciscans reckoned by Propaganda not to exceed four in number; the second was staffed by regulars, primarily Vincentians, between 1651 and 1679; and, the third represented a renewed Franciscan endeavour between 1665 and 1687. What is important in all three of these missions is that they were not speculative, as previous historians have tended to suggest, nor did they materialize out of the blue. From the outset, these missions were facilitated, and it appears engineered, by elements within ClanDonald. A letter dated a full nine months before the first Franciscan missionary arrived in the Western Isles was sent from Cardinal Borghese in Rome to the nuncio in Brussels, who at this time was responsible for the affairs of Scotland, asking him to persuade the Irish Franciscans at Louvain to provide some missionaries for Scotland 'under the guidance of a Scottish laird named MacDonald'.[21] The identification of a particular individual in Scotland before the practical plausibility of such a mission had even been ascertained may indicate that the Scot had submitted a supplication for a mission which he would in turn provide guidance for. Certainly a few years later, between February 1621 and July 1623, additional requests came from Scotland for Irish Franciscans, perhaps from the same source.[22] Some attention needs to be given to the identity of this individual that the Franciscan historian Cathuldus Giblin has identified as 'a Scottish laird named MacDonald'. The original letter describes him as 'Baron di Marandal, scozesse'. Cathuldus attributes this person with being a MacDonald, but with no specification as to who they are.[23]

Just as political factors contributed to the maintenance of Catholicism in the Scottish Lowlands during the seventeenth century, so too they played a prominent part in the reintroduction of a missionary presence in the Isles.[24] Pressures on the traditional power structures of the Western Isles increased from the ascension of James VI to the English throne, particularly through the implementation of the Statutes of Iona in 1609 and their agenda relating to feuds, education and religion. By 1616 more precise mechanisms were in place to ensure that royal authority would be enforced. The rise of client clans such as the MacKenzies and Campbells allowed the possibility for royal authority to be imposed in the Isles without the kind of expense required for the expeditions funded in 1596, 1599, 1605, 1607 and 1608.[25] In this new model of implementing policy the cost of campaigning was carried by the client clans, but they were recompensed by expansion in influence and territory at their victim's expense. One of the primary targets of this royal policy was ClanDonald, who since the reduction of the Lordship of the Isles in 1493 had suffered internally from severe infighting and fragmentation while also facing persistent external pressure from central royal authority and Campbell encroachments. In 1607 the traditional MacDonald territories of Kintyre were given to the seventh earl of Argyll by royal charter and through similar policies Islay later fell into Campbell hands as well. In that same year, the privy council instructed the earl of Argyll to take 'action of blude' against ClanDonald, 'being the strongest piller of all the broken hieland men, quha never in any aige wer civill … bot evir wer assisteris of the northern Irische people … in all their rebellionis'. The order sought the clan's 'ruitteing out and utter suppressing' on the grounds that 'sa long as the said Clan Donald remaynes unremovit furth of the saidis landis, his Majestie nor na otheris sal half any proffeit, and the uncivilitie and barbarities all continew nocht only thair [Ireland] bot in the Iles'.[26] However, contrary to traditional interpretations of the dire straits of Clan Iain Mhòr (ClanDonald South), resulting from internal divisions in the wake of Sorley Boy MacDonnell's death in 1590 and increased pressure from the crown after 1603, ClanDonald began to demonstrate a strong policy of developing and consolidating clan links by the 1610s.[27]

After losing Kintyre in 1607 and facing a similar plight with Islay, Angus MacDonald of Dunyveg appeared in St Giles' Cathedral in 1612 to receive redemption of the island in the face of Campbell attempts to buy it. Present with Angus was Sir Randall MacDonnell, later first earl of Antrim.[28] In stark contrast to the rift ascribed to the Antrim and Dunyveg branches of ClanDonald South, this occasion tends to suggest a united front to Campbell encroachments. Randall's presence and his financial success stemming from his ability to stay in favour with the crown through the Nine Years War and his subsequent grants for planting in Ulster have led Martin MacGregor to posit that he provided the money for Dunyveg's redemption of Islay.[29] This unilateral ClanDonald manoeuvre did temporarily stave off further losses to the Campbells. Randall MacDonnell received a short-term lease for Islay the following year, but the implementation of his business strategies forged in Ulster planting on Islay led to complaints of excessive feus. In addition, it seems probable that there were also tensions from the rank-and-file of the MacDonalds of Islay at the usurpation of the MacDonnells of Antrim, rivals for the cheiftancy of Clan Iain Mhòr, as their superiors, but this does not mean that Angus and Randall had not acted together in a concerted effort to stave off the challenges to ClanDonald. Help from Antrim provided support for Angus at a time when the MacDonalds of Dunyveg suffered from serious internal turmoil relating to the succession of the chieftaincy, including an attempted patricide by immolation at the hands of Sir James MacDonald of Knockrinsay. Likewise, the expansion of his influence helped solidify the position of Randall who faced pressure from elements within the Antrim MacDonnells who were unhappy with his planting policies that brought in large numbers of Protestant Scots and English into Ulster.[30] Clearly the ambitions among clan elites were not always shared among the rank-and-file of the clan. Poems produced in relation to the activities of the chiefs of the Antrim MacDonnells and Glengarry MacDonlads bemoan their interests beyond the clans' traditional bounds.[31]

After the death of Angus in 1613 elements within ClanDonald feuded over the Dunyveg rights to Islay and the chieftancy of Clan Iain Mhòr, including Coll Ciotach who attempted to gain control of the church lands on the island in a negotiated settlement after the rebellion and was associated with the Catholic mission in some of the earliest reports.[32] However, as a result of excessive feus and general unrest, the crown granted the heritable title of Islay to Sir John Campbell of Cawdor in 1614, a clear indication of the crown's commitment to forcibly remove ClanDonald South not only from Kintyre but Islay and Jura as well. As a result of this dispossession the *fine* of the MacBraynes, MacKays and MacEucherns had, by 1618, obliged themselves to become 'dewtiful kinsmen and obedient tennentis' of the Campbells.[33] This change of allegiance threatened not only the power of the MacDonalds of Dunyveg, but of all the clans of ClanDonald South. The reaction 'to the territorial ambitions of ClanCampbell', states Macinnes, proved to be the 'most important polarising factor within Gaeldom prior to the outbreak of the Scottish civil war'.[34]

In the face of this attempt to dispossess ClanDonald the fractured branches made concerted efforts to regain their former glory. Antrim's attempt to secure the MacDonalds of Dunyveg's rights to Islay was not his only intervention. Jane Ohlmeyer has produced an excellent assessment of the unyielding ambitions and various methods employed by the Antrim MacDonnells to maintain what she has defined as their 'MacDonnell Archipelago'.[35] It was a matter that took on an even greater urgency after the death of Sir James MacDonald of Knockrinsay in 1626, the son of Angus and the last claimant to the chieftaincy of the MacDonalds of Dunyveg and the Glens. In 1627 the earl of Antrim made another attempt to reacquire Islay and in 1634 made a bid to buy large swathes of Kintyre and Jura from James Campbell, Lord Kintyre, who was crippled by debt, only to have the deal quashed (retrospectively) through the intervention of the crown on the basis of Lord Lorne's pleas.[36] Lorne's primary argument was that MacDonnell, his son or 'anie of the Clandonald' posed a major risk to the tranquillity of the region and that priests would be imported to 'make the whole people turn papistes'.[37] Although a failure, this event seems to have left an indelible mark on the memory of the MacDonnells of Antrim. A history written c.1700 ignores the fact that the deal was rescinded, recording the first earl 'also bought with ready money the lands of Kintyre and if he lived but four or five years more he would be Lord of Iyla, Kintire and many more lands in Ireland and Scotland'.[38] Despite such efforts to restore traditional territorial boundaries, royal policies and mounting debts within ClanDonald led to significant swaths of ClanDonald's territory falling into Campbell hands and as a result their influence throughout the Isles waned. By 1638 the mainland and island estates of the Clanranald chief from Moidart to South Uist and Benbecula 'had been incorporated entirely within the feudal superiority of the House of Argyll'.[39]

ClanDonald came to identify crown and Campbell aggressions as being carried out under a banner of Protestantism. For instance, in 1615 when Campbell forces under Sir John Campbell of Cawdor put down the rebellion in Islay they specifically destroyed images used in Catholic forms of worship while Cawdor explicitly identified the island's inhabitants as Catholic.[40] This claim represents a justification for Campbell actions against a 'Catholic' population, despite the fact there was no functioning Catholicism on the island because there had been no clerical presence there for decades. Thus it should not be viewed as coincidental that the first concerted Catholic mission to the *Gaidhealtachd* in several generations began in the wake of this political turmoil, that it was precipitated by the intervention of a 'MacDonald', or that the primary motivator moving to finance the preservation of ClanDonald territory, MacDonnell of Antrim, was also the primary financial benefactor of Bonamargy Priory, which served as the base for the mission.[41] The priory became the official base of the Franciscan mission in 1624, but their presence there and the priory's use as an operational base certainly predated that year. The MacDonnells' use of the priory as the centre of family religion and as a sepulchre stretches back to at least the 1580s, as Sorley Boy MacDonnell was interred there in 1589, and perhaps as far back as the fifteenth century. Randall MacDonnell, first earl of Antrim, was buried at Bonamargy in 1636 in new family vaults he had built in 1621.[42] The priory itself, according to some sources, began to be used by the Franciscans early in the sixteenth century.[43] Thus, it appears that the close relationship between the MacDonnells and the Franciscans centred on Bonamargy began long before the mission. That it was officially deeded to the Franciscan mission by Rome in 1624, after a number of requests for the property, may have resulted from Antrim's run in with authorities and his being summoned to Dublin in 1621 for harbouring priests. Upon admitting his error and promising not to do so again in the future, he was let off. The grant from Rome protected the friars' possession of Bonamargy at a time when Franciscans at Carrickfergus were trying to gain control of the priory, while at the same time freeing Antrim from any direct involvement and therefore culpability for their presence there.

In later years, thousands of Scots from the Western Isles were said to cross over to Bonamargy in order to receive the sacraments of the eucharist and, more importantly, confirmation, which only a bishop could facilitate. The bishop of Down and Connor is reputed to have confirmed 700 Scots on a single occasion in 1639. Thus the priory on the Irish coast came to replace Iona as the centre of Scottish Gaelic Catholicism, particularly for the progeny of the Lords of the Isles. In 1626 the missioners requested the priory be granted a privileged altar, which would allow for private masses that included a plenary indulgence for the soul of the individual for whom the mass was offered.[44] Rather than providing a blessing to Catholics in Ireland, the necessity of the altar was deemed to be that the friary sat as the doorway from Scotland. From as early as 1629 there were eight or nine priests at Bonamargy to deal with the crowds that frequented the place, the indication being that they were supported by Antrim.[45] Father Hegarty reported in 1637 'that the people from the Hebrides flock daily to Bonamargy for spiritual aid, so that the friars resident there are always kept busy'.[46] Thus the mission actively sought to draw Scottish Catholics to a new pilgrimage site which was already deeply rooted in the political landscape of the Antrim MacDonnells.

That ClanDonald supported Catholic missions is certain, but the motivations for doing so need to be addressed. There are several reasons why religion should be viewed in the political context of the early seventeenth century as something that could be used to engender corporate identity in the face of attacks on traditional hegemonies. Firstly, it must be noted that legislation limiting traditional aspects of Gaelic life introduced by the government of Scotland was explicitly bound up with the adoption and promulgation of Protestantism. The Statutes of Iona, signed in 1609, required clan chiefs and other elites to stop feuding, provide education in English and endorse the Protestant faith. Despite early attempts by Bishop John Carswell in 1567 to utilize Gaelic as a tool to encourage Protestantism within the *Gaidhealtachd*, ultimately the reformation in Scotland is where the impetus for suppressing Gaelic sprang.[47] Intriguingly, nine of the chiefs who signed the statutes, or their descendants, including Angus MacDonald of Dunyveg, MacLean of Duart, MacLean of Lochbuie, Donald Gorm MacDonald of Sleat, MacLeod of Harris, MacKinnon of MacKinnon, MacLean of Coll, MacDonald of Clanranald, and MacQuarrie acted when the opportunity arose and embraced Catholicism.[48] It may be because these individuals had embraced Catholicism that the privy council appointed a number of them to apprehend Jesuits in their bounds, as a means of heightening pressure on them.[49] Secondly, Catholicism was bound up in the traditional claims of ClanDonald hegemony. Even into the reign of Charles II, a chronicle of the clan's history and origin myth asserted that

Donald, after committing fratricide, went to the pope to seek forgiveness. The pope, because of Donald's sincere contrition, pardoned his transgression and gave him 'rights of all the lands he possessed in Argyll, Kintyre and the rest of the continent'.[50] Under this authority the MacNeills had been imparted portions of Kintyre. Therefore, Rome offered an authority for their traditional rights which stretched back to before Scotland's apostasy when ClanDonald were in their ascendency. The same chronicle also emphasizes the importance of the mass in the ceremonial tradition of succession for the Lord of the Isles.

The role that religion had played in preserving the identity and authority of the Lordship of the Isles prior to 1493, and afterwards for their ClanDonald descendants, should not be underemphasized. According to A.D.M. Barrell, the period of ClanDonald hegemony witnessed 'a remarkable series of stone monuments' including freestanding crosses. Whereas this practice diminished elsewhere in Britain and Ireland it continued in the Hebrides down to the reformation. Barrell argues this likely served 'as antiquarianism deliberately fostered by the lords of the Isles to underpin the Gaelic roots of their lordship, akin to their famous inauguration ceremony which likewise echoed the practices of an earlier period'.[51] In these ways traditional lands previously bound up in the Lordship of the Isles, which were gradually being stripped through government policies carried out by ClanCampbell under the banner of Protestantism, were depicted as the rightful possessions of ClanDonald. The use of genealogies, such as the one noting the pope's grant to Donald, was, according to Martin MacGregor, a way for the extent of ClanDonald rights to be asserted.[52] As such, the resurgence of Catholicism might be seen as both an ideological anti-venom to Protestant and Lowland encroachments as well as a part of a return to a romanticized past. Or, in Curry's words, religiously and linguistically, Gaelic Catholicism 'served to emphasize the difference between such Highlanders [referring here specifically to the MacDonnells of Glengarry] and the rest of mainland Britain'.[53]

Throughout the first Franciscan mission there is ample evidence to demonstrate the hands-on influence of the first earl of Antrim and his son, as well as their keen sense of political manoeuvring. From the late 1620s missionary reports ask if missioners can spend extended periods of time at Bonamargy and, if so, whether during these periods they may act as penitentiaries as St Patrick's Purgatory, despite Propaganda's insistence that the pilgrimage site lay outside the scope of the mission.[54] This is of importance since the first earl was a patron of both Bonamargy and St Patrick's Purgatory.[55] The patronage of sites was not simply an act of personal devotion, but equally a public duty and a means for strengthening traditional support.[56] Although the missionaries were explicitly told that serving St Patrick's Purgatory was not part of their remit, when the missionaries gathered testimonies relating the success of their labours, the testimony of the Irish priest Terrence Kelly states he had seen Ward at the site, presumably inferring that he was ministering there.[57]

While Antrim encouraged the mission, he recognized its sensitive nature and political implications. In 1627 his natural son, Francis, was nominated to serve the Franciscan mission to Scotland. The following year, being keen to have a superior over the mission designated, the missionaries nominated Francis as their favoured candidate. However, the earl seems to have had the appointment blocked fearing it would put the family estates at risk as other Ulster families had recently been deprived for treating with 'foreign powers'.[58] Even more interesting than the earl's politicking is Francis's nomination by those working on the mission. He had not yet even arrived on the mission and had only finished his studies a few years previously. This is certainly indicative of the family's prominent role in the mission. In his request to the nuncio in Brussels for MacDonnell's appointment, Cornelius Ward, one of the missionaries, argues for his suitability on the basis that his father owns Bonamargy, is of a great deal of help to the mission and regularly visits the missioners.[59] MacDonnell was not appointed, but it was suggested in 1634 that he be made bishop of Clogher or Derry on which condition the earl promised to contribute 2,000 scudi to cover the cost of his position.[60] Similar intervention occurred in 1671. When Propaganda ordered Archbishop Oliver Plunkett to visit the renewed Franciscan mission in Scotland, which had begun in 1665, the marquis of Antrim, along with others, dissuaded him from doing so due to the political fears of the Scottish government over a French invasion.[61] Later the marquis demonstrated continuing personal support for another Francis MacDonnell, again a close relative,[62] in a bid to become 'Father of the Province' after fourteen years of service on the mission. The marquis went as far as offering to personally finance the cost of maintaining his bishopric.[63] Thus, in two successive generations the leading members of the MacDonnells of Antrim actively sought to have a kinsman appointed to a high-ranking ecclesiastical position which would affect not only Ulster, but the Western Isles of Scotland as well.

During the more than seventy years the three missions spanned, missionaries worked primarily in traditional ClanDonald territories or those of clans associated with them: South Uist, Barra, Benbecula, Colonsay, Eigg, Canna, Rum, Skye, Mull, Harris, Moidart, Arisaig, Glengarry and Kintyre.[64] In fact, when the mission came into question in the late 1620s and the missionaries were compelled to make lists of converts and attain letters supporting their claims, one Captain Donald MacDonald wrote from Colonsay to testify Ward's ministry had brought many back to the faith. Moreover, MacDonald had personally accompanied Ward to Kintyre, Colonsay and the territories of Clanranald and Glengarry where the priest had administered the sacraments.[65] Another letter from Islay described the mission's successes in similar terms, ascribing work in Kintyre, Arran, Jura, Colonsay, Mull, Barra and South Uist as well as within the territories of the lairds of MacLeod, Lochaber and Glengarry.[66] Work often focused around particular regions. From January 1625 until August 1626 Father O'Neill worked exclusively in 'the territory of MacLeod of Harris' and the adjacent areas.[67] By 1637 Patrick Brady had served the mission for eighteen years in the 'northern parts of Scotland', where he lived, according to Ward, in the house of a leading Catholic and it was believed he had readily available access to hosts for the eucharist.[68] Brady's mission is the most perplexing of the missionaries as none of his reports survive. All that Ward affirms is Brady was generally stationary in a location he had been serving for nine years that, 'bordering the Highlands' approximately '150 miles' from Eigg, took a solid 12-day journey through mountainous terrain.[69] Between September 1636 and April 1637 Ward himself remained in vicinity of Lochaber, Moidart, Sleat and Glenelg.[70]

Besides working within the territories of prominent clan members, the movements of the missionaries seem to have been directed by them. Ward reports being invited to Barra, just as he had been invited to Uist and Moidart by Clanranald.[71] The priests also regularly stayed with leading members of the clans when in their proximity.[72] A report citing hardship on Colonsay specifically states that it was because Coll Ciotach was not there that food was unavailable.[73] On a number of occasions the priests were accompanied on their missions by these individuals.[74] The reports of hardship occurred when travelling between the territories where the missionaries reported there were not towns or other places to find supplies. Another reason to believe that there was direct intervention on the part of the clan chiefs is that the funds from Propaganda were notoriously absent, despite repeated requests. According to one report, Patrick Brady worked on the mission for seven years before it was requested by a superior that he be given a stipend with which to support himself.[75] Without those funds the mission required additional sources of support, especially in light of statements that the Franciscans regularly travelled with one or 'at least two attendants' who carried the necessary accoutrements for celebrating mass or who on occasion were sent to get wine, hosts for the eucharist or other necessary items.[76] This raises the question of who was paying for or providing the services of these attendants. Whereas Giblin argues the missioners received no money from the population and John Campbell suggests they refused money offered, the reports claim no money was ever asked for but that the leading members of the clans had a tendency to offer it.[77] Claims emphasizing the poverty and difficulty of the mission can hardly be unexpected when the missionaries were attempting to elicit long overdue funds from Propaganda. Moreover, the *fine* who were supporting them would have been anxious for continental money as in many circumstances the laity, to minimize legal pressures from the central state, had to pay teinds to the government to support largely absent Protestant clergy.

By 1626 Ward reported to the Archbishop of Armagh that Clanranald and his clan had embraced the faith and looked to propagate Catholicism among the whole of Scotland. Besides Clanranald, MacLeod of Harris, John Campbell of Cawdor and Archibald Campbell of Barbeck (both of whom invoked the great displeasure of the eighth earl of Argyll for their conversions),[78] Coll Ciotach MacDonald, MacLean of Lochbuie (the second most important laird on Mull after Duart)[79], the family of the MacDonald laird of Islay (Cintriae Iliae – here probably referring to Knockrinsay or perhaps Antrim, who had claims over these lands), with all their subjects and with the inhabitants of the islands of the Hebrides (here probably meaning the territories of MacLeod of Harris), Jura, Arran, Uist (Iriod), Canna and Barra (Cintua Barra), had embraced the faith.[80] Moreover, they requested a bishop be ordained into a restored see and that parish priests be provided in order for the firm preservation of the faith for the future. This action, despite the variety of clans listed above, can still very much be viewed as a concerted ClanDonald effort as the leading figure, Clanranald, was connected by marriage with the MacLeods, the MacNeills and the MacLeans of Duart. In terms of his MacDonald connections at this time, Clanranald spells out in a contemporary letter written to the pope that a number of his relations were professing Catholics and willing to militarily defend the faith, including his brothers Ragnall Og, Alasdair Og and Domhnall Glas; his son, Domhnall Dubh (the future thirteenth chief of Clanranald, 1670–86); his uncles Ranald MacDonald of Benbecula (Mac Ailean 'ic Iain) and Iain Ruari; along with Donald Gorm MacDonald of Sleat. Moreover, the missionaries providing clerical services to the individuals were by this time officially based at Bonamargy priory, for which reason it might be assumed the reference to the MacDonald laird of Islay is referring to the first earl of Antrim, the leading figure of Clan Ian Mhòr after the death of Sir James MacDonald of Dunyveg. Thus there appears to be a ClanDonald backbone to the mission stretching from Antrim to Islay, through Coll Ciotach on Colonsay and on to the MacDonalds of Clanranald (spanning from Barra across to Arisaig and Moidart) and Sleat and the MacDonnells of Glengarry.

That there is more to the Catholic revival than just piety might be indicated by a number of instances in which a profession of Catholic faith coincided with an assertion of traditional hegemonies in the face of concerted infringements. For example, Ward claimed the conversion of the last chief of the MacIains of Ardnamurchan in 1625, before the clan was eradicated.[81] Thus Ward places the conversion of MacIain, a part of ClanDonald South, at about the same time as the clan's resistance to Campbell encroachments and a burgeoning notoriety for piracy.[82] A direct link cannot be made here, but there is a similarity with the tactics of Coll Ciotach. In 1616, after his involvement in the Islay rebellion, Coll Ciotach set out on a bout of piracy in the Hebrides. Rather than just for pecuniary gain it has been suggested the expedition may have been intended to find a suitable base to establish a Catholic mission, because the earliest mission report for 1624 and 1625 (those from the years 1619 to 1623 are not extant) records visits to the same islands Coll Ciotach had visited in 1616: Texa, Islay, Colonsay, Mull, Canna, North Uist and Iona.[83] Coll Ciotach's 1616 foray also seems to have had broader ClanDonald intentions as he feasted at the home of the daughter of Angus of Dunyveg (Sir James MacDonald's sister) and visited the foster brother of Antrim.[84] Similarly, clan MacIain was sheltered by Clanranald when royal/Campbell forces struck at the clan and upon their decimation they were assimilated into Clanranald.[85] Both Coll Ciotach and MacIain embraced the Catholic faith while simultaneously exerting their traditional powers through bouts of piracy, a traditional practice, but one of these particular occasions flew directly in the face of royal policies and Campbell ambitions. However, from as early as 1609 the struggle between ClanDonald and ClanCampbell appears to have exhibited a religious element. John L. Campbell argues this had a direct affect on the actions of the clans around them and suggests the alleged murder of the Protestant minister in Benbecula in 1609 was linked to the contested influences of the two clans over the MacNeills of Barra.[86] The culprit of the act was Niall Og, a usurper for control of the clan, who before fulfilling his aspirations refused to convert to Catholicism, but seven years after becoming MacNeill of Barra accepted the faith.[87] The indication is that as a rival to a chief supported by ClanDonald maintaining a nominally Protestant faith allowed for the possibility of Campbell support. Similarly, in relation to the first foray of the Franciscans, John Campbell notes the only chief who was openly hostile to the missionaries in the Hebrides was Hector MacLean of Duart, son of Sir Lachlan MacLean who died a Protestant in 1598, and, of equal importance, was a bitter enemy of the MacDonalds.[88] Here too a rivalry between two closely linked clans sharing the island of Mull may account for inclinations toward religious preferences. Confessional identities tended to mirror kin allegiances or antipathies.

The pattern of mission and the supporting role of prominent clan members sheds important light on the missionaries' reports of conversions and continental claims that they were grossly over-exaggerated. Whereas Donald MacLean argues that the statistics were inflated in order to ensure that the missionaries qualified for their subsidy from Propaganda, Odo Blundell, Campbell and others have demonstrated that 'conversion' did not necessarily entail turning from Calvinism to Catholicism but could simply mean being reconciled to the church.[89] Working in an area formerly of a Catholic persuasion was not the same as working in the New World, Africa or Asia, where conversion would mean a new confession of the faith from a prior position of ignorance. As far as both the kirk and the Catholic Church were concerned, the Western Isles were a religious vacuum due to decades of clerical neglect. Priests had not been in the Western Isles for nearly sixty years, which meant no Roman Catholic sacraments of baptisms, penance, the eucharist or confirmation. However, pre-reformation practices were still rife. Holy wells and other sacred sites, particularly those associated with St Columba or other Celtic saints, remained part of cultural practices.[90] Yet the failure to receive the sacraments for three generations could hardly leave the people 'Catholic' in the eyes of Rome. What remained in the cultural memory of the people was a faith completely untouched by Trent, and the priests recognized this. Yet elements of faith had continued. There are reports from the 1590s of people from Barra making pilgrimages to St Patrick's Purgatory in Ireland, and the very able historian John L. Campbell has argued this is evidence of Catholic survival down to the arrival of Franciscan missionaries.

As a result, 'conversion' should be viewed a very loose term. According to Campbell, a convert could be used to 'describe anyone from a baptised Catholic who had had no chance to practice his religion, to a convinced Calvinist won over', who was brought to the sacraments.[91] In either case, this usually meant a quick crash course in Catholic doctrine, teaching the *pater noster*, *ave* and creed, confession and admission to the mass.[92] Such a basic definition makes the number of conversions claimed by the priests much more credible than MacLean or Macinnes have granted, especially when the priests noted that on occasion it was necessary to listen to confessions for twenty-four straight hours.[93] The Vincentians found a way of speeding up the education process in the 1650s, if not the hearing of confessions. Father Duggan wrote, 'one needed only teach the *Pater, Ave* and *Credo* to one young child in each village and a few days later all in that village knew them, grown-ups as well as little ones'.[94] So conversion might be better read as reconciliation, which perhaps provides one of our clearest pieces of evidence for what was happening during the first Franciscan mission. Rather than courting clan elites, the mission was provoked, directed and facilitated by the elites of ClanDonald and their *fine*.

The account of the missionaries' success in nearly every location they visited is indicative of a social movement in which the adoption of the Catholic faith by a kin group represents a systematic process of group cohesion. Such an interpretation is supported by two Vincentian reports. Father Duggan wrote to St Vincent de Paul in 1652 that arriving in South Uist he found God 'has so softened the hearts there that Clanranald, Laird of a great part of Uist, has become a convert, together with his wife, son and their whole family. This lead has been followed by all the gentry, the tenants and their families'.[95] A subsequent letter dated 1654 claims that 'in Moidart, Morar, Knoidart and Glengarry all are converted or at least resolved to receive instruction when we have an opportunity of visiting them'.[96] This would also explain why someone like Clanranald would need to be 'converted', since he had not seen a priest in his lifetime, even if he was behind the endeavour, as well as explain why Clanranald was so pleased by Ward's reports of success on the island of Eigg in 1626.[97]

Contrary to this position, James A. Stewart argues in his doctoral dissertation on Clanranald that the missions were not in fact carried out by means of any kin influence, because initial conversions on Canna, a Clanranald territory, were minimal.[98] Yet, Canna and Eigg appear to have been susceptible to external pressures in a way that other Clanranald territories were not, partly due to their exposed location halfway between Uist and Moidart as well as their close proximity to Protestant areas of Skye. In 1625 Neil MacKinnon, minister of Sleat, seized Ward on Eigg and in 1630 the Protestant bishop of the Isles, Thomas Knox, seized Patrick Hegarty on South Uist just after he arrived from Canna.[99] On both occasions elements of Clanranald militarily intervened and liberated the Franciscans, the latter incident provoking the ire of both the Privy Council and Charles I.[100] Thereafter, success on Canna and Eigg improved.[101] These circumstances are further enlightening because possession of Canna seems to have been contested. While the island clearly belonged to Clanranald in 1593, the MacLeods of Dunvegan are identified as the possessors in Thomas Knox's report of 1626.[102] This might give greater credence to an argument for confessionalization endorsed by Clanranald both within the clan's bounds as well as in contested areas. Regardless of the political motivations pertaining to Eigg and Canna, the leading role of the laity in preserving Gaelic-speaking Catholicism is repeatedly supported in the surviving evidence. Whereas Fiona Macdonald accepts that the re-emergence of Catholicism became a 'weapon against assimilation into the state', it appears ClanDonald and a number of their neighbours actively introduced a Catholic presence for that very purpose.[103]

Thus, when two Vincentians arrived in 1651 they were missionaries, but they were arriving to an established context. Tradition holds and records indicate that they had been invited to fulfil a particular role among a particular group of people. Historians have quibbled over who requested their services, Clanranald or Angus (or Aeneas) MacDonnell, chief of the MacDonnells of Glengarry, but the two Vincentians worked almost exclusively within their spheres of influence.[104] The missionary work of the Gaelic-speaking regulars continued during the period 1651 to 1679, usually with the presence of two Vincentians in the Highlands.[105] Dermot Duggan worked mainly in the territories of Clanranald, his 1654 report citing visits to Barra, Uist, Canna, Eigg and Skye, and the mainland districts of Moidart, Arisaig and Morar; while Francis White concentrated on the MacDonnells of Glengarry and Strathglass. Even after Rome sanctioned a secular mission to Scotland in 1653 staffed by English-speaking priests under the direction of the first Apostolic

Prefect, William Bannatyne, Irish involvement continued in the Gaelic-speaking west Highlands.[106] But the relationship between these missionaries and their supporters seems to have been even closer than their Franciscan predecessors, except perhaps for Brady. Although White was arrested in 1655 and spent a period of time in prison, a report from Propaganda in 1664 declared there to be 'four thousand Catholics in the mountains of Scotland with only one priest, Father Francis White. For ten years he has worked there without receiving any support from Propaganda.'[107] A report just two years later from Father Winster, the prefect of the Scottish mission, declared the number of Catholics in the Highlands to be 12,000 and confirmed White was working alone. Despite being the lone priest, the work went on.

About 1664 White installed a schoolmaster in Glengarry. His name was Ewan MacAlastair and he had been working for at least the previous three years in Skye, despite being unsanctioned by Propaganda, seemingly funded by Glengarry.[108] He had approximately sixty students in the Skye school, but was forced to relocate due to an increased anti-Catholic sentiment.[109] In Glengarry, MacAlastair was provided a room within Invergarry Castle to re-establish the school. Although the number of students was small in 1665, MacAlastair had hoped they would increase upon the return of Angus MacDonnell, Lord of MacDonnell and Aros, from London.[110] A similar level of support was shown for the work of the Dominican George Fanning in Barra who, according to the Franciscan Francis MacDonnell, ran a school on the island for eight years before the second Franciscan mission 'discovered' him working there. According to Francis, he 'would have perished from hunger before now, were it not that he lived with the laird of Barra. He has not received a sixpence from the Sacred Congregation for the past eight years.'[111]

Such relationships meant a high level of dependence upon the laity, approaching something like a level of patronage that Dominicans and Vincentians, unlike Jesuits, would not normally have embraced. Francis White, likewise, resided in Invergarry Castle for large portions of the year. While not receiving explicit permission from Propaganda to do so on a permanent basis, White was given permission, due to the inclement weather of the region, to stay at Invergarry Castle from October to May – two-thirds of the year.[112] Thus, according to G. Fitzgibbon, Invergarry Castle 'provided a base for Highland mission equivalent to that for the Lowlands at Gordon Castle.'[113] For Lisa Curry, Glengarry's persistent advocacy of Catholicism, like his canny political manoeuvring, were part of his efforts to be recognized as the head of all ClanDonald.[114]

It is in this light that the presence of Catholic priests among the clans of the Western Highlands and Isles, from their arrival in 1619 until the appointment of a vicar-apostolic in 1694, needs to be understood. Rather than counter-reformation in nature, the missions primarily brought Catholicism to kin groups who requested their presence, because Catholicism offered a powerful tool for bringing about cohesion in the face of systematic opposition to traditional Gaelic society. This was confessionalization. It is for this reason that Fiona Macdonald has claimed that, at its root, 'identification with Catholicism [in the Highlands and Western Isles] was far more of a political statement of cultural solidarity than a religious commitment'.[115] This, however, was not a by-product of the mission. It was the purpose of the mission and the reason why clan elites went to great lengths to support it. This highly political nature, over and above purely pious practice, is indicated by the fact that Clanranald invited the missionaries to come into his lands in 1625, but on two separate occasions seems to have been too busy to take the sacraments himself.[116] Thus their presence, from his perspective, does not seem to be simply salvific. Similarly, on occasion clan chiefs who allowed or encouraged missionaries to work among their people outwardly conformed to the Protestant kirk or at least conceded to demands that their children received Protestant educations.[117] Such nominal conformity could serve to diminish pressure from the state, while simultaneously the work of priests functioned in a socially cohesive role among the *fine* and rank-and-file. When either Clanrandald or Glengarry sent to Ireland for priests in 1650, they were procured 'for the superintendence of his people and his immediate neighbours'.[118] Once the priests had arrived, Clanranald sent one of them, Father Duggan, to visit South Uist where he subsequently received invitations from MacNeill to visit Barra as well as from seven other unnamed lairds to visit other locations.[119] According to Father Duggan, 'MacNeil, Lord of the isle of Barra, having heard of me, sent a gentleman to beg me to do for Barra what I had done for Uist'.[120] Thus the presence, distribution and itinerary of priests owed much to the agenda of the gentry.

By the 1640s the kirk recognized the culturally binding nature of Catholicism within Gaeldom. While one of the kirk's ultimate goals remained the 'extirpation' of 'barbaric' Gaelic culture, a distinction was made between long-term goals and short-term expediencies. In the 1640s bursaries were set aside for Gaelic speakers to attend Scottish universities. In 1649 the synod of Argyll authorized a Gaelic translation of the Shorter Catechism and subsequently approved the edition produced by Dugald Campbell and Ewen Cameron in 1651. By 1659 a Gaelic translation of the first fifty Psalms was completed and in 1684 the first complete Gaelic Psalter was produced.[121] This policy of using the medium of Gaelic was, according to Durkacz, necessary for 'holding back the Counter-Reformation'.[122] Yet, as has already been argued, it was less of a process of counter-reformation than one of confessionalization which brought priest and clan into a close-knit and mutually dependent relationship. Father Hegarty's 1640 report gives some indication of just how important the clans must have been to the priests working in isolation. He declared that despite writing numerous reports to Rome over ten years on the mission, he did not receive one reply except for two faculties granting powers, both of which required a bishop which thus made them dead letters.[123]

As a result of the mutuality of the relationship between the clans and the priests close ties were forged. In the absence of promised continental funds the clan *fine* supported the work themselves. This led to a situation, like that in the north-east of Scotland, in which priests were closely linked to patrons. Such was the close-knit relationship between clan and priest that a portrait of Father White hung in Invergarry Castle, in a room referred to as 'Mr. White's Room', until the castle burned down in 1745.[124] On another occasion the kin link preceded the religious one. In 1626 the first Protestant minister on South Uist, Ranald MacDonald, was converted to Catholicism under the influence of the Franciscan missionaries. He travelled to the continent and, after being denied entrance into the Scots college in Douai, completed his studies and was ordained at the Irish college in Louvain in 1629.[125] Both his admission to the college and his return to the Hebrides were carried forth, according to the nuncio, on the agreement that his training and ministry would be funded by 'a well-born' relative in Scotland who would act as his patron, although the issue came to be contested between the mission and Propaganda.[126] He returned to South Uist in 1634, after being arrested in London on his way back to the island in 1630, and served as the first resident post-reformation secular priest in the Western Isles.[127] He ministered to the people of South Uist, rarely leaving the island.[128] Despite reports from Ward claiming MacDonald lived in poverty on a remote part of South Uist, the minutes of the Synod of Argyll suggest he was living in the home of Clanranald.[129] MacDonald had numerous run-ins with the presbytery of Argyll and after being arrested and tried in Edinburgh he made a temporary return to the kirk on the condition of receiving one-third of the rent of Snizort on Skye. The situation demonstrates the challenge of both churches to secure qualified candidates to serve in remote areas. However, upon his return to the Hebrides he carried on in his Catholic ministrations and was eventually excommunicated by the presbytery of Skye.[130] There seem to have been similar kin links elsewhere in ClanDonald. MacBreck relays Donald Macranald 'the Fair' died in 1645, and the Jesuit feared this might diminish the spiritual harvest in the Highlands.[131] Donald was a devout Catholic and, according to MacBreck, his brother-in-law was a Scottish Minim working in the north of Scotland. On at least one occasion, Donald liberated the priest from incarceration.[132] Rather than burning down the house and killing the perpetrators, 'he considered it more pious to pardon them … and had the good satisfaction of hearing them speak in praise of his clemency'.[133]

Such links were based on a degree of reciprocity and shared identity. The bonds between clan and priest meant that, if necessary, the clans physically intervened when priests were in danger. For instance, when the Franciscan Patrick Hegarty was arrested by the Bishop of the Isles in 1630 some clansmen of Clanranald and Benebecula 'followed the said bishop and his company, presented their arms at them, and forcibly took the said priest out of their hands', just as they had five years earlier.[134] This tends to suggest, as Curry argues, that the priests were perceived as part of the clans and they were thus redeemed in a manner consistent with this belief.[135] In fact, there is evidence to indicate that this feeling was reciprocated. The animosity between the Campbells and Clan Donald, along with its religious overtones, had its clearest expression during the 1640s. Campbell incursions in Glengarry were justified by the Clan Donnells being 'proven enemies of religion'.[136] Conversely, when Irish troops under the command of Alasdair MacColla, the son of Coll Ciotach, opened a campaign in Scotland in 1643 under the encouragement of Antrim, they sought revenge on the Campbells as 'the fiercest persecutors and … murderers and assassins of the Catholics, in the north of Ireland and the whole of Scotland'.[137] Although they united with Montrose's force, contemporary accounts recognized the army fighting under Montrose to be a coalition force of 'Catholics and Royalists'.[138] The Catholic side's intentions never strayed beyond Argyllshire for any extended period of time.

During the winter of 1644–45 the MacDonalds compelled Montrose to campaign in Argyllshire where, according to a commanding MacDonald's account, 'we left neither house nor hold unburned, nor corn nor cattle, that belonged to the name of Campbell', singling out the lands of the Campbells of Glenorchy, Inverawe, Lawers and Auchenbreck.[139] In total 895 Campbells were killed without a single skirmish or battle.[140] Patrick Gordon records that Montrose 'would have spared the people', but 'Clan Donald wheresoever they fand any that was able to cary armes, did without mercie dispatch them'.[141] This was a campaign that could have been ascribed as genocide, one that E.J. Cowan calls an 'orgy of blood and plunder', but instead MacColla became known throughout Argyllshire as 'The Destroyer of Houses'.[142] The vehemence of MacDonald hatred of the Campbells was probably best summarized, however, in the wake of MacColla's rout of the Campbells at the Battle of Inverlochy in 1645 by Iain Lom, the bard of Keppoch:

> You remember the place called the Tawny Field?
> It got a fine dose of manure;
> Not the dung of sheep or goats,
> but Campbell blood well congealed.
> To Hell with you if I care for your plight,
> as I listen to your children's distress,
> lamenting the band that went to battle,
> the howling of the women of Argyll.[143]

But there was a religious edge to this event as well. The Jesuit James MacBreck heralded the campaign into Argyll as to 'the greater glory of God that it was by a Catholic army that the persecutor was to be assailed and crushed; that the standard of religion was to be carried into a land whence religion had been wholly expelled'.[144] Before the battle at Inverlochy, MacBreck describes how 'when Montrose reviewed his army, after having placed it in order of battle, he found the men on their knees, with priests behind them imploring the divine protection, signing themselves and their weapons with the cross, entreating the celestial aid of the Queen of Heaven, fervently repeating the names of Saint Patrick, the patron of Ireland, and of Saint Brigid'.[145]

Whereas Iain Lom's account is one of triumph over insidious Campbells, MacBreck rejoiced in the same victory as one of providential dispensation against the chief heretics.[146] Several victories, including Inverlochy, fell on Catholic feast days which were interpreted as divinely ordained, while other feast days were marked by fasting and signs of intense devotion by the troops.[147] Continuity between the Franciscan mission and the campaign was maintained by three of the Franciscans serving as army chaplains along with the Jesuit MacBreck; Patrick Brady, Paul O'Neill and Edmund McCann were all old hands on the Franciscan mission.[148] Importantly, the priests seem to have had some influence in the decision-making process of the campaign and on occasion were consulted in relation to Campbell pleas to spare their lands or even over oaths to be subscribed by the army.[149] They also celebrated mass frequently for the soldiers and for civilians.[150] This has led Alasdair Roberts to interpret MacColla's campaign as a Catholic crusade, however this is only part of the picture.[151] David Stevenson recognizes that Catholicism certainly played an important part 'as the Irish and most of the Highlanders who joined them shared religious motivation', but curbs this by adding 'it was not shared by all the clans involved' (in Montrose's campaign) and instead suggests Royalism was of much greater importance in clan participation.[152] Royalism certainly was an important element of the campaign, but Allan Macinnes gets closer to the point when he asserts that the actions of leading ClanDonald chiefs in supporting the campaigns of Alasdair MacColla were to 'further the cause of the Gael'.[153] There was both an overwhelming sense of Catholic identity and piety, as well as a clear understanding that, as MacBreck puts it, 'the march of the army was in reality directed upon Argyllshire'.[154]

Throughout his description of events, MacBreck emphasizes the two streams contributing to the campaign by lauding both the greatness of the ClanDonald contribution and the triumph of Catholicism over a heretical enemy. MacBreck particularly praises MacColla in the kind of language used to laud great Gaelic heroes of the past, such as Fionn Mac Cumhaill, writing: 'MacDonald was remarkable for zeal in the faith and strength and courage of mind and body … it was thought that no man like him had lived for centuries'. The ClanDonald influence on the campaign is also persistently reiterated in the clerical report. Besides noting the influence of MacColla, Clanranald,

Antrim and Macranald the Fair, MacBreck identifies the contributions of several smaller clans or septs such as the Robertsons, MacNabs and Johnstons as being either MacDonalds or deriving 'their descent and honours from the race of the MacDonalds'.[155] MacBreck then emphasizes the fundamental nature of the campaign by declaring, MacColla's 'very name was a terror to the heretic Campbells'.[156] MacColla's strength and success is repeatedly identified as being rooted in his support for the spiritual work of the priests among his army and is characterized by his immense respect for the priests. He is reported to have fasted three days a week, insisted on Latin prayers before meals and 'even among the greatest tumult and the utmost peril, he always wished to have Mass celebrated'.[157] So to an extent Roberts is correct that from the priest's perspective, and probably to an extent MacColla's as well, this was indeed a religious crusade. But it was also thoroughly cultural and kin-based too. 'The entire conduct of the war', summarized MacBreck:

> and the whole hazard of their cause, turned upon this single point … they considered that they would effect nothing worthy of their efforts unless they crushed the Campbells, devastated Argyll with fire and sword, and administered a terrible and telling chastisement to this hideous receptacle of bandits, plunderers, incendiaries, and cut-throats. The Campbells must be thoroughly intimidated, and their asylum reached and overthrown, or else there would never be any safety in any part of the Highlands. *The King's subjects would not flock to his standards or accept his service, if these assassins … were not hunted down in their strongholds and dens of crime.* In fact the power exercised by Argyll was of the greatest possible importance to the rebels. *He had been named by the King governor of the Hebrides, and exercised there an authority unknown before* … All the Catholics, at the war council, agreed that it was necessary to invade the territory of Argyll.[158]

Rather than the Royalism that Stevenson suggests, what held Montrose's troops together was anti-Campbellism. In light of this, MacBreck constructed a panegyric in his report to Rome in which the Catholic *Gael*, epitomized in the person of MacColla and corporate commitment of ClanDonald, took up arms to destroy the Judas-like Campbells who profited by betraying their neighbours and advancing the cause of the heretic and the *Gall* (Lowland/ non-Gael). As such, the report clearly supports Allan Macinnes's argument that their Highland neighbours, especially from the signing of the Covenant in 1638, believed ClanCampbell policies 'were promoting cultural assimilation with the racially inferior Lowlander'.[159]

There were in fact two separate campaigns in Campbell territories. Whereas the first included the forces of Montrose, the second represented a wholly ClanDonald directed action led by MacColla and involving other clans resistant to ClanCampbell. The second campaign, which witnessed the arrival of Antrim himself in 1646, included a meeting in December 1645 where the leading members of clans involved signed 'a most cruell horrid and bloody band' intent on 'rooting out the name of Campbell'.[160] MacColla spent most of 1646 in the Campbell territories of Lorne, Knapdale and Kintyre. As in the first campaign a clerical accompaniment of 'frieris and seminarie priests' played an active part. According to the synod of Argyll, the priests actively proselytized 'about Kintyre and some of the isles' making converts 'even of the better sort'.[161] In this way priests assisted in the determined action of protecting Gaelic culture. Moreover, it was a commitment that was institutionally supported in Ireland by this time, as the nuncio Rinuccini and Owen Roe O'Neill had usurped control of the Irish Confederacy from Ormond to restore strict Catholic and Gaelic interests over those of the Old English and Royalists. Interestingly, the opposite happened in Scotland. The shift to a pro-Royalist sympathy among large swathes of Scottish Gaeldom was largely the result of the house of Argyll casting its lot with the Covenanters. Whereas the policies of the crown during the reign of James VI and I looked to represent the greatest threat to Gaelic culture, the Covenanters brought Gael and king into a new alliance. Unfortunately, Charles I's settlement with the Covenanters in May 1646 spelled disaster for the clans who had supported him against the Presbyterian regime. The king ordered Antrim to disband the Gaelic forces he had rallied in Scotland. He and the bulk of his army eventually returned to Ireland after a delay of several months, leaving MacColla and a small force to hold key strategic positions in Kintyre. At this point Antrim still believed he would receive Kintyre as reward for his support of the king. In fact, Antrim received an explicit verbal promise from Charles I that he would receive Argyll's estates in Kintyre once the king was in a position to forfeit them.[162] In the face of Leslie's Covenanter forces MacColla's remnant experienced a series of disasters. MacColla himself departed for Ireland in June 1647, where Glengarry took troops as well. In this sense the fight to further the cause of the Gael was exported from the Scottish theatre to an Irish one with an even more complicated coalition of Catholics, Royalists and Gaels. The ClanDonald troops left in Kintyre to maintain a clan presence under the command of Archibald Mor MacDonald of Sanda garrisoned the castle of Dunaverty, but were slaughtered by Leslie's forces, partly due to the influence of a minister of the kirk and the earl of Argyll.[163]

Argyll's estates were not forfeited and by 1648 all of the Western Isles and the bordering Highland regions as far north as Mull were in the possession of the Campbells.[164] From this point ClanDonald resistance to Campbell and Lowland policies shifted from being primarily initiated from ClanDonald South to the northern branches, as was the presence of Gaelic-speaking Catholic clergy. It was precisely at this point that Clanranald and Glengarry sent for priests from the continent. The continuation of clan consolidation and resistance persisted in the appropriation of Catholic identity. With a solid wedge now driven between ClanDonald North and South and Cromwellian dominance of Ireland from 1649 Ireland became a more difficult source of clerical support. But Irish-speaking priests, rather than Lowland English-speaking Scots clergy, were sourced from the continent in the form of Vincentians. What seems to have taken place through Clan Donald involvement between 1619 and 1647 was a fusion between clan identity and religious identity, as well as the roles of clan members and those of the clergy serving them. This was evidenced in the above accounts, but also in the participation of the Catholic clergy in later events. In the wake of the Popish Plot in 1678 the crown ordered all clans to disarm. The MacDonnells of Glengarry refused and with the assistance of 'other Popish chiefs' marched upon the Campbells in 1679.[165] The campaign was thoroughly anti-Campbell rather than religious in its validation, but the fact that these two elements had blurred into one is evidenced by the enlistment of the missionaries Francis MacDonnell and Robert Munro as soldiers in Glengarry's army, taking the ranks of *Caballieri* and *Capitani* respectively.[166] No matter the close pastoral links between the Franciscans and the people of Glengarry, there was no need for priests to serve in a military role. The only explanation is that they viewed themselves as part of the clan and the campaign against the Campbells as having a religious significance. This represented a role more deeply rooted in the intricacies of clan politics than Propaganda would have approved of.

Yet perhaps even more crucial in understanding the way in which Catholicism came to underpin the cohesion of clan networks in Gaelic Scotland and Ireland was the letter written from Clanranald to Pope Urban VIII in 1626. In it the twelfth chief of Clanranald promised, upon receiving four ships and arms for 7,000 troops from the pope, the cooperation of all ClanDonald (both in Scotland and Ireland) in a campaign to conquer Scotland and return the nation to the Catholic faith.[167] Much more than a mere declaration of religious identity or, as Allan Macinnes has argued, a plea for employment for redundant Gaelic mercenary forces, the letter represents 'the re-establishment of their own autonomy, which came above any other kind of loyalty'.[168] This was an appeal to a proprietary relationship with Rome that offered religious justification for political autonomy. In fact, it was essentially the same ideological trajectory that would lead to the formation of the Irish Confederacy in 1642. While Clanranald's crusade never materialized (except for those directed against ClanCampbell), the letter demonstrates the profound turn in fortunes ClanDonald experienced from the deep rifts of the late sixteenth century to the pan-Celtic cooperation of ClanDonald by the mid-seventeenth century. The mission endeavours bankrolled, and possibly masterminded, by elements within ClanDonald transformed the political geography of the Western Isles in the face of concerted Stuart policies for centralization of the political economy.

The process of the mission can be charted through a ClanDonald backbone. Catholicism was reintroduced in ClanDonald lands only after 1619, in what was largely a religious vacuum, at the instigation of leading elements of the clan and served to formulate an alternative identity most clearly exhibited in Clanranald's letter to the pope in 1626; Irish involvement against ClanCampbell in the 1640s; and the service of Catholic priests again against ClanCampbell in 1679. Moreover, the persistent participation of ClanDonald in the Catholic missions to the Western Isles was crucial to the continued presence of the faith. Although likely instigated by ClanDonald South, by the 1650s the epicentre had shifted away from Clan Iain Mhòr's territories to the territories of the Clanranald and Glengarry MacDonnells. This shift coincided with the end of Antrim's hopes of regaining control of Kintyre. Jane Ohlmeyer and Ronald Black argue that Antrim's direct support of the Franciscan mission came to an end upon the arrest of the mission's superior, Patrick Hegarty, in 1641.[169] If this is the case, then it further supports the position that his political ambitions fuelled his support of the mission, for by that time he believed he had received a tacit promise from Charles I to be restored ownership of Kintyre in return for sending troops to Scotland.[170] His ambitions attained, there was less urgency for supporting the mission although support did continue on a lesser scale. By the 1650s the northern branches of ClanDonald became the driving force of the mission as is evidenced by their invitation and then appropriation of missionaries. Through the 1650s and 1660s Angus MacDonnell of Glengarry (Lord Glengarry and Aros, from 1660) actively manoeuvred to be recognized as the head of all ClanDonald, a process that included supporting a resident priest and an essentially illicit school. These efforts led to him being recognized by leading Catholic missioners as one of the two most important contributors to the persistence of the faith. In the late 1660s a letter was sent to Rome requesting Propaganda write to the two greatest proponents and supporters of Catholicism in Scotland and asking that some holy relics be included to encourage their continued support. The first of these individuals was the Marquis of Huntly, who was widely recognized across the continent for his efforts in supporting Catholicism in the north-east of Scotland, the second was Glengarry.[171]

Allan Macinnes argues Catholicism had little lasting influence on the cultural landscape of Scottish Gaeldom as a whole, because only six of the fifty principal clans maintained their Catholic identities into the Jacobite period. However, it is crucial to note that these clans in the minority were the ones who pinned their collective identities and traditional rights to the reintroduction and sustenance of Catholicism nearly a century before. Among these were the Gordons, MacDonalds of Glengarry, MacDonalds of Clanranald, MacDonalds of Keppoch and the MacNeills of Barra, as well as portions of the MacDonalds of Sleat and MacDonnells of Antrim, who, ever the opportunists, were keenly aware of the political landscape before declaring their religious affiliation.[172] These clans remained committed to Catholicism into the turbulent political years of the eighteenth century partly because it continued to provide a degree of political currency. Moreover, in relation to ClanDonald, religion was not the sole point of cooperation between the constituent clans. Just as financial cooperation within ClanDonald pre-empted the mission in 1619, it continued to play its part in the 1670s and 1680s. During the period of the second Franciscan mission ClanDonald set up an extended credit network that protected the interests of the MacDonnells of Antrim, MacDonnells of Glengarry, MacDonalds of Sleat, MacDonalds of Clanranald and MacDonalds of Benbecula. Fiona Macdonald argues this financial cooperation represents one of 'five different types of social bonding – marital, fostering, financial, commercial and cultural recreational' – implemented by the *fine* of ClanDonald during the seventeenth century to protect their traditional hegemonies.[173] Due to the hands-on role of ClanDonald in the process of Catholic missions and their efforts to sustain it in the complete absence of continental funds during the same period, confessionalization needs to be considered as a sixth strand in this wider process of promoting social cohesion.

NOTES

1 A.I. MacInnes, *Clanship, Commerce and the House of Stuart, 1603–1788* (East Linton, 1986), p. 78; D. MacLean, 'Catholicism in the Highlands and Isles, 1560–1680', *Innes Review*, 3 (1952), 5–13.

2 For recent studies on the individual Scots colleges see: B. Halloran, *Scots College in Paris, 1603–1792* (Edinburgh, 1997); M. Taylor, *The Scots College in Spain* (Valladolid, 1971); Raymond McCluskey (ed.), *The Scots College Rome, 1600–2000* (Edinburgh, 2000); T. McInally, 'The alumni of the Scots colleges abroad, 1575–1799', PhD dissertation, University of Aberdeen, 2008.

3 MacInnes, *Clanship*, pp. 78, 173–4.

4 For the political and cultural development of the *Gaidhealtachd* see J. Dawson, 'The Gaidhealtachd and the emergence of the Scottish Highlands', in B. Bradshaw and R. Roberts (eds), *British Identity and Consciousness* (Cambridge, 1998), pp. 259–300.

5 MacInnes, *Clanship*, p. 78.

6 P.F. Anson, *Underground Catholicism in Scotland, 1622–1878* (Montrose, 1970), pp. 17–25, 38–43, 56–60, 69–72; John L. Campbell, 'The Catholic Church in the Hebrides: 1560–1760', *The Tablet*, 206:6032 (December 1955), 655–67; MacLean, 'Catholicism in the Highlands and Isles', 5–13; C. Giblin (ed.), *The Irish Franciscan Mission to Scotland, 1619–1646* (Dublin, 1964), *passim*.

7 A. Bellesheim, *History of the Catholic Church of Scotland*, trans. Oswald Hunter Blair (4 vols, Edinburgh and London, 1887–90), iv, pp. 69–70.

8 Giblin (ed.), *Mission*, no. 49, pp. 150–2.

9 J.L. Campbell, 'The Catholic isles of Scotland: the Catholic church in the Hebrides 1560–1760', *The Capuchin Annual* (Dublin, 1964), 108–12.
10 See Chapter 7 in this volume.
11 See Chapter 7 in this volume.
12 F. Macdonald, *Missions to the Gaels: Reformation and Counter-Reformation in Ulster and the Highlands and Islands of Scotland* (Edinburgh, 2006), pp. 36–96, 133–79; Lisa Curry, *Catholicism and the Clan MacDonnell of Glengarry* (Lewiston, 2008).
13 Macdonald, *Missions to the Gaels*, p. 70.
14 Giblin (ed.), *Mission*, nos 1 and 2; C. Giblin, 'The Irish Mission to Scotland in the Seventeenth Century', *Franciscan College Annual* (Multyfarnham, 1952), 9. Document 1 in Giblin (ed.), *Mission*, indicates a significant number of requests were made directly to the Irish Franciscan College at Louvain. As the college was founded in 1606, this suggests the bulk of requests occurred after that year.
15 U. Lotz-Heumann, *Die doppelte Konfessionalisierung in Ireland. Konflikt und Koexistenz im 16. Und in der ersten Hälfte des 17. Jahrhunderts* (Tübingen, 2000); H. Klueting, 'Problems of the term and concept "Second Reformation": memories of a 1980s debate', in J.M. Headley, H.J. Hillerbrand and A.J. Papalas (eds), *Confessionalization in Europe, 1555–1700: Essays in Honor and Memory of Bodo Nischan* (Aldershot, 2004), pp. 37–50, 48–9. For an excellent assessment of the need for re-evaluating of concepts of confessionalization in relation to Scotland and Ireland see E. Boran, 'Introduction', in E. Boran and C. Gribben (eds), *Enforcing the Reformation in Ireland and Scotland, 1550–1700* (Aldershot, 2006), pp. 1–13.
16 J. Goodare, *The Government of Scotland, 1560–1625* (Oxford, 2004), chapter 4; J. Goodare, *State and Society in Early Modern Scotland* (Oxford, 1999), pp. 235–9.
17 S. Connelly, *Contested Island: Ireland 1460–1640* (Oxford, 2007), pp. 343–4. Connelly argues by the 1630s Ireland had the basic structures for a functional diocesan system, but even before that a reasonably consistent presence enables continuity.
18 M. Forster, 'With and without confessionalization: varieties of early modern German Catholicism', in A. Pettegree (ed.), *The Reformation: Critical Concepts in Historical Studies* (London, 2004), pp. 219–43.
19 Curry, *Catholicism*, p. 13.
20 M.J. Seymour's Foreword to Curry, *Catholicism*, p. ii.
21 Giblin (ed.), *Mission*, no. 4, p. 14.
22 *Ibid.*, no. 1, pp. 7–9.
23 The most likely candidates for this 'Marandal' are: Coll Ciotach MacDonnell, who from 1623 possessed Colonsay and was a claimant to the chieftancy of Clan Ian Mhòr, the southern branch of Clan Donald; Sir James MacDonald of Knockrinsay, the last chief of Dunyveg who had attempted to immolate his father and was involved with the rebellion on Islay in 1614–15, along with MacDonald of Keppoch, after he was dispossessed of the island – both were accused of fraternizing with the Catholic earl of Argyll during their exile in Spain; or Randall MacDonnell, first earl of Antrim. Another plausible, but less likely candidate, is Iain Muideartach, the twelfth chief of Clanranald from 1618 to 1670, as he is

reported to have converted in 1624. For a fuller discussion see R.S. Spurlock, 'Catholic continuance and the role of the laity in Scotland, 1603–1694', in R. Armstrong and T. Ó hAnnracháin (eds), *Insular Christianity 1530–1750* (Manchester, 2013).

24 For discussions of the political nature of lay support for the preservation of Catholicism in the Lowlands see: K.M. Brown, 'The making of a *politique*: the Counter-Reformation and the regional politics of John, eighth Lord Maxwell', *Scottish Historical Review*, 66 (1987), 152–75; R. Grant, 'The making of the Anglo-Scottish alliance of 1586', in J. Goodare and A.A. MacDonald (eds), *Sixteenth-Century Scotland* (Leiden, 2008), pp. 211–36; M. Yellowlees, 'Father William Crichton's estimate of the Scottish nobility, 1595', in J. Goodare and A.A. MacDonald (eds), *Sixteenth-Century Scotland* (Leiden, 2008), pp. 295–311; R. Grant, 'The Brig o' Dee affair, the sixth earl of Huntly and the politics of the Counter-Reformation', in J. Goodare and M. Lynch (eds), *The Reign of James VI* (Edinburgh, 2000), pp. 93–109; R. S. Spurlock, '"I disclaim both Ecclesiasticke and Politick Poperie": lay Catholic practice and experience in early modern Scotland', *Records of the Scottish Church History Society*, 38 (2008), 5–22.

25 A.I. MacInnes, 'Crown, clans and *Fine*: the "civilizing" of Scottish gaeldom, 1587–1638', *Northern Scotland*, 13 (1993), 31–55: 34.

26 R.C. Paterson, *The Lords of the Isles: A History of Clan Donald* (Edinburgh, 2001), pp. 113–14; *RPCS, 1616–19*, pp. 467–8, 507–8; *RPCS, 1604–07*, p. 465.

27 For the internal troubles of Clan Iain Mhòr see J.M. Hill, 'The rift within Clan Ian Mor: the Antrim and Dunyveg MacDonnells, 1590–1603', *The Sixteenth Century Journal*, 24:4 (1993), 865–79. For royal policy against the clan see: MacInnes, *Clanship*, pp. 61–3.

28 C. Innes and J. Frederick V.C. Cawdor (eds), *The Book of the Thanes of Cawdor* (Aberdeen, 1859), pp. 222–4; J.R.N. MacPhail (ed.), *Highland Papers* (4 vols, Edinburgh, 1914), iii, pp. 158–9; J. Goodare, *State and Society*, p. 278.

29 M. MacGregor, 'Statues of Iona', *Innes Review*, 57 (2006), 111–82: 167.

30 D. Stevenson, *Highland Warrior: Alasdair MacColla and the Civil Wars* (Edinburgh, 2003), p. 39.

31 R. Flower, 'An Irish-Gaelic poem on the Montrose wars', *Scottish Gaelic Studies*, 1 (1926), 113–18; A.M. MacKenzie (ed.), *Orain Iain Luim: Songs of John MacDonald, Bard of Keppoch* (Edinburgh, 1973), pp. 90–1, 124–7, 158–61; Stevenson, *Highland Warrior*, p. 298; MacInnes, *Clanship*, pp. 127–8.

32 J.L. Campbell, *Canna – The Story of a Hebridean Island* (Oxford, 1984), pp. 52–3; Macdonald, *Missions to the Gaels*, p. 71; Paterson, *Lords of the Isles*, p. 116; Giblin (ed.), *Mission*, no. 11, pp. 24–52.

33 MacInnes, *Clanship*, p. 63; Paterson, *Lords of the Isles*, p. 122.

34 MacInnes, *Clanship*, p. 95.

35 J. Ohlmeyer, *Civil War and Restoration in the Three Stuart Kingdoms: The Career of Randall MacDonnell, Marquis of Antrim, 1609–1683* (Cambridge, 1993), pp. 20, 288–9.

36 MacInnes, *Clanship*, pp. 75–6.

37 Paterson, *Lords of the Isles*, p. 122.

38 A. MacDonald, 'A Fragment of an Irish MS: History of the MacDonalds of Antrim', *Transactions of the Gaelic Society of Inverness*, 37 (1934–36), 262–85: 282.
39 MacInnes, 'Crown, clans and *Fine*', p. 46.
40 D. Gregory, *The History of the Western Highlands and Isles of Scotland from A.D. 1493 to A.D. 1625* (London and Glasgow, 1881), p. 365; Campbell, 'The Catholic Isles of Scotland', 109; MacPhail, *Highland Papers*, iii, p. 186; Giblin (ed.), *Mission*, p. vii.
41 Ohlmeyer, *Civil War and Restoration*, pp. 215, 277; B. MacCuarta, *Catholic Revival in the North of Ireland, 1603–41* (Dublin, 2007), pp. 101–3. According to a manuscript history of the MacDonnells of Antrim, the earl repaired Bonamargy, built a chapel there and 'gave his own convent of Franciscans forty pounds sterling', MacDonald, 'A fragment of an Irish MS', 262–85: 280. The document also records other acts of Catholic patronage including building roofs over St John the Baptist's (Leinster) and St Bridget's wells, building a structure at St Patrick's Purgatory at Loughderg, and giving £20 to the Franciscans of Ardmarge.
42 G. Hill, *An Historical Account of the MacDonnells of Antrim* (Belfast, 1873), p. 246.
43 *Ibid.*, p. 40.
44 Giblin (ed.), *Mission*, no. 23, p. 98.
45 *Ibid.*, no. 32, pp. 111–12.
46 *Ibid.*, no. 70, p. 178.
47 V. Durkacz, *The Decline of the Celtic Languages* (Edinburgh, 1983), p. 1; C. Kidd, *British Identities before Nationalism* (Cambridge, 1999), p. 126. For early Protestant use of Gaelic see J. Dawson, 'Calvinism and the *Gaidhealtachd* in Scotland', in A. Duke, G. Lewis and A. Pettegree (eds), *Calvinism in Europe, 1560–1620* (Cambridge, 1994), pp. 231–53.
48 Campbell, 'The Catholic isles of Scotland', 109.
49 Innes, *The Book of the Thanes of Cawdor*, p. 269. MacDonald of Sleat, MacLean of Duart, MacLeod of Harris, Lachlan MacKinnon of MacKinnon, MacLean of Coll, Campbell of Cawdor and MacLean of Lochbuie were all appointed.
50 D. Gregory and W. Forbes-Skene (eds), *Collectanea de De Rebus Albanicis* (Edinburgh, 1847), p. 289.
51 A.D.M. Barrell, 'The church in the West Highlands in the late middle ages', *Innes Review*, 54 (2003), 23–46: 24.
52 M. MacGregor, 'Genealogies of the clans', *Innes Review*, 51 (2000), 131–46: 143.
53 Curry, *Catholicism*, p. 206.
54 Giblin (ed.), *Mission*, nos 32, p. 111; 35, pp. 117, 118; 42, pp. 127, 129.
55 MacDonald, 'A Fragment of an Irish MS', 280; Ohlmeyer, *Civil War and Restoration*, pp. 27, 47, 69, 71, 75, 277; Wentworth to Conway, 13 August 1638, WWM, Str. P. 10 A, fol. 172).
56 Ohlmeyer, *Civil War and Restoration*, p. 27.
57 Giblin (ed.), *Mission*, no. 59.
58 C. Giblin, 'Francis MacDonnell, OFM, Son of the First Early of Antrim (d. 1636)', *Seanchas Ardmhacha*, 8 (1975–6), 44–54: 49, 50; Giblin (ed.), *Mission*, no. 20, pp. 50, 52; Macdonald, *Missions to the Gaels*, pp. 84–5.
59 Giblin (ed.), *Mission*, no. 33, pp. 114, 116.
60 Giblin, 'Francis MacDonnell, OFM', 53.

61 C. Giblin, 'St Oliver Plunkett, Francis MacDonnell, OFM and the Mission to the Hebrides', *Collectanea Hibernica*, 17 (1974–5), 64–102: 72; S. MacGuaire, 'Ireland and the Catholic Hebrides', *The Irish Ecclesiastical Record*, 42 (1933), 345–64, 488–507: 493; C. Giblin, 'The mission to the Highlands and Isles c. 1670', *Franciscan College Annual* (Multyfarnham, 1954), 7–20: 17; Macdonald, *Missions to the Gaels*, p. 154.

62 F.O. Blundell, *The Catholic Highlands of Scotland* (12 vols, Edinburgh, 1909) ii, p. 9; Curry, *Catholicism*, p. 99.

63 Macdonald, *Missions to the Gaels*, p. 155; Giblin, 'St Oliver Plunkett, Francis McDonnell', 64–102.

64 The lists provided in the extant missionary reports should not be viewed as complete. Besides the obvious problem of missing reports, there are accounts of conversions when locations are not provided. For instance, Ward reports the conversion of the last chief of Clan MacIain of Ardnamurchan in 1625, but does not specifically list the peninsula in his report (Giblin (ed.), *Mission*, no. 20, pp. 56–7; Macdonald, *Missions to the Gaels*, p. 77). Instead these locations might best be understood as the locations from which mission work was based.

65 Giblin (ed.), *Mission*, no. 39, p. 122.

66 *Ibid.*, no. 40, p. 124.

67 *Ibid.*, no. 21, p. 66.

68 *Ibid.*, nos 20, pp. 55–6; 21, pp. 66–7; 26, p. 102.

69 *Ibid.*, nos 20; 21; 26; 30, pp. 106–7. Giblin interprets this as meaning Sutherland and Caithness (*ibid.*, p. xii). Fiona Macdonald, on the other hand, has speculated that since those regions are actually in the Highlands it is more likely that he resided with Gordon of Cluny in Aberdeenshire (Macdonald, *Missions to the Gaels*, pp. 81, 83). In any case, when he was appointed superior over the mission as the result of his long service the other missionaries complained that he was too far away to be of any regular help (Giblin (ed.), *Mission*, nos 42; 60; 66).

70 *Ibid.*, no. 69, pp. 172–7.

71 *Ibid.*, no. 21, pp. 73–4.

72 *Ibid.*, no. 21, pp. 72–3, 73–4.

73 *Ibid.*, no. 20, pp. 52–3.

74 *Ibid.*, nos 21, pp. 66–9; 36, p. 122.

75 *Ibid.*, no. 16, p. 37.

76 *Ibid.*, nos 15, pp. 32–6; 20, pp. 53–4, 55–6; 21, pp. 66–7; 25, pp. 96–7.

77 *Ibid.*, no. 20, pp. 56–7; J.L. Campbell, 'Some notes and comments on "The Irish Franciscan Mission in Scotland" by Rev. Cathaldus Giblin, OFM', *Innes Review*, 4 (1953), 42–8: 43.

78 Cawdor's conversion came after Ward entered his home under the guise of a bard, however, the Franciscans themselves noted that the conversion of Cawdor and then Barbreck had more to do with the exiled seventh earl of Argyll than their own influence. Macdonald, *Missions to the Gaels*, p. 19; Giblin (ed.), *Mission*, no. 22, p. 80.

79 Campbell, 'Some notes', 47. Hector Mór MacLean of Duart, on the other hand, vigorously advocated Protestantism and opposed the missionaries (Giblin (ed.), *Mission*, no. 22, pp. 81–2; Macdonald, *Missions to the Gaels*, p. 74.)

80 B. Jennings, 'Miscellaneous Docmuents – I', *Archivium Hibernicum*, 12 (1946), 115–16; J.L. Campbell, 'The letter sent by Iain Muideartach, twelfth chief of Clanranald, to Pope Urban VIII, in 1626', *Innes Review*, 4:2 (1953), 110–16: 110.
81 Macdonald, *Missions to the Gaels*, p. 77.
82 MacInnes, *Clanship*, pp. 63–6. The MacIains of Ardnamurchan had been placed under the feudal superiority of Argyll in 1602 and the territory was managed by Campbell of Barbeck-Lochawe during Alasdair (Alexander's) minority.
83 Campbell, *Canna*, pp. 52–3; Macdonald, *Missions to the Gaels*, p. 71.
84 Campbell, *Canna*, p. 52. For additional cooperation between Sir James and Antrim in the wider European political context see David Worthington, *Scots in Habsburg Service, 1618–1648* (Leiden and Boston, 2004), pp. 83–4.
85 MacInnes, *Clanship*, pp. 63–4.
86 J.L. Campbell, 'The MacNeills of Barra and the Irish Franciscans', *Innes Review*, 5 (1954), 33–8: 34.
87 J.L. Campbell, 'South Uist in the Ballentyne Report', *Innes Review*, 9 (1958), 214–15.
88 Campbell, *Canna*, p. 55.
89 MacLean, *Counter Reformation in Scotland*, pp. 154, 159; Blundell, *Highlands of Scotland*, ii, pp. 5–6; Campbell, 'Some notes', 43; MacGuaire, 'Ireland and the Catholic Hebrides', 493.
90 Giblin (ed.), *Mission*, nos 19, pp. 47–50; 20, pp. 50–3; 21, pp. 61, 63–4, 68–9, 73–4; 22, p. 81; 45, p. 143; 47, p. 149.
91 Campbell, 'Some notes', 43; Campbell, 'The Catholic isles of Scotland', 111.
92 MacGuaire, 'Ireland and the Catholic Hebrides', 362.
93 Giblin (ed.), *Mission*, no. 23, pp. 95–6. On a number of other occasions the priests record the great challenge of hearing the necessary number of confessions, *Ibid.*, nos 18, pp. 45–7; 20, p. 51.
94 M. Purcell, *The Story of the Vincentians* (Dublin, 1973), p. 49.
95 MacGuare, 'Ireland and the Catholic Hebrides, p. 360.
96 *Ibid.*, pp. 361–2.
97 Giblin (ed.), *Mission*, no. 21, p. 66.
98 J.A. Stewart, 'The Clan Ranald: history of a Highland kindred', PhD dissertation, University of Edinburgh, 1982, p. 71.
99 In 1626 the Franciscans report that MacKinnon was persuaded to leave the priests and Catholics of Eigg alone in exchange for one-third of the island's teinds. Giblin (ed.), *Mission*, no. 21.
100 Campbell, *Canna*, p. 60; Gregory and Forbes-Skene (eds), *De Rebus Albanicis*, p. 127.
101 Giblin (ed.), *Mission*, no. 43; MacGuaire, 'Ireland and the Catholic Hebrides', 360.
102 Macdonald, *Missions to the Gaels*, p. 289 n. 31; Campbell, *Canna*, p. 63.
103 Macdonald, *Missions to the Gaels*, p. 67.
104 Those that advocate Glengarry are: Campbell, 'The Catholic Isles of Scotland', p. 111; Curry, *Catholicism*, pp. 6–7. Fiona Macdonald follows on from MacGuaire to suggest Clanranald: Macdonald, *Missions to the Gaels*, p. 142; MacGuaire, 'Ireland and the Catholic Hebrides', 358–9. A shared source among all of these is J.F.S. Gordon, who simply identifies the request as coming from 'the Cheiftain of the MacDonnells': J.F.S. Gordon, *Journal and Appendix to Scotichronicon and*

Monasticon (Glasgow, 1867), p. xv. This may add weight to Clanranald's case, because although Glengarry was on the rise his ascendancy and claim to be the head of all of ClanDonald did not reach fruition until 1660 when he was given a charter of nobility as Lord MacDonnell and Aros. From 1660 the Scottish government on occasion referred to him as the leader of all of the MacDonalds. Edward M. Furgol, 'Macdonnell, Angus, Lord Macdonnell and Aros (*d.* 1680)', *ODNB*, www.oxforddnb.com/view/article/67440, accessed 4 December 2009.

105 For a very useful summary of the mission itineraries see: F.A. Macdonald, 'Ireland and Scotland: historical perspectives on the Gaelic dimension 1560–1760', PhD dissertation, University of Glasgow, 1994, pp. 961–90.

106 F. Macdonald, 'Irish priests in the Highlands: judicial evidence from Argyll', *Innes Review*, 46:1 (1995), 17; Purcell, *Vincentians*, pp. 44, 49, 53, 57; MacGuaire, 'Ireland and the Catholic Hebrides', 361. There were increased links with the missionary work of priests in the north-east, with meetings attended at Huntly Castle (Purcell, *Vincentians*, p. 52).

107 Purcell, *Vincentians*, p. 53. Duggan had died in Uist in 1657.

108 C. Giblin, 'The "Acta" of Propaganda archives in the Scottish mission, 1623–1670', *Innes Review*, 54:1 (1954), 107.

109 This might mean the school was within the territory of Sir John Donald of Sleat. He had incurred massive debts by the 1660s and was an absentee landlord. An attack on the school may have been a reprisal by those to whom he owed money. For an account of Sleat's dismal finances, see MacInnes, *Clanship*, p.128.

110 Purcell, *Vincentians*, p. 55.

111 O. Blundell, *Highlands of Scotland*, ii, pp. 10, 17.

112 Purcell, *Vincentians*, p. 57; Curry, *Catholicism*, p. 93.

113 G. Fitzgibbon, 'Robert Munro, secular priest in the Highlands (1645–1704)', *Innes Review*, 48:1 (1997), 165–173: 165.

114 Curry, *Catholicism*, p. 25.

115 Macdonald, *Missions to the Gaels*, p. 75.

116 Giblin (ed.), *Mission*, no. 21, pp. 62–3, 66–7.

117 Macdonald, *Missions to the Gaels*, pp. 74, 175; Campbell, 'The Catholic Church in the Hebrides', 656.

118 MacGuaire, 'Ireland and the Catholic Hebrides', 358–9; Curry, *Catholicism*, pp. 6–7; Gordon, *Scotichronicon and Monasticon*, p. xv.

119 O. Blundell, 'St Vincent of Paul and the Highlands of Scotland', *Dublin Review* 149 (1911), 304–20, 306; Macdonald, *Missions to the Gaels*, p. 143.

120 Purcell, *Vincentians*, p. 46.

121 Kidd, *British Identities*, pp. 130–1; D.C. MacTavish (ed.), *Minutes of the Synod of Argyll* (2 vols, Edinburgh, 1943–44), i, pp. 127, 227; Durkacz, *Decline*, pp. 10, 15–16. For the challenges of printing Gaelic Bibles even at the end of the seventeenth century see: George P. Johnston, 'Notices of a Collection of MSS. relating to the circulation of Irish Bibles of 1685 and 1690 in the Highlands and the Association of Rev. James kirkwood therewith' in *Papers of the Edinburgh Bibliographical Society* (Edinburgh, 1906), iv, pp 1–18.

122 Durkacz, *Decline*, p. 10; Kidd, *British Identities*, p. 130.

123 Giblin (ed.), *Mission*, no. 72, pp. 180–3.

124 Bellesheim, *History of the Catholic Church of Scotland*, iv, p. 85n.
125 Ranald MacDonald apparently arrived at Douai with letters of recommendation from the nuncio in Brussels, but the college took in three English-speaking Scots in preference to him. Giblin (ed.), *Mission*, nos 23, pp. 90–1; 28, p. 104.
126 *Ibid.*, nos 28, p. 104; 35, pp. 117–18; 42, pp. 127–8.
127 *Ibid.*, no. 45, pp. 144–5.
128 Campbell, 'Some notes', 45; Giblin (ed.), *Mission*, no. 69, pp. 174–5.
129 MacTavish (ed.), *Minutes of the Synod of Argyll*, i, p. 37; Macdonald, *Missions to the Gaels*, p. 136.
130 Macdonald, *Missions to the Gaels*, pp. 109–11; MacTavish (ed.), *Minutes of the Synod of Argyll*, ii, pp. 69, 71–2, 74, 172, 185.
131 'Donald Macranald, the Fair' is an enigmatic figure. MacBreck describes him as 'a soldier of high reputation in the wars in Belgium and Germany. He belonged by birth to the clan MacDonald, and had been educated by his parents in the faith of his forefathers. Prompted by his anxiety to serve his clansmen, and his care for the welfare of Catholics, he undertook to show them [MacColla's recently arrived Irish army] the way into the part of the country where the officer in chief command of the King's army [Montrose] was most likely to be'. Moreover, he makes several comments linking the Macranalds directly to Clanranald and that this Macranald is in fact a chief. W. Forbes Leith, *Memoirs of Scottish Catholics during the XVII and XVIII Centuries* (2 vols, London, 1909), i, pp. 291, 301–2, 304–5. Despite the fact that he was nearly 100 this seems to be referring to Donald Gorm MacDonald, uncle of Angus of Glengarry, or perhaps Donald MacDonald of Keppoch.
132 Forbes Leith, *Memoirs*, i, pp. 330–1, 334; MacInnes, *Clanship*, p. 6.
133 Forbes Leith, *Memoirs*, i, p. 331.
134 Anson, *Underground Catholicism*, p. 38.
135 Curry, *Catholicism*, p. 107.
136 Purcell, *Vincentians*, pp. 45–6; Curry, *Catholicism*, p. 6.
137 Forbes Leith, *Memoirs*, i, p. 306.
138 Forbes Leith, *Memoirs*, i, pp. 315, 322, 350.
139 Hill, *MacDonnells of Antrim*, p. 90; Stevenson, *Highland Warrior*, pp. 147–8; T. Carte, *A collection of original letters and papers concerning affairs ... found among the duke of Ormonde's papers* (2 vols, London, 1739), i, p. 75. David Stevenson has this report coming from MacColla himself, whereas John MacLean attributes it to an Irish officer named Colonel James MacDonald. John A. MacLean, 'The sources, particularly the Celtic sources, for the history of the Highlands in the seventeenth century', PhD dissertation, University of Aberdeen, 1939, pp. 16–17.
140 A. MacBain and J. Kennedy (eds), *Reliquiae Celticae* (2 vols, Inverness, 1892–4), ii, p. 183.
141 P. Gordon, *A Short Abridgement of Britain's Distemper, 1639–1649*, ed. J. Dunn (Aberdeen, 1844), p. 98; MacLean, 'The sources', p. 17.
142 E.J. Cowan, *Montrose: For Covenant and King* (London, 1977), p. 117; Stevenson, *Highland Warrior*, p. 148; MacLean, 'The Sources', pp. 16–17.
143 Roderick Watson, *The Poetry of Scotland: Gaelic, Scots, and English, 1380–1980* (Edinburgh, 1995), pp. 218–25.

144 Forbes Leith, *Memoirs*, i, p. 308.
145 *Ibid.*, i, p. 321.
146 *Ibid.*, i, p. 320; Stevenson, *Highland Warrior*, p. 158.
147 *Ibid.*, p. 199; Forbes Leith, *Memoirs*, i, pp. 320, 343, 348, 355, 357, 358.
148 Macdonald, *Missions to the Gaels*, p. 139.
149 Forbes Leith, *Memoirs*, i, pp. 303–8, 312, 324–5; Stevenson, *Highland Warrior*, pp. 146, 152,
150 Forbes Leith, *Memoirs*, i, pp. 299, 303, 310, 311. 319, 340, 341. Priests accompanied the Irish forces and held masses in which soldiers and civilians were in attendance. Among those who attended these services were 'Catholics of the Ogilvie clan from Angus'. Forbes Leith, *Memoirs*, i, p. 334, 341, 344; Macdonald, *Missions to the Gaels*, p. 137.
151 A. Roberts, 'The "Irishes" in Scotland, 1644–7', *The Glynns*, 14 (1986), 41.
152 Stevenson, *Highland Warrior*, pp. 122, 267.
153 A.I. MacInnes, 'The First Scottish Tories', *Scottish Historical Review*, 67:183 (1988), 56–66, 60.
154 Forbes Leith, *Memoirs*, i, p. 303.
155 *Ibid.*, i, pp. 303, 308–9, 317.
156 *Ibid.*, i, p. 292.
157 *Ibid.*, i, pp. 302, 303, 350.
158 *Ibid.*, i, p. 306–7. Added emphasis.
159 MacInnes, *Clanship*, p. 99.
160 Stevenson, *Highland Warrior*, p. 215; NAS, GD 14/19, pp. 113–14, 30; H. McKechnie, *The Lamont Clan* (Edinburgh, 1938), p. 170.
161 A.F. Mitchell and J. Christie (eds), *Records of the Commission of the General Assembly of the Church of Scotland* (3 vols, Edinburgh, 1892–1909), i, pp. 66–8, 70–2; Stevenson, *Highland Warrior*, p. 228.
162 Ohlmeyer, *Civil War and Restoration*, p. 178; Hill, *MacDonnells of Antrim*, p. 306; Stevenson, *Highland Warrior*, p. 227; Paterson, *Lords of the Isles*, p. 144;
163 Stevenson, *Highland Warrior*, p. 236.
164 *Ibid.*, p. 240.
165 B.A. Lang, *The Highlands of Scotland in 1750. From Manuscript 104 in the King's Library, British Museum* (Edinburgh, 1898), pp. 103–4; Curry, *Catholicism*, p. 35.
166 Macdonald, *Missions to the Gaels*, pp. 155, 174; Curry, *Catholicism*, p. 105; P. Hopkins, *Glencoe and the End of the Highland War* (Edinburgh, 1986), pp. 65–7.
167 Campbell, 'The letter sent by Iain Muideartach', pp. 110–16.
168 Macdonald, *Missions to the Gaels*, p. 75; MacInnes, *Clanship*, p. 79.
169 Ohlmeyer, *Civil War and Restoration*, p. 75; R. Black, 'Coll Ciotach', *Transactions of the Gaelic Society of Inverness*, 48 (1972–74), 201–43: 221–3.
170 W. Knowler (ed.), *The Earl of Strafforde's Letters and Despatches with an Essay towards his Life by Sir George Radcliffe* (2 vols, London, 1739), ii, pp. 225–6, 319, 325; Ohlmeyer, *Civil War and Restoration*, p. 79; A. Clarke, 'The earl of Antrim and the first Bishops' War', *Irish Sword*, 6:23 (1963), 108–15.
171 Giblin, 'The "Acta" of Propaganda', p. 68 n. 106, p. 71 n. 119.
172 MacInnes, *Clanship*, pp. 174, 248–9. The Chisholms persisted in their Catholicism into the Jacobite period. Catholicism is believed to have become embedded in

Strathglass from the 1660s. John Boyd Antigonish, *A Short Memoir of the Mission of Strathglass* (Malignant Cove, Inverness, 1850).

173 Macdonald, 'Ireland and Scotland: historical perspectives on the Gaelic dimension 1560–1760', pp. 654–64: 663.

* A version of this chapter has appeared in *Recusant History*, 31:2 (2012), published by the Catholic Record Society

7

The Irish Franciscan mission to the Highlands and Islands

JASON HARRIS

In 1612, the infant and impecunious Irish college at Louvain began to be drawn into two courses of action contrary to its founding bull and statutes. First, impoverished by their own success at attracting new recruits, the members of the college requested a licence to beg in the streets in order to supplement their annual stipend from the Spanish crown.[1] This heightened tensions with rival mendicants in Louvain and the surrounding areas. Yet at the same time the college was drawn into involvement in Scottish affairs. A Scottish resident of the college, John Ogilvie, departed for Scotland with the intention of establishing a mission there and of providing information to the Irish in Louvain to facilitate that end.[2] The combination of these two courses of action, with their conflicting pressures, is indicative of the dilemma facing the young college. Founded rather more on energy than finance, it had to be dynamic and expansive in its outlook and activity in order to secure continued patronage and pay. Thus, although chronically insolvent, the college could not afford to languish for fear of obsolescence.

After the arrival of the first Irish friars in 1619, the mission seemed to go very well. However, persecution and arrests limited the effectiveness of the friars, and in 1623 three further Irish missionaries were sent to Scotland to supplement the mission. From 1626 onwards the friars took control of a derelict friary at Bonamargy in North Antrim as an organizational base and a refuge for the Catholic communities in western Scotland. Despite persistent problems with resources and shortage of manpower, the mission continued in Scotland until 1637, although from 1630 onwards the activities of the friars were very limited. Operations at Bonamargy continued even after the cessation of direct missionary activity, but, apart from a brief revival in 1647 under the influence of the proto-nuncio to Ireland, Francesco Scarampi, the mission effectively ceased to exist in 1641 with the arrest of the prefect of the mission, Patrick Hegarty, at Bonamargy. Thus, despite reports of considerable success, both religious and political, the mission died out after roughly twenty-five years, and the direct involvement of the Irish at Louvain lasted less than twenty years.

To understand why the Irish Franciscans found themselves in this predicament, and why, in particular, they were charged with undertaking a mission to Scotland in addition to their Irish duties, and why the mission ultimately fell into abeyance, it is necessary to consider the political and cultural pressures acting upon Irish and Scottish Catholics abroad. These pressures inevitably played themselves out through the complex webs of ecclesiastical patronage and rivalry as well as through the congeries of diplomatic networks. Also, one must keep in mind the varying degree of importance that Irish and Scottish affairs held for the Curia during the first half of the seventeenth century. Developing alongside and interacting with the Ulster Plantation, the Spanish match, the Scotic debate, and the flourishing network of Irish colleges on the continent, the Irish mission to the Highlands and Islands is central to understanding the relationship between Scottish and Irish Catholics in the seventeenth century, but it was not always of equal importance to papal strategy with regard to Northern Europe.

The origins of the Irish Franciscan mission to Scotland have been described in outline form elsewhere, and in considerable detail recently in the work of Fiona Macdonald.[3] In the wake of the gunpowder plot, persecution of Scottish Catholics intensified, and, accordingly, appeals for foreign assistance likewise increased. The Jesuits were already active and attempts were made to expand their mission. In 1610, Patrick Anderson, later rector of the Scots College in Rome, claimed to have found 100 potential missionaries who were ready to serve, subject to official support and funding.[4] The Irish were already involved, most notably the prominent Jesuit author Christopher Holywood, for whom James I reserved singular animosity.[5] Outside the Jesuit order, the picture was obscured and complicated by the lack of any local church hierarchy through which an effective command structure could operate.[6] Rome was poorly informed about Scottish Catholics and was only just beginning to coordinate a coherent response to the situation after half a century of indifference and neglect. In part, this stemmed from a failure to conceive of appropriate means for an ordinary to operate in the absence of diocesan and provincial structures.[7] Yet, above all, what was required was a greater determination to address the plight of Scottish Catholics. When the Cardinal Protector of Scotland, Camillo Borghese, was elected pope in 1605, the situation looked set to change; in fact, however, his prior knowledge of James VI led rather to a focus on the king's new English dominion than to any sustained attempt to cultivate his old Scottish territories.[8] The initiative in the establishment of Scottish missions came consistently from the exiles themselves rather than the church hierarchy, which, though not uninterested, was phlegmatic and easily distracted. Thus, when the first petitions of Scottish exiles for help from the Irish Franciscans in Louvain were delivered in 1611, no immediate pressure came from Rome to promote the cause.

The logic behind requesting Irish assistance was simple – language. Most of the Scottish Jesuits were Lowlanders and preferred to work in towns or in the households of the southern nobility where direct political influence could be sought. Although some of the leading Gaelic lords could communicate through Scots, any mission to the Highlands or Hebrides had to be conducted in Gaelic.[9] There is no doubt that some competent Gaelic speakers could have been found on the continent; however, ethnic and regional politics ensured that the Scots exiles largely refused to participate in the mission, excusing themselves both on the grounds of language and by suggesting that the Gaelic Scots were, on the whole, unreliable, naturally inclined to sin, and thus unworthy of missionary efforts.[10] In any case, from a continental perspective the Irish were the obvious choice for such a mission, since in curial circles Scots Gaelic was known simply as the Irish language. For the most part, the Irish themselves acceded to this usage, which suited the broader concern of the Louvain Franciscans who, in their hagiographical scholarship, were anxious to emphasize that medieval Scotia was, in fact, Ireland, and that the name – and language – had only passed to Scotland subsequent to the Dál Riada invasion.[11] The linguistic reality was somewhat more complicated. The missionaries themselves often distinguished the language from their own as 'Scots-Irish' and noted that they were immediately recognizable as foreigners on account of their speech, for which reason their instructions from the nuncio urged them to try constantly to improve their command of the 'Scottish' tongue. According to one missionary, Cornelius Ward, only well-educated Irish speakers [*linguae peritia instructos*] could be sent to the Highlands.[12] Yet, these attempts to distinguish between Irish and Gaelic are only ever made in the context of articulating the difficulties facing the missionaries. The common assumption was that Scots Gaelic was simply a form of Irish and thus, whatever the difficulties in dealing with local dialect, the Irish were thought to be best equipped to undertake the mission.

Although this assessment clearly found favour in Rome, not everyone concurred, including some of the Irish in Louvain. Indeed, the inception of the mission was delayed for seven years because of the difficulties that arose in negotiations. The objections of the Irish Franciscans are spelled out in a letter that Aodh Mac Aingil wrote in 1618 to the nuncio in Brussels. He highlights the college's concerns about resources – both the limited number of people available for the mission, and the fear that some of the college's benefactors in Ireland would not appreciate their funds being diverted away from Irish affairs to fund a Scottish mission.[13] How legitimate were these objections?

It is certainly the case that the Franciscans in Louvain were short of funds for new recruits. On the other hand, this seems partly to have been a matter of priorities. In 1610 they were able to buy premises, instead of continuing to rent; in the following year they established a printing press and procured an Irish language font; and in 1616 they purchased land for a new house and chapel, construction of which began in May 1617.[14] True, substantial assistance was provided by Colonel Henry O'Neill; nevertheless, it is clear that the petitions for financial aid emanating from St Anthony's in the 1610s need to be understood in the context of the college's rapid expansion.

The second concern, that funds which came from Ireland would cease if it seemed that they were going to serve another nation, leaving Ireland short of missionaries [*le limosine che ci mandano d'Irlanda mancherebbero se vedessero che andassimo a servir ad altri, lasciando loro in gran penuria d'operarii*], is harder to assess.[15] By the time the mission had begun, confirmation had come from the archbishop of Dublin that it was supported in Ireland, so perhaps the objection was undercut by reports from Ireland or had simply ceased to be relevant because of the increased number of missionaries then available.[16] There is no doubt that establishing a mission on the basis of such limited resources as were available in the 1610s was ambitious to the point of naivety, as Mac Aingil himself, somewhat prophetically, noted.[17] But by the end of the decade the situation had improved greatly, both because of the increasing success of St Anthony's and because the mission in Ireland itself had been placed upon firmer footing.

Yet it is possible that the hesitancy of the Irish was caused by more than mere financial caution. After all, the 'others' to whom funds were to be diverted were Scots who had been committed to the charge of the Irish college because of the linguistic affinity between the two groups of *Gaeil*. For the Irish, the *Gaeltacht* was evidently a less compelling focus of loyalty or identity than Ireland itself. There is nothing remarkable in this. Although Scots Highlanders referred to themselves as *Gaeil* and Lowlanders as *Gaill*, Irish attitudes towards the Scottish *Gaeil* are not easy to pin down, especially since such a strong sense of kinship and regional identity shaped concepts of ethnic identity within the broader category of *Gael*. For example, the Irish classed the Gaelic Scots mercenaries who settled in Ireland as *Gallóglaigh*, which, although it means warriors from *Insi Gall*, nevertheless carried the original sense of 'foreigner'.[18] In addition, the record of Irish troops employed by the English crown to fight in Scotland is marked by sufficient brutality to suggest that whatever sense of commonality proceeded from the shared linguistic and literary culture of Gaeldom could readily disappear in the midst of rivalry and mutual antagonism.[19] Yet, setting aside questions of Gaelic unity, a further problem was the mixed ethnic make-up of Irish Catholicism. Even if the Gaelic Irish could be relied upon to support a mission to Scotland, it is not clear why the Old English should share their interest. In Ulster, geographical proximity provided a strong argument for fostering Catholicism in western Scotland, which might then provide a refuge from persecution; but the wealthy towns in the south had no such incentive.

Because of the limited resources available for the mission in Ireland itself, regional and ethnic rivalries among the Irish were becoming an endemic problem within ecclesiastical networks. The Roman authorities were thoroughly familiar with the problem because of the repeated charge of nepotism in the appointment of bishops and in the granting of places within the Irish colleges. In an Irish context, nepotism was understood as ethnic favouritism that extended beyond the immediate kin group. The case of Christopher Cusack, the rector at Douai who was accused of favouring the Old English, even reached the attention of the cardinal nephew himself in Rome.[20] By the end of the decade, similar attacks had been directed against Peter Lombard and Luke Wadding, so that in the 1620s it became standard policy for papal officials to note the ethnic character of every Irish candidate for promotion, and, when possible, to appoint prelates or bishops from among the majority ethnic group within each diocese.[21] Given the acrimony surrounding patronage and the allocation of resources, it is not surprising that the Louvain Franciscans were chary about being told to redirect some of their energies towards the Scots. Yet, while ethnic and regional tensions might affect the provision of funds from Ireland, the deployment of resources within the Franciscan order was a matter of provincial management, thus the friars argued that the burden of missionary work in Scotland should naturally be borne by the Scottish province rather than the Irish.[22] This brought them outside the sphere of intestinal dispute among the Irish and into the middle of another argument that was brewing among Catholic exiles as they vied with one another for limited resources – the Scotic debate.

For over a century, Scottish scholars had published histories of their nation that claimed every medieval saint or scholar designated 'Scotus' [or *Scottus*] as a Scot, whereas in fact until around the end of the tenth century the term normally meant an inhabitant of Ireland. The *Scoti* were the medieval Gaelic Irish, but the establishment of the Dál Riada kingdom meant that the term *Scotia* came to be employed for both Ireland and Scotland, until eventually the older usage died away and only the Scots were known as *Scoti*.[23] For most of the sixteenth century the Irish, who scarcely participated at all in the first century of printing, left the field to the Scots who therefore secured international recognition for their claim that the medieval *Scoti* were all Scots. This meant that potential patrons in France, Italy, the Low Countries and Germany believed that it was the Scots, not the Irish, who had established monasteries and preserved Christian learning across northern Europe during the middle ages.[24] In the last quarter of the sixteenth century, however, the arrival on the continent of large numbers of Irish exiles in search of asylum resulted in a furious debate over the legacy of medieval Scotia. The work of the Jesuits Richard Fleming, Henry Fitzsimon and Stephen White led to the publication of Fitzsimon's *Catalogue of the Principle Saints of Ireland* in 1611, just when the Irish Franciscans in Louvain were being asked to undertake an arduous and expensive mission to Scotland. Within a few years, the Louvain Franciscans had entered the lists on behalf of Ireland and St Anthony's College soon became the leading centre of medieval Irish hagiography.[25] It would not be at all surprising if the animosities aroused by the Scotic debate impeded the formation of the Irish mission to Scotland. Although the mission was first suggested by Scots, probably from the small Gaelic-speaking community resident among the Irish in Louvain, other Scottish exiles opposed it from the outset on the grounds that the Irish were foreigners. Yet the latter group refused to undertake the mission themselves on the grounds that too many obstacles stood in the way, and they can probably be equated with the group who criticised the religious character of the Gaelic Scots.[26] The most likely centre of such opposition was the Scots college in Paris, where riots would break out in 1620 in response to Irish claims regarding St Brigid. This was probably the largest and most vocal community of Lowland Scots exiles on the continent, and it had the most to lose from the presence of the Irish, who challenged Scottish claims to have been instrumental in founding the university of Paris.[27] It is hard not to surmise that the Highlanders and islanders were left hanging while the Irish and the Lowland Scots jostled for prestige and position on the continent.

Under these circumstances, outside intervention was required to drive forward the projected mission. Scottish petitions were not only delivered to the Irish in Louvain, but also to the nuncio in Brussels and to the pope himself.[28] This reveals something of the administrative mechanism for starting an initiative of this kind in an area of multiple over-lapping jurisdictions. Prior to the establishment of Propaganda Fide in 1622, the mission most naturally fell to the remit of the cardinal protector of Scotland, Maffeo Barberini; but if the Irish were to be called upon then the cardinal protector of Ireland, Fabrizio Veralli, ought to be consulted. However, for information on Ireland and Scotland, the Curia generally relied upon the nuncio in Brussels who was the nearest senior-ranking prelate. From 1607–15 this was the distinguished archbishop of Rhodes, Guido Bentivoglio. On his promotion to the nunciature of France, he was replaced by the lesser figures of Ascanio Gesualdo (1615–17), Lucio Morra (1617–19), and, after a gap of nearly six months, Lucio San Severino (1619–21).[29] However, Bentivoglio was still occasionally consulted regarding the Scotic mission after he returned to Rome from France in 1621, partly because of his particular expertise in the matter but also owing to prominence within the Curia and his broad grasp of European diplomacy.[30] Since the Irish who were to be assigned to the mission were Franciscans, it was necessary to gain the permission of several key figures within the Franciscan order – the minister general of the order, the minister general of the ultramontane province, the Commissary General of the German-Belgian province to which the Irish belonged, the provincial of the Irish province, and, of course, the guardian of St Anthony's college. Each of these men worked according to different budgets, represented rival power blocks, and often pursued competing policies. Given the complexity of these overlapping jurisdictions, it is no wonder that the Irish mission to Scotland took a long time to get going. Nevertheless, these hierarchical or jurisdictional structures were primarily sources of red tape, rather than avenues through which policy was formulated. They served to connect two key locations where the plans were actually conceived and the issues debated – Belgium and Rome.

In Belgium, the two primary sources of power were the archdukes, Albert and Isabella, and the nuncio, though both were subject to Spanish influences that were often channelled through the Spanish ambassador, cardinal Alfonso de la Cueva, or special emissaries who held key local positions, such as the confessor to the archduchess Isabella and commissary general of the Franciscan Order, Andrea de Soto, or the provincial of the Irish Franciscans and, subsequently, archbishop of Tuam, Florence Conry, who founded the convent of St Anthony's at Louvain. In Rome, prior to 1622, local knowledge relating to Ireland and its mission was provided most prominently through the archbishop of Armagh, Peter Lombard, often derived from his vicar-apostolic in Ireland, David Rothe. Other senior figures also contributed information, most notably the exiled earls of Tyrone and Tyrconnell, and their associates. Numerous reports and petitions from prelates within Ireland were delivered via these routes or directly to the cardinal protector; the only other major supply line was the Jesuit order. The other major stake-holders in Rome were the members of the Spanish faction among the cardinalate, owing to Spanish involvement in English and Irish affairs. In major matters of policy, particularly when they were politically sensitive or required papal funding, the cardinal protector had to turn to the papal nephew, Scipio Borghese, who was effectively the head of the Curia. He was therefore also, however, the target of petitions by the pro-Spanish cardinals, as well as by the rival French faction. Occasionally, Pope Paul V himself intervened in the minutiae of Irish and Scottish affairs, perhaps reflecting sustained interest that stemmed from his position as cardinal protector of Scotland prior to his election to the papacy.

The commencement of the Scottish mission, once the objections of the Irish had been overcome, was brought about through the timely coalescence of these various interest groups. In May 1617, the cardinal nephew, Scipio Borghese, ordered the newly appointed nuncio in Brussels, Lucio Morra, to pursue the matter with Donough Mooney, the former guardian of St Anthony's and current father provincial of the Irish Franciscans. Although Mooney's response was the standard objection that the college had insufficient resources to undertake the mission, he used the opportunity to suggest that an increase in the college's funding might allow him to reconsider.[31] Construction work upon new premises for the college was well under way at this stage and it is likely that Mooney was merely chancing his arm in pursuit of more money to secure the investment and allow the intake of more students. This would fit in with his wider initiative to gain increased support for the Irish Franciscan missions. The customary stance of the cardinal nephew was that the papacy could not afford sustained financial support of any enterprise in Ireland or Scotland.[32] Six months later, however, Borghese replied that the pope had personally intervened to guarantee some level of funding and to secure the compliance of the relevant provincials of the order.[33] Accordingly, the nuncio applied further pressure, this time enlisting the aid of the commissary general, Andrea de Soto, and Florence Conry, newly arrived in Brussels from Spain upon diplomatic business.[34] To such weighty intervention, no further objection could be made by the Louvain Franciscans. Since the church in Ireland was in a far better condition than that in Scotland, and given that the first generation of students to have studied at the continental Irish colleges had now matured sufficiently to undertake missionary activity, it is not surprising that the weight of opinion now leant in favour of the Irish beginning a Scottish mission. In Rome, a sensitive approach was made to the father general of the Jesuits to gauge the scope of his own order's mission in Scotland and to ensure that no offence was caused by the proximity of the new mission to the Jesuit one. Discussion of the already well-established Jesuit mission also afforded Borghese the opportunity to argue for sending fewer Franciscans, thereby limiting the overall expense. Thus, in early 1619, three missionaries (Patrick Brady, Edmund McCann and John Stuart) arrived in Scotland to supplement the work of Ogilvie, and shortly afterwards a fourth (Sylvester Robertson) joined them.[35]

This turn of events was clearly driven by a new initiative from Spain, as is made clear by the timely intervention of two Spanish agents, Andrea de Soto and Florence Conry, to lend weight to Morra's advocacy of the mission in Brussels. Although Scotland was traditionally more a concern of France, the Franco-Spanish *détente* left the Spanish freer to pursue an interventionist religious policy in Scotland and Ireland, and in this they were further aided by the presence of a pro-Spanish nuncio in Paris – Guido Bentivoglio, the former nuncio in Brussels who had first dealt with the plans for a mission to Scotland. Spanish interest in the Hebrides was not merely theoretical, and in 1612–13 plans were put in place for an uprising that would be coordinated between the lords of the Isles, the Ulster earls, and Spanish agents, with the intention of subverting the Ulster Plantation and restraining the persecution of Catholics in both Scotland and Ireland.[36] Although the rebellion went ahead, it remained largely a local affair because the Spanish flirtation with the affair was undercut by the concern to stay on good terms with England. Despite the advocacy of Hugh O'Neill and Florence Conry, Spain was unwilling to back a larger-scale uprising to drive the English out of Ireland with Scottish aid because it was considered more realistic to seek toleration of Catholicism through maintenance of the Anglo-Spanish peace.[37] By 1617, that policy had come to depend upon the potential success of the proposed marriage of Prince Charles to the Spanish infanta. Although this alliance was viewed with suspicion by the papacy, the cardinal protector of Scotland, Maffeo Barberini, was one of the key negotiators, and the Spanish had required the mitigation of the persecution of Catholics as one of the preconditions for the proposed marriage.[38] The papacy thus had every reason to believe that the time was propitious for undertaking a mission to restore Catholicism in the west of Scotland, on the assumption that a relaxation of persecution was imminent.

Ironically, it was the diminished possibility of Catholic insurgency that paved the way for the Franciscan mission. The failure of the Macdonald rebellion, the relative success of the crown in pacifying Argyll, and the increased dominance of the royalist Campbells and their clients throughout south-western Scotland seemed to have secured the most vulnerable strategic weak spot in James's realm. Further, the death of Hugh O'Neill in 1616 removed a key sponsor of sedition, although in latter years he had been more of a symbolic than a military threat. O'Neill's desire to leave Rome, to travel either to Spain or Flanders, was consistently regarded by the Spanish and English alike as a destabilizing element in their attempts to maintain the peace and enshrine it through a dynastic alliance. O'Neill's death therefore removed a major embarrassment to the Spanish; but from James's perspective, it combined with the slow but visible progress of the Ulster Plantation and the pacification of the Gaelic lords of Scotland to allow James to feel relatively confident that the Gaeltacht no longer presented a serious threat to his authority.[39] Conversely, from a Catholic perspective, missionary work replaced military resistance as the main avenue for aspirations towards religious toleration.

South-western Scotland had, by this stage, been impoverished by economic decline combined with the debts and devastations derived from the recent rebellions.[40] The activities of the Irish missionaries were fashioned by these circumstances as much as by the lack of an existing ecclesiastical infrastructure. The guiding principle upon which their mission was based was that they should operate at minimal expense both to the church and, more particularly, to the local community. This was, of course, a rule of thumb for mendicants in all situations, but was normally honoured more in the breach than the observance. In this instance, however, the missionaries could often beg only for a night's accommodation and the most meagre scraps of food. They went without food, wine or beer for long stretches at a time, frequently slept rough in caves and were often forced to return to Ireland for a respite from these conditions, as well as to evade perseuction.[41] The itinerant character of their mission, particularly on the islands, must be understood in this context – even where large numbers of conversions were reported, they could not afford to stay long for fear of over-taxing local resources or attracting the attention of Protestant ministers.

The result was that in most instances the missionaries briefly passed through areas to which they could perhaps only hope to return in a matter of weeks, but sometimes not for several months. They encountered ignorance of the rudiments of the Catholic faith, but also often a complete lack of awareness of mendicancy. Their first steps in such communities were devoted to explaining such basic things as their own clothing and accoutrements, as well as the basic character of the sacraments and sacramentals such as holy water, signs of benediction, and consecrated chalices. Most of the islanders were unfamiliar with Catholic observance, and those who were old enough to remember it found the new post-Tridentine rites confusing.[42] The missionaries did not engage in Catholic apologetics or polemic, but rather concentrated upon the administration of the sacraments and the normalization of Catholic observance, rendering it familiar so that it might come to seem the natural form of religious expression.[43] The term 'conversion' needs to be understood in this context, and doing so helps to resolve the controversy about whether the reports of the Franciscans were greatly inflated or not. For example, the missionaries reported that by 1633 they had converted 6,627 people from Calvinism and had baptized a further 3,010.[44] The first figure merely represents the number who were willing to confess and receive communion from the friars; the second denotes the number of children who were baptized. Given the remoteness of the locations involved and the limited sense of confessional awareness among the laity, it is not surprising that over the course of fifteen years many would turn to the friars when other ministers were not present to perform these basic rites.

A deliberate choice to embrace and persist in one confession is another matter altogether. This is best measured in communities within which Protestant ministers were present either continuously or frequently. In these cases, the friars did engage in a form of religious debate. Although the friars avoided any public confrontation with ministers, they would attend Protestant services incognito to hear the sermon and would then address the same topics in their own preaching during subsequent days so that they could provide some redress to the Protestant message. It also seems that the friars relied upon the sacramental elements in Catholic devotion to counter local superstitions, such as belief in the people of the *sídh*. Ward reports that Catholicism was deemed more efficacious in this regard than Protestantism, and if this reflects anything other than his own bias it may be that the ritualistic use of the Catholic sacramentals (for example, holy water) was better able to replace the talismanic elements in local belief than the more austere practices of the Presbyterians.[45] At any rate, if Ward reported this to Rome it is likely that he proclaimed it to the islanders as a way of countering the appeal of Protestantism. The willingness of the community to harbour the friars and even to go to considerable lengths to help them evade persecution suggests genuine committment to Catholic observance. However, it is equally likely that their sympathies reflect the sense of excitement and adventure that the missions brought to the local communities. Also, the ministers themselves were often not native to their parishes, and it would be surprising if anticlericalism and village feuds were less a feature of parish life in western Scotland than they were elsewhere in Europe. Thus, many factors may have aroused sympathy for the friars, but given the itinerant nature of their mission, it is unlikely that they did more than to introduce a form of multiple observance into these regions. In remote areas throughout early modern Europe, villagers could not afford to be choosy and had little interest in being so when they did have the opportunity. They took their sacraments as and when they could get them with little regard to the theological subtleties that the clergy urged upon them. It is doubtful that many among the Scottish islanders would have viewed the evidently understaffed Franciscan mission as anything other than a supplement to normal observance. The missionaries must have been aware of this, but it is not surprising that it did not feature in their reports.

To circumvent these limitations upon their work, the friars tried to establish a basis for more sustained support for their work. Their attempts to do so may be divided into three broad classes: first, the targeting of key figures within the community who could sponsor the mission on a more substantial basis and attract international recognition of the political potential of the mission; secondly, the establishment of institutional structures to underpin the mission; and thirdly, the promulgation of Columban propaganda to promote the achievements of the missionaries. Each of these aspects will be considered in turn before examining the final culmination of the mission and its broader significance.

While much of the missionary zeal expressed in the preparatory stages of the mission, and, indeed, in the reports of the missionaries, was directed towards the notion of saving the souls of the poor, faithful, but remote inhabitants of western Scotland who had been unwillingly cut off from and neglected by the universal church, in fact the efforts of the friars were astutely built around flirtation with the local nobility rather than the devout peasantry.[46] The reasons for this were simple and pragmatic – the peasantry could not provide long-term political or economic support for the mission. Local nobility could more readily house the friars and conceal them from the search parties of the Protestant ministers. The difficulty was how to approach them. In many instances, the friars appear first to have approached lesser nobility, relying upon kinship connections to draw them into the sphere of more prominent figures. Most famously, however, Cornelius Ward disguised himself as a bard (he was, of course, from a bardic family) and, accompanied by a singer with a harp, spent three days at a poetic contest hosted by Sir John Campbell of Cawdor before revealing that he was a missionary. Ward instructed Cawdor as to the errors of Protestantism, but the latter did not immediately convert, owing to the presence of other Protestant lairds, and merely promised to do so at a later date. His conversion is subsequently reported through his reception of absolution at the hands of Patrick Hegarty, leading Ward to report that he had beome Catholic – a fine demonstration of the pragmatic approach to religious matters demonstrated by some local 'converts'.[47]

While Campbell of Cawdor may merely have been hedging his bets in the salvation stakes, other nobles were more committed, and their actions reveal an extra dimension to the rationale behind wooing the nobility. Ranald Macdonald, a scion of the ruling family of Uist, had been the local Protestant minister, but was converted to Catholicism by Ward.[48] Macdonald was quite a coup and was trumpeted far and wide by the missionaries when he travelled to the continent to seek ordination as a priest.[49] He represented two key strands of strategy: the foundation of a body of native clergy and the revival of Catholic political hopes in the southern Hebrides. The latter prospect was raised by John of Moidart, also of Clanranald, in a letter to the papacy in 1626, although his Franciscan colleagues did not report directly on the matter themselves.[50] This should not be taken to mean that they were not privy to or promulgators of the plans. On the contrary, Cornelius Ward foolishly revealed the political dimension of the mission during a sojourn with his friend Sir Charles Coote in Galway in 1624.[51] The project to foment Catholic rebellion in the Hebrides was, however, a controversial one, and could easily be seen to detract from the cure of souls in the missionary enterprise.

In reporting to the *Congregatio de Propaganda Fide*, the Franciscans were always cautious to emphasize the positive pastoral impact of their work, omitting, as we have seen, any hint that their conversions might be either superficial or politically motivated. From the perspective of the church, the friars probably judged correctly. Even with the sudden shift of Stuart foreign policy towards preparations for war with Spain after the failure of the negotiations for a Spanish match, there was little immediate prospect of sustained support for an uprising in the Hebrides. Indeed, the secrecy that local lords employed in their dealings with the friars ensured both that the mission could transgress the limits of faction and that it could not easily become the basis of a factional uprising. It was certainly to the advantage of the mission in the short term that the friars were able to woo members of rival clans and, more particularly, to gain support from mutual enemies even in the midst of conflict. For example, after having converted Campbell of Cawdor, Ward was also able to gain the support of his enemy Alasdair MacIain, who had been evicted from Ardnamurchan by Campbell's half-brother, and who had embraced piracy by late 1624, which may have been why Ward, with a note of anxiety, noted that MacIain was still a Catholic in 1625.[52] The down side of operating across the boundaries of faction was that the leading converts could hardly be expected to work together towards a Catholic political rising. Clanranald was perhaps exceptional in this regard. Not only did Ranald Macdonald publicly abjure Protestantism, but the strength in depth of the Clanranald conversions allowed the chief to dream of rebellion.[53] Even if this remained a pipe-dream, or a project to provide employment for roving bands of *buannachan*, the appearance on the continent of a member of the Scottish nobility suing for ordination while the leader of his clan petitioned for military support, provided the *Congregatio* with concrete evidence of the incredible success stories emanating from western Scotland and enticed them with the idea that a sustainable Catholic presence in western Scotland might be possible.

The need to establish resident parish clergy was evident to everyone involved with the mission. A Franciscan mission might lay the basis for this, but could not substitute for it indefinitely. There were two primary reasons for this: finance and faculties. The mission was essentially a subsistence-level operation that had to be continually maintained by church sponsorship, whereas a parish clergy supported by local nobility might, if it came to replace the Protestant parish structure, eventually sustain itself or even potentially generate revenue. Most importantly, however, the itinerant mission was dogged by a lack of infrastructure through which resources could be channelled. The case of Ranald Macdonald indicates both the strengths and the weaknesses of the system. The striking austerity and fragility of the mendicant mission prompted sympathy even as it whetted local appetites for a direct connection with Rome, given the lack of national avenues towards patronage; but Macdonald had to travel to receive instruction and ordination, because the Franciscans had neither the resources nor the power to prepare him for the priesthood in Scotland.[54] Not only had the training of priests been allocated to the new seminary system established by the Council of Trent, but the power of ordination lay in the hands of the relevant ordinary, normally a bishop. In other words, a diocesan structure could not be home grown, but could only be established through the faculties of an existing ordinary. Thus, when Macdonald returned to Scotland he was too isolated and impoverished to sustain pastoral labours beyond the most rudimentary level. The locals could not afford to support him with tithes, which they already paid to the kirk, and so, according to Ward, instead of providing the basis of a parish structure, he was forced to fish, gather shellfish and try to cultivate barren land in order to keep himself alive in a remote corner of Uist.[55] In order to remedy the situation, the missionaries sought, not the faculty of ordination, but of appointment to parishes.[56] To concede this, however, would have been tantamount to abandoning the establishment of a diocesan structure in the short to medium term, something the papacy was not willing to do at this point.

The lack of a local bishop also caused other practical problems such as the need to consecrate holy water, other sacramentals, and disused churches; to replace consecrated chalices when lost; to be allowed to say mass at night, to dispense with servers, candles and similar paraphernalia that were hard to come by on the mission; to dispense with the Franciscan habit when necessary, to eat dairy foods and eggs on fast days, to ride horses, and so forth.[57] Further, each of the missionaries was under obligation to send frequent reports to Rome, yet they lacked the infrastructure to do so, hence they requested that one of them be appointed director of the mission to coordinate their efforts and that, further, a Franciscan superior should be chosen to whom they could send their reports. There was some confusion in this matter. When the *Congregatio* tried to resolve this problem by appointing Patrick Brady as senior missionary, the others objected, despite having previously recommended him, on the grounds that he worked in the Highlands, remote and cut off from them.[58] Finally, the lack of infrastructure meant that the reports of the missionaries, and the replies of the *Congregatio*, frequently failed to reach their intended recipients. Indeed, the money allocated to the missionaries seems rarely to have reached them without substantial delays. Worse, the loss *en route* of the missionaries' reports caused suspicion in Rome that they had not been written, which resulted in delays in approving further finances, so that the mission was consistently under-funded.

Most importantly, however, the friars needed a bishop to provide dispensations for marriages contracted within the forbidden degrees of consanguinity. This was an acute problem, because kinship relations and the remote locations of the Hebrides had resulted in large numbers of marriages that the Church deemed illegitimate. Not only did this present a problem in terms of convincing potential recruits to embrace Catholicism, but it also meant that these people could not receive the sacraments while living in what was officially regarded as a state of sin. This was not only a problem for the friars but also preoccupied the Calvinist ministers. Although the latter could offer divorce as a means to resolve the difficulty, they were reluctant to do so because of a desire to promote the sanctity of marriage over its traditional function as the means to extend and propagate the kin group.[59] Thus, if the missionaries could offer a better solution, either by dissolving or legitimizing the marriages as occasion demanded, they stood a very good chance of luring large numbers away from their rivals. Securing dispensations from Rome was, however, a slow process ill-suited to the transient visits of the friars to each island. Thus, they repeatedly asked to be granted special faculties, pending the appointment of an ordinary who could service the mission, in order to circumvent what were evidently extreme restrictions upon their work.[60] Not surprisingly, Rome demurred. Some of the reasons for this were political, and these will be discussed later in the chapter, but the main problem was that the church was preoccupied with acrimonious debates about some of the same issues in Ireland, where hostility between the mendicants and the secular clergy was threatening to undermine the entire project to rebuild a basic diocesan infrastructure.[61] The problem in Ireland was that friars, specifically the Franciscans, had been operating without a parish structure for a long time and did not want to cede space and resources to a new body of local clergy. They had also been granted special faculties to pursue the mission and they were loathe to give these up in favour of local ordinaries because they would thereby lose influence within the community. If the Church wished to appoint bishops, they argued, it should draw them from the ranks of the Franciscans who could build upon the missionary achievements and contacts already established within Ireland. The regulars and the secular clergy thus revived a polemic among themselves that had flared up at intervals for the past two hundred years. In Rome this dispute divided along institutional lines, with the advocates of the secular clergy gaining more support in Propaganda Fide and the regulars relying more on the Holy Office and the Datary.[62] One consequence of this fracas was that, at the very moment when the friars were requesting special faculties for their work in Scotland, the papacy had become freshly aware of the difficulties involved in any transition from mission to diocesan church, thus the reports of the friars were subjected to detailed scrutiny and grudging, limited concessions despite the apparent success of their mission so far.

No resolution of this problem could be found in the absence of a bishop and the Franciscans themselves repeatedly sent petitions to this end. As such, the supervision of the Scottish mission became subject to broader discussions about the appointment of bishoprics within Ireland as a whole. Several difficulties beset these negotiations, not least the regionalism and ethnic tensions that cut across all Irish Catholic policy in this period. Most importantly, several high-ranking advocates of the Gaelic Irish argued that bishops should be chosen from among those native to the diocese – Ulstermen for Ulster dioceses, and so forth.[63] On the other hand, the religious orders also sought to gain due representation in the episcopate and sent lists of candidates to Rome for consideration. Finally, Ireland had its own minor investiture controversy in these decades as the expatriate nobility sought to retain its traditional role in the appointment of senior prelates.[64] These disputes stalled the whole process of appointment for a short while, particularly in Gaelic areas, but, perhaps more significantly, they also established principles that could only present obstacles in the case of western Scotland. Simply put, there were no natives of the region who could be appointed ordinaries there. If an outsider were to be chosen, the obligation of residence within the diocese would be both unappealing to potential candidates and difficult to maintain in practice. If, on the other hand, the missionaries were to be considered as candidates, the problem was that they were not high-ranking ecclesiastics and their records or achievements could not easily be scrutinized except on the basis of their own reports.

It was only in 1640 that the missionaries eventually secured agreement from the *Congregatio* that a bishop was necessary, could be afforded, and could be drawn from among the missionaries who had worked in Scotland. The focus of these discussions centred around the proposed appointment of Patrick Hegarty to the bishopric of Sodor, which was the old diocesan see of the Isles. Although Hegarty had spent over a decade continuously at work on the mission, doubts were raised by the *Congregatio* about his qualifications for the position. The council objected that he had seldom sent the required reports on his activities and complained that he had spent most of his time in Ireland avoiding persecution since 1631. Finally, it deferred taking a decision until Hegarty had proven himself in his new role as prefect of the mission.[65] Subsequently, events took over, with the advent of war in Scotland and Ireland, so that Hegarty never attained his bishopric. This was typical of the processes which undermined the mission throughout its 25- year lifespan. Inadequate communication and a climate of suspicion frustrated even the best of intentions at an administrative level and among the functionaries in Scotland.

From the reports submitted by Cornelius Ward, the most frequent and extensive writer to the *Congregatio*, it is possible to glean something of the difficulties that faced the church hierarchy with regard to interpretation of the missives that arrived from Scotland. From at least 1625 onwards, Ward seems to have engaged in an attempt to create a parallel between his own mission and that of St Columba, the apostle of the Western Isles in the sixth century.[66] This may originally have begun as a missionary device, since Ward relates that the inhabitants of the Hebrides showed great devotion to the saint's memory, and he notes that he visited the sites of Columban ruins and tried to explain to locals that he preached the same faith as that of Columba.[67] The locals pointed out to Ward that Columba had driven out poisonous animals from the islands and performed many miracles, so it is perhaps no coincidence that by 1626 Ward himself had begun to report that visions and miracles were now occurring through and around the missionaries. Thus, a man on the island of Barra reported having a detailed vision of three of the missionaries meeting many miles away on South Uist, while another had an apocalyptic vision of the armies of heretics lining up against the soldiers of Christ. A third vision was reported of a Protestant farmer who had criticised a statue of the Holy Trinity that was reported to have miraculous properties. The farmer had a dream in which he chose to follow Christ rather than the Devil, who then afflicted him with a wound in the side. When the farmer awoke, the wound was visible, so he repented his sins and converted to Catholicism. Several miracles seemed to cluster around Ward himself, though he did not claim to have performed them himself, with one exception – he called upon God to punish a blasphemer, who died shortly afterwards.[68] The reports of these visions and miracles were intended to legitimate the mission and underscore the importance of continuing to support the missionaries.[69] It was an imaginitive two-pronged strategy: while Ward played Protestant criticism of the cult of saints against local Columban traditions, he marketed his efforts abroad as a replaying of the original Irish conversion of Scotland.

It is hard to know what impact Ward expected these reports to have in Rome. The successes of the first missionaries had already led to an expansion of the mission in 1623, resulting in the assignment of three new friars to the mission, including Ward himself, who arrived in Scotland in 1624. However, broken lines of communication thereafter began to frustrate the enterprise and provide cause for irritation in Rome. From the perspective of the *Congregatio*, the missionaries were being remiss in their duty to report regularly; but the missionaries felt that Rome was being tardy in the provision of financial aid. Ward thus appears to have felt the need to inflate the significance of the mission in order to attract swifter and surer support from the *Congregatio*. Yet Ward also joined the mission during the height of the Scotic debate, and it is therefore no surprise that the activities of St Columba in Scotland were at the forefront of his mind, since the Scots had already controversially tried to claim that Columba was Scottish. It is Ward who focuses most attention upon the tensions between the Gaelic- and the Anglo-Scots in his reports to the *Congregatio*, and his criticisms of the latter surely reflect the sensitivities of the Irish, particularly in Louvain, to Anglo-Scottish politics and historiography in the 1620s.[70] Yet, in the context of the Scotic debate, the Columban propaganda in his reports to Rome was not just foolhardy but inflammatory. The new pope, Maffeo Barberini, and his cardinal nephew Francesco, had long-standing connections with the Lowland Scots exiles on the continent; indeed, the latter had replaced the former as cardinal protector of Scotland. Not long after this, rumours began to circulate in the Curia that Ward's reports were unreliable and that the Franciscan claims to have converted thousands were fictitious.

Ward appears to have somewhat over-played his cards. The successes of the mission in the 1620s attracted a great deal of attention as a supplement to the work of the Louvain friars in restoring Catholicism within Ireland. In 1626, an astute administrative reform granted to the nuncio in Brussels the power of granting licences and missionary faculties at his own discretion in order to streamline the command structure behind the mission.[71] This coincided with the high-point of the mission: a disused friary at Bonamargy was made available as a refuge and a base from which to supply the mission, and it seems that the friars had opened up a pilgrimage route to Patrick's Purgatory, which site was now flourishing such that they requested permission to base one of the missionaries there when resting from the hardships in Scotland (though this was refused on the grounds that it distracted from the mission).[72] The establishment of further Irish colleges on the continent was a strong indication of papal approval for the enterprises undertaken so far. Indeed, the success of the Scottish mission was mentioned in key correspondence behind the foundation of the Irish college in Prague in 1629. Hugh Ward specifically referred to it in a letter to the Archduchess Isabella, which became the template for Isabella's own recommendation of the Prague project, and the pope himself was said to be inclined to favour the new college on the basis of the Scottish mission's success.[73] Yet, within a few short years, the mission seems to have fallen into disfavour such that in February 1630 the *Congregatio* demanded evidence of the veracity of the friars' reports. It seems that a report which Ward had written in late 1628 or early 1629, covering the previous two years of the mission, was lost some time after he handed it to the nuncio in Brussels.[74] The *Congregatio* was suspicious. When the request for more information was not complied with to their satisfaction, they ceased to send money to the friars, and since the money sent in 1629 did not reach its target, the friars received no financial support for nearly four years until late 1633.[75] In the meantime, Cornelius Ward and Ranald Macdonald were arrested and held in London, and Patrick Hegarty left Scotland to reside in Bonamargy from 1631 onwards, requiring Scottish Catholics to come to him rather than the other way round. Although the site was relatively convenient for this purpose, and Hegarty reported large numbers flocking to the place, his withdrawal is evidence that, instead of life becoming easier for the missionaries as they established a local following, the hardship of avoiding persecution and trying to survive without funding from Rome forced the friars to beat a tactical retreat. Only Patrick Brady was able to remain in Scotland throughout the 1630s, but he was hidden in a nobleman's house in the southern Highlands and was rarely in contact with his colleagues, and so his work is poorly documented.[76]

Much of the problem seems to have been that Ward, having been sent to report on the mission, was arrested and held in English custody for nearly three years. His loose tongue in earlier years had drawn unfavourable attention upon him, focused around rumours of a political agenda behind the mission. While King James had consistently dismissed the political threat that his ministers claimed to perceive in the activities of the friars, rumours of foreign machinations against Protestantism in Scotland were enough to keep Ward locked away until the intervention of the Polish ambassador saved him, on the grounds that he travel to Poland and never return to England or Scotland.

Ward instantly, of course, broke these terms and began campaigning to revive the mission.[77] Opposition plagued his efforts all the way. He complained, in particular, about the frosty reception he received among the Franciscans in both Madrid and Rome, and one report claimed that he had lost his mind during his captivity in England.[78] To prove that he had not simply invented the material in his earlier reports, he was required to compile lists of the names of all those converted to Catholicism. When he managed to provide substantial lists – no mean feat – several individual entries were queried. Eventually, however, he managed to secure the release of the finances promised to the missionaries, including backpayments, and he returned to the mission. The backbone of the project had, however, been broken.

What had happened? A process of attrition through persecution had undoubtedly contributed to the decline of the mission. In 1623 there were eight Franciscans (five Irish, three Scots) active in Scotland. However, the Scottish laybrother John Stuart was arrested in 1624 and died shortly after his release. Edmund McCann had been arrested in late 1620, and broke his leg trying to escape, so although he returned to the mission in 1624, he was unable to progress further than Ireland, where he resided in a friary until his death.[79] In 1626/27 Paul O'Neill withdrew to Ireland, probably because of the limited resources and support available to mitigate the appalling conditions in which the friars were working.[80] Although the *Congregatio* seemed willing to replace O'Neill in order to keep four Irish friars in the field, he himself received no word of this and so remained in Ireland awaiting instructions.[81] The intended replacement, Francis Macdonnell, was not permitted to risk joining the mission in Scotland by his father, the earl of Antrim, so that effectively the number of active missionaries sponsored by Louvain was reduced to three by 1629.[82] In that year, the mission suffered collateral damage from the government crackdown on recusancy in both Ireland and Scotland. While it had always been difficult to transmit information to Rome, this period seems to have been particularly troublesome, and very little evidence survives to reveal what was happening. The friars, starved and demoralized, spent more and more time in Ireland, while the cardinals in Rome turned their attention more fully to preserving the Irish church, reserving mainly suspicion for the friars' activities in Scotland. Thus, although the persecution of recusants in western Scotland did not translate into prosecutions, it should not be assumed that it had little impact upon Catholicism in the region, since it appears to coincide with the collapse of the friars' communication with Rome and their effective withdrawal from Scottish territory.[83]

The breakdown in communication might not have proven fatal if the mission had not faced a smear campaign in Rome. It is not clear exactly who among the Lowland Scots orchestrated this, though the finger is normally pointed at George Conn, because he was named by the *Congregatio* as the person who had to be consulted regarding the veracity of Cornelius Ward's reports.[84] In fact, this might equally suggest that he was regarded by the cardinals as an independent party who could be trusted to adjudicate. The *Congregatio* naturally turned to resident experts who could be expected to be familiar with the details of the mission; for example, Cardinal Bentivoglio, the former nuncio in Brussels and Paris, was consulted because of his prior involvement in the mission.[85] Nevertheless, Conn is still a plausible candidate, since he was well connected within the Curia, being a member of the cardinal nephew's personal court, and was something of a rising star, who would be dispatched on a high-profile embassy to the English court from 1636 to 1639. His support of the Jesuits and diplomatic influence through recusants at the court of Queen Henrietta-Maria, and his earlier participation in the Scotic debate as a former pupil of the irascible Hibernophobe Thomas Dempster, make him a plausible candidate. It is also possible that there was Irish opposition to the mission, whether on the basis of resource allocation or as an extension of the ethnic battles within the Irish exile church. St Anthony's in Louvain was not exempt from these in the early 1630s, and it is possible that the frosty reception that Ward found among the Franciscans in Madrid and Rome was related to this.

Troubles within the Franciscan order regarding the activities of Joseph Bergaigne, the commissary general of the Belgian province, doubtless contributed to the reception Ward found among the ultramontane friaries. Bergaigne was accused of fomenting schism within the order by acting without recourse to the appropriate superiors, and, given the close involvement of the Louvain Franciscans in defending Bergaigne, it is likely that Ward encountered some of the disgruntlement of the southern friars about the behaviour of the Belgian province.[86] Still more acrimonious within ecclesiastical circles was the growing fracas over Jansenism. The Irish were caught in the cross-fire of the debate surrounding Jansen, to the extent that few Irish clergy escaped suspicion at some stage or other.[87] The Scots College in Paris was also centrally involved in the developing controversy with the result that serious damage was done to the Scottish missions.[88] Although there was little reason to connect these feuds with the Irish Franciscan mission to Scotland, its close association with Louvain, one of the birthplaces of the Jansenist movement, cannot have helped to expedite the requisition of funding to renew the mission. In a climate clouded with conspiracy theories, even influential figures like Luke Wadding could become the target of accusations, especially because of the Jansenist leanings of many other Irishmen.[89] The combination of all these difficulties combined to hinder Ward's funding drive, so that by the time he had convinced the members of the *Congregatio* that the accusations laid against the missionaries by the Anglo-Scots were false the mission was essentially moribund. Despite the release of further funds to support the friars, the initiative in missionary matters had been transferred to other, potentially more lucrative, projects, such as the reconversion of England or the promotion of the extra-European missions.

The Irish Franciscan mission to Scotland was not, however, without fruit. The list of clans that remained largely Catholic into the eighteenth century is composed mostly of those that the Franciscans converted, such as the MacNeill of Barra, the Macdonalds of Glengarry, Keppoch and Clanranald, and elements of the Macdonald of Sleat.[90] While some of their high-ranking converts were disenfranchised warlords – such as Alasdair MacIain and Rory Mór MacLeod – who were unable to provide lasting institutional support for the missionaries, and while they failed to establish the basis for a parish structure that might have transformed the Scottish mission into a church, nevertheless the missionaries appear to have fared rather well in their pastoral efforts to sew a Catholic fringe onto the frayed ends of the kirk in western Scotland, at least until their work was undone by the Cromwellian wars.[91] Yet what is most significant about the mission is that it reveals an unexamined aspect of papal relations with the Stuarts. The priority of both James I and Charles I with regard to western Scotland was to ensure stability while the Plantation of Ulster proceeded. While the policy of plantation was partly designed to scythe the Scottish from the Irish *Gaeltacht*, the belief of Irish Catholic leaders that this was a matter of religion was inaccurate, and Rome knew it. From a royal perspective, religion was secondary to the primacy of political obedience and financial gain, though the policy-hacks in parliament and at court did not always agree. The Franciscan mission to the Hebrides and Highlands was a cheap way for the papacy to exploit this situation during the Anglo-Spanish flirtation, while the friars themselves might be allowed to flirt with more aggressive options through cultivating disaffected rulers at a convenient distance from crown control. The political trappings of the mission attracted lucrative sponsors, but the papacy was not about to jeopardize its relations with the Stuart kings by stirring up rebellion without a chance of lasting success. It was a sleeper operation, one that proved more troublesome to run than had been hoped. Poor planning and inflexible structures combined with ecclesiastical rivalries to scupper the entire enterprise. When the papacy was faced with a number of prominent Catholic Scots, hostile to the mission, who were willing to undertake more direct initiatives at the royal court, they were happy to sacrifice the friars to the greater good of the church. The alternative strategy proved equally fruitless, yet by the time George Conn's mission at the English court had fallen apart in 1638, it was too late to salvage the sleeper operation in Scotland where more dynamic and immediate developments were catapulting the country towards civil war.

NOTES

1 B. Jennings (ed.), *Louvain Papers 1606–1827* (Dublin, 1968), no. 41.

2 C. Giblin (ed.), *Irish Franciscan Mission to Scotland 1619–1646* (Dublin, 1964), nos 1 and 2.

3 F. Macdonald, *Missions to the Gaels: Reformation and Counter-reformation in Ulster and the Highlands and Islands of Scotland, 1560–1760* (Edinburgh, 2005); H. Concannon, 'Irish missions to Scotland in penal days', *Irish Ecclesiastical Record*, 14 (1919); S. MacGuaire, 'Ireland and the Catholic Hebrides', *Irish Ecclesiastical Record*, 42 (1933), 345–64; C. Giblin, 'The Irish Franciscan mission to Scotland in the seventeenth century', *Franciscan College Annual* (Multyfarnham, 1952), 7–24; C. Giblin, 'The Franciscan mission to Scotland, 1619–1647', *Proceedings of the Irish Catholic Historical Committee 1957* (Dublin, 1957), pp. 15–24; and Giblin (ed.), *Mission*, pp. vii–xvi; J.L. Campbell, *The Catholic Church in the Hebrides, 1560–1760* (Glasgow, 1983); and W. McLeod, *Divided Gaels: Gaelic Cultural Identities in Scotland and Ireland, c.1200-c.1650* (Oxford, 2004), pp. 204–12.

4 For Anderson's projects, including the desire to found a Scots seminary in Paris, see Archivio Segreto Vaticano, Rome, MS Borghese, I, 594, f. 57rv. See also M. Dilworth, 'Beginnings 1600–1707', in R. McCluskey (ed.), *The Scots College Rome 1600–2000* (Edinburgh, 2000), pp. 19–42.

5 For Holywood, see E. Hogan, *Distinguished Irishmen of the Sixteenth Century* (London, 1894), pp. 395–501.

6 A list of 23 secular priests active in Scotland between 1612 and 1637 was compiled by Thomas Innes and published with annotations as Appendix V of M.V. Hay, *The Blairs Papers (1603–1660)* (London, 1929), pp. 247–9. On the Dominicans and Minims, see A. Ross, 'Dominicans and Scotland in the seventeenth century', *Innes Review*, 23:1 (1972), 40–75; J. Durkan, 'The career of John Brown, Minim, and "brown's confession"', *Innes Review*, 18:2 (1967), 164–170; and J. Durkan, 'Early letters of John Brown, Minim, and report to Propaganda, 1623, by Scots Minims', *Innes Review*, 52:1 (2001), 63–79. Note also, P.F. Anson, *Underground Catholicism in Scotland 1622–1878* (Montrose, 1970).

7 W.J. Anderson, 'Rome and Scotland, 1513–1625', *Innes Review*, 4:2 (1959), 173–93.

8 On Paul V's policies with regard to northern Europe, the best synoptic view is still Ludwig Pastor, *History of the Popes*, trans. and ed. E. Graf (40 vols., London, 1891–1953), xxvi, pp. 117–217.

9 The linguistic character of the Scottish clergy is referred to in Giblin (ed.), *Mission*, nos 1–5; 19; 23, p. 90; and 31. As regards the state of Catholicism in western Scotland during this period see Anson, *Underground Catholicism in Scotland*; Campbell, *The Catholic Church in the Hebrides;* J. Kirk (ed.), *The Church in the Highlands* (Edinburgh, 1998); D. Maclean, 'Catholicism in the Highlands and Isles, 1560–1680', *Innes Review*, 3:1 (1952), 5–13; A. MacInnes, 'Catholic recusancy and the Penal Laws, 1603–1707', *Records of the Scottish Church History Society*, 23(1987), 27–63. A survey of the Scottish Jesuits and the Scots Colleges in the seventeenth century is given by Hay, *The Blairs Papers*, pp. 52–181; for the beginnings of the mission see T. McCoog, *The Society of Jesus in Ireland, Scotland,*

and England 1541–1588: "our way of proceeding?" (Leiden, 1996) and M. Yellowlees, *'So Strange a Monster as a Jesuite': The Society of Jesus in Sixteenth-Century Scotland* (Colonsay, 2003). On the linguistic situation in western Scotland see J. MacInnes, 'The Scottish Gaelic language', in G. Price (ed.), *The Celtic Connection* (Gerrards Cross, 1992), pp. 101–30; and W. Gillies (ed.), *Gaelic and Scotland* (Edinburgh, 1989).

10 These insinuations are referred to and refuted by Aodh Mac Aingil in a letter to the nuncio at Brussels in 1618 and by Cornelius Ward in a report submitted to the *Congregatio de Propaganda Fide* in 1624: Gibbin (ed.), *Mission*, nos 1 and 5. A detailed description of the differences between the Gaelic- and Anglo-Scots can be found in Giblin (ed.), *Mission*, no. 23, p. 91.

11 For reference to Gaelic as 'Irish', see, for example, *ibid.*, nos 1, 2 and 4–6.

12 For references to 'Scots-Irish', see *ibid.*, nos 1 and 9; the nuncio's instructions are contained in no. 11; Ward's letter is no. 19.

13 *Ibid.*, no. 5.

14 Jennings (ed.), *Louvain Papers*, nos 34, 37, 48–51, 56, 65.

15 Giblin (ed.), *Mission*, no. 5.

16 See the letter reproduced in J. Hagan, 'Miscellanea Vaticano-Hibernica, 1580–1631 (VA: Borghese Collection)', *Archivium Hibernicum*, 3 (1914), 318.

17 Giblin (ed.), *Mission*, no. 5; see also no. 69, the report for the year 1637.

18 See J. MacInnes, 'The Gaelic perception of the Lowlands', in Gillies (ed.), *Gaelic and Scotland*, pp. 89–100; and McLeod, *Divided Gaels*, pp. 14–52: 25, 43–4.

19 See, for example, J.S. Brewer (ed.), *Letters and Papers, Foreign and Domestic, of the Reign Of Henry VIII: Preserved in the Public Record Office, the British Museum, and Elsewhere* (19 vols., London 1862–), xix, pt. 1, no. 654; *Ibid.* 2, nos. 284, 562, 819 and 1046; *Ibid*, xxi, pt.1 no. 1279.

20 For the attack on Cusack, see J. Hagan, 'Miscellanea Vaticano-Hibernica, 1420–1631 (VA: Borghese Collection)', *Archivium Hibernicum*, 4 (1915), 284–6.

21 For the attack on Lombard, see *Wadding Papers*, no. 11; for Wadding see B. Jennings, 'Miscellaneous documents I: 1588–1634', *Archivium Hibernicum*, 10 (1946), 184–7; and Franciscan Fathers dún Mhuire and Killiney (eds), *Father Luke Wadding: Commemorative Volume* (Killiney, 1957). For policy with regard to appointment of bishops, see, for example, the letters reproduced in *Wadding Papers*, nos 70–1, which were sent by the nuncio in Flanders, Guido del Bagno, to the Cardinal Assessor of the Holy Office, in relation to the appointment of archbishops of Armagh and Cashel. The documents are available in translation in Historical Manuscripts Commission, *Report on the Franciscan Manuscripts Pr eserved at the Convent, Merchants' Quay, Dublin* (Dublin, 1906), pp. 87–92.

22 Giblin (ed.), *Mission*, no. 5.

23 For discussion of this complex development see M. Anderson, *Kings and Kingship in Early Scotland* (Edinburgh, 1973); and M. Anderson, 'Dalriada and the creation of the kingdom of the Scots', in D. Dumville, R. McKitterick and D. Whitelock (eds), *Ireland in Early Medieval Europe* (Cambridge, 1982), pp. 106–32; J. Bannerman, *Studies in the History of Dalriada* (Edinburgh, 1974); M. Herbert, 'Sea-divided Gaels? Constructing relationships between the Irish and Scots, c.800–1169', in B. Smith (ed.), *Britain and Ireland 900–1300: Insular Responses to*

Medieval European Change (Cambridge, 1999), pp. 87–97; and M. Herbert, 'Rí Éirenn, Rí Alban, kingship and identity in the ninth and tenth centuries', in S. Taylor (ed.), *Kings, Clerics and Chronicles in Scotland* (Four Courts, 2000). For an alternative view of the origins of the Gaelic Scots see E. Campbell, 'Were the Scots Irish?', *Antiquity*, 75 (2001), 285–92.

24 The most thorough recent discussion is David Caulfield, 'The *Tenebriomastix* of Don Philip O'Sullivan-Beare: Poitiers, MS 259 (97)', PhD dissertation, University College Cork, 2004. On Scottish identity and political thought see R. Mason, *Kingship and the Commonweal: Political Thought in Renaissance and Reformation Scotland* (East Lothian, 1998).

25 For an account of the Scotic debate see P. Grosjean SJ, 'Un Soldat Irlandais au service des "Acta Sanctorum"', in *Analecta Bollandiana*, 81, Fasc. III–IV (Brussels, 1963), pp. 418–30; P. Grosjean, 'Sur quelques pièces, imprimées et manuscrites, de la controverse entre Ecossais et Irlandais au debút du xviime siècle', *Analecta Bollandiana*, 81, Fasc. III–IV (Brussels, 1963), pp. 430–46; R. Sharpe, *Medieval Irish Saints' Lives* (Dublin, 1991); P. O'Riain, 'The Catalogus praecipuorum sanctorum Hiberniae, sixty years on', in A.P. Smith (ed.), *Studies in Early and Medieval Irish Archaeology, History and Literature in Honour of Francis J. Byrne* (Dublin, 2002), pp. 396–430; Caulfield, 'The *Tenebriomastix* of Don Philip O'Sullivan-Beare: Poitiers, MS 259 (97)'; David Caulfield, 'The Scotic debate: Philip O'Sullivan Beare and his *Tenebriomastix*', in J. Harris and K. Sidwell (eds), *Making Ireland Roman* (Cork, 2009), pp. 109–25.

26 Giblin (ed.), *Mission*, no. 1.

27 For the Scots college, see B. Halloran, *The Scots College Paris, 1603–1792* (Edinburgh, 1997). The Paris affair was sparked off by David Rothe, whose *Brigida Thaumaturga* (Paris, 1620) was an elaboration of the speech he gave at the Irish college in Paris, during which he attacked the Scottish historian Thomas Dempster. A polemic debate ensued in the following publications: Thomas Dempster, *Scotia Illustrior* (Lyon, 1620); Donatus Roirk [David Rothe], *Hibernia Resurgens* (Rouen, 1621); George Con, *Praemetiae, sive Calumniae Hirlandorum indicatae* (Bologna, 1621); G.F. Veridicus Hibernus [David Rothe], *Hiberniae, sive antiquioris Scotiae Vindiciae adversus immodestam Parechbasim Thomae Dempsteri* (Antwerp, 1621).

28 Giblin (ed.), *Mission*, no. 1.

29 The correspondence of the nuncios has been edited: R. Belvederi, *Guido Bentivoglio, Diplomatico* (2 vols., Rovigo, 1947); L. van Meerbeck (ed), *Correspondence des Nonces Gesualdo, Morra, Sanseverino avec la Secretaire d'Etat Pontificale (1615–1621)* (Rome, 1937); B. de Meester (ed.), *Correspondence du Nonce Giovanni-Francesco Guidi di Bagno (1621–1627)* (2 vols., Rome, 1938); L. van Meerbeck (ed.), *Correspondence du Nonce Fabio de Lagonissa, Archeveque de Conza (1627–1634)* (Rome, 1966).

30 See the comprehensive study by R. Belvederi, *Guido Bentivoglio, e la politica eurpea del suo tempo (1607–1621)* (Padua, 1962).

31 Giblin (ed.), *Mission*, no. 3.

32 For example, see M. Kerney-Walsh, '*Destruction by Peace*': *Hugh O'Neill after Kinsale* (Armagh, 1986), nos 77 and 79; also, Hagan, 'Miscellanea Vaticano-Hibernica, 1420–1631', 281.

33 Giblin (ed.), *Mission*, no. 4.

34 *Ibid.*, nos 5–6.

35 *Ibid.*, nos 7, 9.

36 *CSPI, 1615–25*, no. 71; see J. Hagan, 'Miscellanea Vaticano-Hibernica, 1420–1631', 270–5.

37 See Kerney-Walsh, '*Destruction by Peace*', nos 219A, 221, 230, 234, 236, 236A, 238.

38 See the preface to George Con's *Vita Mariae Stuarti* (Rome, 1624) for praise of the efforts made in the doomed negotiations by Barberini, who had been elected pope in 1623. There are several recent studies of the negotiations: G. Redworth, *The Prince and the Infanta: The Cultural Politics of the Spanish Match* (New Haven, CT, 2003); A. Samson, *The Spanish Match* (Aldershot, 2006); but see also Robert Cross's rather critical review of Redworth's book, 'Pretense and perception in the Spanish match, or history in a fake beard', *Journal of Interdisciplinary History*, 37:4 (2007), 563–83.

39 On James's policies with regard to western Scotland see A. MacInnes, *Clanship, Commerce and the House of Stuart, 1603–1788* (East Linton, 1996), pp. 56–87; K.M. Brown, 'The Scottish aristocracy, Anglicization and the court, 1603–38', *The Historical Journal*, 36:3 (September 1993), pp. 543–76; M. Lynch, 'James VI and the "Highland problem"', in J. Goodare and M. Lynch (eds), *The Reign of James VI* (East Lothian, 2000), pp. 208–27; S. Adams, 'James VI and the politics of south-west Scotland, 1603–1625', in *ibid.*, pp. 228–40. For helpful redress of earlier misconceptions about James's religious policies see W.B. Patterson, *King James VI and I and the Reunion of Christendom* (Cambridge, 1997); C. Hibbard, 'Early Stuart Catholicism: revisions and re-revisions', *The Journal of Modern History*, 52:1 (March 1980), 1–34; and, specifically with regard to Scotland, A. MacInnes, 'Catholic recusancy and the Penal Laws, 1603–1707', *Records of the Scottish Church History Society*, 23 (1987), 27–63 (though note that MacInnes's interpretation perhaps underestimates the impact of the crack-down in the 1630s).

40 See F.J. Shaw, *The Northern and Western Islands of Scotland: Their Economy and Society in the Seventeenth Century* (Edinburgh, 1980); K.M. Brown, 'Aristocratic finances and the origins of the Scottish Revolution', *English Historical Review*, 104:410 (1989), 46–87; D. Watt, '"The laberinth of thir difficulties': the influence of debt of the Highland elite *c.*1550–1700', *Scottish Historical Review*, 85:1, no. 219 (April 2006), 28–51.

41 Giblin (ed.), *Mission*, no. 69, provides a vivid description of the hardship faced by the missionaries.

42 See, for example, *Ibid.*, no. 21.

43 *Ibid.*, nos 11, 13, 15.

44 The numbers are reported in *ibid.*, nos 48, 49.

45 *Ibid.*, no. 23.

46 The nuncio's instructions for the new recruits in 1623 focused upon contacts with the nobility: *Ibid.*, no.11. For a good example of how this was put into practice, see the summary of the missionaries' reports that was compiled in 1625: *Ibid.*, no. 22.

47 *Ibid.*, no. 20.
48 *Ibid.*, nos 21, 28, 69.
49 For a contrasting view, expressing considerable scepticism about Macdonald's career and motivation, see Macdonald, *Missions to the Gaels*, pp. 24, 89, 109, 136 and 245.
50 J.L. Campbell, 'The letter sent by Iain Muideartachd, Twelfth Chief of the Clanranald, to Pope Urban VIII, in 1626', *Innes Review*, 4 (1953), 110–16.
51 *CSPI, 1615–25*, no. 1221. Ward carried Moidart's letter to the continent and informed Aodh Mac Aingil about it: Jennings, 'Miscellaneous documents I', 115–21.
52 Giblin (ed.), *Mission*, no. 20.
53 J.L. Campbell, 'The letter sent by Iain Muideartachd', 110–16; David Stevenson, 'The Irish Franciscan Mission to Scotland and the Irish Rebellion of 1641', *Innes Review*, 30:1 (1979), 54–61; and Anson, *Underground Catholicism in Scotland*, pp. 18–25, 38–43.
54 Giblin (ed.), *Mission*, nos 23, 28, 30.
55 *Ibid.*, no. 69.
56 *Ibid.*, no. 23, p. 92.
57 A summary list is provided in *Ibid.*, no. 24.
58 *Ibid.*, nos 20, 32, 35.
59 MacInnes, *Clanship*, pp. 77–8; T. McCaughey, 'Protestantism and Scottish Highland culture', in James Mackey (ed.), *An Introduction to Celtic Christianity* (Edinbuirgh, 1989), pp. 172–205; J. Dawson, 'Calvinism and the Gaidhealtachd in Scotland', in A. Pettegree, A. Duke and G. Lewis (eds), *Calvinism in Europe, 1540–1620* (Cambridge, 1994), pp. 231–53; and J. Dawson, 'Clan, kin and kirk: The Campbells and the Scottish reformation', in N. Scott Amos, A. Pettigree, and H. van Nierop (eds), *The Education of a Christian Society: Humanism and the Reformation in Britain and the Netherlands* (Aldershot, 1999), pp. 211–42.
60 For example, see Giblin (ed.), *Mission*, nos 10, 13, 15–16, 24–7, 32–5, 42, 66.
61 See A. Forrestal, *Catholic Synods in Ireland 1600–1690* (Dublin, 1998); C. Giblin, 'The "Processus Datariae" and the appointment of Irish bishops in the seventeenth century', in Franciscan Fathers Dún Mhuire and Killiney (eds), *Father Luke Wadding: Commemorative Volume*, pp. 508–19; H. Kearney, 'Ecclesiastical politics and the Counter-reformation in Ireland', *Journal of Ecclesiastical History*, 11 (1960), 202–12; P. Corish, 'The reorganisation of the Irish Church, 1603–41', *Proceedings of the Irish Catholic Historical Committee*, 3 (1957), 9–14; and P. Corish, *The Catholic Community in the Seventeenth and Eighteenth Centuries* (Dublin, 1981), pp. 25–8. Similar disputes can be found elsewhere in the early seventeenth century; for example, see J. Bossy, 'The English Catholic Community, 1603–1625,' in A.G.R. Smith (ed.), *The Reign of James VI and I* (London, 1973), pp. 91–105.
62 See P. Corish, 'An Irish Counter-reformation bishop: John Roche', *Irish Theological Quarterly*, 25 (1958), 14–32, 101–23; xxvi (1959), 101–16 and 313–30.
63 For example, see the documents reproduced in Jennings, 'Miscellaneous documents I', 159–60, 164–82 *passim*.
64 Giblin, 'The "Processus Datariae"', pp. 508–19; J.J. Silke, 'Primate Peter Lombard and Hugh O'Neill', *Irish Theological Quarterly*, 22 (1955), 15–30; Corish, 'An Irish

counter-reformation bishop', 14–32, 101–23, and 126 , 101–16 and 313–330; Kearney, 'Ecclesiastical politics', 202–12.

65 Giblin (ed.), *Mission*, nos 70–72.

66 *Ibid.*, no. 19. For further discussion see Macdonald, *Missions to the Gaels.*

67 Giblin (ed.), *Mission*, no. 20, p.52; no. 21, p. 68.

68 *Ibid.*, no. 23.

69 See Macdonald, *Missions to the Gaels.* For a contrary view, see McLeod, *Divided Gaels*, p. 211.

70 For example, see Giblin (ed.), *Mission*, no. 23; but see also H. Ward's comments in *ibid.*, no. 42.

71 *Ibid.*, no. 25.

72 *Ibid.*, nos. 26, 32 and 37.

73 B. Jennings, 'Documents of the Irish Franciscan College at Prague', *Archivium Hibernicum.*, 9 (1942), 173–5, 202–24, 226–9.

74 Giblin (ed.), *Mission*, no. 66.

75 See the minutes for minutes for 26 February 1630 and 30 September 1633 in B. Jennings, 'Acta Sacrae Congregationis de Propaganda Fide, 1622–1650', *Archivium Hibernicum*, 12 (1959), 50–1, 74–5.

76 F. Macdonald, 'Irish priests in the Highlands: judicial evidence from Argyll', *Innes Review*, 46:1 (1995), 15–33; Macdonald, *Missions to the Gaels.*

77 Giblin (ed.), *Mission*, nos 45 and 46.

78 *Ibid.*, no. 66; Jennings, 'Documents of the Irish Franciscan College', 266.

79 Giblin (ed.), *Mission*, no. 66.

80 The threat to leave for this reason was mentioned in Ward's report of August 1626: *Ibid.*, no. 23.

81 *Ibid.*, nos 29–30.

82 *Ibid.*, no. 33. See C. Giblin, 'Francis MacDonnell, OFM, son of the first earl of Antrim (d. 1636)', *Seanchas Ardmhacha*, 8 (1975), 44–54.

83 For a contrary view, see MacInnes, *Clanship*, pp. 78–9; and MacInnes, 'Catholic recusancy and the Penal Laws, 1603–1707', *Records of the Scottish Church History Society*, 23 (1987), 27–63.

84 Giblin (ed.), *Mission*, no. 50.

85 *Ibid.*, no. 49.

86 See Jennings (ed.), *Louvain Papers*, nos 150–4.

87 T. O'Connor, *Jansenists in Seventeenth Century Ireland* (Dublin, 2008).

88 B. Halloran, *The Scots College Paris.*

89 L. Ceyssens, 'Florence Conry, Hugh de Burgo, Luke Wadding, and Jansenism', in Franciscan Fathers Dún Mhuire and Killiney (eds), *Father Luke Wadding*, pp. 295–404.

90 For an approximate list, see MacInnes, *Clanship*, pp. 247–9.

91 Macdonald, *Missions to the Gaels.*

8

The Scottish response to the 1641 rebellion in Connacht: the case of Sir Frederick Hamilton[1]

AOIFE DUIGNAN

Sir Frederick Hamilton encapsulates the complexities of the Scottish presence in early seventeenth-century Ireland. Despite a strong Catholic strain in his immediate family background, Hamilton staunchly defended Protestant interests in a politico-military career that spanned the Irish, British and European stages. The current focus is one episode in a colourful public life – Hamilton's military response to the outbreak of violence in north Connacht during late autumn 1641. Probing the remaining evidence facilitates a rare glimpse into the on-the-ground reality of pursuing Catholic insurgents in the turbulent and chaotic early phase of the Confederate Wars. Hamilton's reaction is located in the broader context of contemporary military practices and norms of behaviour, the overall response from the settler community in the region, and his attitude towards those of his own nation, and kin, whose survival strategies deviated from his own. Further, probing Hamilton's experience of violence in the western province in the early 1640s in turn facilitates analysis of the factors that motivated a settler under attack in Ireland's remote western province.

In comparative terms, the settler community in Connacht was smaller and more scattered than elsewhere in the country.[2] Despite its relatively limited scope, however, the newcomers who settled in the region included a Scottish element, particularly in north Connacht, Sir Frederick Hamilton's hinterland. Proximity to planted Ulster located Hamilton within a broader Scottish community that transcended provincial boundaries. Bordering Fermanagh, it had experienced an influx of both English and Scottish settlers after 1610, and while the number of Scots living in neighbouring Cavan was comparatively smaller than elsewhere in the northern plantation, a network of Scottish planters had been established within the county.[3] In his recent survey of Scottish migration to Ireland during the seventeenth century, Patrick Fitzgerald has cautioned against viewing the contemporary Scots presence in Ireland as confined to the officially planted Ulster counties. Rather he argues that internal migration did not respect county or provincial boundaries, and in this context highlights the overspill of Scottish settlement from Ulster into north Connacht, particularly Counties Leitrim, Sligo and Mayo.[4]

Mary O'Dowd chronicles this migratory pattern in her examination of landownership in early modern Sligo. The majority of new settlers who came to Sligo town after 1603 are identified as being of Scottish origin, while the Scottish presence increased among Ballymote's mercantile community in subsequent decades. O'Dowd speculates that while the Scots may have originally come to Ireland with the intention of settling on plantation lands, they subsequently moved to Sligo as its commercial potential proved more attractive than Ulster's remoter reaches. A second wave of immigration formed part of a wider movement of Scottish settlers into north Connacht during the 1620s and 1630s, which was in turn connected with a revival of emigration from Scotland at that time.[5] The regularisation of appointments to diocesan and parish vacancies within the established church in the north-west also contributed to a growth in the local Scottish population. The united diocese of Killala and Achonry was presided over by successive Scotsmen – Archibald Hamilton from 1623 to 1630, and Archibald Adair from 1630 to 1640. Their impact on the ethnic profile of appointees at lower levels within the diocese is evidenced by Alan Ford's reference to the transformation of the diocesan clergy into a largely Scottish ministry by the mid 1630s.[6]

Leitrim, Hamilton's place of residence, was the only county in Connacht to experience a formal plantation.[7] Seven Scottish undertakers were granted proportions in the scheme. This figure included non-residents such as Sir Arthur Forbes, who lived in Longford, and the Cavan-based planter, Sir James Craig.[8] By 1622, only four of the original British grantees actually lived in the county, including Hamilton and his fellow Scot, Walter Harrison.[9] While the Leitrim plantation neither envisaged nor resulted in a dramatic transformation of the county's ethnic composition, records indicate a Scottish presence on the ground by 1641.[10] At national level, Perceval Maxwell has alluded to the general difficulties in quantifying Scottish penetration prior to this date and this is particularly true of the remote western province.[11] However, the accounts of attacks on members of the settler community found within the 1641 Depositions for Connacht attest to a Scottish presence in the north-west of the province, and specifically in Co. Leitrim.[12]

Thus, Hamilton was not in a unique position as a Scotsman in Ireland's north-western reaches. The extent to which his reaction to the outbreak of violence in 1641 was influenced by his identification with a Scottish, or indeed a broader settler communal group in the locality will be explored later. In the meantime, it is useful to examine his personal background.

Sir Frederick Hamilton was the youngest son of Claud Hamilton, first Lord Paisley. This branch of the Hamilton clan, based at Renfrewshire, Scotland, inclined towards Catholicism, with Claud himself received into the faith in 1580 by a Jesuit cleric, James Tyrie.[13] Despite this religious background Frederick's older siblings were key beneficiaries under the Ulster Plantation scheme. Among them, James Hamilton, created first earl of Abercorn in 1603, was one of the chief Scottish undertakers in the northern province, significantly improving the lands allocated to him in Strabane barony, Co Tyrone.[14] Ultimately, however, the most notable feature to emerge from the Hamilton presence in Strabane was the family's role in the promotion of Catholicism in the area. In particular, Frederick's brother, Sir George Hamilton of Greenlaw, was identified by contemporaries as a key instigator of recusancy. George became guardian to the heirs of Abercorn and those of another brother, Sir Claud Hamilton of Schawfield, and reared the minors in the Catholic faith. During the reign of King Charles, George and the second earl of Abercorn drew Catholic immigrants from Scotland, establishing a hub of Catholicism in Scottish Ulster, with George personally making numerous converts.[15] His family's profession and active propagation of the Roman faith renders Frederick's military adventures on the continent during the 1630s and his reaction to unrest among the Catholic population in north-west Connacht during the early 1640s, all the more striking.

The Hamilton clan's involvement in plantation projects was not limited to Ulster, with Frederick emerging as one of the major beneficiaries of the scheme to plant Co. Leitrim in the 1620s.[16] Initially granted approximately 1,500 profitable acres, Hamilton engaged in major land expansion over the next decade and a half, so that his holdings by 1641 were estimated to be over 8,000 acres. This energetic land acquisition, coupled with the physical changes he brought to the local environment, saw Frederick defined as a key player in a new group of Leitrim-based settlers, who had a major impact on that county's human landscape.[17] His hard-line military response to the outbreak of unrest among his Catholic neighbours in October 1641 ensured that his memory and legend would endure in local history and popular folklore long after the physical markers of his presence in Leitrim had faded.[18]

The arrival of insurrection in the western province was signalled by an attack on Sir Charles Coote's iron works on the Leitrim–Cavan border, a mere two days after the 1641 rebellion broke out in Ulster. This attack, led by Colonel Owen O Rourke and Colonel Con O Rourke, under the direction of Captain Rory Maguire, marked the start of a series of robberies perpetrated against Leitrim's settler population.[19] The remainder of this chapter focuses on Hamilton's reaction to the outbreak of violence within his locality and bordering regions. Analysis is primarily based on an anonymous pamphlet, published in 1643, which offers a diary-style account apparently written by one of his followers.[20] It is a problematic source, designed for propagandist purposes and peppered with blatant exaggeration.[21] However, in light of the general dearth of evidence on the settler response in north Leitrim, it offers the only detailed account of the activities of the Manorhamilton garrison from the outbreak of rebellion until April 1643, when entries cease.

Hamilton is portrayed as initially securing his own property, which would become a place of shelter for Protestant refugees, including some of those settlers, mainly English, who took flight after the attack on Coote's ironworks.[22] He subsequently engaged in pro-active forays against those who took up arms, and those he perceived in rebellion, in the broader north-western region. Hamilton was in Derry when news of rebellion broke. He departed for Manorhamilton immediately, with a battalion of 20 Scottish horsemen, relieving Ballyshannon Castle, Co. Donegal, on the return journey.[23] On arriving in Leitrim, he gathered together a force of 50 horsemen, made up from among his servants and tenants, and was also assisted by six of his soldiers newly arrived from Carlisle – five Scots and one Irishman. Throughout early November, his men were dispatched on expeditions into neighbouring baronies, apprehending alleged rebels and bringing prisoners back to Hamilton, along with plunder. At the end of the month, when his Irish tenants disobeyed his summons to court, Hamilton took the view that rebellion had arrived on his doorstep. Having appealed in vain to central and provincial government highlighting his own situation and emphasizing the need to defend neighbouring Sligo town and garrison, Hamilton took matters into his own hands. In response to his tenants' apparent treachery and defiance, he erected a gallows in a prominent location on a hilltop near Manorhamilton castle, and hanged eight of the prisoners captured while relieving Ballyshannon.[24] So began in earnest Hamilton's offensive in the north-west.

His efforts were placed on a more official footing when, on 30 December 1641, the lords justices commissioned Hamilton to reinforce his foot company and to 'make diligent search and inquiry throughout the Counties of Leitrim and Sligoe, and the Borders adjoining thereunto, for all Traitors'. Any apprehended should be hung under martial law.[25] Hamilton responded to his brief with relish. The first half of 1642 saw his men embark on a scorched earth policy, burning houses and crops, taking prisoners and killing those in rebellion and their supporters as far as the borders of Fermanagh to the north, and into Co. Sligo.[26] This is not, however, to suggest an unreciprocated onslaught. Throughout the account of his campaign we see Manorhamilton under attack by rebels from Leitrim, Sligo, Donegal, Fermanagh and Cavan, often cooperating with each other against the garrison. The diary account affords one such example in late January 1642, with claims that up to 1,500 rebels burned the town of Manorhamilton and its mills. However, those within the walls of Hamilton's castle and bawn remained safe.[27]

In her study of contemporary Sligo, O'Dowd has argued that Hamilton's military campaigns exacerbated tensions in that county, and that the murder of a group of settlers housed in Sligo jail in January 1642 must be viewed in the context of Hamilton's offensive on the Sligo–Leitrim border, and a genuine fear among the insurgents that he could take over Sligo town.[28] That apprehension appeared justified when, on 1 July, Hamilton and his men burned the town. There followed a major victory by Hamilton's forces against a large party of rebels, whom they encountered on their return journey to Manorhamilton. The diarist commented on the extent of devastation wreaked by Hamilton and his soldiers in the night's activities in typically effusive fashion, stating that they had destroyed 'neere 3 hundred soules by fire, sword and drowning, to God's everlasting great honour and glory and our comforts'.[29]

However, from mid-summer 1642 a decline in the fortunes of the Manorhamilton garrison is evident. In July, Hamilton and his men made an abortive attempt to gain control of Dromahair castle. Their lack of success, according to the diarist, was in no small way attributable to the non-intervention of a number of Sir William Cole's soldiers, who were present at the time.[30] Such allegations cannot be taken at face value but must be viewed in the context of Hamilton's subsequent public spat with Cole, commander of the garrison at Enniskillen. The Manorhamilton garrison also suffered from depleting manpower at this stage, arising out of defections to the Fermanagh camp. In the account of Hamilton's campaign, this exodus is attributed to the Manorhamilton men having witnessed the 'liberty and disorderly government and discipline of those Enniskillen soldiers'.[31] A more plausible explanation, however, is that the growing pressure from struggling to maintain an isolated garrison, surrounded by hostile rebels, exacerbated by diminishing supplies and little hope of aid, encouraged desertions. By spring 1643 conditions in the garrison had deteriorated considerably. Manorhamilton was at this stage besieged by between ten and twelve rebel companies under the command of Lord Taaffe and Bryan MacDonough, and assisted by Owen O Rourke. The diarist continues to report small-scale victories against the rebels, but the language used is considerably less triumphal.[32] At this point the account of Manorhamilton's garrison ends, and references to Hamilton's public involvement primarily relate to his activities in Ulster and Scotland.

Thus, Hamilton is portrayed as an effective military force in the Leitrim–Sligo region. Additionally, the diary account of his campaign facilitates tentative estimates on his contribution, and that of his men, to the body count in the region during the early years of conflict. Given the paucity of source material, and the frequently biased nature of what remains, this is not an exact science. However, calculating all enumerated references to insurgent deaths through raids and military skirmishes brings us to a cautious estimate of well over 1,000 dead in the period between December 1641 and April 1643. The diarist also provides a list of 57 individuals executed at Manorhamilton in this period. Along with the methodological difficulties in calculating a specific figure on the basis of the information provided in the diary, the author's definite tendency towards exaggeration must also be taken into account.[33] Furthermore it appeared at a time when Hamilton wished to portray himself valiantly battling to defend the British presence in the north-west. Thus these figures cannot be taken as a definitive total of his casualties. However, even taking all of the above qualifications into account, the picture that emerges is one of effective engagement with local insurgents and slaughter of local civilians.

Throughout, Hamilton is depicted as eager to go into combat despite being outnumbered, pursuing a proactive offensive rather than merely reacting in a defensive manner. It is reported that on St Patrick's Day 1642, he tried to goad the rebels into battle by staging a mock execution of a captured rebel, hanging an effigy on the gallows, in the hope of enticing the rebels to come forward and rescue their imprisoned associate.[34] Further, Hamilton's men are depicted expressing contempt at their opponents' military abilities. When a rebel camp was taken over in April 1642, their weaponry was derided, 'bringing from the Rogues a great many Iron-crowes and such like instruments, made and marked with the signe of the Crosse, making their poore churles beleeve, that with those Irons they were to pull downe our Colonels Castle and Bawne'.[35]

Hamilton's disinclination to tread cautiously went beyond military encounters with his Catholic neighbours in arms. On 15 March 1642, Hamilton had received correspondence from Teige O Connor Sligo justifying the latter's decision to take up arms alongside his co-religionists. O Connor also urged Hamilton to conclude a truce with surrounding insurgents, emphasizing the good relationship that he had enjoyed with O Connor's father.[36] Hamilton's curt and decisive response to this letter is worth quoting in its entirety. He wrote,

> Your loyalty to your King, your faith to your friends once broke, never more to be trusted by me, but revenged as God shall enable the hands of him who was loving to your loyall Predecessours, whose curse will contribute to your destruction, for extingishing the memory of their loyalties, Thus I rest with contempt and scorn to all your base bragges. Your scourge if I can. F.H.[37]

In an era when most correspondence was concluded with exaggerated declarations of love and affection, irrespective of its content, Hamilton's candour is reflective of his unveiled hostility towards those in arms. While it could be argued that by March 1642 the unrest had entered a second more organised phase and that, in turn, general settler responses had evolved, the vocal opposition expressed in Hamilton's letter had been reflected in his proactive military campaigning from the outbreak of unrest.[38]

In such deliberate provocation, Hamilton's behaviour is in stark contrast with the bulk of the settler population throughout Connacht. On 1 November 1641 the Lords Justices wrote to the old English magnate, Ulick Burke, fifth earl of Clanricarde, thanking him for his endeavours to restore order in Galway. However they were critical of the response from that county's elite, 'Although we like well that the gentlemen of that county should endeavour to secure their houses against the rebels, yet we dislike they should so shut up themselves therein.'[39] A much more suitable approach, according to the Dublin administration, would be to cooperate with their counterparts under threat, 'being so united in considerable parties, they might be the better able to defend the county, and consequently secure their houses more safely'.[40] Clanricarde himself articulated similar anxieties. Commenting on the settler response in Counties Leitrim and Roscommon, he referred to 'many English of quality shutting themselves up in forts, no enemy appearing'.[41] While Hamilton did not respond to the official plea for a unified front against the rebel threat – frequently coming into conflict with his fellow settlers – he certainly could not be accused of adopting a siege mentality.

Along with amassing a large body count, Hamilton and his men were notable for their ruthlessness and ferocity. Military successes are described in great detail, as are the treatments received by the enemy upon capture. In a number of cases when insurgents were killed, their heads were brought back to Hamilton. Non-combatants, including women, were also targeted.[42] Another feature emerging from the account of Hamilton's campaign is the parallels between the behaviour of his forces as described by the diarist and actions attributed to the insurgents by the Deponents, used in the latter context to illustrate the depravity of those in arms. The bodies of those killed by his soldiers were often stripped.[43] The significance of the practice of stripping victims by the Catholic insurgents has been discussed recently in the context of both its practical and symbolic functions.[44] This aspect of Hamilton's campaign demonstrates that stripping was not limited to one side, thus displaying a comparable desire to degrade and dehumanize the enemy.

The brutality described in the account of Hamilton's campaign was not novel, rather a regular feature of conflict in early modern Ireland.[45] However, the graphic descriptions facilitate deeper examination of the style of war fought by a newcomer, and representative of the official interest, in a remote corner of north-west Ireland. In the context of contemporary patterns of conflict, historians point to the regulation of military practices in Europe from the late sixteenth century, with the concept of military honour informing codes of conduct between combative forces. This found practical expression in the exchange of prisoners, negotiation of surrenders, and in the treatment of enemy troops. However, while such standards were increasingly observed in England, the style of war employed by the Irish, involving ambushes from woods and bogs, was perceived as un-English, base and an inhuman form of combat. Consequently the Irish enemy was perceived as savage, and so ethical constraints on the conduct of war could be removed. Tom Bartlett makes specific reference to Hamilton's behaviour in the north-west in the context of the ferocious treatment meted out to Irish prisoners of war. On 10 November 1642 a large rebel party approached Manorhamilton and engaged with Hamilton's forces. A rebel captain, Charles McGuire, was captured and his legs broken. According to the diarist, Hamilton ordered that McGuire be brought to the gallows in a wheelbarrow and executed immediately. McGuire objected that having fought in continental armies he should be afforded a soldier's death, and proclaimed 'that it was the Devill brought him from his former honourable service to this base and miserable end'.[46]

However, recent analysis of governmental military strategies in Ireland, with particular emphasis on codes of conduct and how they were, or were not, applied to the native insurgents, has challenged the orthodox view that Ireland in the 1640s was entirely a place apart, where the burgeoning rules of war did not extend.[47] Micheál Ó Siochrú has argued that late 1642 saw a moderation of the military excess which typified the early days of the 1641 rebellion. He argues that this trend was influenced by the increased professionalism of the armies involved and the threat of retaliation. It found expression in the absence of major massacres; the fact that terms of surrender were, for the most part, honoured; and the regular exchange of prisoners.[48] The detail included in the account of Hamilton's campaign facilitates analysis of whether such a shift occurred in the pattern of this particular local conflict. Up until January 1642 the targets of Hamilton's men are depicted as loose bands of rogues and rebels, but after spring 1642 the account presents their adversaries as more organised units, with definite military leaders identified, although references to the chaotic nature of the Irish efforts persist.[49] However, while the latter months of 1642 saw a significant reduction in the number of diary entries, the patterns of interaction that emerge do not suggest any significant change in the garrison's attitude towards their opponents, with references to fatal assaults on a number of 'rogues' as they harvested corn; the hanging of a female prisoner; and the stripping of Irish killed in combat.[50]

The sense that Hamilton did not moderate his behaviour towards his opponents is further substantiated by the fact that some of his contemporaries viewed Hamilton's actions as transcending the boundaries of honourable behaviour, even in time of military crisis – and particularly when its targets could not be deemed base savages. Clanricarde wrote to Hamilton in October 1643 reporting the astonishment and concern expressed in Dublin at Hamilton's attitude towards Viscount Taaffe. This arose out of Hamilton's forces reputedly having burned Taaffe's seat in Sligo, and either hanging, or at the least detaining Taaffe's messenger. Clanricarde emphasised Taaffe's gallantry, and the honour he had attained in England, in his correspondence with Hamilton.[51]

However, it is worth noting that the account of Hamilton's campaign does contain one indication that the contempt which Hamilton and his men held for the local rebels was not universal. Commenting on an encounter between Hamilton's forces and the rebel army headed by Lieutenant Colonel Brian MacDonagh on 1 April 1643, the diarist notes the latter's death. MacDonagh is described as 'one of the greatest fire-brands in Connaght', but the subsequent commentary implies some recognition of his professional merit as a soldier.[52] The author acknowledges his determination, stating that MacDonagh 'fought most desperately as ever man did, divers being with shot and pike beaten to the ground, yet he did fight upon his knees', and concludes, 'pity so great courage should have beene in so Arch a Traitour'.[53]

Any analysis of Hamilton's style of war in north Connacht must take into account his previous military experience on the continent. Hamilton fought in the Swedish army from 1631, at the tail end of what has been categorized as the period of most intense Swedish military recruitment in Britain.[54] Serving as a colonel in a Scottish Irish battalion under the command of General Ake Todt, the bravery of this unit was commented upon during an assault on Draconfeldt.[55] Contemporary service in foreign armies proved particularly attractive for members of cadet branches of noble families or younger sons of nobles, such as Hamilton, who did not benefit under the primogeniture system.[56] Analysis of Scottish involvement in the Swedish military highlights systematic promotion structures as an incentive for participation. Throughout his career Hamilton displayed a considerable drive for self-improvement, and in all likelihood viewed the continental stage as offering great potential for personal gain. But research in this area has also indicated that Scots who fought in the Swedish army were not exclusively motivated by materialism. Rather there existed a contemporary perception of Sweden as the true saviour of Protestant Europe, and Frederick Hamilton cannot have been immune from such sentiments.[57]

But what of the impact of this experience on the military tactics employed by Hamilton in Connacht? The diary account depicts Hamilton's troop as a well-oiled machine – disciplined and effective, in no small part due to the effective leadership of their colonel. However, his behaviour in Connacht may also reflect his Scottish background. In analyzing the impact of the Swedish experience on the Scottish Covenanter army, Furgol identifies the continental pre-occupation with fortresses and garrisons. But he also refers to the long-standing Scottish tradition of 'fire and sword' – burning crops, food stores and houses, and killing enemy supporters, irrespective of age and sex.[58] As shown earlier in the chapter, this constituted a key element of Hamilton's strategy in the north-west. However, his pursuit of a scorched earth policy also reflects a more general government tactic for the suppression of native unrest increasingly utilized from the sixteenth century.[59]

Hamilton's relentless pursuit of those in arms extended to members of his own nation who had sought to preserve themselves by succumbing to rebel pressure. This is evident in the case of Thomas Abercromy, a Scot with family ties in Ulster, who had gained lands in the Leitrim plantation.[60] Following the outbreak of violence Abercromy 'being misled by a treacherous Jesuiticall kinsman of his owne' abandoned his house and took refuge in the castle of Con O Rourke. Abercromy and his family were subsequently turned out by Hamilton's men when they raided O Rourke's camp.[61] Sir William Cole subsequently alleged that Hamilton's behaviour in this matter was motivated by long-standing malice towards Abercromy and his father-in-law, Sir John Dunbar. However, Hamilton ardently rebuffed this charge, stating that he was motivated solely by Abercromy's alliance with the rebels.[62] Similarly, one James Wetherspin, 'a Scotch-man married to an Irish woman', who was captured at Sligo and confessed to having been one of O Connor Sligo's soldiers, was hanged in July 1642.[63] Cole later accused Hamilton of having tortured Wetherspin, intimating that long-standing suits between Hamilton and Wetherspin in Ireland and England influenced his behaviour. Hamilton again denied this charge, stating that Wetherspin's actions in joining the rebels made him unworthy of the Scottish nation.[64]

Hamilton also proved unwilling to make concessions even where it might have meant preserving the lives of his fellow countrymen. Sir Robert Hannay, a Scot who had been clerk of the Nichills in Ireland during the 1630s, surrendered Beleek castle in Sligo to the rebels on the understanding that he and the other inhabitants would be safely transported to Ballyshannon. However, his party were subsequently captured by a group of rebels and held captive at Dromahair castle, Co. Leitrim.[65] Hannay and his fellow prisoners wrote to Hamilton requesting that he sanction the release of O Rourke prisoners in exchange for their own freedom. If this were not granted, they feared death. Hamilton expressed sympathy for their plight but stated that he would not concede to rebel demands. Even in the event of his own sons' captivity he declared, 'I had rather they should die gloriously for the cause of Christ, then should so abase themselves with such traitours to God and his majesty.'[66] Cole subsequently alleged that on receiving Hannay's letter, Hamilton hanged one of the chief O Rourke prisoners in view of the rebel messenger, a charge repudiated by Hamilton.[67] However, following Hamilton's refusal to exchange prisoners, three of Hannay's prisoners, including two Protestant ministers, were brought to the Irish camp near Manorhamilton and executed.[68]

That shared ethnicity was not sufficient to encourage Hamilton's deviation from a hardline policy towards negotiation with the insurgents, raises questions over his attitude towards members of his immediate family whose political and religious viewpoints deviated from his own. Significant variations in allegiance did emerge.[69] We have already noted the strong Catholic tendencies among this branch of the Hamilton family in Ulster. Frederick's afore-mentioned brother, Sir George Hamilton, had married Mary, daughter of Walter, eleventh earl of Ormond in 1630, and was granted the manor, castle, town and lands of Roscrea, Co. Tipperary a year later.[70] George's nephew, George the younger, son of the first earl of Abercorn, was also based in Co. Tipperary, at Nenagh. He too had strong Butler connections, marrying another Mary, sister of James Butler, twelfth earl and first Duke of Ormond.[71] George the younger would play an active role on the royalist side in Ireland during the 1640s and was in frequent correspondence with the Connacht-based earl of Clarnicarde.[72]

Records of interaction between Frederick and his immediate family in Ireland are scant, but there does appear to have been some contact with his brother, Sir George. In late October 1643 Clanricarde wrote to Frederick enclosing a letter from his 'noble brother'. Clanricarde advised Frederick that George had visited him in the recent past and reported improvements in the latter's health.[73] In late August 1645 Sir George Hamilton corresponded with Clanricarde requesting that his former motion regarding Manorhamilton should be brought to Ormond's attention. At this point Theobald, Viscount Taaffe, was commanding a joint royalist-confederate offensive in Connacht, against those who had contravened the 1643 cessation, which made considerable progress in the west throughout August and September 1645.[74] In the event of Manorhamilton being taken, George requested that it be held either in Clanricarde's or in Ormond's name 'as I be not discovered herein'. Should Frederick submit and receive royal pardon, and consequently be restored to his estate, George requested that it be legally charged to ensure speedy payment of Frederick's debts, which George had provided surety for.[75] Thus, there had been financial arrangements between the brothers in the past, with George acting as a guarantor for his younger brother's borrowing. George had a pattern of lending money to family members. Manning has reported that he loaned £4,102 to William Hamilton, son of his brother Sir Claud, in 1625.[76] Also interesting is George's request that the castle not be held in his name, suggesting a reluctance to come into open conflict with his brother, whose political allegiance had deviated from his own. In the absence of direct evidence we can only speculate about Hamilton's attitude towards his family's politics. However, it does not seem a leap too far to surmise that his relentless opposition to those who had taken up arms, and unwillingness to compromise even if it meant safeguarding those with whom he might be expected to empathize, would have alienated him from those family members whose allegiance deviated so far from his own.

Finally, it is worth considering the factors that motivated Hamilton's hardline policy towards the Catholic rebels in the north-west, and towards those who capitulated in the face of their threat. Such analysis necessitates treading a fine line between the frequently contradictory version of events from Hamilton and those accounts provided by his contemporaries. His involvement in public life prior to and after this interlude also bears relevance. While his experiences in the Swedish army influenced the style of war propagated in Connacht, the remaining evidence also intimates that both the personal characteristics and the motivations which led Hamilton to fight on the continent in the first place also influenced his actions in the north-west. Though perhaps not the sole factor, defence of Protestantism must have influenced his decision to fight under the Swedish flag in the 1630s. This leads us to question whether his military activities following the outbreak of violence in 1641 bear the characteristics of a religious crusade. Aspects of the diary account of Hamilton's war in Connacht do suggest a religious dimension. Throughout the pamphlet, victories, particularly when his men are depicted as outnumbered, are attributed to God's providence.[77] However it is important not to overstate this point. Rather the providential nature of the seventeenth-century mentality, with both positive and negative developments attributed to an interventionist God, must also be borne in mind.[78]

Recent analysis posits that Hamilton's diary facilitates an insight into local settler contempt for the Catholic religion, specifically citing the attempt by Hamilton and his men to goad the rebels by feigning an execution in 'honour' of St Patrick, thereby ridiculing the Irish saints and Catholic religious practices.[79] Similar derision is evident in the attack on Sligo in July 1642, with Hamilton's forces specifically targeting the Catholic friary and destroying the symbols of their faith.[80] But while native beliefs were mocked, settler convictions were honoured. Referring to a successful engagement with the rebels in late November 1642 the diarist noted that the victory had taken place on St Andrew's Day, in honour of their Scottish patron.[81]

Hamilton's response to Sir Robert Hannay's request for assistance has already been discussed in the context of the former's attitude to his fellow Scots under attack. The language attributed to Hamilton in this regard is also notable. Articulating his inability to aid Hannay, Hamilton presents his own position as a defence of religion, as well as the established political order, specifically referring to 'glorious death' in the 'cause of Christ'.[82] Thus to some extent Hamilton perceived, or wished to have others perceive, his actions as religiously motivated.

Biblical echoes in the account of his campaign also point to a religious aspect. Prior to the onslaught on Sligo Hamilton is reported to have ordered that 'no man presume upon pain of death to enter any house for plunder, but with fire and sword to destroy all we could come at'. The fact that his men were given explicit directions not to pillage and bring their spoils back to Manorhamilton, as they would normally have done, suggests a crusading undertone to this particular engagement.[83] This notion of putting aside any material gain accruing from victory so as not to debase the real purpose of the mission was not unique among seventeenth-century Protestants. Following the defeat of the Cromwellian expedition to Hispaniola in 1655, the Commonwealth leadership was accused of incurring God's displeasure by seeking to promote private agendas and personal gain. Contemporary critics drew Biblical parallels, citing the Book of Jericho, when the Israelites transgressed by availing of 'the accursed thing' and were punished with the defeat of their expedition to Bethel.[84]

Hamilton himself subsequently looked to the Bible when pursuing his suit against Sir William Cole. He concluded his statement to parliament with reference to the Book of Kings and the profit Micaiah. Hamilton drew parallels between his own situation and that of the one true visionary, who had spoken out against the false prophets, and advised the King of Israel against targeting Ramoth in Gilead. Micaiah was imprisoned for his pronouncements, but his prediction was ultimately vindicated by the king's subsequent death at the hands of the Syrians.[85] In this familiarity with Biblical text and his invoking scripture to justify his own position, Hamilton displayed tendencies associated with what has been loosely defined as puritan strains within contemporary Protestantism.[86]

Hamilton's subsequent role in propagating the Solemn League and Covenant in Derry in 1644 also appears to support the notion of religion as the driving force in his earlier campaign in the north-west. We have seen how defence of the Protestant faith featured in his military forays, both prior to and following the outbreak of violence in 1641. However, it would be an over-simplification to present religion as the only motivating factor. Recent analysis suggests that Hamilton's desire to secure the governorship of Derry was of major significance in his support for the Covenant.[87] Then having proven unsuccessful in securing power in Ulster, Hamilton turned his attention to Connacht once more, trying in vain to secure official parliamentary command in Counties Sligo and Leitrim in 1645.[88] Prior to 1641 Hamilton had done well in Leitrim and when the area became de-stabilized he fought hard to defend his material interests. His strategy was very much a unilateral one, which did not involve cooperation with his settler neighbours. While defence of his faith and the established order acted as a spur during the 1640s, he also pursued a personal agenda and tried to use the developing political environment to his own ends.

In attempting to analyze motive behind Hamilton's actions in the 1641–43 period, his personality cannot be ignored. The notion of 'fury' or psychosis, invoked by contemporaries to help comprehend acts of extreme and unprecedented violence in early modern Ireland, has recently been examined.[89] That Hamilton could have been subject to passions leading him to behave in a rash and excessive manner appears substantiated by evaluations of his character in the years preceding 1641. Wentworth was particularly harsh in his judgement, describing Hamilton as 'a Gentleman of a strange extravagant Humour and Judgment as any other indeed I know'.[90] His difficult nature may have been something of a family trait – his father, Lord Claud, was described by a contemporary as 'an ambitious, cruel and dissembling' man.[91] Into the 1640s, Clanricarde's caution against Hamilton's excesses has already been noted, while Thomas Carte referred to Hamilton's 'violence, rapines, cruelties, and insupportable insolencies'.[92] Exploring motives for land speculation in Ulster at the turn of the seventeenth century, John McGurk has made particular reference to the covetousness of younger sons, whom he has defined as 'angry young men, embittered due to their exclusion from inheritance by the primogeniture system'.[93] Hamilton was such a younger son, seeking to make his mark through military service abroad and later in extensive property acquisition throughout Ireland. When external forces sought to undermine his efforts, he responded with vigour.

While a conclusive understanding of the forces driving Hamilton is beyond our reach, it would be an injustice to dismiss him as merely belligerent. In many ways Hamilton epitomized the isolated Protestant settler, far from government assistance in the remote north-west, surrounded by hostile forces. However, in contrast with the bulk of his settler neighbours, his reaction was not to flee, nor to barricade his castle gates.[94] Rather, from the outset, he sought to actively engage with the insurgents. As we have seen, Hamilton's zealous drive to stamp out the rebel threat resulted in a ruthless campaign which left numerous rebel and civilian casualties. Ultimately, however, Hamilton's desire to vanquish his Catholic foes would not prove sufficient to transcend his private agenda and engage in effective military cooperation with his settler neighbours, not even with his fellow Scots in the west.

NOTES

1 I wish to acknowledge the funding received from the Irish Research Council for the Humanities and Social Sciences, which facilitated the research on which this chapter is based. Thanks to Dr Kevin Forkan and Dr Carole Holohan for their constructive comments on earlier versions.

2 This has been attributed to its geographical distance from Britain, and, with the exception of Leitrim, the absence of formal plantation at provincial level, N. Canny, *Making Ireland British, 1580–1650* (Oxford University Press, 2001), p. 384.

3 We will see later in this chapter that Sir James Craig also received lands under the Leitrim Plantation scheme. Both he and his fellow Scot, Sir Francis Hamilton, provided leadership to the Cavan settler community following the outbreak of violence in 1641. J. Johnston, 'The Scotch settlement of Co. Fermanagh, 1610–30', *Clogher Record*, 10:3 (1978), 367–73; C. McCoy and M. Ó Siochrú, 'County Fermanagh and the 1641 Depositions', *Archivium Hibernicum*, 9 (2008), 66; W. Roulston, 'The Scots in plantation Cavan, 1610–42', in B. Scott (ed.), *Culture and Society in Early Modern Breifne/Cavan* (Dublin, 2009), pp. 131, 143.

4 P. Fitzgerald, 'Scottish migration to Ireland in the seventeenth century', in A. Grosjean and S. Murdoch (eds), *Scottish Communities Abroad in the Early Modern Period* (Brill, 2005), pp. 32, 43.

5 James Smith, Andrew Ferguson, and William Wilson were among those identified as Scottish merchants in Ballymote. M. O'Dowd, *Power, Politics and Land: Sligo, 1562–1688* (Belfast, 1991), pp. 96, 103, 152; Canny, *Making Ireland British*, p. 385.

6 One of the Scottish clerics in the north-west was William Oliphant, vicar of Ballysadare and Enagh, who was killed during the siege of Templehouse in Sligo during the insurrection. Deposition of Jane Browne, (TCD, MS 830, fol. 121); Deposition of Andrew Adair (TCD, MS 831, f. 174); O'Dowd, *Power, Politics and Land*, p. 108; Canny, *Making Ireland British*, p. 386; A. Ford, *The Protestant Reformation in Ireland, 1590–1641* (Frankfurt, 1985), p. 137.

7 B. Mac Cuarta, 'The plantation of Leitrim, 1620–41', *Irish Historical Studies*, 32:127 (2001), 297–320.

8 D. Mac an Ghalloglaigh, 'Leitrim, 1600–41', *Breifne*, 4:14 (1971), 241, 246; M. Perceval-Maxwell, *The Scottish Migration to Ulster in the Reign of James I* (London, 1973), p. 185.

9 Following the outbreak of violence in 1641, Harrison would take shelter with the Sligo based English settler, Robert Parke. Hamilton came into conflict with Parke in February 1642, accusing him of colluding with those in arms and attempting to entrap Hamilton's men. *A true relation of the manner of our Collonell Sir Frederick Hamiltons returne from Londonderry in Ireland, being 60 miles from his Castle and Garrison, where he was at the beginning and breaking out of this Rebellion, with the particular services performed by the Horse and Foote Companies which he commandes garrison'd at Manor Hamilton in the county of Leitrim in the Province of Connaught.* (NLI, Joly Pamphlets, 2095, pp. 22–3, 29). Also see *The information of Sir Frederick Hammilton, Knight, and Colonell, given to the Committee of Both Kingdoms, concerning Sir William Cole, Knight, and Colonell; with the scandalous answer of the said Sir William Cole, Knight* (London, 1645), pp. 83, 85, http://eebo.chadwyck.com, accessed 22 February 2007; O'Dowd, *Power, Politics and Land*, p. 121; B. Mac Cuarta, 'Leitrim Plantation Papers, 1620–22', *Breifne*, 9:35 (1999), p. 131.

10 Mac Cuarta, 'The plantation of Leitrim', 304–6.

11 M. Perceval-Maxwell, 'Ireland and Scotland, 1638–48', in J. Morrill (ed.), *Scottish National Covenant in its British Context* (Edinburgh, 1990), pp. 193–4.

12 The following accounts attest to a Scottish presence in counties Sligo and Mayo in 1641: Deposition of Elizabeth Holliwell (TCD, MS 830, fol. 3b); Deposition of Jane Browne (TCD, MS 831, fol. 63); Deposition of William Walsh (TCD, MS 831, fol. 66b); Deposition of Jane Stewart (TCD, MS 831, fol. 73); Deposition of John Shrawley (TCD, MS 831, fol. 75b); Deposition of Oliver Albanagh (TCD, MS 831, fol. 81); Deposition of Elizabeth Beucannon (TCD MS 831, fol. 143b); Deposition of James Bayley (TCD, MS 831, fol. 242). The following depositions refer to a Scottish presence in Leitrim: Deposition of James Stevenson (TCD, MS 831, fol. 6); Deposition of Gilbt Corbin (TCD, MS 831, fol. 8); Deposition of John Winder (TCD, MS 831, fol. 8); Deposition of Anthony Mills (TCD, MS 831, fol. 8); Deposition of Suzanna Stevenson (TCD, MS 831, fol. 14b); Deposition of Mary Carr (TCD, MS 831, fol. 16).

13 Claud was also an ardent supporter of Mary, Queen of Scots throughout his lifetime. P. Holmes, 'Hamilton, Claud, 1st Lord Paisley (1546–1621(?))', *ODNB*, www.oxforddnb.com/view/article/12057, accessed 20 February 2007; B. Mac Cuarta, *Catholic Revival in the North of Ireland, 1603–41* (Dublin, 2007), p. 103.

14 A similarly zealous trend is evident in Frederick's subsequent activities in Leitrim, with his stone castle at Manorhamilton lauded as the strongest fort in Connacht. Another brother, Sir Claud Hamilton of Schawfield was granted 3,000 acres in Strabane. W. Trimble, *The History of Enniskillen with Reference to Some Manors in Co. Fermanagh: and other Local Subjects*, I (Enniskillen, 1919), p. 251; Perceval-Maxwell, *The Scottish Migration*, pp. 130–1, 344.

15 *Ibid.*,p. 272; Mac Cuarta, *Catholic Revival in the North of Ireland*, pp. 103–4.

16 See Mac Cuarta, 'Plantation of Leitrim, 1620–41', 297–320.

17 *Ibid.*, p. 315; D. Rooney, *The Life and Times of Sir Frederick Hamilton, 1590–1647* (Dublin, 2013), p. 24.

18 Mac an Ghalloglaigh's narrative of Hamilton's Leitrim campaign includes a section on his place in popular folk memory. He notes that Hamilton's reputation in the area was such that his name was used as a term of abuse until the late nineteenth century. Additionally, W.B. Yeats's short story 'The Curse of the Fire and of the Shadows' offers a fictionalised account of Hamilton's attack on Sligo. W.B. Yeats, *Mythologies* (New York, 1959); D. Mac an Ghalloglaigh, 'Sir Frederick Hamilton', *Breifne*, 7:9 (1966), 96–7; Rooney, *Sir Frederick Hamilton*.

19 Canny, *Making Ireland British*, p. 492; Deposition of Andrew Adair (TCD, MS 831, fol. 174b); Deposition of Nicholas Ward (TCD, MS 831, fol. 2); Deposition of George Bowker (TCD, MS 831, fol. 2b); Deposition of Edward Bichpam (TCD, MS 831, fol. 3); Deposition of John Browne (TCD, MS 831, fol. 4).

20 *A true relation*; Rooney, *Sir Frederick Hamilton*.

21 The pamphlet has recently been characterised as a 'vainglorious recitation of indiscriminate killings'. In the same volume, however, Kenneth Nicholls has pointed to the potential benefit in a systematic examination of contemporary pamphlets for evidence of violence and massacres perpetrated against the Irish during the early 1640s, positing that such analyses would be likely to produce much credible material. D. Edwards, P. Lenihan and C. Tait, 'Introduction', in D. Edwards, P. Lenihan and C. Tait (eds), *Age of Atrocity: Violence and Political Conflict in Early*

Modern Ireland (Dublin, 2007), p. 26; K. Nicholls, 'The other massacre: English killings of Irish, 1641–2', in *ibid.*, p. 182.

22 *A true relation*, p. 16; Manorhamilton is also cited as a place of refuge for Protestants fleeing violence in the Sligo Depositions. Deposition of Edward Braxton (TCD, MS 831, fol. 61); Deposition of Richard Jones (TCD, MS 831, fol. 70).

23 *A true relation*, p.17. Hamilton had married Sidney, daughter of Sir John Vaughan, a servitor and former mayor of Derry, who had died in 1634. Frederick eventually inherited his father-in-law's Derry properties. V. Treadwell, *Buckingham and Ireland, 1616–1628* (Dublin, 1998), pp. 56–7.

24 *A true relation*, pp. 17–19.

25 *Information of Sir Frederick Hamilton*, pp. 90–1.

26 The diary account notes intense and sustained campaigns of pillage and burning by Hamilton's men in early January, throughout April and into May, and in July 1642. *A true relation*, pp. 21, 25–7, 31–2.

27 *Ibid.*, pp. 20–1.

28 O'Dowd, *Power, Politics and Land*, p. 120.

29 *A true relation*, p. 31. Wood-Martin also documents Hamilton's attack on Sligo, but does not give a casualty figure. W.G. Wood-Martin, *History of Sligo, county and town, from 1688 to the present time* (3 vols, Dublin, 1892), iii, pp. 64–6.

30 *A true relation*, pp. 33–43.

31 *Ibid.*, p. 36.

32 *Ibid.*, pp. 44–6; Deposition of Will Welshe (TCD, MS 831, fol. 66).

33 Frequently, the diarist offers conveniently rounded figures for the numbers killed, which detracts somewhat from its sense of reliability as an accurate tot. For instance, the figures 8, 20, 40 and 60 occur repeatedly, on occasion in consecutive entries. I am grateful to David Edwards for raising this point. For purposes of calculation, unspecific references to more than one rebel casualty, for example 'some rogues', has been taken to mean two. Where the diarist has stated that a given number or more have been killed, or offered two potential figures for casualties in a particular encounter, for example where he states '7 or 8' have been killed, it is the lower figure that is included in the calculation. On this basis, the approximate figure may be an under-estimate.

34 Similarly in May 1642, Hamilton's men are portrayed as eager to go into battle, despite numerical disadvantage. To this end they brought out a rebel prisoner, pretending that he was one of the insurgent leaders, and hanged him in view of the rebel camp. When this did not elicit the desired response, Hamilton ordered that 200 cattle be driven towards the rebels, goading them with proclamations that the cattle had been recently seized from the rebel, Owen O Rourke. *A true relation*, pp. 25, 28.

35 *Ibid.*, pp. 20, 25.

36 *Ibid.*, p. 53.

37 *Ibid.*

38 For analysis of the emergence of organisation among the Catholics in arms at national level see M. Ó Siochrú, *Confederate Ireland, 1642–49: A Constitutional and Political Analysis* (Dublin, 1999), pp. 27–42; P. Lenihan, *Confederate Catholics*

at War (Cork, 2001), pp. 14–42. For information on the formalization of unrest within Connacht see A. Duignan, 'All in a confused opposition to each other: politics and war in Connacht, 1641–9', PhD dissertation, University College Dublin, 2006.

39 U. Bourke, *The Memoirs and Letters of Ulick, Marquiss of Clanricarde* (London, 1757), p. 10.

40 *Ibid.*

41 *Ibid.*, p. 6. O'Dowd discusses the tendency of pro-government landowners to barricade themselves inside their castles and try to remain neutral, in Sligo and in Connacht generally, and the implications this had for the growth of the insurgents' cause. O'Dowd, *Power, Politics, and Land*, pp. 121–2.

42 *A true relation*, pp. 20, 26.

43 *Ibid.*, pp. 23, 29, 31–2, 36.

44 Canny initially discusses stripping as a form of theft, but then refers to second phase stripping, when the victim was in such poor condition there could be no material benefit from the act. In this context he contends that the objective was to degrade the victim. He also refers to a metaphoric appeal for the Catholic insurgents, as such stripping 'symbolised the departure of these intruders from the properties on which they had settled in the same penniless state in which they arrived'. Further, the practice is located in its broader European context, and comparisons made with the 'cultural rites of purification' practised during the wars of religion in sixteenth-century France. Canny, *Making Ireland British*, pp. 542–5.

45 Beheadings were a feature of military aggression on both the Irish and English sides during the sixteenth century. While conflict in the seventeenth century increasingly claimed civilian casualties, Kenneth Nicholls makes particular reference to instances of English Protestant forces deliberately targeting female members of the Irish gentry in the early 1640s. D. Edwards, 'The escalation of violence in sixteenth-century Ireland', in D. Edwards, P. Lenihan and C. Tait (eds), *Age of Atrocity: Violence and Political Conflict in Early Modern Ireland* (Dublin, 2007), pp. 47, 56–7; J. McGurk, 'The pacification of Ulster, 1600–1603', in *ibid.*, pp. 119–29; Nicholls, 'The other massacre', p. 179.

46 B. Donagan, 'The web of honour: soldiers, christians and gentlemen in the English Civil War', *The Historical Journal*, 44:2 (June, 2001), 365–89; T. Bartlett, *The Military Academy of Warre. Military Affairs in Ireland, 1600 to 1800* (Dublin, 2002), p. 24.

47 For discussion of the government's use of martial law in the immediate aftermath of the outbreak of violence see R. Armstrong, *Protestant War: The "British" of Ireland and the Wars of the Three Kingdoms* (Manchester, 2005), pp. 14–42.

48 M. Ó Siochrú, 'Atrocity, codes of conduct and the Irish in the British Civil Wars 1641–53', *Past and Present*, 195 (May 2007), 62–3.

49 For example the following description of a rebel onslaught in May 1642, 'the Rogues … fell to stripping themselves, and with a great noyse and a cry came running towards us.' *A true relation*, p. 28. Hints at their lack of professionalism, and consequent ineptness, are counterbalanced by numerous references to their vast manpower and the extent to which they outnumbered Hamilton's

beleaguered garrison, thus depicting the latter's military success as all the more laudable.

50 Between 19 October 1642 and 1 April 1643, the point at which diary entries cease, there are only fourteen entries, much less than for the earlier period. *A true relation*, pp. 38–46.

51 Hamilton's purported disrespect towards Taaffe was all the more striking given that the latter would not join the confederates until 1647. 24 October 1643, Portumna, Clanricarde to Sir Frederick Hamilton. J. Lowe (ed.), *Letter Book of the Earl of Clanricarde, 1643–47* (Dublin, 1983), p. 10; Ó Siochrú, *Confederate Ireland*, p. 253 n. 11.

52 MacDonagh would have received formal military training as he had been made a captain in one of the two regiments raised in Connacht as part of Strafford's Irish army. O'Dowd states that MacDonagh served under Sir Henry Bruce in this context, but subsequently suggests that he was an officer in Coote's regiment. Evidence from manuscript sources supports the former. List of new army, endorsed 23 April 1640 (Bodleian Library, Oxford (hereafter Bod. Lib.) Carte MS 1, fol. 183); O'Dowd, *Power, Politics and Land*, pp. 113, 119.

53 *A true relation*, p. 46. This encounter is also referred to in the Deposition of William Walsh, taken in February 1644. Walsh, an occasional foot soldier with the Manorhamilton garrison, stated that he was present at the skirmish and noted the 'greate number of armed men' commanded by MacDonagh, and Captain Luke Taaffe. Deposition of William Walsh (TCD, MS 831, fol. 65).

54 M. E. Ailes, *Military Migration and State Formation: the British Military Community in Seventeenth-Century Sweden* (Lincoln, NE, 2002), p. 15

55 'Sir Frederick Hamilton of Manorhamilton', 1184, http://www.st-andrews.ac.uk/history/ssne, accessed 24 February 2007; Rooney, *Sir Frederick Hamilton*, pp. 60–70.

56 Ailes, *Military Migration and State Formation*, p. 30

57 J. Mackenzie, 'Foreword', in A. Mackillop and S. Murdoch (eds), *Military Governors and Imperial Frontiers c.1600–1800* (Leiden, 2003), p. xxxiv.

58 E. Furgol, 'Scotland turned Sweden: The Scottish Covenanters and the military revolution in 1638–9', in J. Morrill (ed.), *Scottish National Covenant in its British Context* (Edinburgh, 1990), p. 146.

59 Edwards, 'The escalation of violence in sixteenth-century Ireland', p. 45.

60 Mac Cuarta, 'Plantation of Leitrim', p. 315.

61 Subsequently, Abercromy's aforementioned Catholic cousin, and namesake, attempted to rescue a number of rebel prisoners captured by Hamilton's men, and was 'apprehended as a dangerous Instrument'. *A true relation*, pp. 19–20.

62 *Information of Sir Frederick Hamilton*, pp. 19, 39.

63 *A true relation*, p. 31.

64 *Information of Sir Frederick Hamilton*, p. 36.

65 Wood-Martin, *History of Sligo*, ii, p. 58; A. Clarke, *Prelude to Restoration in Ireland: The End of the Commonwealth, 1659–60* (Cambridge, 1999), p. 173 n. 12.

66 *A true relation*, p. 57.

67 *Information of Sir Frederick Hamilton*, pp. 20–1, 56–7.

68 Deposition of John Layng (TCD, MS 831, fol. 84); Examination of Captain Andrew O'Adare (TCD, MS 831, fol. 97); Wood-Martin, *History of Sligo*, ii, p. 59.

69 The widow of Frederick's nephew, Claud Hamilton, married Sir Phelim O'Neill in the late 1640s. Her son by Claud, who was named James, would fight alongside his stepfather, O'Neill, against the forces of parliament in 1650. This James was Frederick's grand-nephew – his father Claud was the son of Frederick's brother, the first earl of Abercorn. Mac an Ghalloglaigh mistakenly identifies this James Hamilton as Frederick's brother. However, Frederick's brother, James, died on 23 November 1618. C. Manning, 'The two Sir George Hamiltons and their connections with the castles of Roscrea and Nenagh', *Tipperary Historical Journal* (2001), 154, n. 40; Mac an Ghalloglaigh, 'Sir Frederick Hamilton', p. 59, n. 13; Perceval-Maxwell, *The Scottish Migration*, p. 326.

70 Manning, 'The two Sir George Hamiltons', p. 150.

71 T. Carte, *An History of the Life of James, Duke of Ormonde* (4 vols, London, 1736), i, p. lxvii; J. Lodge, *The Peerage of Ireland: or, a genealogical history of the present Nobility of that kingdom. With engravings of their paternal coats of arms* (7 vols, Dublin, 1789), iv, p. 40; Manning, 'The two Sir George Hamiltons', p. 150.

72 2 September 1645, Nenagh, Sir George Hamilton to Clanricarde; 16 August 1647, Kilcolgan, Clanricarde to Digby, Kilcolgan. Lowe (ed.), *The Letter Book of the Earl of Clanricarde*, pp. 185, 469; 16 March 1650, Manorhamilton, Sir George Hamilton to Clanricarde, Bod. Lib., Carte MS 27, fol. 116(86).

73 Clanricarde to Sir Frederick Hamilton, Portumna, 24 October 1643. Lowe (ed.), *Letter Book of the Earl of Clanricarde*, p. 11.

74 September 1645, Breviate of Taaffe's commission as commander of king's army in Connacht (Bod. Lib., Carte MS 15, fol. 714); 1 August 1645, By lord viscount Taaffe (Bod. Lib., Carte MS 15, fol. 324); J.T. Gilbert, *History of the Irish Confederation an d the war in Ireland, 1641[–1649] containing a narrative of affairs of Ireland* (7 vols, Dublin, 1882–91), iv, pp. 16–18.

75 Rooney, *Sir Frederick Hamilton*, p 72. Manorhamilton was not captured at this point, but George remained hopeful of gaining custody. The following June, Clanricarde wrote to Ormond renewing George's petition to be granted custody of his brother's house. 30 August 1645, Roscrea, Sir George Hamilton to Ormond (Bod. Lib., MS Carte 15, fol. 541); 15 June 1646, Loghreagh, Clanricarde to Ormond (Bod. Lib., MS Carte 17, fol. 518).

76 Manning, 'The two Sir George Hamiltons', p. 150

77 See *A true relation* pp. 23–8, 30, 32, 41 for examples.

78 Martin Ingram discusses the prevalence of this 'providential framework of thought' in the context of Tudor and Stuart England. Belief in an interventionist God spanned the confessional divide in Connacht, with both rebels and settlers attributing their success and defeat to divine will. Duignan, 'All in a confused opposition', p. 147; M. Ingram, 'From reformation to toleration: popular religious cultures in England, 1540–1690', in T. Harris (ed.), *Popular Culture in England, c. 1500–1850* (London, 1995), p. 109.

79 B. Scott, 'Reporting the 1641 rising in Cavan and Leitrim', in B. Scott (ed.), *Culture and Society in Early Modern Breifne/Cavan* (Dublin, 2009), p. 203.

80 *A true relation*, pp. 30–1.

81 *Ibid.*, p. 41.

82 *Ibid.*, p. 57.

83 *Ibid.*, pp. 30–1. I am grateful to Kenneth Nicholls for this observation.

84 B. Worden, 'Oliver Cromwell and the sin of Achan', D. Beales and G. Best (eds), *History, Society and the Churches* (Cambridge, 1985), pp. 135–8.

85 *The information of Sir Frederick Hamilton*, p. 61.

86 C. Durston and J. Eales, 'Introduction: the puritan ethos, 1560–1700', in C. Durston and J. Eales (eds), *The Culture of English Puritanism, 1560–1700* (London, 1996), pp. 16–17, 31.

87 W.D. Killen (ed.), *A True Narrative of the Rise and Progress of the Presbyterian Church in Ireland, 1633–1670* (Belfast, 1886), pp. 415–17, 427; J.S. Reid, *The History Of The Presbyterian Church In Ireland: Comprising the Civil History of the Province from the Accession of James the First* (3 vols, Dublin, 1837), ii, p. 22; Armstrong, *Protestant War*, p. 113; K. Forkan, 'Scottish-Protestant Ulster and the crisis of the three kingdoms, 1637–1652', PhD dissertation, National University of Ireland, Galway, 2003, pp. 114–16; Rooney, *Sir Frederick Hamilton*, pp. 170, 185–7.

88 'A remonstrance of Sir Frederick Hammilton, knight and colonell to the right honourable the committee of both kingdoms', Wing (2nd edn)/ H477B, http://eebo.chadwyck.com, accessed 24 February 2007.

89 Edwards, Lenihan and Tait (eds), 'Introduction', p. 22.

90 The previous year, in the context of complaints made against Hamilton by his neighbours, Wentworth stated that while his behaviour might be deemed acceptable in a Swedish army it could not be tolerated in a 'civil commonwealth'. 7 April 1635, Dublin, Wentworth to Mr Secretary Coke; 18 August 1634, Dublin, Wentworth to Mr Secretary Coke. W. Knowler (ed.), *The Earl of Strafforde's Letters and Dispatches* (2 vols, London, 1739), i, pp. 281, 407; Lord Deputy to the Lord Conway and Killultagh, 12 March 1635, *CSPI, 1633–47*, p. 100; Mac an Ghalloglaigh, 'Sir Frederick Hamilton', pp. 60–9.

91 'Hamilton, Claud, 1st Lord Paisley (1546–1621(?))', *ODNB*, www.oxforddnb.com/view/article/12057, accessed 20 February 2007.

92 T. Carte, *The Life of James, Duke of Ormond* (3 vols, Oxford, 1751), iii, p. 164.

93 McGurk, 'The pacification of Ulster', p. 120.

94 Some comparison may be made, on this level, between Hamilton and Sir William St Leger, provincial president of Munster at the outbreak of unrest, who engaged in a pre-emptive strike at the first rumblings of trouble, leading his forces into Tipperary and Waterford and killing indiscriminately. E. Murphy, '"God's Providence" Inchiquin and the survival of Protestant Munster, 1641–9', MLitt dissertation, University College Dublin, 1999, p. 4; D. Dickson, *Old World Colony: Cork and South Munster, 1630–1680* (Cork, 2005), pp. 31–4.

9

The Scots of Ireland and the English Republic, 1649–60[1]

ROBERT ARMSTRONG

Bonnets, it seems, were part of the problem: or so thought one commentator on Ulster around 1659. 'It would be convenient for this part of Ireland that all the Scotch who now wear bonnets did wear hats. This would bring a trade now in Scotland into Ireland, which would be at least £10,000 yearly', but more to the point, 'it would not be so visible to themselves in a short time that they [the Scots] were so numerous nor so great a discouragement to the English, who in all fairs and markets see a hundred bonnets for one hat, which is a great prejudice and doth wholly dishearten the English there already'.[2] A few years earlier Major Anthony Morgan had worried that 'the Scotch in the North keep up an interest distinct in garb and all formalities, and are able to raise an army of 40,000 fighting men at any time'.[3] Garb mattered. Scots in Ireland, apparently, must at least look English. But the nub of things lay not with dress, trade or even fighting men but with another term employed by Morgan, 'interest'. Concern at the potential threat of a 'Scotch interest' in Ulster was one which dogged the rulers of Ireland from before the plantations to the aftermath of the Williamite wars. Such fears were not unchanging, but proved particularly potent and protean for the regimes which held power in the 1650s. Responses, too, were not simple but partook in full of the energy, imagination, ready implacability, recurrent confusion and relapsing compromise which characterized the interregnum governments. Treatment of the Scots of Ulster reflected the ongoing tensions between impulses tending towards the promotion of security and stability, with all that promised in terms of restoring revenue and cutting costs, as against transformation and godly reformation to shape a new Ireland. Attempts to formulate or implement 'policies' were caught in the coils of a politics stumbling from Commonwealth to Protectorate and back again, while fumbling at the task of organising the affairs of its subject nations within a notionally unitary, but practically devolved, and at best partially coordinated, state structure.[4] But most of all the republican regimes' thoughts and deeds were shaped by the particular manner in which a 'Scotch interest' had emerged in the early months of 1649.

Over the preceding decade the military and political mobilization of Protestant society had not overwhelmed national distinctions.[5] The social and economic power of the Scottish landowners in Ulster, embedded in 'Scottish microcosms' bound by kinship and credit, and enhanced by its translation into military power after 1641, sat alongside, and sometimes jostled, the more formidable military might of the army despatched to Ulster from Scotland in 1642.[6] If that army was a declining force by the later 1640s, it had formed a third nuclei for a Scottish interest in the Ulster presbytery – a cloud no smaller than a man's hand until the mid-1640s, it would soon overshadow Ulster, from an English republican perspective. The presbytery had moved far beyond its base in general Monro's army: it had engaged with a patchwork of local communities by the provision of spiritual services; it had spurred their integration within themselves, and propelled their integration with each other, through congregational elders administering discipline and gathering with the ministers in meetings of presbytery; it had cultivated an 'ideological' distinction by its ownership of the Solemn League and Covenant, widely accepted in Protestant zones in Ulster in 1644, though not without opposition, from the elite of English Ulster in particular.[7] And in 1649 it allied itself to the lords and lairds in defiance of the regicide republic which had taken power in England.[8]

That new regime considered itself the heir of the wartime Long Parliament, ally of the Scots of Scotland and of Ulster, as well as legatee of royal power over Ireland. The armed confrontation now brewing between the Scots of Ulster and the military commanders loyal to the new English republic, Sir Charles Coote in the north-west and George Monck in the north-east, was more than a little local difficulty.[9] If the Scottish government, like their countrymen in Ulster, had moved to recognize Charles II as king of England and Ireland as well as Scotland, the republic hoped that tensions with its northern neighbour could be held short of armed confrontation, even if that meant acceptance of Charles II as king of a separate Scotland. Events in Ulster brought resistance onto what London regarded as 'English' soil. Moreover the accommodation, albeit temporary, between the different elements of the Scottish community in Ulster was in advance of any like arrangement in Scotland itself where deep rifts divided the more thoroughgoing Presbyterians in power with those tainted as royalist 'malignants'. In Scottish Ulster, the republic faced an alignment which might turn 'Cavalierish' and reach out to the royalist coalition being pieced together around the royal lord lieutenant, Ormond. Perhaps even more dangerously, it took Presbyterian resistance to regicide and republic, fierce and articulate in England as well as Scotland, grounded it in Ireland, and gave it guns.[10]

Before it could grapple militarily, the republic determined to assail its opponent in print. John Milton's 'Observations' on the *Necessary Representation of the present evills* ... issued by the Ulster presbytery,[11] resonated with the stance adopted by the English republic towards Scotland, and engaged with 'a crucial phase of English domestic politics, the attempts by the Rump to discredit Presbyterian leaders while retaining at least the acquiescence of the rank-and-file supporters of Presbyterian persuasion'.[12] Milton redeployed his well-honed criticisms of 'Presbyters' as 'busie Bodies' who could not avoid 'Medling' in 'affaires of State', not far short of what 'the Pope hath for many Ages done'. If the Ulster ministers were adamant that their call was to 'cordially endeavour the preservation of the Union amongst the well-affected in the Kingdomes, not being swayed by any Nationall respect', Milton was clear that the '*Scottish* Inhabitants of that Province are actually revolted', and denounced those 'who from a ground which is not thir own dare send such defiance to the sovran Magistracy of *England*, by whose autoritie and in whose right they inhabit there ... a Countrey better than thir own ... ingratefull and treacherous guests to thir best friends and entertainers'.[13] Milton's attack did not stand alone: it had been preceded by the anonymous *Necessary Examination of a Dangerous Design and Practice against the Interest and Soveraignty of the Nation and Common-wealth of ENGLAND, by the Presbytery at BELFAST*, which also adopted the format of a reprint of the February text with commentary. Here was a vociferous blend of anti-Presbyterianism, depicting presbytery as the latest manifestation of anti-Christian persecution, with a strain of anti-Scottishness if anything more virulent than Milton's, directed at an upstart 'company [of] *Scotch Priests*, who have there set up, and do exercise a jurisdiction over the *bodies* and *souls* of men, according to the *pattern* that hath been shewed them in *the Mountains of Scotland*', even though such 'Men are Inhabitants of *Ireland*, and that subject to the jurisdiction and soveraignty of *England*'.[14]

A succession of London-published works seeped out in the coming months, presenting and editorializing Ulster Presbyterian documents. When the ministers of the presbytery and the leading Scottish landowner Hugh, viscount Montgomery of the Ards, fell to mutual denunciation, the exchange of letters was published 'by Authority' in London and depicted Ards, for all his folly, as led astray, since 'his Ghostly Fathers *instigated* him' though now 'poore Viscount *Montgomery* lyes under their Prophesies and Fulminations'.[15] A year later the long-running exchanges between the presbytery and two dissident ministers, James Kerr and Jeremy O'Quin were published with a brief preface insisting that '*for sottish, barbarous, bold, ignorant stuff, Tyrannically imposing upon their Brethren, and Treasonably acting and prescribing against the State, perhaps you will hardly finde one to have out-gone them, though you should search all the Crown of the Doctors of the Canon-Law, who have acted the Officials under the Bishops, whether Popish or Protestant*', adding '*Read the Book, and see the pitiful slavery they lie under, where a Presbytery is Established*'.[16] By now, in the summer of 1650, the English republic had launched its invasion of Scotland, accompanied by an onslaught in print which, as earlier towards Ulster, charged Presbyterians with muddying their cause by dabbling with 'malignants' but culminated in the army's August 1650 declaration wherein, it has been suggested, they 'proclaimed liberation from religious oppression as the primary motivation for the invasion', with 'the language of slaying the beast of the antichrist … formerly used to attack Prelacy' now 'levelled … against the Presbyterian kirk'.[17]

Hostility on the part of the state towards the spiritual 'tyranny' and 'sedition' of Scottish Presbyterianism might diminish in intensity in the years ahead, but would never entirely cease buzzing in the background. The power of presbytery was apparent when internal fractures appeared among the Ulster Scottish coalition, with viscount Ards being accused of moving too far in accommodating royalist interests. The resulting trial of strength brought victory not only to the ministers but to a covenanted movement which bound them to other men of local influence – army officers, congregational elders, and the representatives of the 'Country' in east Ulster – in interlinked civil, military and spiritual bodies. The call of the ministers was heeded, too, by the bulk of the rank and file who deigned not to align with either 'malignants' or the 'sectaries' and king-killers of the English republic, who were winning some support amongst English Protestants in Ireland. Yet for the Scots of Ulster denunciation from London, followed by the disintegration of their precarious coalition, was followed in turn by defeat at the hands of Colonel Robert Venables, moving north from the main English invading army at Drogheda, in tandem with Coote, moving west from Derry. By August Coote was able to report from western Ulster that he had received offers of submission, 'some professing their readiness to obey my Authority without conditioning, others upon Condition that they may not be forced to any thing against the ends of the Covenant; or otherwise, That they may have liberty to depart this Country with Bag and Baggage'.[18] In the east of the province Ards, beaten in battle, departed south to join Ormond with only an 'inconsiderable Partie' of those who might be considered 'preaching proof', 'most of them officers and gents'.[19] In December Monck, cooling his heels in Exeter, wrote to his former subordinate in Ulster, major George Rawdon, to tell him how he was 'glad to hear of the good success you have had against your neighbours the blue caps. I hope now you have gotten the mastery of them you will make them your servants and not your masters again.' He warned that the likes of Ards and his fellow commander James Hamilton, Viscount Clandeboye (or earl of

Clanbrassill), should 'enjoy not their estates again, and that you suffer no Scots ministers to preach in that country again. I doubt if this be not observed you will be once more slaves to the Scots and then none of your friends will pity you ...'[20]

Prospects for the Scots were not entirely bleak. The Presbyterian minister Patrick Adair recalled, some decades later, that in the first flush of conquest Venables, 'did emit declarations to encourage ministers of the country, giving all encouragement to the well-affected, and those who had been in opposition to the malignant party before, and declaring that it was for their preservation he was sent to Ireland'. That Venables, 'not yet fixed in the country' tended not to press the ministers, whom he had found 'sober and religious', and that he sought to 'insinuate upon them' seems plausible, though Venables was doubtless concerned that the ministers continued to pray for the new king and to 'declare against the sectarian party'.[21] As for the last remnants of Ards's contingent, now serving far to the south of Ulster, they came in under the 'General articles for the Protestant party in Ireland' authorised by Oliver Cromwell on 26 April 1650, terms later allowed to those, like Clandeboye, who had surrendered earlier, in Ulster.[22] Thereby they were allowed to move 'to the several places they desire' within Ireland, 'they engaging themselves not to do anything to the prejudice of the parliament or Commonwealth of England'. The articles embodied a fair degree of ambiguity as to possession of estates, demitting the question of terms for 'present possession' to commissioners of revenue, 'untill either the pleasure of Parliament be knowne concerninge them respectively, or until there be Commissioners or rules settled by authority from the Parliament for the fines or compositions of persons in theire quallity of delinquency ...'[23] Pacification was succeeding. The appeal of the Ulster Irish to their 'fellow-subjects', the sadly 'misled' Scots to join them, fell on stony ground,[24] though it was claimed that Venables had written that, with the Irish advance into the north-west '*the* Scots *there com under the Enemie, and contribute to their relief, and that hee himself durst not leav those parts where hee is, lest they should rise in Arms*', while the warning of the Ulster Irish that 'ere long none of the *Scottish* will bee suffered, either Gentrie, or Commonalty to inhabit in any part of this Province, Bordering on their native Kingdom of *Scotland*' was prescient.[25]

June 1650 saw the Ulster Irish army go down to defeat at Scarrifhollis, though Venables and Coote still had to contend with ongoing Catholic military resistance.[26] That same month, Venables attempted, unsuccessfully, to secure written undertakings from the ministers of the presbytery that they would not promote '*sedition or trouble*, or touch upon any other thing of State matters' in return for exercise of 'their Ministerial Functions'.[27] Some ministers were rounded up, and later Presbyterian accounts relate an extended debate between Venables and the detainees.[28] The colonel's maximum position was to secure assent to the 'engagement' mandated by the Rump parliament in London, 'I Do declare and promise, That I will be true and faithful to the Commonwealth of England, as it is now Established, without a King or House of Lords'. His interlocutors denied even the alternative of pledging 'a *non-acting against*, or a permissive sufferance' of the present power, since to do so would mean that 'we *wrong others* with whom we are bound in solemn Covenant' and rendered the ministers, in conscience, unable to do their duty if 'Lawful Authority may have a door open'd for the RESTAURATION thereof'. Unsurprisingly the upshot was an order that the ministers 'must be gone' signed not only by the English officers Venables and Robert Barrow, but also by Coote and his brother Chidley.[29] The ministers showed some sophistication in political argument, worryingly so, from the state's perspective, and doubly so in echoing stances adopted elsewhere. In England Presbyterians developed overt and sustained criticism of the engagement, with the ministers as 'key opponents' of the measure, sparking debates which ranged over the legality and legitimacy of the Commonwealth, and, at least as significantly, over moral and conscientious questions, notably that of the continuing obligations of earlier oaths, especially the Solemn League and Covenant, with its mandate to uphold the king.[30]

In the meantime Coote may have felt some need to guard his own back. In a declaration issued with his council of war in August 1650, at least in part 'for preventing such Misreports as some wou'd Charge us withal', he complained of the failure of 'several admonitions, private and public intimations' to move the ministers to 'adhere to their former Dispensation of the word without these *frequent oblique Calumnies upon that Government and Power* under which they live …'[31] He and his associates were not the only local Protestants to be drawn into the embrace of the republic. The arrival, in January 1651, of commissioners from the parliament of England, gave greater impetus to the implementation of the republic's ambitions for Ireland, greater scope to move from mere pacification to what might be considered a settlement. The commissioners were empowered to appoint 'officers and other persons' to assist them, notably in the assessment and collection of revenue, and these 'commissioners of revenue', assigned to regional 'precincts' appeared in early 1651 and were to accumulate a wide range of powers and duties.[32] In Ulster the incorporation of local Protestants alongside English army officers seems to have proceeded more rapidly than elsewhere.[33] Particularly prominent in the Belfast precinct was Colonel Arthur Hill, serving alongside his former subordinate Major George Rawdon. Both men had bobbed about on the turbulent waters of wartime politics, between the Protestant royalists of Dublin and the English parliamentarian–Scots alliance, as they upheld the English and Protestant interest, and if they gravitated into the Commonwealth camp with apparent ease, were soon evidencing episcopalian sympathies. Neither had shown much sympathy for specifically Scottish, covenanting or Presbyterian concerns, indeed in Rawdon's case the spectrum ran from barely concealed suspicion to undisguised hostility.[34] Any Scottish presence within the ranks of regional government then or later in the decade was almost undetectable, with the anomalous exception of Lieutenant-Colonel James Traill, a long-standing associate of the Clandeboye family.

This was hardly surprising given the view of the parliamentary commissioners, on their visit to Ulster in the summer of 1651, that 'the Scots, who do inhabit the greatest part of this country … are generally disaffected'.[35] It was not their greatest worry, given the persistence of armed resistance among the Irish, spiralling costs, 'economic near-collapse' and the exacerbation of these problems by the tardiness of their political masters in London in delivering some firm settlement of the country, and particularly of the question of property, or even promises of security for those who could feed the country, and the army, by their labours.[36] Something could be gained through control of the property of those deemed enemies by the state, and this not only meant giving effect to legislation confiscating the lands of Catholic 'rebels' but also implementing wartime measures directed against parliament's other foes.[37] Revenue commissioners had been told to ensure that those who sought to escape sequestration made proof of 'constant adherency and good affection' to the parliament and Commonwealth of England since 1641.[38] English royalists, like the wealthy Viscount Conway, were put at risk, though in his case his loyal agent, George Rawdon, ensured that steps were soon in train to counter the threat by appealing to the terms agreed in 1647 for the surrender of Dublin from Protestant royalist to parliamentarian control.[39] Scots, whose political sins post-dated 1647, had no such recourse, and the property of leading figures likes Ards and Clandeboye was seized.[40]

Sequestration was also to apply to ecclesiastical property, on the same lines as in England, from the lands of bishops or deans and chapters, to tithes now devolved to the hands of the state or impropriate to delinquent landowners, tithes which had in some cases been enjoyed by Presbyterian ministers planted in the 1640s. The parliamentary commissioners had been mandated to pursue financial recuperation alongside spiritual reformation, 'the advancement of religion and the propagation of the gospel'.[41] Ecclesiastical assets, redirected to state treasuries, were to be disbursed to support preaching ministers and schoolmasters and in August 1651 the Ulster revenue commissioners were authorized to appoint 'Godly and able persons, who shall be fit to preach the Gospell', and schoolmasters, in the key locations of Derry, Lisburn, Belfast, Carrickfergus and Dundalk, and to recommend 'what Godly able persons they can find fitt to be employed' elsewhere.[42] Some key appointments were rapidly made – the Independent Timothy Taylor at Carrickfergus, and the more radical Andrew Wyke at Lisburn.[43]

Could Presbyterians qualify as 'godly' and fit ministers? For one thing they faced the insistence that ministers, like 'all others that bear any office or receive any salary from the Commonwealth are to subscribe the Engagement'.[44] Within the general grammar of Protestantism, the idiom of language used by the parliamentary commissioners was telling. Writing to colonels Venables and Barrow, and Timothy Taylor, they pointed out that 'because there is great scarcity of persons fitly qualified to be sent out to preach to the people, we desire you to countenance and encourage frequent Christian meetings, both publicly and privately, to confer with each others about Gospel duties, and declare unto one another their experiences of the Lord's love and gracious dealing to them, to exercise their gifts in prayer and exhortations for the refreshing and edifying one another … avoiding vain and unnecessary questions and disputations, which administer strife …'[45] Exhortations to unity and liberty translated as support for the gathering together of the godly, apart from ecclesiastical structure, indeed regardless of clerical intervention, even as in Scotland where the kirk had discerned the appeal made by the English army as directed to a godly minority, rather than to a godly national church, and where the official intention 'to promote the preaching of the Gospel … and to advance the power of true Religion and Holinesse … ' meant, in practice, an encouragement of religious Independency.[46] Presbyterian fortunes declined, as the number of ministers, subject to arrest and despatch to Scotland, dwindled to about half a dozen in Counties Antrim and Down, serving 'little societies' in 'remote or private places' yet retaining a commitment to the 'public ordinances' of a settled church.[47] In the spring of 1652 these were drawn into a confrontation with Taylor and Wyke, mirroring the form and content of debates and disputes in both Scotland and England, with Adair defending the orthodox Presbyterian position: 'They were for visible saints, or such as in ground of charity had positive holiness. We took in all those who were willing to profess the truth, and be subject to Christ's ordinances'.[48]

Things were only going to get worse.[49] As late summer turned to autumn the parliamentary commissioners reiterated that no ministers could receive state support or tithes in Ulster without taking the engagement, adding that 'if you find that any of them carry on the Scotch interest, or principle the people against the present Government of the Commonwealth of England, you are to further secure them, and send them up to us in safe custody …'[50] Concerned to establish firmer communication with their counterparts in Scotland,[51] they picked up allegations 'that the Scotch Ministers do preach as violently against the Parliament as ever', while the 'Scotch gentry' in Ulster were 'meeting by 50 or 60 at a time, sometimes under the pretence of hunting'. Those on the spot must 'use some course for the timely prevention of such numerous and tumultuous assemblies of disaffected and discontented people'.[52] The revenue commissioners summoned the ministers to another prolonged and fruitless poring over the engagement and other 'ensnaring' documents, with a six-week breathing space, when the revenue commissioners appealed to Dublin and the ministers to the senior ministers in Scotland.[53] The exasperated response from Dublin failed to give further directions concerning the ministers 'unless there be some proof made against them', but tellingly added that no 'officers of the Scottish nation, that have borne arms against the Parliament, and refuse to subscribe the Engagement' be permitted 'to live within your quarters'.[54] As Westminster finally moved to set some certainty to conditions in Ireland, passing the Act for the Settling of Ireland in August, so its servants in Dublin were poised to consider a more drastic response to their Scottish problem, mooting a scheme for large-scale transplantation.[55]

For the commissioners in Dublin, the 1652 Act provided the necessary framework and conferred the required powers.[56] If only a handful of leading Protestants were among those singled out to be 'excepted from pardon for Life and Estate',[57] and if the act proved less unrelenting towards those caught up the 'War of Ireland' than those engaged in the first flush of 'Rebellion' in 1641–42, it still presaged severe terms for the Scottish population of Ulster. Those who had borne arms against the English parliament or Commonwealth faced the loss of two-thirds of their property, 'to be assigned in such places in Ireland, as the Parliament … shall think fit', the senior commissioned officers among them to be banished. Only among non-combatants were clear distinctions made on the basis of religion: Catholics would lose one-third of their lands, but Protestants who failed in having 'manifested their good Affections to the Interest of the Parliament of England' would only lose one-fifth. Pardon would be extended to 'all and every person or persons (having no real Estate in Ireland, nor personal Estate to the value of Ten pounds) that shall lay down Arms' upon taking the engagement, while the parliamentary commissioners made it clear that the requirement placed on landowners to 'declare and evidence their submission to the power and authority of the Parliament' meant they must subscribe the engagement too.[58]

By the spring of 1653 reports were again seeping through of simmering discontent in Scotland, liable to spill over into Ulster. The Dublin authorities responded as they had in the previous October, but this time with more precision, informing Venables that 'things are under consideration for removing all such persons of the Scottish nation as have been officers and commanders in arms against the Parliament or their forces, or such others as may likely be most active in these late counsels; for the execution of which you shall suddenly receive a commission, with some others …'[59] The commission duly followed, naming Venables alongside two other English officers, Major Anthony Morgan and Adjutant-General William Allen, and two Irish-based Protestants, Arthur Hill and Henry Jones, erstwhile bishop of Clogher. Plans would evolve through dialogue between these men and the commissioners in Dublin.[60] Those deputed to Ulster summoned all who had borne arms and reckoned 'the greatest part of them' had signed the engagement 'but we cannot say out of conscientious grounds', others 'a negative paper', though some 'will neither promise nor give bond to disturb the present government'. They believed 'the temper of this people … are more or less perverse according to the temper of their respective ministers' and what they recommended, as 'ways of gentleness and meekness' was the 'transplanting all popular Scots into some other part of Ireland' as 'no visible expedient to preserve these parts in safety' could otherwise be found.[61] As with the plans for transplantation of Catholic landowners – plans which had emerged by July 1653[62] – the emergence of more settled conditions did not obviate, but rather induced, efforts to make such plans effective. Security not only meant getting the Scots away from the north coast, it could also be enhanced by 'strengthening your hands against the common enemy' elsewhere given the Scots were 'sufficiently averse from the Irish'.[63]

Dublin assigned Kilkenny, Tipperary and parts of Waterford[64] for settlement, though Jones and his colleagues worried about the assignment of 'contiguous' locations and recommended dispersal across Leinster and Munster to 'render their conjunctions less powerful in opposition at any time against the State'. Dublin determined that resettlement would match 'the Qualification which they fall in the Act of Settlement' and chose to distinguish 'those who are to be transplanted and provided for on account of the Commonwealth', still assigned to Tipperary and Kilkenny, and all others,'left to the liberty for taking land from any proprietor in the respective counties of the Province of Leinster, respect being had to their numbers in every of the said counties'. The significance lay in the indication that more than just the landed, but also 'many … of mean condition' were to be removed. The commission in Ulster had even pondered whether the 'Scotch inhabitants' of Derry city might not be relocated to 'some of your towns in the south, if we can find fit grounds for their removal, their number being at present almost equal with the English, which we judge very dangerous to be allowed'.[65] It fell to the Ulster commission to draw up lists of those to be removed, presumably focusing on those once in arms – certainly no exemptions were to be given to any who 'contrived, counselled, aided or assisted' the assault on Derry in 1649, the ousting of Monck from Dundalk, or other feats of arms against the forces of parliament.[66] Lists were duly incorporated in a proclamation, dated 23 May, and to be issued over the names of Jones, Venables and the others, but which they baulked at setting forth because of 'the great mistake of the printing the names' along with problems in the time schedule.[67]

Consideration was given to the detailed terms for removal, to matters of timing, of the rights to crops in the ground, or the burden of future taxes, and these were discussed with agents whom the 'transplanters' were empowered to appoint and directly with 'some gentlemen of both counties' (Antrim and Down), though hints of accommodation always betrayed a glint of menace.[68] That settlement in the south was to be upon 'very good lands waste' reflected recurrent concerns of government about the stunted development of 'husbandry', prompting shortages of produce but also shortfalls in revenue. Such concerns had prompted detailed orders to revenue commissioners across Ireland (February 1653) to set waste and untenanted lands to officers and soldiers, on especially good terms if they planted English tenants, orders extended in May to all English Protestants with lands in Ireland 'constantly faithfull to the Interest of the Commonwealth'.[69] So the transplantation scheme was intended not only to promote the 'future planting of these parts [of Ulster] with English and thereby securing the same' but also profit from the resettlement of Scots in 'those wastes'.[70] Perhaps unsurprisingly the agents of those designated for removal pressed 'that so many of our tenants and tradesmen, whom we can persuade to come with us may have the benefit of the conditions granted to ourselves, and our servants be compelled to come with us'; at least the former request was granted. Favour was shown, too, to the notion that the displaced Scots 'may choose their own ministers, provided they be such as are peaceable-minded men towards the authority they live under and not scandalous'.[71] Might the upshot not have been a patchwork of identifiable Scottish communities, a splintering rather than a dissolution of a Scottish interest?

It was not to be. Transplantation of the Scots did not happen, but nor is it clear that it was ever formally abandoned. Three years later, one prominent Scot, Lieutenant-Colonel Brice Cochrane, suggested that he and his brother could gather fifty or sixty families, and 'some precious men of the ministry' to begin the move south, though he admitted that the earlier plans found the Scots in Ulster 'altogether unwilling' to move.[72] The process of summoning and assembling the Scottish population, of mandating identifiably Scots agents, had served to further brand a national identity upon elements of the population of Ulster. But resistance to the plans, by dogged legal challenge and active politicking, was not communal but the personal campaigns of the two greatest Scottish landowners in the province, viscounts Ards and Clandeboye. Despite the terms of the 1650 articles both men had suffered sequestration of their estates and, in Ards's case, temporary exile.[73] Clandeboye's challenge to the transplantation plan through appeal to the commissioners in Dublin was brushed off,[74] but like Ards he took his case to London. For all the prolonged and tortuous nature of the subsequent proceedings, both men's cases really came down to two questions: were they encompassed within the 1650 articles, and if so, did this nullify transplantation?[75] The first was certainly simpler, and in validating their case both lords appealed directly, and successfully, to Oliver Cromwell himself, the man who had authorized the surrender terms back in

1650.[76] For the Dublin government, though, these terms set holding arrangements only until parliament gave a final ruling on property rights, a ruling, it was contended, made good in the 1652 act, which in turn allowed for partial confiscation and complete reallocation of lands.[77] The counter-case not only challenged the arguments made, but sought to exploit alternative mechanisms of authority and to prod one of the tender points of civil–military relations, the matter of honour attached to upholding terms agreed with defeated enemies.[78] First Ards, then Clandeboye, appealed to the commissioners for articles of war in London who issued judgment, speaking the language of 'the faith of the army' and the 'honour and justice' of the nation and the parliament, that upholding the articles meant blocking transplantation.[79]

Of course the matter did not end there.[80] But while wrangles persisted, actions to transplant the two largest Scottish landowners in Ulster were stalled. Cromwell, who had written to block Clandeboye's transplantation in July, wrote again in December, now with the authority of the office of Lord Protector, arguing that Clandeboye be excepted from 'the general rule of transplanting' since this 'is not like to be hazardous or prejudiciall to the publicke peace' and because 'his case in many ways varying so much that what is done in his behalfe cannot be drawne into president for very few, if any'.[81] In March 1654 it was still envisaged that Protestant delinquents would have their lands taken with 'satisfaction elsewhere'[82] but continued lobbying, by Viscountess Clandeboye in particular, seems to have led to a reconsideration of the whole question. By April her husband's case had been mulled over and a recommendation issued that he be allowed to pay a composition to regain his property, subsequently set at two years' (pre-war) value.[83] It was the same rate later applied to Protestant delinquents in general, and there is some indication that actions taken to resolve the Clandeboye case were connected to the emergence of an ordinance, passed in September, which offered freedom from 'Sequestration, Confiscation or Forfeiture' for Protestant delinquents on payment of the requisite fine.[84] Yet days before it passed into law the Dublin authorities had made a pre-emptive move and granted out chunks of Montgomery and Clandeboye land to the leading adventurer, Erasmus Smith, and to Henry Whalley, judge-advocate in Scotland and brother to Major-General Edward Whalley. More players thus entered the game, further queering matters for Ards and Clandeboye.[85]

The two lords' cases spanned the transition from Commonwealth to Protectorate. That transition would shake up the government in Dublin, from August 1654 lodged in the hands of a lord deputy, Charles Fleetwood, and council.[86] It also witnessed a span of months marked by 'a wide-ranging legislative programme' enacted by the Protector and his Council in England, carrying forward a number of measures 'long … in the public domain' and not least a 'clutch' of measures 'to improve the administration and quality of the state church in England and Wales', instituting bodies of triers, to approve ministerial candidates, and ejectors, to purge inadequate pastors,[87] the former also empowered to vet those planning to travel to Ireland to serve in the church there.[88] The mood of the moment reflected the Protector's own religious temperament, being inclined towards unity among the 'godly', solid settlement of the church, and maintenance of due respect of the temporal power.[89] At the same time, in the spring of 1654, the initiative was taken to try to implement a more inclusive church settlement in Scotland, but the resulting arrangements, superficially similar, ran up against more staunch Scots notions of the autonomy of the church and, rather than proving more inclusive, were reckoned to privilege one faction among the deeply riven Presbyterian majority, aided by an assortment of 'sectaries'.[90] Developments elsewhere could hardly but spill over into Ulster where the presbytery faced three interlocking challenges: staving off the danger of internal rifts on Scottish lines; managing some acceptable accommodation with the state; maintaining, extending and deepening that integration of kirk and local community which had begun in the 1640s and which reflected the presbytery's particular vision of the advancement of the kingdom of Christ.[91] For the moment, 1654 seemed to bring a 'new sunshine of liberty of all ordinances' and the opportunity for ministers and elders to meet 'presbyterially'.[92]

Patrick Adair proved cagey in delineating divisions within the small presbytery, but he was clear that they were there, along the lines of the sharp and bitter controversy between Protesters (or Remonstrants) and Resolutioners in Scotland. Under the Commonwealth, the English regime in Scotland had looked more favourably upon the former, as more unrelenting in their attitude towards the house of Stuart and, as proponents of a pure and purged church, possibly more inclined towards sympathy with 'gathered' or voluntary forms of church order. In April 1654 revenue commissioners in Ulster were told that, given the 'want of godly and well-affected ministers in most parts of Ulster' and that it 'ought to be our care to lay hold upon all opportunities' they should inquire into 'such persons of the Scots nation … as you have reason to believe godly, of peaceable, not of turbulent dispositions, but qualified for that service'.[93] Six Presbyterians have been identified as being in receipt of state salaries in early 1654, of whom four have been reckoned to be 'certainly Protesters'. Indeed, five of the six were located in the west of Ulster, where Adair allowed that the 'protesting way' took root more readily.[94] The upshot was the agreement known as the 'Act of Bangor' whereby the presbytery resolved to permit 'no mutual contestings about the differences in Scotland, nor any owning of them on either side in public preaching or prayer, nor in conference among the people as siding with one party more than another'. Incoming candidates for the ministry were not to be 'violent in either of those ways' but to be commended by both sides in Scotland, and to subscribe to the terms of the Bangor resolution.[95] Thus Gilbert Simpson, admitted to Ballyclare by the presbytery in August 1655 'did declare himself cordiall for peace, and in token thereof did subscrybe to ye Coppie of the Act … made at Bangor'; so, in the same month, did John Douglas, called to Braid.[96]

Both Douglas and Simpson would subsequently appear as salaried preachers on the civil list.[97] Over the course of 1654–55 arrangements had been put in place, at least partly brokered by the Presbyterians' old friend, the Antrim landowner, Sir John Clotworthy, which allowed for a batch of Presbyterian ministers in east Ulster to become salaried within the state church by November of that year.[98] Not least important was the fact that the ministers would not be obliged to recognise the present 'usurping power', and indeed the 1649 legislation enforcing the engagement had been repealed.[99] The desire of the ministers, and others, for the full restoration of tithes was not conceded, and Lord Deputy Fleetwood was clear that present arrangements were preferable in ensuring the ministry's 'dependence on the state' and thereby ensuring a restraint on 'troublesome spirits, which may bee too apt to give disturbances to the publique peace; of which there have bine sad experience in the North'.[100] But the ministers had developed a casuistry capable of recognizing that their legal right, the parish tithes, had been taken 'by powers then uncontrollable' but would now come back to the ministers as payments so that 'what they got from the treasury was but getting their own again'.[101] In a miniature version of arrangements in England or Scotland, the government determined that where presentation was in state hands,[102] 'if the inhabitants of those places shall present the names of able godly ministers qualified for preaching the Word all due care shall be taken for making of provision … and for the supply of destitute places with persons qualified'; meanwhile 'persons fitly qualified for gospel-preaching' or present incumbents 'not scandalous or delinquents' were to be assessed by Colonel Barrow, Lieutenant-Colonel James Traill and Timothy Taylor, minister at Carrickfergus, and if 'approved by us they shall immediately be provided for with a comfortable sufficient maintenance'.[103]

Fleetwood's 1655 arrangement, if modified in details, was to provide the basis for the incorporation of Scottish Presbyterian ministers within the state church in Ireland.[104] It was premised upon an incorporation of Presbyterians, as individual godly ministers, not of Presbyterianism. Indeed the years to follow would see the development of what might be regarded as parallel systems in Scottish-dominated parts of Ulster or, perhaps, as a church-within-a-church. As the presbytery grew, so it devolved some of its functions to three (later five) geographically organized 'meetings' of ministers and elders.[105] Primarily concerned with the exercise of discipline, particularly over breaches of sexual morality, the treatment of issues of ecclesiastical order suggest a self-contained system. Meetings were to process the 'supplications' of vacant parishes for ministers, ensure bonds for the maintenance were in place ('during the sequestration' of the tithes),[106] and put candidates to their trials, over a period of months, assessing their preaching, their mastery of doctrine and their ability in cases of conscience.[107] Local communities, and particularly parochial elites, were bound in: elders were sworn in where absent,[108] local landowners on occasion lent assistance in securing ministers' maintenance,[109] and clerical candidates were identified by the despatch of 'commissioners' to Scotland.[110] The presbytery and its meetings were wary of congregational autonomy: in August 1656 a delegate was sent off to Lisnaskea in Co. Fermanagh to 'try Mr Johnstowns conversation, the unanimity of his call to that place, And that peoples subjection' to the Presbytery. Several of the parish reckoned that 'haveing his owne consent & maintenance for him' they had was no need of more, but with Johnston 'declaring himself to be for the Presby[tery], And they being enformed of the Presbyteries way of admission, [they] consented to suffer the same to be done'.[111] The presbytery, and its participant congregations, or at least their elders, were authorizing ministers according to their own rules, exercising a discipline superior to that of the congregation, and yet securing an income by means of a state system premised on different foundations.[112]

An effective concordat did not mean that suspicion, even animosity, was at an end. The cases of the Scottish lords, too, had rumbled on. Ards failed to secure access to composition under the 1654 ordinance,[113] and in March 1655 Fleetwood's council repeated the view of their predecessors in Dublin that the 1652 act provided a final settlement, that the court of articles in London had no jurisdiction to overturn it, or earlier rulings, and that if they were overturned this would hamper the process of settling soldiers and adventurers. Even so, having consulted the judges, and 'finding much difference in opinion' among themselves, the council appealed to the Protector for 'final adjudication' on the articles and Ards's case.[114] In the interim Fleetwood was effectively displaced, and his successor, Henry Cromwell, would in due course oversee further incorporation of the 'old' Protestants of Ireland within the structures of power, and demonstrate increasing sympathy for their preferred religious tendencies at the expense of more novel and exclusive bodies, like the Baptists and Independents, even if at first he was curbed by limitations on his power. Yet Scots, and Scots Presbyterians, were awkward accomplices – Henry Cromwell's 'policy was based on realism rather than enthusiasm for the Scots Presbyterians' who 'remained uncertain supporters of the regime'.[115] At first, indeed, he was inclined to consider the Scots of Ulster 'a packe of knaves', and he resolved to 'have an eye on them and such like'.[116] Over the winter of 1655–56 Fleetwood, displaced to London but still holding the office of lord deputy, continued to pepper his letters with remarks to 'Have a care of Ulster', and that the 'more care you take of the north the better',[117] while Henry Cromwell and his fellow reformer, Lord Broghill, president of the council in Scotland, corresponded about the danger of renewed disorder in Scotland affecting Ireland.[118]

In London, the council of state's committee of Irish affairs, concerned at the multitude of Scots in Ulster, resolved that a re-grant of County Londonderry to the London Companies be made conditional on an undertaking to plant only English for three years.[119] As it mulled over Ards's interminable case, recommendations received seemed to tilt towards the viscount, not least when matters financial came into play, and the prospect of a handsome composition payment was weighed against the possibility that the state owed Ards for the services he and his family had done, and the monies they had spent, during the wars against the Irish.[120] Fleetwood reported, on 22 January, a 'great debate' on Ards's case, the only resolution being that it was fitter to be determined in Dublin 'which I fear you will find troblesome'.[121] The implications were spelt in new instructions which were issued to the council in Dublin in March 1656. As well as the requirement that church livings in Ulster, as they fell vacant 'be from time to time supplied by ministers of the English nation', plans to exclude Scots from Ulster (and County Louth) were again put forward, covering all who had come to Ireland since June 1650, or who would come over in future. But the tangle which had ravelled around property rights determined that it was those who had 'at any time been in arms or hostility against the State' but who were not 'freeholders or having lands of inheritance, or articles whereby they are freed and acquitted of their delinquency' who must now face removal, or composition payments.[122] Dublin had been less than impressed about how those already required to compound had acted, noting that only 'some few persons (the most of them being of the Scottish nation) have made their compositions' and if inclined to take a hard line with defaulters were open to considerations of mercy.[123] The Ards and Clandeboye cases were raised in the parliament of 1656–57, which brought Irish and Scottish as well as English MPs to Westminster. Henry Cromwell's associates pressed for 'some expedient' to satisfy Whalley and Smith since Clandeboye had compounded and parliament 'ought to be tender, likewise, in the articles which Lord Ardes pretends to', but Anthony Morgan, 'one of his most trusted subordinates',[124] continued to warn of the dangers of a Scottish 'interest' and made clear his preference that the new grantees be left in possession and the Scottish lords have 'their estates … assigned them in some other part of the nation'.[125] Eventually the matter was laid to rest: Whalley and Smith were recompensed with lands in Co. Galway, Ards and Clandeboye regained possession of their estates, if burdened by fines and debts, and were reduced to selling large chunks of their properties.[126]

Yet even in the later Protectorate, approaches towards the Scots of Ulster were less redolent of inclusion than of containment. Even as local governance increasingly fell into the hands of local Protestants, not many Scots can be identified as MPs, JPs, revenue commissioners or participants in urban government.[127] Colonel Thomas Cooper, governor of Ulster, indeed urged that, 'for the peace of Ireland' it were better that 'in all townes of strength at leaste, noe Scotch minister be admitted, except hee bee a knowne friend to the present government', and particularly not to Derry, Coleraine, Carrickfergus, or Belfast. Indeed 'if it could well bee done, it wear adviseable, that noe Scotchmen might live in those townes, at least for some years; for your lordship knows, ther is more dainger to be expected from that interest, then the Ireish in Ulster'.[128] Restrictions on migration to Ireland remained in force.[129] Recurrent clashes occurred, in 1656, 1657 and 1658, as the ministers of the presbytery refused to participate in fast days called by the state, or insisted on their own mandate to call such occasions.[130] Reports reached Dublin of disorder allegedly sparked by Presbyterian aggressiveness and intolerance.[131] At the interface between kirk and state reliance was increasingly being laid upon a handful of ministers – some, like John Drysdale and John Hart (Heart), of known Protester inclinations.[132] Hart, for example, was one of those who took part in Henry Cromwell's 1658 convention which eased the passage towards a fuller restoration of tithes, a desideratum of a full-blown Presbyterian order.[133] Hart, too, showed himself particularly zealous in pursuing 'scandalous' ministers in his backyard, in north-west Ulster, ministers not affiliated to the presbytery and whom he was willing, eager even, to deal with in cooperation with state authorities.[134] It was, perhaps, indicative of his ecclesiological views, for Protesters in Scotland were less squeamish in dealing with even an illegitimate regime in pursuit of a pure church. Spats in the Laggan would play themselves out in the years ahead, when Hart's opponents would brand him an associate of the 'great Remonstrator' Patrick Gillespie, given 'charge of all the churches of the north-west'.[135]

By 1658 regulations for the admission of ministers seem to have allowed for a reliance upon a 'Testimonial in writing under the hands of two or more godly able Ministers of the Gospel',[136] and in December 1658 Drysdale and Hart can be found presenting a slate of nine Presbyterian candidates.[137] (Some, of different inclinations, were expressing concerns about the 'stamp' of those sent from Scotland to Ulster as mostly 'Remonstrators, amongst whom Mr Hart is a leading man'.)[138] By 1659–60 there were something of the order of seventy to eighty Presbyterian ministers in Ulster, many ministering within the state system, a large proportion of them now funded by tithes.[139] Mapping their locations shows a pronounced overlap with well-established Scottish zones. In Co. Down ministers are almost all to be found in the east of the county, mostly in the baronies of upper Clandeboy, Ards and Dufferin, precisely the areas owned by the houses of Ards and Clandeboy before the wars. In Antrim, ministers are spread, for the most part, in a band across the middle of the county, from Larne through Ballymena to Ahoghill, leaving aside the Macdonnell country in the north-east and the more English south of the county. A further cluster in north-west Antrim spilt over into adjacent north-west Londonderry (nucleus of the future Route presbytery), and a fourth concentration lay on the Laggan country where Counties Donegal, Londonderry and Tyrone meet, an area assigned for Scottish settlement back to the plantation grants at the start of the century. Presbyterian ministers remained notably absent from the garrison towns which troubled Colonel Cooper. At Magheralin in Co. Down, on the other hand, petitioners insisted that a great part of the parish was English, unlike neighbouring Donaghcloney, full of 'Papists and Scots, who are so bound up to their own judgements that they will not admit of any other' and were troubling the minister, Andrew Wyke, whose services the petitioners desired.[140]

If Richard Cromwell's brief hold on power was marked by something of an inclination towards Presbyterians, soon plunged beneath a wave of radical reaction in the latter part of 1659, the collapse of the Commonwealth in 1660 signalled some consideration of a Presbyterian settlement for Ireland by those assembled in the Irish convention. It was, though, a development all too aligned with what was suspected of prevailing trends in England – as the wind blew in an Episcopalian direction, so it blew away the haze of a Presbyterian establishment.[141] Yet in terms of Ulster Scottish developments, perhaps such moves had only ever been of marginal importance. With the return of the bishops the ministers were ousted once more – the 'sectaries time' was not unlike the 'prelates time'.[142] But the very concentration of Presbyterian ministers, overlapping with Scottish settlement, and the strong institutional bonds they had created, allowed for sustenance even under state disfavour. It was the republic which had incubated Presbyterianism.

The regimes of the 1650s set their face against a Scottish 'interest' in Ireland, an 'interest' militarily threatening, but also sustained in its peevish behaviour by its 'seditious' ministers. That interest could be faced down, confronted, dismantled or simply contained, and it was the latter approach which proved most constant as republic morphed into protectorate. Curiously enough, it was in the state-sponsored church, not the apparatus of the state, that the Scots made more of a space for themselves in the 1650s, as they had in the 1620s and 1630s. Yet although some of the early Scots ministers may have been less than fully conformist, the situation in the 1650s was far different from that of thirty years before. From being almost extinguished, the Presbyterians – not only ministers, but elders and lay supporters – constructed their 'settled' church notionally within the loose state structures but in reality as a church-within-a-church. The 'Scottish interest' was not destroyed, and further waves of Scottish settlement would sweep over Ulster in the decades ahead. But it had changed in character. When a funeral sermon was preached for Ards (now earl of Mountalexander) in 1663, his constant devotion to the 'Church of England' was singled out.[143] Elite support for, or more often discreet countenance of, Presbyterians would not vanish in 1660, any more than a complete identification of Scots and Presbyterians would be effected.[144] But the balance within the Scottish population in Ulster had shifted. The great families of the Montgomerys and the Clandeboye Hamiltons were perhaps fatally weakened by the onerous impositions of the 1650s,[145] even while their persistent and insistent struggles during those years had contributed to sustaining the integrity of Scottish Ulster. It was not simply a case of ministers versus magnates – it had not even been that in 1649. The Presbyterian system had bound in the very types of persons who had faced transplantation in 1653.[146] The mesh that had been woven in the 1640s by the nascent presbytery was spun with many more strands in the ensuing decade. It was to tightly knit together much of the Scottish population of Ulster for the remainder of the century, making the 'dissenting interest' at least as threatening in the eyes of the powers that be as the 'Scottish interest' had been to their predecessors a little earlier.[147] Perhaps they still wore bonnets.

NOTES

1 I am grateful to Dr Crawford Gribben and Dr Tadhg Ó hAnnracháin for reading and commenting on this chapter. Its shortcomings are my own.

2 TNA, SP 63/305/113; *CSPI, 1660–62*, pp. 164–7. I owe my knowledge of this document to Michael Perceval-Maxwell, 'The Scots migration to Ulster', Multitext Project in Irish History, http://multitext.ucc.ie/d/The_Scots_Migration_to_Ulster.

3 J.T. Rutt (ed.), *The Diary of Thomas Burton Esq.* (4 vols, 1828), i: July 1653–April 1657, pp. 1–11, www.british-history.ac.uk/report.aspx?compid=36738, accessed 8 April 2008.

4 T.C. Barnard, *Cromwellian Ireland: English Government and Reform in Ireland 1649–1660* (Oxford, 2000), chapter 2; P. Little, 'The Irish and Scottish Councils and the dislocation of the Protectoral Union', in Patrick Little (ed.), *The Cromwellian Protectorate* (Woodbridge, 2007), pp. 127–35.

5 For a telling discussion of 'English' and 'Protestant' interests see T.C. Barnard, 'The Protestant interest, 1641–1660', in J. Ohlmeyer (ed.), *Ireland from Independence to Occupation 1641–1660* (Cambridge, 1995), pp. 218–40. Important interpretations emphasizing the emergence of a strong 'English interest' in the 1640s are John Adamson, 'Strafford's ghost: the British context of Viscount Lisle's lieutenancy of Ireland', in Ohlmeyer (ed.), *Ireland from Independence to Occupation*, pp. 128–59 and P. Little, 'The Irish "Independents" and Viscount Lisle's lieutenancy of Ireland', *Historical Journal* 44:4 (2001), 941–61.

6 For detailed discussions of developments within the Protestant community in Ulster during the 1640s see especially D. Stevenson, *Scottish Covenanters and Irish Confederates* (Belfast, 1981); K. Forkan, 'Scottish-Protestant Ulster and the crisis of the three kingdoms, 1637–1652', PhD dissertation, National University of Ireland, Galway, 2003; R. Armstrong, *Protestant War: The 'British' of Ireland and the Wars of the Three Kingdoms* (Manchester, 2005); K. McKenny, *The Laggan Army in Ireland 1640–1685* (Dublin, 2005).

7 R. Armstrong, 'Ireland's puritan revolution? The origins of Ulster Presbyterianism reconsidered' *English Historical Review*, 121:493 (2006), 1048–74.

8 For a detailed discussion of events in 1649 see R. Armstrong, 'Viscount Ards and the Presbytery: politics and religion among the Scots in Ulster in the 1640s', in W.P. Kelly and J.R. Young (eds), *Scotland and the Ulster Plantations* (Dublin, 2008), pp. 18–40. See also K. Forkan, 'The Ulster-Scots and the Engagement, 1647–1648', *Irish Historical Studies*, 35:140 (2007), 455–76.

9 Monck failed to come to terms with the Scottish alliance in the province, and by July 1649 had surrendered his last stronghold, Dundalk, to royalist forces under the king's lord lieutenant, Ormond, and had taken ship for England. To stave off disaster he had made an accommodation with the Ulster Catholic commander, Owen Roe O'Neill, an expedient also resorted to by Coote, besieged in Derry city.

10 E. Vernon, 'The quarrel of the covenant: the London Presbyterians and the regicide', in J. Peacey (ed.), *The Regicides and the Execution of Charles I* (Basingstoke, 2001), pp. 202–24.

11 J. Milton, *Articles of Peace, made and concluded with the Irish Rebels ... And a Representation of the Scotch Presbytery at Belfast ... Upon all which are added Observations* (London, 1649), 'Publisht by Autority' in May 1649. Milton also commented on Ormond's recent treaty with the confederate Catholics and Ormond's letters to the parliamentary commander, Colonel Michael Jones. The text, and that of the *Necessary Representation* can conveniently be found in J. Milton, *Complete Prose Works* (8 vols, New Haven, CT, 1953–82), iii, pp. 296–9, 300–34.

12 T.N. Corns, 'Milton's *Observations upon the Articles of Peace*: Ireland under English eyes', in D. Loewenstein and J.G. Turner (eds), *Politics, Poetics and Hermeneutics in Milton's Prose* (Cambridge, 1990), pp. 123–34, 125. Cf. W. Maley, *Nation, State and Empire in English Renaissance Literature: Shakespeare to Milton* (Basingstoke, 2003), chapter 7.

13 Milton, *Complete Prose Works*, iii, pp. 299, 318–20, 333–4 (original emphases).

14 *A Necessary Examination of a Dangerous Design and Practice against the Interest and Soveraignty of the Nation and Common-wealth of ENGLAND, by the Presbytery at BELFAST* (London, 1649), pp. 3, 5.

15 *The Complaint of the Boutefeu Scorched in his own Kindlings* (London, 1649), pp. 7, 14.

16 *News from Ireland Concerning the Proceedings of the Presbytery in the County of Antrim in IRELAND* ... (London, 1650), sig. A2. Thomason's date for the pamphlet is 9 July.

17 R.S. Spurlock, *Cromwell and Scotland: Conquest and Religion 1650–1660* (Edinburgh, 2007), pp. 22–3, 28, 30–1. See Chapter 1 in general for an account of the polemical exchanges between the Scottish church and the English army and its supporters.

18 He stated that he had agreed terms with a delegation empowered to 'Treat with me for the whole ... That all, excepting Commission-Officers, as well Soldiers as Countrymen, submitting themselves to the Authority of the Parliament and State of ENGLAND, and delivering up their Arms and Ammunition, should be suffered to remain quietly and peaceably in this Country, they paying such

Contributions towards the maintenance of the Army, as was formerly laid upon them', *A true relation of the transactions between Sir Charls Coot ... and Owen-Roe-O-Neal ...* (London, 1649), pp. 10–11.

19 Sir James Montgomery to Ormond, 20 August 1649, Bod. Lib., Oxford, Carte MS 25, fol. 312; G. Hill (ed.), *The Montgomery Manuscripts* (Belfast, 1869), pp. 191, 193.

20 HMC, *Report on the Manuscripts of the late Reginald Rawdon Hastings, esq.* (4 vols, London, 1928–47), ii, p. 361. Hamilton, the second viscount Clandeboye, had been awarded the earldom of Clanbrassill by Charles I in 1647, but this was not recognized by the English parliament or the regimes of the 1650s, who continued to refer to him as viscount Clandeboye, which title will be used here.

21 P. Adair, *A True Narrative of the Rise and Progress of the Presbyterian Church in Ireland*, ed. W.D. Killen (Belfast, 1866), pp. 175, 177–8.

22 J. T. Gilbert (ed.), *A Contemporary History of Affairs in Ireland* (3 vols, Dublin, 1879), ii, 393–6; TNA, SP 63/286/95, order of the committee for relief on articles of war in case of Lord Clandeboye, 1653.

23 Gilbert, *Contemporary History*, ii, pp. 394–5.

24 It was later alleged that Ards had made contact with the Ulster Irish, though he claimed that he wrote, with permission, to secure the recovery of some of his goods. The incident, reported by Coote to Lord Deputy Ireton, proved sufficient to merit an order banishing Ards from Ireland for six months, TNA, SP 63/286/62, Venables's report on viscount Ards, 1652.

25 *A Declaration of the Irish Armie in Ulster ...* (London, 1650), p. 1 (letter from Attorney-General William Basill to Speaker William Lenthall, 20 June 1650), 2–4 (declaration of 20 May 1650, also in Gilbert, *Contemporary history*, ii, pp. 418–20).

26 I. J. Gentles, *The New Model Army in England, Ireland, and Scotland, 1645–1653* (Oxford, 1991), pp. 380–1.

27 Venables stated that if they could not give such assurances they would be free to depart for Scotland: J. Kirkpatrick, *An Historical Essay upon the Loyalty of Presbyterians* (Belfast, 1713), p. 288; Adair, *True Narrative*, pp. 178–9.

28 Kirkpatrick claims to print the manuscript drawn up by the four ministers, 'Omitting such passages in it as are not material to the business in hand, to prevent its being tedious', Kirkpatrick *Historical Essay*, pp. 289–97. His 'business in hand' is clear from the title of his work. Adair, *True Narrative*, p. 179 for other ministers who escaped to Scotland or lay low locally.

29 Adair, *True Narrative*, p. 180 (original emphasis).

30 E. Vallance, *Revolutionary England and the National Covenant: State Oaths, Protestantism and the Political Nation, 1553–1682* (Woodbridge, 2005), pp. 161–5, 170–1. Vallance notes how the English situation also witnessed the use of equivocation or limited subscription, in attempts to find some means of securing some form of allegiance, Vallance, *Revolutionary England*, pp. 168–76.

31 Kirkpatrick, *Historical Essay*, pp. 297–8 (original emphasis).

32 R. Dunlop (ed.), *Ireland under the Commonwealth* (2 vols, Manchester, 1913), i, pp. 1–4 (instructions for commissioners, October 1650). The origin of the commissioners of revenue appears to have lain in the December 1650 assessment ordinance which empowered the parliamentary commissioners to lay a monthly

assessment and appoint officials to give it effect, C.H. Firth and R.S. Rait (eds), *Acts and Ordinances of the Interregnum, 1642–1660* (3 vols, 1911), ii, pp. 494–5.

33 Dunlop, *Commonwealth,* i, pp. 40–1 and n. 2, 76 and n. 1, for lists of revenue commissioners for the precincts of Belfast (September 1651) and Derry (November 1651) respectively.

34 Barnard, *Cromwellian Ireland,* pp. 151, 291. For some suggestive remarks on, and a detailed case study of, how a shared anti-Scottish and anti-Presbyterian position could bring together former royalists and thoroughgoing parliamentarians in northern England see, respectively, D. Scott, 'The wars of the three kingdoms, 1642–1649', in Barry Coward (ed.), *A Companion to Stuart Britain* (Oxford, 2003), pp. 322–4, and D. Scott, 'The Barwis Affair: political allegiance and the Scots during the British civil wars', *English Historical Review,* 115:463 (2000), 843–63.

35 Commissioners to Sir Henry Vane, 2 August 1651, in Dunlop, *Commonwealth,* i, pp. 23. Coote's decision to employ 'seven score' Scots in the Laggan district, given his, and his forces', absence in Connacht, was overturned when the commissioners visited Derry, having 'but little confidence' in the force 'being all Scots': see Commissioners to Council of State, 2 August 1651, in Dunlop, *Commonwealth,* i, pp. 19–20.

36 Gentles, *New Model Army,* p. 380; C.H. Firth (ed.), *The Memoirs of Edmund Ludlow* (2 vols, 1894), i, pp. 486–7, 499. In Scotland, too, 'sweeping provisions' were made for confiscation in October 1651, but by the following March parliamentary commissioners had recommended that these 'be reduced to the naming of specific persons', something not done until 1654: F. Dow, *Cromwellian Scotland 1651–1660* (Edinburgh, 1979), pp. 31, 57–8.

37 Instructions for commissioners, October 1650, in Dunlop, *Commonwealth,* i, pp. 1–4.

38 BL, Egerton MS 1761, fols 53–5 (16 July 1651). Commissioners in Ulster were specifically urged to ensure the sequestration of the estates of all who had aided the 'rebellion' against parliament in Ireland or in England, and Hill was told that sequestration was to extend to all 'that have been sequestered in England' but also to 'others … so far as the same appear to be for the advantage of the State and increase of the Public Revenue', BL Egerton MS 1761, fols 55–64; Dunlop, *Commonwealth,* i, pp. 71–2 (October 1651).

39 *CSPI, 1647–60,* pp. 383–4. Rawdon hinted that the earl of Cork might provide a test case; Cork duly secured a two-year reprieve in early 1652, and in 1653 the right to compound under the 1647 articles, a concession 'extended to all royalists who had not actively supported the king after 1647', P. Little, *Lord Broghill and the Cromwellian Union with Ireland and Scotland* (Woodbridge, 2004), pp. 69–70.

40 *CSPI, 1647–60,* pp. 383, 390, 398.

41 Dunlop, *Commonwealth,* i, pp. 1–2. See Barnard, *Cromwellian Ireland,* pp. 153–6 for discussion of tithes, glebes and state initiatives for the maintenance of ministers.

42 BL Egerton MS 1761, fos 36–7 (21 May 1651), 83–4 (11 August 1651).

43 Dunlop, *Commonwealth,* i, p. 60, n. 2; A. Hessayon, 'Wyke, Andrew (*fl.* 1645–1663)', *ODNB* (61 vols; Oxford, 2004), lx, pp. 633–4. Taylor had been a close associate of the leading Cheshire Independent Samuel Eaton, co-authoring

defences of the Independent church order: S. J. Guscott, 'Eaton, Samuel (*d.* 1665)', *ODNB*, xvii, pp. 612–13.

44 Commissioners to revenue commissioners at Derry, 11 November 1651, Dunlop, *Commonwealth*, i, p. 76. In April 1651 all revenue commissioners, governors of garrisons and other officials were ordered to administer the engagement not only to all suitors for office, employment or preferment, but to all who sought to travel out of Ireland, or who came to offer to take the same, BL Egerton MS 1761, fol. 21 (transcript of Commonwealth records).

45 4 October 1651, Dunlop, *Commonwealth*, i, p. 61.

46 Spurlock, *Cromwell and Scotland*, pp. 23, 30–1, 44–7, 50–1, 99, 119.

47 Adair, *True Narrative*, pp. 182–3.

48 *Ibid.*, pp. 183–9 at p. 189. For similar arguments deployed in Scotland see Spurlock, *Cromwell and Scotland*, pp. 41, 54, 59–69, 88, 93–4.

49 Adair reckoned the public dispute did usher in a 'little respite' when ministers could act 'more confidently and openly', Adair, *True Narrative*, p. 191.

50 Dunlop, *Commonwealth*, i, p. 256.

51 *Ibid.*, pp. 256–7.

52 R.M. Young, *Historical Notices of old Belfast* (Belfast, 1896), p. 76. No indication is given of the authors or recipients of the letter, but it fits the sequence of correspondence between the parliamentary commissioners and the Ulster revenue commissioners.

53 Adair, *True Narrative*, pp. 191–4.

54 Dunlop, *Commonwealth*, ii, pp. 292–3.

55 For brief discussions see Stevenson, *Scottish Covenanters and Irish Confederates*, pp. 286–9; McKenny, *Laggan Army*, pp. 117–9.

56 Firth and Rait, *Acts and Ordinances*, ii, pp. 598–603.

57 Though these did include individuals centrally involved in the fighting in Ulster in 1649 – Viscount Ards, his uncle Sir James Montgomery, Sir George Monro and Sir Robert Stewart (the other Protestants were Ormond, Inchiquin and bishop Bramhall).

58 Dunlop, *Commonwealth*, ii, pp. 283–2 (11 October 1652).

59 The rising out in Scotland was Highland-based and drew more on former royalists than Presbyterians, facts noted by the Dublin commissioners, who nonetheless insisted all Scots who had borne arms against parliament were to be removed, Dunlop, *Commonwealth*, ii, pp. cxxxv, 325–6; Dow, *Cromwellian Scotland*, pp. 74–5, 80–2.

60 By 14 June the commissioners confessed their commission was 'determined' and Morgan and Allen had already departed; Jones, too, was in Dublin by the end of the month, when he and Allen served on a further committee to whom were referred all relevant papers and propositions, and who met agents from counties Antrim and Down; active membership also included Richard Lawrence, governor of Waterford, and Philip Carteret, advocate-general to the army (and later judge-advocate in transplanting the Irish), Dunlop, *Commonwealth*, ii, pp. 346, 351–4, 360.

61 Jones, Hill, Venables and Morgan to commissioners, in Dunlop, *Commonwealth*, ii, pp. 329–32 but without the signatories' names, which can be found in Young,

Historical Notices, pp. 78–9 and TCD, MS 844, fols 141a–142a. The same four men, plus Allen, signed a letter from Derry on 24 April, Dunlop, *Commonwealth,* ii, pp. 338–9. Adair insisted that the ministers continued to resist the engagement, Adair, *True Narrative*, pp. 196–9.

62 Dunlop, *Commonwealth,* ii, pp. 355–9.

63 *Ibid.*, p. 330.

64 Waterford was later removed, at the request of the transplantees, as being too far distant, though Lawrence was involved in plans for settlement of Protestants in the county, and any Ulster Scots 'who desire to reside there' were to be permitted to do so, *ibid.*, p. 360; Toby Barnard, 'Lawrence, Richard (*d.* 1684)', *ODNB* (61 vols; Oxford, 2004), xxxii, pp. 487–9.

65 Dunlop, *Commonwealth,* ii, pp. 333–4, 338–9, 349, 351–2, 360–1.

66 *Ibid.,* pp. 360–1. McKenny, *Laggan Army*, pp. 113–15 reckons 32 'settlers' were scheduled to lose their lands in north-west Ulster, all but one (who died in 1648) being besiegers of Derry in 1649.

67 Dunlop, *Commonwealth,* ii, pp. 346–7, 348, 352. The proclamation can be found in *Mercurius politicus* 158 (16–23 June 1653), pp. 2520–5; J.S. Reid, *History of the Presbyterian Church in Ireland* (3 vols, Belfast, 1867), ii, pp. 187–90.

68 Dunlop, *Commonwealth,* ii, pp. 346–9, 351.

69 BL Egerton MS 1779, fols 25a–27a, 87b–90a, 97a.

70 Dunlop, *Commonwealth*, ii, pp. 349, 353, 361.

71 *Ibid.*, pp. 339, 349, 353–4, 361.

72 *CSPI, 1647–60*, pp. 662–3. Cochrane had served in Monro's army but had aligned himself with the 'kirk party' in Ulster from 1648, and subsequently returned to Scotland to face the English forces; captured in 1650 he was condemned for subscribing the engagement to the republic, E.M. Furgol, *A Regimental History of the Covenanting Armies 1639–1651* (Edinburgh,1990), pp. 86–7, 318–19.

73 Council of state's committee for examinations, report on Ards's case, 24 February 1652, TNA, SP 63/286/61, Venables's report on Ards, 29 December 1652, TNA, SP 63/286/62; *CSPI, 1647–60*, pp. 580–2.

74 Dunlop, *Commonwealth*, ii, pp. 352–3.

75 In Ards's case there was the further complication that he had been named as one of those 'excepted' from pardon for life and estate under the 1652 Act, but a further clause allowed that any so named could escape the assigned penalty if they had been mistakenly included, having obtained exemption under articles. The Dublin authorities conceded that Ards fell into this category, leaving him, like Clandeboye, instead facing the loss of part of his estates and transplantation.

76 TNA, SP 63/286/63, certificate by Cromwell for viscount Montgomery of the Ards, 10 March 1653. Cromwell's certificate for Clandeboye is mentioned in the order of the committee for relief on articles of war, 22 August 1653, TNA, SP 63/286/95.

77 Commissioners for Ireland, 27 July 1653, TNA, SP 63/286/66.

78 Gentles, *New Model Army*, pp. 412–21.

79 TNA, SP 63/286/65, SP 63/286/68 (rulings on Ards case), SP 63/286/95 (ruling on Clandeboye case). The Clandeboye document is reproduced in C.W. Russell and J.P. Prendergast, *The Carte Manuscripts in the Bodleian Library Oxford: A*

Report (London, 1871), pp. 135–7. The commissioners for the articles argued that the conditional clause in the articles awarding temporary possession until rules were determined for composition meant that composition had been implicitly conceded.

80 The commissioners for the articles ordered transplantation to be halted, but sought to learn further as to how far the 'publique safety' was concerned in the plan, TNA, SP 63/286/68 (ruling on Ards case). It was later claimed that the commissioners in Dublin had never agreed to the decree issued by the commissioners for articles, and in 1655 the council in Dublin still maintained that the 1652 Act blocked any such decrees, TNA, SP 63/286/73, lord deputy and council to Lord Protector and council, 1 March 1655.

81 Russell and Prendergast, *Carte Manuscripts*, p. 137.

82 Dunlop, *Commonwealth*, ii, p. 410, responses to queries concerning the distribution of land to disbanded soldiers. Orders issued in July 1653 for removal of landowners to Connacht and Clare were not to encompass Protestants, but this did not preclude alternative arrangements for at least some categories of Protestant delinquents, Dunlop, *Commonwealth*, ii, p. 356.

83 TNA, SP 63/286/95 (undated petition by viscountess Clandeboye to the Lord Protector), SP 63/286/96 (report by colonels Mackworth and Montague, April 1654, apparently drawn up in response to this petition), SP 63/286/94 (draft order of Lord Protector and council); Russell and Prendergast, *Carte Manuscripts*, pp. 137–8; *CSPI, 1647–60*, pp. 598–9.

84 Russell and Prendergast, *Carte manuscripts*, pp. 138–139; Firth and Rait, *Acts and Ordinances*, ii, pp. 1015–16. A separate ordinance was passed to take account of the peculiar circumstances of the Protestants of Munster.

85 For documents concerning the arguments between Whalley and Smith, and Ards, in 1655, see TNA, SP 63/286/70, 71; *CSPI, 1647–60*, pp. 585–8.

86 Little, 'Irish and Scottish Councils', p. 129; Barnard, *Cromwellian Ireland*, pp. 17–19.

87 P. Gaunt, '"To create a little world out of chaos": the protectoral ordinances of 1653–3 reconsidered', in P. Little (ed.), *Cromwellian Protectorate*, pp. 107, 110–11, 117; J.R. Collins, 'The church settlement of Oliver Cromwell', *History*, 87 (2002), 24–8.

88 'An ordinance for the further encouragement of the adventurers for lands in Ireland, and of the soldiers and other planters there' (June 1654), in Firth and Rait, *Acts and Ordinances*, ii, pp. 924–9.

89 Collins, 'Church settlement', pp. 20, 22–3. For Cromwell, it has been claimed, 'the godly … were, by and large, presbyterians, independents and baptists', Anthony Fletcher, 'Oliver Cromwell and the godly nation', in J. Morrill (ed.), *Oliver Cromwell and the English Revolution* (Harlow, 1990), p. 211.

90 The resulting measure, generally referred to as 'Gillespie's charter' after the Protester leader Patrick Gillespie, was passed in August 1654, and can be found in Firth and Rait, *Acts and Ordinances*, iii, pp. cxiv–cxv. For developments in Scotland see Dow, *Cromwellian Scotland*, pp. 101, 146; Spurlock, *Cromwell and Scotland*, pp. 94–7 (Protectorate policy), 140–7 (Gillespie's charter).

91 The best account of operation of the presbytery, and its ecclesiological thought is in C. Gribben, *God's Irishmen: Theological Debates in Cromwellian Ireland* (Oxford, 2007), Chapter 3.
92 Adair, *True Narrative*, p. 207.
93 Dunlop, *Commonwealth*, ii, pp. 414–15.
94 St. J.D. Seymour, *The Puritans in Ireland* (Oxford, 1921), p. 98; Adair, *True Narrative*, pp. 208–9.
95 Adair, *True narrative*, pp. 209–11.
96 PRONI, D 1759/1A/1, fol. 45.
97 Seymour, *Puritans*, pp. 211, 220.
98 *Ibid.*, pp. 98–100 largely follows the account in Adair, *True Narrative*, pp. 216–21 as do all subsequent accounts.
99 Partially repealed in November 1653, and in full by ordinance of January 1654, Firth and Rait, *Acts and ordinances*, ii, pp. 774, 830.
100 Fleetwood to Thurloe, 23 November 1654, in Thomas Birch (ed.), *State Papers of John Thurloe* (7 vols, 1742), ii, p. 733.
101 Adair, *True narrative*, pp. 220–1. Cf. Kirkpatrick, *Historical Essay*, p. 301.
102 Rights of presentation were regained by those, like Sir John Clotworthy, no longer under state disfavour, Barnard, *Cromwellian Ireland*, p. 150.
103 Seymour, *Puritans*, pp. 99–100.
104 Little, *Lord Broghill*, pp. 98–9, 105, 108–9 suggests connections between the arrangements in Ulster and those subsequently overseen by Broghill in Scotland.
105 The records of the Antrim meeting survive and can be found in PRONI, D 1759/1A/1.
106 PRONI, D 1759/1A/1, pp. 7–8.
107 See, for example, the processes for John Douglas, PRONI, D 1759/1A/1, pp. 3, 5, 11, 26, 34, 40, 45, 51; Thomas Crawford, PRONI, D 1759/1A/1, pp. 6, 7, 13, 26, 36, 46, 51, 52; Gilbert Simpson, PRONI, D 1759/1A/1, pp. 6, 8, 13, 22, 26, 40, 45.
108 PRONI, D 1759/1A/1, pp. 179, 189, 195.
109 PRONI, D 1759/1A/1, pp. 18, 24, 123–4 (Upton at Templepatrick), 23, 26 (Edmoundston at Broadisland), 32, 34, 36, 52, 53 (Sir Robert Adair at Ballymena).
110 PRONI, D 1759/1A/1, pp. 84, 94, 95, 122, 157, 167, 179. Commissioners required a letter from a minister deputed by the meeting, clarifying that all was in order – this was not always given.
111 PRONI, D 1759/1A/1, pp. 130, 140, 154. Seymour, *Puritans*, p. 101 mentions the 1655 petition from Johnston asking that he be established at Lisnaskea, where preaching for some time; he was soon after awarded a salary.
112 For the notions of church order underpinning the 'civil list' of 'ministers of the gospel' see especially Gribben, *God's Irishmen*, pp. 105, 113–14.
113 Petition on behalf of viscount Ards, June 1655, TNA, SP 63/286/70; an undated draft of Ards's case, including the arguments advanced by Whalley and Smith, and counter-arguments from Ards's side, provides the fullest state of the case to 1655, TNA, SP 63/286/71, mostly in *CSPI, 1647–60*, pp. 586–8.
114 TNA, SP 63/286/73. For efforts, in April, to press the Protector to make a resolution, TNA, SP 63/286/72. Representations made on behalf of Whalley

(and Smith) and of Ards continued to elaborate on earlier arguments, TNA, SP 63/286/74, 75 (June 1655).

115 T.C. Barnard, 'Planters and policies in Cromwellian Ireland', *Past & Present,* 61 (1973), 36, 48–9, 55, 56.

116 Henry Cromwell to Thurloe, 14 November 1655, in Birch (ed.) *State Papers of John Thurloe*, iv, p. 198. The previous day Thurloe had written to Henry Cromwell referring to what Henry Cromwell had reported as being a matter of 'the Scotts comeinge into the north of Ireland' 'a matter of a very great consideration' and 'a growing evill', in Birch (ed.) *State Papers of John Thurloe*, iv, p. 191.

117 P. Gaunt (ed.), *The Correspondence of Henry Cromwell, 1655–1659* (Cambridge, 2007), pp. 81, 93, 94–5, 97.

118 P. Little, 'An Irish governor of Scotland: Lord Broghill, 1655–1656', in A. Mackillop and S. Murdoch (eds), *Military Governors and Imperial Frontiers c.1600–1800* (Leiden, 2003), pp. 88–90.

119 *CSPI, 1647–60*, p. 819.

120 TNA, SP 63/286/77 (December 1655), SP 63/286/78 (undated).

121 Fleetwood to Henry Cromwell, 22 January 1656, Gaunt (ed.), *Correspondence of Henry Cromwell*, p. 97.

122 Dunlop, *Commonwealth*, ii, pp. 580–1.

123 Council of Ireland to the Protector, 1 April 1656, in Birch (ed.) *State Papers of John Thurloe*, iv, p. 668.

124 P. Little, 'Morgan, Sir Anthony (1621–1668)', *ODNB*, xxxix, pp. 96–7.

125 Rutt (ed.) *Diary of Thomas Burton Esq, i*: July 1653–April 1657, pp. 1–11, www.british-history.ac.uk/report.aspx?compid=36738, accessed 8 April 2008. Morgan insisted that Clandeboy 'hath done you more service than disservice'.

126 Gaunt (ed.), *Correspondence of Henry Cromwell*, p. 298; R. Gillespie, 'Landed society and the interregnum in Ireland and Scotland', in Rosalind Mitchison and Peter Roebuck (eds), *Economy and Society in Scotland and Ireland, 1500–1939* (Edinburgh, 1988), pp. 39, 41–2, 44.

127 Barnard, *Cromwellian Ireland*, pp. 64, 289–91; *CSPI, 1647–60*, p. 623. Gillespie, 'Landed society', p. 43 argues for a high turnover in families holding positions as MP, JP or sheriff in Ulster from before to after the 1650s. Patrick Little, 'Irish representation in the Protectorate parliaments', *Parliamentary History*, 23 (2004), 354–6 provides a list of all MPs from Ireland elected to the three Protectorate parliaments – the only identifiable Scot is James Traill, elected MP for Antrim, Down and Armagh in 1656.

128 Cooper to Henry Cromwell, 15 June 1657, in Birch (ed.) *State Papers of John Thurloe*, vi, p. 349. The focus of his criticism was on the minister, John Greg, 'a man of a veary turbulent spirit, and extreamly disafected to the present government', and on Carrickfergus, which 'hath many Scotts in it; and the English there have to much a Scotch spirit, by reason of Mr. Grigg's formerly beinge their minister'.

129 *CSPI, 1647–60*, p. 853.

130 Gribben, *God's Irishmen*, pp. 99–100, 105–8.

131 Seymour, *Puritans*, pp. 137–8; Dunlop, *Commonwealth*, ii, pp. 670–1.

132 Seymour, *Puritans*, pp. 138–9. Hart, then at Hamilton, had taken part in the emergence of the Protester faction as a signatory of the 1651 protest against the

actions of the general assembly. He is found in contact with Johnston of Wariston during the 1650s, G.M. Paul (ed.), *Diary of Sir Archibald Johnston of Wariston* (3 vols, Scottish History Society, 1911–40), ii, p. 93, 279; iii, p. 39.

133 Seymour, *Puritans*, pp. 152–6; Barnard, *Cromwellian Ireland*, pp. 126–7.

134 The 1658 convention had begun the process, Seymour, *Puritans*, pp. 155–7, 168–9. See also Gaunt (ed.), *Correspondence of Henry Cromwell*, pp. 381–2; Representative Church Body Library, Dublin (hereafter RCB), MS LIBR 20, Seymour transcripts from Commonwealth records, pp. 14–15.

135 Seymour, *Puritans*, pp. 199–200.

136 *Mercurius Politicus*, pp. 205, 225 February to 4 March 1657/58, p. 366. The alternative was to secure approbation from the triers in England, as indicated in the 1654 ordinance for the further encouragement of adventurers.

137 RCB, MS LIBR/20, pp. 97–8.

138 James Sharp, the resolutioners' agent in London, to Robert Douglas, 1 March 1659, in W. Stephen (ed.), *Register of Consultations of the Ministers of Edinburgh and some other Brethren for the Ministry, 1652-60* (2 vols, Scottish Historical Society, 1921–30), p. 154.

139 For lists of ministers, by precinct, in the later 1650s see RCB, MS LIBR/20, pp. 203–16. Seymour, *Puritans*, pp. 206–24 provides a list of all ministers he was able to identify as in receipt of state payment with his, admittedly tentative, identification of allegiances.

140 RCB, MS LIBR 20, p. 99 (September 1659).

141 A. Clarke, *Prelude to Restoration in Ireland* (Cambridge, 1999), pp. 243–7, 251–3, 278–85, 310–12.

142 Adair, *True Narrative*, p. 215.

143 G. Rust, *A Sermon Preached at New-town ... at the funeral of ... Hugh Earl of Mount-Alexander ...* (Dublin, 1664). I am grateful to Professor Jane Ohlmeyer for bringing this pamphlet to my attention.

144 T. Barnard, 'Identities, ethnicity and tradition among Irish dissenters c.1650–1750', in K. Herlihy (ed.), *The Irish Dissenting Tradition 1650–1750* (Dublin, 1995), pp. 33–5.

145 Gillespie, 'Landed society', p. 44.

146 Interestingly the records of the Antrim meeting, as well as accounts like that of Adair, are replete with references to individuals (elders, commissioners, sympathetic landowners) with military titles derived from their service in the local forces raised in the 1640s.

147 For the situation in Derry see Barnard, 'Identities, ethnicity and tradition'; R.L. Greaves, *God's Other Children: Protestant Nonconformists and the Emergence of Denominational Churches in Ireland, 1660–1700* (Stanford, CA, 1997), pp. 47–8, 59.

Index

Lightning Source UK Ltd.
Milton Keynes UK
UKHW010930120619
344251UK00003B/378/P